The question of modernity has provoked a vigorous debate in the work of thinkers from Hegel onwards, through figures such as Heidegger, Habermas, Benjamin, Blumenberg, Rorty, and Lyotard. Our own self-styled postmodern age has seen no end to this debate, which now receives a major and wide-ranging intervention from the theorist and critic Anthony J. Cascardi. Whereas existing analyses of subjectivity and modernity accept the Cartesian model of self-consciousness as dominant even where they argue against it, Cascardi shows how the modern subject is positioned within a field of conflicting cultural discourses. Offering an historical analysis of the origins and transformations of the modern subject beginning with such seventeenth-century figures as Descartes, Cervantes, Hobbes, Pascal, and the Don Juan myth, Cascardi carries his argument through to the twentieth century across the fields of epistemology, literature, political science, religion, and psychology.

Drawing critically on Max Weber's concept of "world disenchantment," Cascardi undertakes a searching analysis of modernity's sense of its own absoluteness, divorced from an archaic "enchanted" world. He proposes in its place a more fruitful model that integrates historical analysis and theoretical speculation. Contesting the views of Habermas as well as the postmodern thinkers Habermas has sought to criticize, Cascardi develops a constructive rethinking of modernity around the concepts of recognition, transformation, and aesthetic liberalism. Cascardi's challenging work offers a stimulating alternative to the current orthodoxies regarding the place of the subject in the modern world and opens new ground for analysis in criticial theory.

The subject of modernity

Literature, Culture, Theory

❖❖

General editors

RICHARD MACKSEY, *The Johns Hopkins University*

and MICHAEL SPRINKER, *State University of New York at Stony Brook*

The Cambridge *Literature, Culture, Theory* series is dedicated to theoretical studies in the human sciences that have literature and culture as their object of enquiry. Acknowledging the contemporary expansion of cultural studies and the redefinitions of literature that this has entailed, the series includes not only original works of literary theory but also monographs and essay collections on topics and seminal figures from the long history of theoretical speculation on the arts and human communication generally. The concept of theory embraced in the series is broad, including not only the classical disciplines of poetics and rhetoric, but also those of aesthetics, linguistics, psychoanalysis, semiotics, and other cognate sciences that have inflected the systematic study of literature during the past half century.

Title published

Return to Freud: Jacques Lacan's dislocation of psychoanalysis

SAMUEL WEBER

(*translated from the German by Michael Levine*)

Wordsworth, dialogics, and the practice of criticism

DON H. BIALOSTOSKY

The subject of modernity

ANTHONY J. CASCARDI

Onomatopoetics: theory of language and literature

JOSEPH GRAHAM

Other titles in preparation

Paratexts

GERARD GENETTE

(*translated from the French by Jane Lewin*)

The object of literature

PIERRE MACHEREY

(*translated from the French by David Macey*)

Parody: ancient, modern, and post-modern

MARGARET ROSE

Kenneth Burke: a rhetoric of the subject

ROBERT WESS

Narrative of narratives: the reflexive tradition in the English novel

JEFFREY WILLIAMS

The subject of modernity

ANTHONY J. CASCARDI

Professor of Comparative Literature
University of California, Berkeley

CAMBRIDGE
UNIVERSITY PRESS

Published by the Press Syndicate of the University of Cambridge
The Pitt Building, Trumpington Street, Cambridge CB2 1RP
40 West 20th Street, New York, NY 10011-4211 USA
10 Stamford Road, Oakleigh, Melbourne 3166, Australia

First published 1992
Reprinted 1994, 1995

Printed in Great Britain by Athenæum Press Ltd,
Gateshead, Tyne & Wear

A catalogue record for this book is available from the British Library

Library of Congress cataloguing in publication data
Cascardi, Anthony J.
The subject of modernity / Anthony J. Cascardi.
p.   cm. – (Literature, culture, theory)
Includes bibliographical references and index.
ISBN 0 521 41287 0 (hardcover). – ISBN 0 521 42378 3 (paperback)
1. Subjectivity.   2. Philosophy, Modern.   3. Civilization, Modern.
4. Literature, Modern.   I. Title.   II. Series.
B841.6.C37   1992
126–dc20   91-12689   CIP

ISBN 0 521 41287 0 hardback
ISBN 0 521 42378 3 paperback

Contents

Acknowledgments

I am fortunate to have had the help and advice of numerous colleagues and friends while this book was in preparation. In particular, I would like to thank Bernard Williams for his initial puzzlement over what I had to say about Descartes and history; Richard Eldridge and John Caputo for helping me see the relevance of "aesthetic liberalism" to the critique of modernity; Stanley Rosen for challenging discussions of the Platonic alternatives to the views sketched here; Richard Shusterman for incisive comments on my efforts to conjoin Weber and Heidegger; Ralph Cohen, Joseph Margolis, Jeff Kline, and Joan-Ramon Resina for probing comments on my discussion of Lukács and the theory of the novel; Ruth El Saffar for provocative discussions of the relationship between Cervantes and Descartes; Pat Dust for his invitation to explore the connections between Ortega y Gasset and modernity; and Tony Giddens and John O'Neill for their enthusiastic comments on the manuscript as a whole. Richard Macksey warmly received the proposal to include this study in the "Literature, Culture, Theory" series. Michael Sprinker and Doug Collins provided suggestions for revision that have substantially improved the book. Charles Altieri deserves special thanks for his sustaining intellectual companionship over the years and credit for having mapped out some of the terrain covered in a rather different way in the concluding pages of my final chapter.

I wish also to thank my hosts and audiences at Williams College, Boston University, Temple University, Swarthmore College, Haverford College, and The University of Washington at Seattle, as well the American Society for Aesthetics and the International Association for Philosophy and Literature, where some of the material included here was first presented in the form of lectures and colloquia.

I am grateful to Denis Dutton as editor and to Johns Hopkins University Press, publishers of *Philosophy and Literature*, where the nucleus of chapter 1 first appeared under the title "Genealogies of Modernism," for permission to incorporate portions of that study; to Reed Way Dasenbrock and the University of Minnesota Press for permission to draw on material first published as my Afterword to *Redrawing the Lines: Analytic Philosophy, Deconstruction, and Literary Theory* (1989); to the publishers and editors of *Tirso's Don Juan: The Metamorphosis of a Theme* (Washington: Catholic University of America Press, 1988) for permission to use in chapter 5 material that first appeared under the title of "Don Juan and the Discourse of Modernism"; to Michel Meyer for permission to include as part of chapter 6 material on Kant that was first published in the *Revue Internationale de Philosophie* under the title of "Aesthetic Liberalism and the Ethics of Modernity"; and to Marx Wartofsky and the *Philosophical Forum* for permission to incorporate into chapter 2 brief sections of an essay that originally appeared under the title of "Narration and Totality." The University of California, Berkeley, granted funds through its Committee on Research, which, together with the award of a Humanities Research Fellowship, provided for a sabbatical leave during 1988–89.

My family has provided the necessary encouragement, and the even more necessary distractions, without which this book would never have been written. It is dedicated to Matthew and Elisa.

Introduction

When we reflect on the modern age, we are questioning concerning the modern world picture. We characterize the latter by throwing it into relief over against the medieval and the ancient world pictures. But why do we ask concerning a world picture in our interpreting of an historical age? Does every period of history have its world picture, and indeed in such a way as to concern itself from time to time about that world picture? Or is this, after all, only a modern kind of representing, this asking concerning a world picture?

Heidegger, "The Age of the World Picture"

The object of the present study is an interpretation of the category of subjectivity as central to the understanding of what Heidegger calls the "world picture" of modernity. In Heidegger's view, the emergence of the modern world picture cannot adequately be explained as long as we attempt to understand it simply in terms of a contrast with the Ancient or medieval worlds. This is because what is at stake in the emergence of the subject is the activity of "world-picturing" itself, a form of representation that helps secure modernity as something wholly new. As Heidegger goes on to say, "the fact that whatever is comes into being in and through representedness transforms the age in which this occurs into a new age in contrast with the preceding one."[1] Heidegger's essay provides a useful frame of reference for a study of modernity insofar as it questions the belief that the emergence of subjectivity is simply the result of a break in historical time. What remains of course to be seen is whether the self-understanding of modernity that subjectivity founds can any better be understood in terms that are strictly philosophical or, for that matter, social-theoretical. Indeed, the framing structure of my

1 Heidegger, "The Age of the World Picture," in *The Question Concerning Technology and Other Essays*, trans. William Lovitt (New York: Harper and Row, 1977), p. 130; the epigraph to this chapter may be found on pp. 128–29.

1

argument is suggested by the fact that the paradigm of modernity is *more* than historical, just as it requires understanding in terms that are *more* than philosophical in nature; this is because the phenomenon that grounds modernity (the subject) is itself more than any of these things. As I hope to show, the subject exists at the intersection of a series of discourses or cultural spheres, each of which is essential for an understanding of modern culture and none of which can define modernity as a whole. Hence my criticism of Habermas, who interprets modernity largely as a function of its "philosophical discourse."

Somewhat more specifically, I propose to investigate the relationship between historical formations and theoretical discourses and so to explore the manifold cultural paths through which the contradictory self-consciousness of the modern subject/ has taken shape. As the following chapters I hope will make clear, this requires *effort to combine* a focus that is at once historical and theoretical. The discourse on modernity that has been conducted by contemporary thinkers such as Lukács, Heidegger, Blumenberg, and Habermas goes to show that what is at stake in our engagement with the problem of modernity at the theoretical level is essentially a description of the subject. However, our conception of the contradictory ways in which subjectivity is lived needs to be situated in relation to specific discursive formations, each of which may be understood in historical terms. The condition of subjectivity is defined through the (contradictory) discourses of philosophy, literature, the "science" of politics, religion, and psychology; as anchored by the paradigmatic figures of Descartes, Cervantes, Hobbes, Pascal, Milton, and the myth of Don Juan these discourses mark off the social and historical contexts in and through which the subject-self is shaped. These figures and discursive fields provide the organizing structure of the book and articulate one of its overarching themes: the splitting of the subject and the division of discourses in the modern age. I argue that whereas existing analyses of the relationship between subjectivity and modernity accept the Cartesian model of self-consciousness as the dominant one even where they argue against it, the modern subject is in fact positioned within a field of conflicting discourses, such that modern culture can best be imagined as a "detotalized *oxymoron* totality" (Sartre's phrase). As borne out in the chapters that follow, which treat the origins and transformations of the subject with respect to each of these discursive fields, this description is meant to encapsulate rather than perpetuate what are in fact a series of structural contradictions internal to the culture of modernity.

For example, the "philosophical" subject understands itself in terms that are quite distinct from and indeed opposed to those invoked by the "literary" subject, and both of these seek to differentiate themselves from the secular and political subject. Thus the story that is told about the modern conception of reason, including not only the formulations of Descartes but also their later "empiricist" corrections and Kant's "Copernican" reply, may with equal legitimacy be narrated from the perspective of the mobile psyche of modernist desire and its socio-cultural "containment" as imagined in various versions of the myth of Don Juan; it may be told from the vantage point of the structures of terror and authority at work behind the authority of the modern State, as revealed by Machiavelli and theorized by Hobbes; and it may be viewed in terms of the shifting and unequal balance of faith and science, as seen for example in the writings of Milton and Pascal. As attempts to account for the conditions of modernity history and theory remain sharply divided realms: as Hegel's philosophical critique of modernity would later bear out, historical processes resist complete comprehension by the subject, just as the Cartesian theory of reason, which claimed universal applicability to motions in the sublunary world, remained unable to account for its own genesis on an historical plane.

To rephrase these points: we may guard against interpreting the problem of modernity as strictly a problem for philosophy if we keep in mind the fact that the modern subject is defined by its insertion into a series of separate value-spheres, each one of which tends to exclude or attempts to assert its priority over the rest. Subjective experience is itself the conflictive "totality" described by all of these. At one level, these conflicts seek resolution in terms of the efforts of different spheres of culture to constitute themselves as autonomous and independent, and as having a commanding authority over the whole of social or cultural life. But since the condition of subjectivity is intimately tied to individuals, who through the organizing power of social institutions inhabit these cultural and discursive spheres, the autonomy of the various discourses in the modern age inevitably shows up as contradictions within the subject-self. The attempt to understand the culture of modernity as a "detotalized" whole thus may not be resolved but may be made tractable if we keep in mind the seventeenth-century figures mentioned above, who are para-

3

digmatic insofar as they serve to differentiate the conflicting areas of "modern" discourse. Thus the present investigation of subjectivity makes reference not only to the writings of Descartes as crucial to the development of modern philosophy, but also to Cervantes' *Don Quixote*, which establishes the novel as the dominant literary genre in the modern world; to Hobbes, who claims to have instituted politics as a science in *De Cive* and the *Leviathan*; to Milton and Pascal, whose writings are essential to an understanding of the residual place of belief in an increasingly secularized world; and to the myth of Don Juan, which offers a representative example of the nature of the psyche and the problem of desire in the modern world. In and through the numerous contradictions among them, these figures help articulate a paradigm for the divided culture that comes to dominance in the modern age.

How may this approach to the problem of subjectivity be integrated with an understanding of modernity as something "new"? At first glance, it would seem that the social structures in which the modern subject is set may be contrasted with those of "traditional" society and with the forms of substantive rationality and charismatic authority discussed at length by Max Weber; similarly, the principles of subjective selfhood dominant in modernity might initially be understood in contrast with the ethics of "virtue," as brought to light in, among other places, Alasdair MacIntyre's characterization of the Ancient world; likewise, the dominant literary mode of subjectivity, the novel, may with Lukács's help be seen as a transformation of the values once in force in heroic epic literature. We will examine these and other claims about modernity at some length in the chapters to follow. However we shall in the process see that characterizations of the pre-modern world as "traditional" or "heroic" serve principally as fictions for the characterization of a reality that is socially and historically complex. While my aim is not a critique of pre-modern societies, an understanding of these "fictions" as potentially dangerous abstractions is nevertheless central to a comprehension of the self-consciousness of the modern age, for they themselves form part of the framework through which the historical contingencies bearing on the subject could be reduced. This is to say that approaches to the problem of modernity that presuppose the unity of "traditional" society fail to recognize the fact that concepts like "tradition" and "virtue" may be the inventions of a modernizing historical ideology; they tend to represent the totality in terms of the unity of philosophy and literature (MacIntyre), or the primordial oneness of "soul" and "world" (Hegel, Lukács). As Heidegger's account reveals, the modern subject's self-image is built upon the premise of its incommensurability with any pre-existing paradigm. In the Cartesian philosophy that Heidegger seeks to criticize, so great is the transformation that the invention of subjectivity brings that what stands prior to it cannot be recognized as constituting a "world view" at all.

The philosophical conception of the subject as marking a radical break in historical time forms the groundwork of the self-consciousness of the modern age. Reading Jacob Burckhardt on the Renaissance, however, or Hegel's *Aesthetics* on the individual in Shakespearean tragedy, one comes to recognize a radically different view, viz., that subjectivity *qua* self-consciousness gradually emerges over the course of the *longue durée* of the Renaissance, and culminates in the "individualism" expressed in the writings of such figures as Shakespeare, Cervantes, Machiavelli, and Montaigne. My argument is that neither of these positions succeeds in capturing the relationship between reason and history underlying the invention of subjectivity in the modern age. On the one hand, it cannot be denied that the formation of subjectivity is an historically contingent (and, as we shall see, highly unstable) response to a series of transformations that emerged within a pre-existing social sphere of long standing. The concept of the Renaissance as a mediating historical conjuncture is central to this view. As highly stratified societies, relatively secure in their conception of the good and in principle closed to the possibility of revision from within, met a series of destabilizing conditions, the underlying groundwork of authority and the fabric of social relations came to be challenged in fundamental ways. As a result, it became necessary to reconstitute the self on new grounds. But as we see in the philosophical writings of Descartes, the understanding of selfhood as subjectivity came to acquire a normative and legitimizing force, and served to validate under the semblance of a false necessity what must in the first instance be seen as an historically contingent phenomenon. Thus despite the fact that the invention of subjectivity depends on the rejection of the "naturalistic" vision of society – that there is an essential, internal order of things – it remains difficult for the subject to accept its place within a contingent order of events. In response the subject attempts to transform contingency into necessity, as part of an effort to legitimize itself.

5

The historical positioning of the subject just described may in turn be linked to a series of substantive claims about the nature of the modern world. The first of these is that the modern "world picture" is marked by the denial of any fixed and rigid conception of the good, and by the rejection of attempts to bind the principle of the good to any pre-existent or naturally occurring features of the world. In the most rigorous sense, "representation" is a form of world-construction that is dependent on the belief that there are no intelligible essences, no preordained qualities, and no "auratic" presences in the world. The disappearance of such qualities yields a vision of the world as potentially open to transformation from within, but also raises fears that the world may be governed by no authoritative perspective or controlling point of view. As we shall see at greater length in the chapters below, the principles of subjectivity are aligned in a variety of ways to the values of individual freedom and autonomy; the attempts to secure and ground these values conceptually in rational self-consciousness and politically in the liberal State stand among modernity's more prominent goals. And yet it also remains clear that the modern subject is hard pressed to resolve the problem of authority which any social order must face. Societies founded on the principles of virtue or tradition may be able to answer the question of authority by invoking a stable ranking of ends, but the social order with which they are aligned fails to offer the individual the freedom for self-revision that lies at the heart of the modern age; in M. I. Finley's description of the Homeric world, "the basic values of society were given, predetermined, and so were a man's place in the society and the privileges and duties that followed from his status."[2] It is thus possible to see that the "totality" of heroic society is an ideological effect, one requirement of which is that the dominant heroic or "virtuous" groups feel relatively secure and unthreatened in their power. Likewise, the alternatives to modernity that have been presented under the guise of the "virtues" of heroic society or the "wisdom" of the Ancients offer a relatively stable world, but they inevitably translate their vision of the good into a series of fixed social hierarchies and ranks; they tend to deny the openness of society to modification and change. And yet it is the additional burden of the present study to show that the modern subject confronts a situation that is at least as difficult to resolve as this – that

2 Finley, *The World of Odysseus* (New York, Viking Press, 1954), p. 134.

of imagining purposive and coherent possibilities for self-transformation where the ends of action are no longer fixed according to nature and where the terms of transcendence have been rendered suspect. Thus Lacan for example explains that he is unable to treat the problem of alienation (which is itself a consequence of the "disenchantment" of the world) without introducing the concept of freedom, and goes on to admit that what grounds the function of freedom in the subject is that, for it, the signified "kills all meanings."[3]

Because of its inherent schematism, however, the contrast between traditional and modern remains useful only insofar as it may suggest that each type of society has a particular focal point, a sometimes hidden center of contradictions that may at some level be enabling but whose ideological dimensions are made manifest as such at moments of social change. Modern, liberal society is for example vulnerable to the consequences of an instability in the relationship between freedom and authority; a continual struggle between the desire for freedom and the need for order is embedded within the modern world. As Roberto Mangabeira Unger has explained, this has direct consequences for the problem of legitimation: some groups in modern society will in fact have more power than others, and yet no group seems entitled to dominate the rest.[4] Whereas Unger's analysis assumes that the conflicts within society must always be between different social groups, however, the contradictions I see within modernity are lodged within the divided subject, who may act in different functional roles and as a member of various social groups and who may speak in different "voices" when in pursuit of different ends or when making different value-claims.

Because social formations can never be free of ideology, we can at best say that there exist a series of unequal and unreconcilable trade-offs between traditional, pre-modern societies on the one hand and the liberal modern order on the other. In order to understand this contrast in less than schematic terms, we must ask how transformations of these social orders were brought about. For Hegel, whose theories have been taken as seminal in this regard, the wholeness of "traditional" society is bound to break down because of a structural weakness internal to it, viz., the immediate identification

---

3 Lacan, *The Four Fundamental Concepts of Psychoanalysis*, trans. Jacques-Alain Miller (New York: Norton, 1981), p. 252.

4 Unger, *Law in Modern Society: Toward a Criticism of Social Theory* (New York: The Free Press, 1976), pp. 151–52.

of particular roles with the universal good. In Hegel's analysis of traditional society, any given role as performed by an individual invariably comes into conflict with other equally sanctioned roles. This leads people to separate the particularity of their roles from the wholeness of the social universe, and threatens the order of society as it stands. In the words of one recent critic of modernity who has focused explicitly on Hegel, "what had been fused together and provided the identity for the individual self falls apart. The individual self no longer has a clear definition on either side."[5] Conventional accounts of the modern world might lead one to expect that the results of the splitting apart of the individual role and the social order would be a society that is simply fragmented, but this is not exactly the case. Not only is the subject split among the various discursive formations mentioned above; by virtue of a conflicting desire for autonomy and a need for organization the subject experiences the unique and potentially devastating consequences of modernity as an alienated individual subjected to a bureaucratic order. Indeed, beginning in the seventeenth century, the subject has come to preside over a world in which the good is interpreted increasingly in terms of procedural justice and formal rationality. As we shall see in connection with our discussion of Weber in chapter 1 below, this yields a rigid separation of substance and form, and constitutes one of the most visible effects of the process of social rationalization that Weber described.

In the chapters that follow, Weber's exposition of the problem of "world disenchantment" is framed by the discussion of a series of sometimes contrasting critiques whose contemporary sources range from the members of the Frankfurt School to relatively conservative thinkers like Leo Strauss, Stanley Rosen, and Alasdair MacIntyre. My aim is to reformulate these somewhat disparate critiques in terms of an overarching and constitutive antinomy – that of the subject as an abstract and potentially empty underlying ground (whose political analogue may be located in the organization of the modern bureaucratic State), set in a world that has become increasingly disenchanted or "rationalized." MacIntyre's call for a reformulation of the Aristotelian ethic of virtue, and Rosen's insistence on a Platonic unity of reason and the good, provide pungent criticisms of the

5 David Kolb, *The Critique of Pure Modernity* (Chicago: University of Chicago Press, 1986), p. 26.

modern paradigm and serve in addition to articulate ideals that are not in principle unattractive. But both of these alternatives will remain at best abstract possibilities unless we recognize the historically embedded nature of the problems that the subject faces. Max Weber's analysis of rationalization may in this respect provide a more useful guide, even though it is sometimes easy to forget that Weberian social theory is itself a symptom of some of the historical problems it is attempting to address. Weber and his followers can nonetheless help us see that insofar as the subject is positioned in a rationalized world, the possibility of linking values to the world, or for that matter of establishing a self through the pursuit of a particular course of values in that world, is placed seriously in doubt. Any solution to the problem of modernity that concentrates selectively either on the position of the subject, or on the problem of rationalization, but that fails to see the link between these two, is bound to remain incomplete.

Insofar as Weber's "rationalization" theorem provides a point of departure for the chapters that follow, it is important to say that "rationalization" does not describe the spontaneous generation of Reason, even though that is the way in which philosophy has sometimes pictured the emergence of subjective self-consciousness. As Norbert Elias reminds us, "rationalization is not something that arose from the fact that numerous unconnected individual people simultaneously developed from 'within', as if on the basis of some preestablished harmony, a new organ or substance, an 'under-standing' or 'reason' which had not existed hitherto. What changes is the way in which people are bonded to each other. This is why their behavior changes, and why their consciousness and their drive-economy, and, in fact, their personality structure as a whole, change. The circumstances which change are not something which comes from men from 'outside': they are the relationships between people themselves."[6] Still less does rationalization indicate an absolute heightening of the level of reason in human culture. As Weber helps us see, the process of rationalization describes a change in social organization that in turn has consequences for the relationship between reason and value in the world. And yet it would be wrong to think that the problem of rationalization is historically or socially driven in any narrowly causal way. For it is equally the case that the subject attempts to refashion society in order to honor a series of

6 Norbert Elias, *Power and Civility*, trans. Edmund Jephcott (New York: Pantheon, 1982), p. 276.

positive commitments to the values of freedom and autonomy, as made visible in the process of social transformation and as articulated through the Enlightenment's progressive goals.

But even as a principle of exposition, reference to "the subject" as a disembodied substance or to "modernity" as an autonomous order of concepts must remain procedures of restricted scope. The disadvantage of understanding modernity strictly in terms of its "philosophical discourse" (Habermas) is that the invention of subjectivity is something that only transformations in the structure and organization of social values could have produced; indeed, questions relating to the "Cartesian conception of reason" or the "nature of representation" are indicative of the problems of modern culture only insofar as they were accompanied by large-scale transformations of social life. What is required in describing the culture of modernity is thus not to ascertain the veracity of an abstract order of concepts or to establish the validity of a series of autonomous historical "facts" but to comprehend the way in which the subject is positioned between these two orders. Although Weber's social theory is recognizably a product and symptom of the modern age, the Weberian emphasis on the mediating power of institutions may profitably be invoked in at least this respect, for to posit the formation of "subjectivity" at the convergence of historical and theoretical paradigms would itself be inconceivable were it not for this function of institutions. For instance, when Weber described modern society as "rationalized," and spoke of the "disenchantment" of the world, he was neither giving an account of personal experience nor was he speaking in speculative terms about the relationship between a certain conception of reason and the nature of values or qualities in the world. He was, rather, describing the ways in which an institutional realm served to mediate between abstract ideas and socially constituted interests, thus lending "subjective" experience its peculiar shape.[7]

Weber's perspective on the problem of rationalization suggests the need to mediate between a series of theoretical statements about the nature of reason on the one hand and the objectifiable practices of social life on the other. Having said this much, it may be useful to provide a somewhat more detailed indication of my position on modernity *vis-à-vis* that of Habermas, who also relies on Weber, and

---

7 See Wolfgang Schluchter, *The Rise of Western Rationalism*, trans. Guenther Roth (Berkeley: University of California Press, 1981), p. 27.

who in the face of postmodern challenges has professed a continuing commitment to modernity's central goals. Whereas I take the problems of social, historical, and personal transformation as central to modernity, as raising in a crucial way the questions of cultural authority, social order, and personal recognition with which modern society must deal, for Habermas the "normative content" of modernity bears no central connection with the possibility of self-revision but depends almost exclusively on the normative claims of rational enlightenment, as interpreted in accordance with the principles of clear speech. In addition, Habermas's analysis of the modern age begins with the eighteenth century and largely ignores the problems of social and historical change that come to light when we look at the seventeenth. To be sure, Habermas has acknowledged the role of tradition in transmitting social and cultural norms in some of his earlier writings,[8] but in his most important work on modernity (*The Philosophical Discourse of Modernity*) the contrast with traditional society largely drops out. Instead, Habermas seeks to locate, confirm, and perfect the modern project as exemplified in what he describes as "the increasing reflexivity of culture, the generalization of values and norms, and the heightened individuation of socialized subjects, the enhancement of critical consciousness, autonomous will formation and individuation – that is, the strengthening of the moments of rationality once attributed to the practice of subjects." These take place "under conditions of an ever more extensive and ever more finely woven net of linguistically generated intersubjectivity."[9]

In contrast to the analysis that Habermas presents, it is my goal to show that modernity is built around a series of deeply contradictory aims. For example, the subject tends on the one hand to accept the principles of science as reflecting the indisputable truths of reason, while on the other hand the subject assents to the proposition that disputes about value and desires cannot be resolved according to the standards of rational truth. And while Habermas believes that we can return, through the theory of communicative action, to a mode of consensus that represents a path available but not taken in the modern age, it is my argument that Habermas fails to recognize the embeddedness of the contradictions of modernity within the social

---

8 See, for example, *Legitimation Crisis*, trans. Thomas McCarthy (Boston: Beacon Press, 1973).

9 Habermas, *The Philosophical Discourse of Modernity* (henceforth, *PDM*), trans. Frederick Lawrence (Cambridge, MA: MIT Press, 1987), pp. 345–46.

and historical world, so that his version of the theory of communicative action offers at best either an "intersubjective" version of Descartes and Kant or a utopian projection, a possibility that is destined to remain both speculative and abstract.

For the reasons I have suggested above, a critique of modernity cannot be undertaken exclusively through a critique of reason. And yet it would be wrong to forget that the process of rationalization is centrally bound up with the development of the particular form of modern reason that is manifested in modern science. Descartes takes the accomplishments of science (and their basis in mathematics) as a philosophical ideal. Heidegger is in this respect a particularly insightful guide to the difference between the Ancient and modern worlds, for he suggests how the modern conception of reason as a form of mathematically grounded science is intimately bound up with the development of the framing power of representations and with the elaboration of method as a form of purely "instrumental" reason. Indeed, it would not be too much to say that the Cartesian preoccupation with method constitutes one of the earliest symptoms of what underlies the problem of social rationalization. For Plato, the use of a dialectical "method" is grounded in the ideal of an order which transcends the purely instrumental context; and the dialectic is itself only intelligible in terms of "higher" reasons and purposes.[10] In Descartes, by contrast, it is method with which one begins. More accurately, the Cartesian subject begins with nothingness, as imaged in skepticism's radical doubt; method provides a beginning where no natural beginnings exist.[11]

Understood in these terms, the implications of Cartesian science extend considerably deeper than Habermas would admit. Beginning with Descartes, and continuing in Hobbes, nature is no longer understood in terms of the firstness that is Being, or as a series of pre-existing hierarchies or ranks, but rather as the site of the isolation and dissociation of individuals. For Hobbes, the disgregation of individuals is engendered by nature's concrete brutishness: nature is dispersed

10 For further contrasts see Stanley Rosen, *The Ancients and the Moderns: Rethinking Modernity* (New Haven: Yale University Press, 1989).

11 Alan Blum puts the point nicely: "Method is a technique that is uprooted from the soul of the user even while it is grounded in a description of soul; yet it is a description of soul which still leaves soul untouched because it is a description." See *Theorizing* (London: Heinemann, 1974), p. 153. For a discussion of the connection between Cartesian method and nothingness, see also Stanley Rosen, *Nihilism* (New Haven: Yale University Press, 1969).

12

and fragmented in such a way that social and political unity can only be achieved through some external operation performed upon it. The radical character of this operation is rooted in the primary fact of disenchantment – that the essential order of nature has been withdrawn. For this same reason, the autonomy and self-assertion of the subject are bound to the formation of a State: because there is nothing higher than man, social bonds must be maintained through an external force whose legitimacy is bound at the same time always to be at stake. What may be said for the State dominated by the ideals of formal rationality may be said of Cartesian method itself: the "rationality" of method, its universal accessibility and intelligibility, guarantee the certitude of conventional agreement required to reincorporate otherwise disgregated subjects within a framework of reasonable and peaceful social relations. Indeed, the authority of the Cartesian method is much like the authority of the sovereign as formulated by Hobbes. Science appears and acquires its power as a means of resolving the problem of order by requiring that every valid assertion reproduce this external authority within the subjects themselves. Science perpetuates itself ideologically in this world out of the need to establish a community of speakers where none in fact "naturally" exists. In the words of one recent critic, "method as force is the only way to compel people to listen to one another in such a world."[12]

In this way it may be seen that the Habermassian emphasis on the ethics of speech and the goodness of communication follows more directly from the philosophy of Descartes than is commonly recognized. Our reading of Descartes may thus help reveal the hidden passion and fear that drive the Habermassian search for the principles of free and open (i.e., undistorted) speech. In Descartes, the dialectic of science as grounded in the rejection of all prior assumptions about the nature of things and as reflected in the premise of radical doubt generates fears and anxieties about the consequences of disorder. The problem of order is resolved in the establishment of a method, but in such a way that reason (or "science") is not absolutely immunized against this fear, but becomes itself an organized repression of it, as reformulated in rules, method, and procedure. In the case of Habermas, this fear leads good speech to be identified with successful "communication."

12 Blum, *Theorizing*, p. 157.

As the foregoing remarks will have suggested, the modern reformulation of reason as subjectivity is a more-than-historical event whose consequences cannot be contained within the purview of the early modern age, but extend throughout modernity and influence our "postmodern" condition as well. With but a few exceptions, however (the work of Charles Altieri is one), the debate over modernity and postmodernism has amounted to a fiercely ideological contest.[13] In the writings of Habermas, Rorty, and Lyotard,[14] this debate has been characterized by those on the one side who warn of the impending collapse of rational structures, and who threaten that as long as we believe that reason lacks normative authority we will be destined to face the terrors of relativism, decisionism, and emotivism. On the other side, the opposition gathers strength under the banner of a splintered or decentered subject. Energized by the potentially liberating power of the aesthetic imagination that Habermas links to surrealism, certain proponents of the postmodern stance attempt to project possible transformations beyond the bounds of reason in the form of what Lyotard calls a "postmodern sublime." They take what little post-metaphysical comforts they may need from the claim that the culture of modernity is itself so heavily indebted to "Western metaphysics" that only a post-historical critique of reason or a post-theoretical critique of history could possibly overcome the domination they see as inherent in the practices of the modern West.

The critique of modernity undertaken here should allow us to cut across these oppositional stances insofar as it forces us to question the widespread belief that whatever follows the culture of enlightened modernity must in some way be the rejection of it; instead it leads us to see that what we have come to call "postmodernism" may be understood in a dual sense: first, postmodernism represents the consequence of tendencies embedded within the paradigm of modernity; and second, postmodernism is the site of those transformations that remain open to us through a re-interpretation of the modern age. Thus my concluding chapter offers a re-interpretation of Kant's conception of aesthetic judgment in an attempt to draw out

13 See, for example, Altieri's *Painterly Abstraction in Modernist American Poetry* (Cambridge: Cambridge University Press, 1989). Altieri's work is notable for, among other reasons, his insights into the poverty of ideological interpretation.
14 A good summary of these positions is available in Richard J. Bernstein, ed., *Habermas and Modernity* (Cambridge, MA: MIT Press, 1985).

the postmodern possibilities for positioning subjects with respect to heterogeneous discursive spheres. As I hope this study will show, we are inevitably the heirs of modernity, and are as such drawn to live out the consequences of modernity's commitments to the values of freedom and autonomy implicit in the rejection of the "naturalistic" thesis about society and the self. History remains important to this project insofar as it can provide an interpretation of those consequences and can offer substantive images of how such commitments might be met. Yet we are at the same time the beneficiaries of a critical perspective on modernity and so seek to fashion a world in which we might resist the modern legacy, together with its grand historical *récits*. For this reason, history's claim to set the limits of our reflection and judgment cannot be taken as absolute. It would indeed be more accurate to say that there are enduring demands that both history and theory make on us but that neither can satisfy, and that the need to fashion a mode of discourse, a practice of judgment, and a model of selfhood in response to these demands in turn provides a measure of the possibilities that remain open in the postmodern age. As I hope to explain in the concluding pages of this study, these possibilities can best be drawn out through a reinterpretation of the function of "aesthetic judgment" initially outlined by Kant. For it is in connection with a reinterpretation of Kant's third *Critique* that we shall finally see how a solution to the otherwise devastating antinomies of modernity may be achieved through the reintroduction of a principle of judgment that is itself neither historical nor theoretical but "aesthetic" in the sense that it provides models for moving among the various categories that the culture of modernity typically divides.

❖❖

The "disenchantment" of the world

❖❖

Historical self-assertion

The fate of our times is characterized by rationalization and intellectualization, and, above all, by the "disenchantment of the world." Precisely the ultimate and most sublime values have retreated from public life.　　　　　　　　　　　Max Weber, "Science as Vocation"

"The disenchantment of the world" is a phrase that I take from Max Weber, who spoke of the eclipse of magical and animistic beliefs about nature as part of the more general process of "rationalization" which he saw as the defining feature of modernity in the West.[1] In the lecture entitled "Science as Vocation" (1917) and in the prefatory remarks to his studies on the sociology of religion written at the very end of his life (1920), Weber posed the following questions:[2] How can we account for the fact that there developed in the West a series of interrelated practices and beliefs predicated on the a priori accessibility of nature to rational calculation and control? Why was the process of secularization also accompanied by an increase of purposive-rational (*zweckrational*) action in the West? What has been the impact on the modern system of values of a concept of perfection that was uprooted from its sacred context and became interpreted as

---

1　Weber may in turn have known the phrase "die entgöttertur Natur" from Schiller's poem "Die Götter Greichenlands."

2　The date of "Science as Vocation" has been the subject of much confusion and debate. While it had long been considered that both this and "Politics as Vocation" were given in 1918 (and published in 1919), more recent research has shown "Science" to have been delivered in 1917. For a complete discussion of the relevant sources, see Wolfgang Schluchter, "The Question of the Dating of 'Science as a Vocation' and 'Politics as a Vocation'," in Schluchter and Guenther Roth, *Max Weber's Vision of History: Ethics and Methods* (Berkeley: University of California Press, 1979), pp. 113–16. The essays are reprinted in H. H. Gerth and C. Wright Mills, eds., *From Max Weber* (New York: Oxford University Press, 1946).

a form of inner-worldly progress, at once technological in nature and potentially infinite in scope?

The list of phenomena that Weber subsumes under the heading of "rationalization" is remarkably diverse. It only begins with the presupposition that theoretical knowledge can be expressed in mathematical form and tested empirically in controlled experiments. Looking beyond these essays to the remainder of his work, we can see that for Weber Western rationalism extends to encompass everything from the development of a fixed perspective in painting and architecture, to the institutionalization of art in theatres and museums and the development of tempered keyboard instruments. Weber further sees Occidental rationalism as marked by the emergence of the modern State and as bound to the standards of scientific jurisprudence, administered by professionally trained jurists according to the principles of rational natural law. Only in the West, Weber claims, is law divided into a series of separate spheres – sacred and secular, private and public, civil and criminal. Notoriously, Western rationalism develops in close connection with Protestant asceticism, whose attitude of world-mastery Weber regards as the foundation of modern vocational culture (*Berufskultur*). Finally, Weber cites the emergence of capitalism and its attendant structures of action and belief as "the most fateful force in our modern life."[3] For example, it is paramount for Weber's case to see that the Absolute monarchies of the early modern age introduced a series of institutions that appear to be preeminently capitalist in nature – a permanent governmental bureaucracy, a system of national taxation, a codified law, and a unified economy. The emergence of capitalism as Weber understands it came to draw on opportunities for exchange which had come to be institutionalized as in principle universally accessible and continuous in scope and that would have been impossible without the development of a type of rational accounting that allowed for the exact comparison of money spent with money earned. It was built on the basis of freely available labor, organized and attuned to the existence of this regular marketplace.[4] Yet whereas Marx saw the

3 Weber's "Vorbemerkungen" are reprinted as the "Introduction" to *The Protestant Ethic and the Spirit of Capitalism*, trans. Talcott Parsons (New York: Scribner's, 1958), p. 17. See also Louis Dumont, *Homo Aequalis: Genèse et épanouissement de l'idéologie économique* (Paris: Gallimard, 1977), pp. 15–16.

4 Wolfgang Schluchter attempts to give some systematic coherence to the various phenomena Weber understands in terms of "rationalization" in "The Paradox of

rationalization of society as originating directly at the level of productive forces – in the development of new manufacturing techniques, in the expansion of empirical knowledge, and in the abstract quantification of work as "labor power" – and only then as affecting those institutions that control and distribute social power, Weber regards the institutional structure of modern society as expressing a tendency toward rationalization that may anticipate and control the transformation of productive forces.[5]

As an antidote to what has been perceived as the latent idealism of Weber's position, subsequent Marxist historians like Perry Anderson have attempted to reinterpret Weber's theories in light of the causal power of material history while challenging Marx's idea that the rise of modern society coincides with the simple disappearance of serfdom, which was considered the core institution of the pre-capitalist mode of production in Europe. For Anderson, the Absolute States arose principally from a shift in the relationship between the nobility and the monarchy; more specifically, the rule of Absolutism was a reflection of the need of the feudal nobility to consolidate its power in the epoch of transition to capitalism.[6] As Anderson notes, and as we shall see in our discussion of the State in chapter 4 below, the resolution of this situation yielded a precarious harmony between class subjects and State interests. For now it must simply be said that neither the Marxist nor the Weberian position allows us to explain the relationship between the individual as subject

---

Rationalization," *Max Weber's Vision of History* (Berkeley: University of California Press, 1981), pp. 14–15.

5 For systematic contrasts between Marx and Weber, see the essays gathered in Robert J. Antonio and Ronald M. Glassman, eds., *A Marx–Weber Dialogue* (Lawrence: University of Kansas Press, 1985); as well as Karl Löwith, "Max Weber und Karl Marx," *Archiv für Sozialwissenschaft und Sozialpolitik*, 67 (1932), 175–214; S. N. Birnbaum, "Conflicting Interpretations of the Rise of Capitalism: Marx and Weber," *British Journal of Sociology*, 4 (1953), 125–41; Herbert Marcuse, "Industrialization and Capitalism in the Work of Max Weber," *Negations*, trans. Jeremy J. Shapiro (Boston: Beacon Press, 1968), pp. 201–26; Anthony Giddens, *Capitalism and Modern Social Theory: An Analysis of the Writings of Marx, Durkheim and Max Weber* (Cambridge: Cambridge University Press, 1971); and Fredric Jameson, "The Vanishing Mediator; or, Max Weber as Storyteller," *New German Critique*, 1 (1973), 52–89, rpt. in *The Ideologies of Theory: Essays, 1971–1986*, II (Minneapolis: University of Minnesota Press, 1988), pp. 3–34. Some of the methodological background and implications are treated in George Lichtheim's essay "Marx or Weber: Dialectical Methodology," *From Marx to Hegel* (New York: Seabury Press, 1974), pp. 200–18.

6 See Anderson, *Lineages of the Absolute State* (London: Verso, 1979), p. 42.

and the collective modes of production or the institutionalized forms of social life. To be sure, Weber was concerned that the rationalization of society might lead to an entrenchment of purely bureaucratic forms of behavior, to a reification of social relationships, and to the curtailment of individual freedoms at the hands of normalizing social institutions. The wage laborer might thus be in principle free to dispose of his labor-power on the open market, but he is at the same time *compelled* to do so in order to survive within capitalist society. In Weber's example,

The Puritan wanted to work in a calling; we are forced to do so... when asceticism was carried out of monastic cells into everyday life, and began to dominate worldly morality, it did its part in building the tremendous cosmos of the modern economic order. This order is now bound to the technical and economic conditions of machine production which today determine the lives of all the individuals who are born into this mechanism, not only those directly concerned with economic acquisition, with irresistible force. Perhaps it will so determine them until the last ton of fossilized coal is burnt.[7]

The element of "compulsion" present within these and other orders nonetheless remains for Weber an expression of the normalizing authority of social institutions themselves. For this and other reasons, neither Weber nor contemporary thinkers like Jürgen Habermas who take their bearings by him, allow us to view the concept of rationalization as carrying a wholly negative charge.[8] They regard the normative dimension of the concept of rationalization – conceived as an increase or heightening in the level of reason, in the establishment of modes of authority whose motives would in principle be transparent to all, and in the corresponding ability to master the world – as having provided modern institutions with a positive reorientation for themselves. Correspondingly, it is in the normative status of reason that, for Weber, the modern individual's commitment to values must be found. To be sure, an increase in the level of rationality holds the promise of expanded opportunities for self-legitimation in politics, of increased economic fairness, and of more effective and efficient forms of "social engineering." Yet why do

7 Weber, *The Protestant Ethic*, p. 181.
8 Habermas speaks of his task as "a theory of the pathology of modernity from the viewpoint of the realization – the deformed realization – of reason in history." See Axel Honneth, Eberhard Knödler-Unte, and Arno Widmann, "The Dialectics of Rationalization: An Interview with Jürgen Habermas," *Telos*, 49 (1981), 7.

contemporary interpretations of the Weberian thesis obscure the fact that what eventually became institutionalized as the "philosophical discourse of modernity" (Habermas) has failed to provide a value-orientation for modern society as a whole? Why do these interpretations not allow us to perceive the contradictory and sometimes antinomic nature of "modern" discourse?

Perhaps the most obvious answer to these questions is that the method of "value-free" social science as practiced by Weber was itself an expression of the culture that constituted the ostensible object of his critique. The belief that the validity of scientific theories is independent of the acceptance or rejection of any commitments of an ethical or religious nature, as well as the corollary of this view – that reason is insufficient to ground such commitments – are themselves symptomatic of the very phenomenon that Weber was attempting to diagnose.[9] In his analysis of rationalization, for instance, Weber took religion as a paradigmatic expression of value; but Weber viewed religion from the perspective of one who no longer himself believes, and for whom the social-science ethic was rather like an aftereffect of religious conviction that serves at best to remind us what it was like to behave in concert with belief. For Weber, of course, it is this very detachment from values that permits Value itself to come into view as the object of a sociological critique. Weber would accept the premise that value-freedom constitutes a value in its own right, but it is this very attempt to hold values in suspension that finally places the very notion of value in doubt. Accordingly, Weber regards value-conflict as an irreconcilable expression of our cultural fate: "We live as did the ancients when their world was not yet disenchanted of its gods and demons, only *we live in a different sense.* As Hellenic man at times sacrificed to the gods of his city, so do we still nowadays, only the bearing of man has been disenchanted and denuded of its mystical but inwardly genuine plasticity. Fate, and certainly not 'science' holds sway over these gods and their struggles."[10]

9 See the remarks on Weber in Andrew Arato, "The Neo-Idealist Defense of Subjectivity," *Telos*, 21 (1974), 108–61; and Russell Keat, *The Politics of Social Theory: Habermas, Freud and the Critique of Positivism* (Chicago: University of Chicago Press, 1981).

10 "Science as Vocation," in *From Max Weber*, p. 148. Heidegger in effect both diagnoses and confirms Weber's views when he locates the origins of "disenchantment" in the position of the subject: "Because this position secures, organizes, and articulates itself as a world view, the modern relationship to that

In his analysis of culture, Weber was further driven to posit an antinomic relationship between context-shaping institutions and the value-ideas that they may express. On the one hand, the ideas and interests that take shape through politics, economics, religion, law, and art define concrete social structures insofar as they are subject to judgments and receive the imprint of values. "Empirical reality," or the fiction thereof, is for Weber transformed into "culture" as it receives the impress of such evaluative judgments.[11] Yet on the other hand these same values and the institutions which they inform admit of no determinations of validity or truth; thus the Weberian ideas expressed as "values" must paradoxically remain outside the sphere of evaluative discourse and resist all transformative efforts. Weber can claim that judgment of the validity of values is a matter of faith, but must recognize that this faith has been withdrawn from the "disenchanted" world: "The realm of values is dominated by insoluble conflict, hence by the necessity for continuous compromises. Nobody can definitively decide how the compromises should be made, unless it be a "revealed' religion."[12] It can thus be said that Weber regards values as contextual and artefactual but also, because of the secularizing logic of modernity, as beyond our control. They amount to irreducibly competing ideals:

The fate of an epoch which has eaten of the tree of knowledge is that it must know that we cannot learn the meaning of the world from the results of its analysis, be it ever so perfect; it must rather be in a position to create this meaning itself. It must recognize that general views of life and the universe can never be the products of increasing empirical knowledge, and that *the highest ideals, which move us most forcefully, are always formed only in the struggle with other ideals which are just as sacred to others as ours are to us.*
(*Methodology of the Social Sciences*, p. 57; emphasis added)

which is, is one that becomes, in its decisive unfolding, a confrontation of world views; and indeed not of random world views, but only of those that have already taken up the fundamental position of man that is most extreme, and have done so with the utmost resoluteness." Heidegger, "The Age of the World Picture," in *The Question Concerning Technology and Other Essays*, trans. William Lovitt (New York: Harper and Row, 1977), pp. 134–35; emphasis added.

11 See Weber, "Objectivity in Social Science and Social Policy," in *Max Weber, The Methodology of the Social Sciences*, ed. Edward A. Shils and Harry A. Finch (New York: The Free Press, 1949), especially pp. 55, 95–96. See also Gillian Rose, *Hegel Contra Sociology* (London: Athlone Press, 1981), pp. 13–21.

12 The first citation is from Weber's "Objectivity in Social Science and Social Policy," p. 55; the second is from his letter to Robert Wilbrandt, April 2, 1913, in Wolfgang Schluchter, *The Rise of Western Rationalism*, trans. Guenther Roth (Berkeley: University of California Press, 1981), p. v.

Thus while the postulate of "value-freedom" is correctly understood as part of Weber's rejection of all philosophies that seek to convince us of a teleological movement immanent in the apparently chaotic and random processes of social and historical existence, the inner logic that Weber attributes to the rationalization process would seem to deprive us of the grounds for reflection on those values that have been historically institutionalized as "facts." As a result, Weber induces us to accept the false semblance of necessity, the characteristic "absolutism," in terms of which the values of modernity initially asserted themselves.

The normative challenge posed by the Weberian thesis would be to explain how the postulate of *Wertfreiheit* is an ethically appropriate position in the modern world and not itself the product of rationalization or, worse still, a consequence of fate. Yet the Weberian model cannot by its own lights do this much, in part because Weber was unable to recognize his own stance toward values as itself a product of the very logic he attributed to the "disenchantment" of the world. Thus Habermas has taken on the task of rewriting Weber in the language of "communicative action" in the hope of supplying what Weber himself could not – an intersubjective grounding for normative science, one that would overcome the negative consequences of rationalization while preserving modernity's progressive goals.[13] An analysis of rationalization should be able to tell us why a phenomenon that was initially the bearer of positive and revisionary ideas about society and the self should have led to a crisis of values and why the progressive ideology of early modern times, originally oriented toward the transformation of the social and natural worlds, should have led to the closure of contexts and the reduction of opportunities for social change. While I would argue that modernity is a more than historical phenomenon, I would also say that even Habermas, who is aware of the limitations of Weber's thought on questions of social and political legitimation, has failed to appreciate the historical dimensions of the problem, viz., that the modern concept of reason, as embodied in the position of the subject, was initially configured in such a way as to legitimate but finally to limit modernity's revisionary goals. Since Habermas stands among those

13 See especially Habermas's discussion of Weber in volume i of *The Theory of Communicative Action: Reason and the Rationalization of Society*, trans. Thomas McCarthy (Boston: Beacon Press, 1984), pp. 143–271.

who would accept the historical legitimacy of the modern age, his reinterpretation of Weber's concept of modernity as the period in which the theoretical, practical, and symbolic spheres of culture each began to develop their own "inner logic" can be called into question on the grounds that it does not explain the historical beginnings or the subsequent self-contradictions of the rationalized cultures of the West.[14] Yet I shall argue that it is only by first inquiring into the articulation of a new program of reason, and by asking how a sense of false necessity was generated as part of the project of a self-enlightened critique, that we can begin to link the broad spectrum of phenomena that Weber called the "rationalization" of society and the "disenchantment" of the world with the self-consciousness of epoch that Hans Blumenberg has described as the "historical absolutism" of the modern age.[15] We can then begin to see that the role of reason

14 This was not true of Habermas's work of the early 1970s. For instance, in writing about legitimation crises Habermas claimed that "Bourgeois culture as a whole was never able to reproduce itself from itself. It was always dependent on motivationally effective supplementation by traditional world-views. Religion, having retreated into the regions of subjective belief, can no longer satisfy neglected communicative needs, even in conjunction with the secular components of bourgeois ideology (that is, an empiricist or rationalist theory of knowledge, the new physics, and the universalistic value systems of modern natural law and utilitarianism)." *Legitimation Crisis*, trans. Thomas McCarthy (Boston: Beacon Press, 1975), pp. 77–78.

15 On the subject of false necessity, see Roberto Mangabeira Unger, *False Necessity: Anti-Necessitarian Social Theory in the Service of Radical Democracy* (Cambridge: Cambridge University Press, 1987). On "historical absolutism," see Blumenberg, *The Legitimacy of the Modern Age*, trans. Robert M. Wallace (Cambridge, MA: MIT Press, 1985). Cf. Heidegger, "The Age of the World Picture," in *The Question Concerning Technology*, pp. 115–54. At one juncture in his argument, Habermas regards the historical absolutism of the modern age as potentially *protected* from consequences that would upset the tradition-securing modes of belief or religious contemplation: "In order to remove this barrier," Habermas writes, "it was first necessary to generalize the level of learning that was attained with the conceptual apparatus of religious-metaphysical worldviews, that is, to apply the modes of thought achieved in ethical and cognitive rationalization consistently to profane domains of life and experience. This was possible in turn only with the reversal of just those uncouplings to which the high forms of religious ethics of conviction and theoretically grounded cosmology owe their emergence. I am referring to the break of the ascetic search for salvation with the profane orders of this world and the separation of contemplative devotion from those same orders" (*The Theory of Communicative Action*, 1, p. 214). Yet nowhere does Habermas countenance the possibility that the concept of "rationalization," in its normative dimension, might itself have been marshalled in order to legitimize modernizing historical goals.

in the "disenchantment" of the world was not simply to eradicate the magical, superstitious, or religious practices of pre-modern societies. Indeed, many of these were carried forward into modernity in some secularized guise, where they continued to weigh against the "historical absolutism" of the modern age and to provide evidence of the contradictory nature of the rationalization process itself.[16]

The modern concept of reason, understood as subjective self-consciousness and formulated in terms of quasi-mathematical representations of the world, was originally put forward as a vehicle of human emancipation in a number of domains. As seen by Descartes, reason was to provide the means by which man could become the "master and possessor" of the natural world; similarly, reason called for man to rise above the natural passions and control them in accordance with its own laws.[17] Moreover, the "foundational" project of modernity embodied a self-enlightened critique of history that was directed at overcoming the traditions of the past. If the process of rationalization is understood not only as involving the technological domination of nature and the transformation of the world into a representation of the mind, but also as having provided the culture of modernity with a structure of beliefs in which nature, tradition, society, and the self could be positively revised, then those simplified conceptions of modernity as a wholly degenerative phenomenon, i.e. as an historical epoch in which a denatured form of reason rose to power, must indeed be reexamined and recast.[18] Here and in the chapters that follow I shall argue that the nature of modernity is marked not only by the emergence of the subject and

16 Thus in relation to the development of a "Protestant ethic," Weber describes the substance of disenchantment as having displaced and devalued the achievement of salvation through the sacraments of the Church. But needless to say those sacraments continued to be performed.

17 Spinoza makes a related argument the basis of Part IV of the *Ethics*, "Of Human Bondage," and articulates the basic modern belief that the passions must be mastered (later, repressed): "Human infirmity in moderating and checking the emotions I name bondage; for, when a man is prey to his emotions, he is not his own master, but lies at the mercy of fortune." (Trans. R. H. M. Elwes [New York: Dover, 1955], p. 187.)

18 Cf. Habermas's engagement with what he describes as "the pathology of modernity from the viewpoint of the realization – *the deformed realization – of reason in history'*; "The Dialectics of Rationalization," *Telos*, 49 (1981), 7; emphasis added.

the mathematical ground which lends it support, or by the development of "sciences of order in the domain of words, being, and needs," as Foucault claimed,[19] but by a redistribution of the authority of reason and value, by a consolidation of the position of the individual as subject to the authority of the sovereign in the liberal-Absolutist State, by the simultaneous increase in the mobility of the psyche and a heightening of the repressive powers of society, and by a reconception of the relationship between nature and the literary work of art. For while modernity may initially be described in terms of the "rationalization" of society or the "disenchantment" of the world, the relationship of its various elements can best be conceived as that of mutually opposing terms.

Before proceeding to develop this thesis, however, it is important to note that while Weber sought to identify the origins of Occidental rationalism as a social and historical phenomenon distinct from anything in the pre-modern and non-Western worlds, the relationship between modernity and rationality remained for him both necessary and unquestioned. In light of the radical questionings of reason that have intervened since Weber's time, however, this no longer is the case. On the one hand, the metaphysical concept of reason has been submitted to a series of critiques that have placed in doubt the possibility of making normative claims about social and historical arrangements. History has at the same time become the mirage of such omnibus conceptions as "Reason" or "Western metaphysics" as a whole. Yet on the other hand, the more radical forms of historicism that branch out from Marx and Weber have threatened to eliminate the claims of rational consciousness *tout court*. And once the historicist critique of reason is radicalized to a sufficient degree – as occurs, for instance, in some of the work of Foucault – reason is robbed of its speculative dimension and becomes reduced to an illusion created by the shifting alliances of power and institutional control. Phrased in other terms, it could be said that the twin postmodern critiques have rendered reason and history equally, and mutually, suspect. Little wonder, then, that so much postmodern theory has not yet understood the degree to which it is itself implicated in the "disenchantment" of the world.[20]

19 *The Order of Things* (New York: Vintage Books, 1970), p. 57.
20 See A. J. Cascardi, "Genealogies of Modernism," *Philosophy and Literature*, 11 (1987), 207–25, and, from quite different perspectives, the essays in John Fekete, ed. *Life After Postmodernism* (New York: St. Martin's Press, 1987).

The preceding remarks are meant to suggest that the post-metaphysical critique of history and the post-historical critique of metaphysics will both be found methodologically unsuited to the project undertaken here. My aim in this chapter is to understand the emergence and subsequent self-contradictions of the rational subject, and with these a certain consciousness of historical epoch, as providing the legitimizing context for modern culture in the West. Insofar as the issues of self-consciousness, political legitimation, desire, and belief are central to this analysis I would argue that an analysis of modernity requires an interpretation that is more than historical (and, for that matter, more than philosophical) in scope. Thus it should at the outset be said that my interpretation of modernity takes its bearings by (and is at the same time critical of) Hegel, for whom the modern age is characterized by the modes of collective and individual consciousness in force during the period from roughly 1500 until the French Revolution.[21] Here, I wish to make the case that the cultural phenomenon that Hegel described may provisionally be understood in relation to the rational and historical goals articulated by Descartes. In the *Meditations*, the *Discourse on Method*, and the *Rules for the Direction of the Mind*, Descartes advanced a program of self-criticism that called for the rejection of the wisdom of the Ancients and the accumulated experience of the past in favor of those truths of reason that could be certified by the self-reflective mind. In Hegel's estimation, Descartes marks the beginning of modern philosophy insofar as he "recommenced the whole subject from the very beginning and constituted afresh the groundwork on which Philosophy is based, and to which, after a thousand years, it once more returned. The extent of the influence which this man exercised upon his times and the

21 Hegel chose 1500 because of three events: the discovery of the New World, the Renaissance, and the Reformation. See Hegel's *Lectures on The Philosophy of History* and Habermas, *The Philosophical Discourse of Modernity*, trans. Frederick Lawrence (Cambridge, MA: MIT Press, 1987), pp. 5–11 and 23–44. Still it must be said that this leaves open the question of the "new age" *(die neue Zeit)* that is ushered in with the French Revolution and that inspires Hegel in a work like the *Phenomenology of Spirit*. There Hegel writes that "ours is a period of transition to a new era. Spirit has broken with the world it has hitherto inhabited and imagined, and is of a mind to submerge it in the past, and in the labor of its own transformation...The gradual crumbling that left unaltered the fact of the whole is cut short by a sunburst which, in one flash, illuminates the features of a new world" (trans. A. V. Miller [New York: Oxford University Press, 1977], sec. 11, pp. 6–7); henceforward I abbreviate *PhS*.

culture of Philosophy generally, cannot be sufficiently expressed; it rests mainly in his setting aside all former presuppositions and beginning in a free, simple, and likewise popular way."[22] Taken together, the will to begin philosophy entirely anew and the conception that free and rational activity consists in making accurate representations of the world comprise what has sometimes been referred to as Descartes's "foundational" project, i.e., the will to formulate a context for thought that would transcend the immediate historical conditions in which the thinking act takes place. For Descartes, foundational thinking avails itself of mathematics, which provides the means to overcome the deceptions of sense experience; as for Plato, the philosopher's confidence in the certainties of *mathesis* is an expression of resolve in the war of resistance against the conditions of genesis that prevail in the historical and material worlds. In the words of Descartes, "attempting to overcome all the difficulties and errors that prevent our arriving at knowledge of the truth is indeed a matter of fighting battles; we lose a battle whenever we accept some false opinion concerning an important question of general significance, and we need much more skill afterwards to regain our former position than we do to make good progress when we already have principles which are well-founded" (*Discourse*, VI, p. 145).

Yet it would be just as accurate to say that Descartes construes history as open to radical revision by the powers of speculative thought. Descartes's search for the foundations of knowledge is placed in the service of what Blumenberg has called modernist "self-assertion." As an explanatory principle, the concept of self-assertion is meant to secure the legitimacy of the modern age and to justify its own interpretation as an historical order independent of any sacred or secular paradigm whose original substance and meaning would be found in the past. We might hasten to add that modern self-assertion also entails the creation of new historical possibilities through the self-legitimizing generation of new ideas. For Blumenberg, establishing the legitimacy of the modern age does not mean beginning *ex nihilo*, as if through a process of immaculate conception, although that is in fact the image that Descartes invokes as he explains in the *Discourse* the presuppositions at work in his treatise *De Mundo*:

---

22 Hegel, *Lectures on the History of Philosophy*, III, trans. Elizabeth S. Haldane and Frances H. Simson (London, 1896), pp. 220–21.

I decided to leave our world wholly for them to argue about, and to speak solely of what would happen in a new world. I therefore supposed that God now created, somewhere in imaginary spaces, enough matter to compose such a world; that he variously and randomly agitated the different parts of this matter so as to form a chaos as confused as any the poets could invent; and that he then did nothing but lend his regular concurrence to nature, leaving it to act according to the laws he established ... I expressly supposed that this matter lacked all those forms or qualities about which they dispute in the Schools.

(Discourse, v, p. 132)

The characteristically "founding" gestures of modernity that are evident in Descartes's rejection of intelligible essences and of the authority of the past are nonetheless ones that Blumenberg transforms into a thesis in which pre-modern positions are carried forward in the form of questions to which the modern age continues to respond.[23] Yet if the legitimacy of the modern age is not derived simply from the accomplishments of reason, it is in Blumenberg's formulation derived from the more startling claim of the *necessity* of these accomplishments (*Legitimacy of the Modern Age*, p. 99). By speaking of "necessity" in this context, Blumenberg apparently means to suggest that reason in the modern age is empowered not only to mark a break with the past, but also to legitimize the content of the history that will ensue. Conceived in this more radical way – as marking an historical rupture that legitimizes a context for human projects and aims – the concept of self-assertion indicates a project of self-creation that reaches well beyond the will to distance or simply revise the past. In Blumenberg's view, the modern age does not see itself as a secularized version of Christianity or a refashioning of Ancient patterns of thought; it has legitimized and will continue to validate itself through the invocation of a series of self-justifying if pragmatic solutions to ongoing existential situations. Self-assertion is "an existential program, according to which man posits his existence in a historical situation and indicates to himself how he is going to deal with the reality surrounding him and what use he will make of the possibilities that are open to him" (*Legitimacy of the Modern Age*, p. 138). Accordingly, the pragmatic and scientific impulse in Descartes may be seen as transforming the "modernizing" intentions of earlier figures such as Galileo and Cervantes – the former's assertion of the

---

23 Blumenberg writes that "the modern age does not have recourse to what went before it, so much as it opposes and takes a stand against the challenge constituted by what went before it" (*Legitimacy of the Modern Age*, p. 75).

unprecedented nature of the discoveries of the "new science" and the latter's claims to have been the first to "novelize" – into the metaphysical foundations of a self-authenticating age.[24]

To be sure, the project envisioned in the Cartesian texts was meant to provide the groundwork for a program of self-revision that has continued to provide a positive orientation for the modern age. In support of science, Descartes established the absolute certainty of mathematical representations as exemplary of rational activity and conceived his philosophical method as modeled after them; the mathematicians alone, he said, "have been able to find any demonstrations – that is to say, certain and evident reasonings."[25] Furthermore, Descartes did not lose sight of the fact that the end of reason lies in praxis, or that the basis of action is human freedom, which knowledge was meant to secure. The work of reason is directed towards the satisfaction of what Habermas has called "emancipatory" interests, which operate through the transformation of nature, history, society, and the self. Yet the exercise of freedom with regard to history commences for Descartes with the prior abandonment of the encumbrances of the past: "regarding the opinions to which I had hitherto given credence, I thought that I could not do better than undertake to get rid of them, all at one go, in order to replace them afterwards with better ones, or with the same ones once I had squared them with the standards of reason" (*Discourse*, II, p. 117). Similarly, Hobbes will claim that political science was no older than his own work *De Cive*,[26] and in the *Discourse on Method* Descartes will recommend razing the faltering edifice of received opinion for the purpose of building anew:

Admittedly, we never see people pulling down all the houses of a city for the sole purpose of rebuilding them in a different style to make the streets

24 Cervantes asserts his priority among Spanish authors in the Prologue to the *Novelas ejemplares* (1613). For Galileo, see *The Sidereal Messenger* (1610), trans. Edward Stafford Carols (London: Dawsons, n.d.), p. 7. Alban Forcione provides a necessary corrective to the thesis of self-assertion in his "El desposeimiento del ser en la literatura renacentista: Cervantes, Gracián y los desafíos de *nemo*," *Nueva revista de filología hispánica*, 34 (1985–86), 654–90.

25 Descartes, *Discourse*, II, in *The Philosophical Works of Descartes*, trans. John Cottingham, Robert Stoothoff, and Dugald Murdoch (Cambridge: Cambridge University Press, 1984), I, p. 120. Further references, by volume and page, will be incorporated into the text.

26 Hobbes, *English Works*, ed. William Molesworth (London: John Bohn, 1839) I, ix. Hegel interprets this as a crucial claim in his section on Hobbes in the *Lectures on the History of Philosophy* (III, 315).

more attractive; but we do see many individuals having their houses pulled down in order to rebuild them, some even being forced to do so when the houses are in danger of falling down and their foundations are insecure.

(*Discourse*, II, p. 117)

History had been used by pre-modern philosophers in order to illustrate the norms or standards in existence in nature and capable of apprehension by reason. But for Descartes, history is no longer a reflection of pre-existing norms and no longer supplies examples worthy of imitation, as it might have for the rhetorical tradition of Aristotle, Quintilian, and Cicero.[27] This is confirmed in the first part of the *Discourse on Method*, where Descartes classifies works of history together with the exemplary fables of the past; both may present compelling ideals, but they fail to meet the criteria of certainty that the philosopher would invoke:

I thought I had already given enough time to languages and likewise to reading the works of the ancients, both their histories and their fables. For conversing with those of past centuries is much the same as travelling. It is good to know something of the customs of various peoples, so that we may judge our own more soundly and not think that everything contrary to our own ways is ridiculous and irrational, as those who have seen nothing of the world ordinarily do. But one who spends too much time travelling eventually becomes a stranger in his own country; and one who is too curious about the practices of past ages usually remains quite ignorant about those of the present. Moreover, fables make us imagine many events as possible when they are not. And even the most accurate histories, while not altering or exaggerating the importance of matters to make them more worthy of being read, at any rate almost always omit the baser and less notable events; as a result, the other events appear in a false light, and those who regulate their conduct by examples drawn from these works are liable to fall into the excesses of the knights-errant in our tales of chivalry, and conceive plans beyond their powers.[28]

To be sure, the "overcoming" of history by philosophy does not emerge full-blown with Descartes. It was itself provoked by a cultural crisis evident in the efforts of Renaissance writers to assert themselves

---

27 See Aristotle, *Rhetoric*, II, 20; Quintilian, *Institutio Oratoria*, x, 1, 34ff; and especially Cicero, *De Oratore*, II, 9, 36 ("Historia vero testis temporum, lux veritatis, vita memoria, nuntia vetustatis").

28 Descartes, *Discourse*, I, pp. 113–14. On the Cartesian critique of historiography, see Lucien Lévi-Bruhl, "The Cartesian Spirit and History," in *Philosophy and History: Essays Presented to Ernst Cassirer*, ed. Raymond Klibansky and H. J. Paton (New York: Harper and Row, 1963), pp. 191–96.

by means of and against the example of the Ancients. Already for figures like Petrarch, Machiavelli, Cervantes, and Montaigne, historical examples were the source of considerable unease: on the one hand, these writers feel the anxiety of history, which is produced by their reflection on the irrecuperable distance between the present and the past; and on the other hand, they experience the anxiety of reason, which finds itself at a loss when faced with the need to comprehend the disparity between lawlike generalizations and the unpredictable diversity of historical actions and events.[29] Hobbes attempts to address this anxiety when he criticizes "men that take their instruction from the authority of books, and not from their own meditation."[30] This is part of Hobbes's wider program of "self-assertion," in which the accomplishments of reason are seen as self-justifying insofar as they reflect the successful actualization of human aims, intentions, and designs (Hobbes: "Good successe is Power... which makes men either feare him, or rely on him"[31]). As Leo Strauss said in his interpretation of Hobbes, "induction from history can lead to discovery of the norms in only one way – that it teaches one to distinguish between aims which justify themselves and lead to success, and aims which come to grief. The 'receipts' to be gained from history bear only on success or failure, not on moral goodness or baseness. If discovery of the norms is in any way expected from history, then – explicitly or implicitly – moral goodness must have been identified with success, and virtue with prudence."[32] The implications for the new "science" of politics are fairly clear: once the rules for success have been established, political science may supersede history; or, by what amounts to the same logic, history may be seen as having produced the standards for its own self-overcoming in the modern State, which political science

29 Karlheinz Stierle provides an illuminating discussion of Montaigne in "L'Histoire comme exemple, l'exemple comme histoire," *Poétique*, 10 (1972), 176–98. See also Marcel Gutwirth, *Michel de Montaigne ou le pari d'exemplarité* (Montréal: Presses de l'Université de Montréal, 1977), and Michael Wood, "Montaigne and the Mirror of Example," *Philosophy and Literature*, 13 (1989), 1–15.

30 See Gary Shapiro, "Reading and Writing in the Text of Hobbes's *Leviathan*," *Journal of the History of Philosophy*, 18 (1980), 152. This does not, of course, explain the paradox of the instructive powers that Hobbes claims for his own book.

31 Hobbes, *Leviathan*, ed. C. B. Macpherson (Harmondsworth: Penguin, 1968), I, 10, p. 151.

32 Strauss, *The Political Philosophy of Hobbes* (1936; rpt. Chicago: University of Chicago Press, 1984), p. 94.

founds. But insofar as the political scientist remains a detached observer who surveys the course of events and reports their meaning, the standards it establishes are not norms in the traditional sense, but reflections of the success and failure of human plans. Based on assumptions such as these, one moves with relative ease from the "political science" of Hobbes to the "value-free science" of Weber.

By laying bare and criticizing previously authoritative beliefs, the *Leviathan* proposes to offer a true and final understanding of political life. In it, Hobbes discovers the crucial modern truth that no essential order binds men from the origin to the end of all things. For Hobbes, the proof of this truth lies in the evidence of progress itself:

Time, and Industry, produce every day new knowledge. And as the art of well building, is derived from Principles of Reason, observed by industrious men, that had long studied the nature of materials, and the divers effects of figure, and proportion, long after mankind began (though poorly) to build: So, long after men have begun to constitute Common-wealths, imperfect, and apt to relapse into disorder, there may, Principles of Reason be found out, by industrious meditation, to make their constitution (excepting by externall violence) everlasting. And such are those which I have in this discourse set forth."   (*Leviathan*, II, 30, p. 378)

Hobbes's principles of politics are the end-point of progress inasmuch as they result in the "constitution everlasting" of an "Absolute" state. It may thus be said that the place of reason with respect to history is fully revealed only when it is seen that reason is not in fact independent of history, but that history itself – as the coming to be and passing away of human things and an expression of the instability of genesis – validates reason as the measure of human events.[33]

And yet it remains nonetheless clear that this self-legitimizing project, as evidenced in the self-grounding claims of the particular form of reason that Descartes describes, cannot fully comprehend the process of its own historical origination. Thus, rather than say categorically that history is absent from the *cogito*, it would be more accurate to say that history is rendered unreadable by it. Even Blumenberg, who remains convinced of a need to secure and protect the legitimizing interests of modern self-assertion, recognizes the contradictions involved in the modern attempt to mark an absolute beginning in time:

33 See Barry Cooper's chapter on Hobbes in *The End of History* (Toronto: University of Toronto Press, 1984), especially pp. 26–29 and 39–40.

Reason's interpretation of itself as the faculty of an absolute beginning excludes the possibility that there could appear even so much as indications of a situation that calls for reason's application now, no sooner and no later. Reason, as the ultimate authority, has no need of a legitimation for setting itself in motion; but it also denies itself any reply to the question why it was ever out of operation and in need of a beginning. What God did before the Creation and why He decided on it – where reason was before Descartes and what made it prefer this medium and this point in time – these are questions that cannot be asked in the context of the system constituted by their basic concepts.   (*Legitimacy of the Modern Age*, p. 145)

In response to these contradictions, which are evident within his own thought, Descartes establishes the *cogito* as an entirely self-contained form of reflection and "founding" act of thought; Descartes's version of "foundational" reflection closes off history as a valid cognitive and moral domain. Thus already in the early *Rules for the Direction of the Mind*, when Descartes set himself the task of a fully rational critique, he invokes the notion of a *prior* division of history and reason ("science"), i.e., a division of which reason declines to give an account; there he says that "all the arguments of Plato and Aristotle" do not constitute philosophy: "what we would seem to have learnt [in studying them] would not be science but history" (*Rules*, III, p. 13). In this case, the characteristically modern desire to seek the absolute foundations of knowledge mirrors a crisis in the relationship between reason and history that is powerfully resolved by the will to begin entirely from oneself. Yet the latter impulse, it must also be said, is tantamount to the wish to begin from nothing at all.

In the gesture of historical absolutism meant to secure and legitimize the position of the subject as quintessentially modern, Descartes substantially revises the judgment of someone like Bacon, for whom the present age is burdened by a consciousness of its historical age: "These times are the ancient times," writes Bacon, "and not those which we account ancient *ordine retrogrado*, by a computation backward from ourselves."[34] Yet at the same time it appears that Cartesian foundationalism runs substantial risks. In taking up a position whose assertions of truth depend on its claimed immunity to history, the subject assumes a stance that can only be abstract. It is indeed much like the stance described in the painters'

---

34 Bacon adds: "Antiquitas saeculi juventis mundi" ("The antiquity of time is the youth of the world"). *The Advancement of Learning*, I, in *Selected Writings*, ed. Hugh Dick (New York: Modern Library, 1955), p. 189.

manuals of the time, barren and formal. Both perspective and the *cogito* assure a uniformity and regularity of proportion, and provide a vision that could in principle be held by *anyone*, but both define the subject's relation to the world in purely formal terms. (In the visual arts, one would say that perspective predicates relatively little about the specific ways in which lines, planes, and points in space will then be transformed into the semblance of a world of experience, but nonetheless makes it possible for such a semblance to exist.) Indeed, since no degree of abstraction can adequately define a relationship to the world of social and historical experience, the subject is prone to fill out this relationship by an assertion of the power of its will over the world, or by an exertion of its will-to-power in the world. But since Descartes cannot a priori assert the supremacy of consciousness over nature he must imagine the emergence of a "new world," created as if by a surrogate God: "I decided to leave our world wholly for them to argue about, and to speak solely of what would happen in a new world. I therefore supposed that God now created, somewhere in space, enough matter to compose a world" (*Discourse*, v, p. 132). A further expression of the will to power, the founding of Cartesian "science" is modeled after the creation of the world out of chaos. In the words of one recent critic, "for a Cartesian self any representation of the world is finally a representation of its formative powers."[35] We might add that these formative powers are located not in reason but in an unmasterable will. As is well known, Descartes imagines himself as "master and possessor" of the natural world. The imperative to master nature represents an attempt to reduce nature's apparent alterity to consciousness. But the result, as formulated in the *cogito*, reasserts the division between consciousness and the world.

Heidegger expressed one aspect of this general problem when he said that as a consequence of the view of man as subject the world was transformed into a representation or "picture," so that the epoch or "age" of the modern world-picture corresponds to the age of the world seen *as* a picture. In Heidegger's view, the notion that rational activity consists in forming objective representations of the world is intimately bound up with the historical consciousness, the self-

---

35 J. M. Bernstein, *The Philosophy of the Novel: Lukács, Marxism and the Dialectics of Form* (Minneapolis: University of Minnesota Press, 1984), p. 179.

assertion, of a "new age." As Heidegger said in his essay on the "world picture," "The age that is determined from out of [representation] is, when viewed in retrospect, not only a new one in contrast with the one that is past, but it settles itself firmly in place expressly as the new. To be new is peculiar to the world that has become picture."[36] Yet while the subjective understanding of reason may be taken as a definitive characteristic of the modern age, modernity is by no means reducible to it. Indeed, the *internal* structure of modernity is better revealed in the tensions between the speculative or "transcendental" position of the subject and a series of inwardly differentiated social and historical formations in and through which "subjective" experience is shaped. The culture of modernity constitutes a "detotalized totality" and is marked by the splitting of the subject across a series of autonomous value- or interest-spheres. Habermas sees modernity as characterized by the development of the "inner logic" of each of these spheres, and regards it both substantively and historically as coextensive with the Enlightenment, viz., as that period in which reason came to assert itself as the natural destiny of man. On these grounds he attempts a reconstruction of modernity from within its own "centered" point of view, in order to preserve its rational goals. By contrast, I take modernity as an originally "detotalized" whole, which is to say as a cultural totality whose various facets could only be held together at the level of a historically abstract and substantively empty subject.

Understood in these terms, the genealogy of the modern age encompasses the philosophy of Descartes as well as those who set themselves the task of challenging Cartesian rationalism and who stand in apparent opposition to Cartesian ideas. My claim is that the traditions represented by thinkers like Descartes, Hume, and Kant on the one hand, and by Nietzsche, Heidegger, and Derrida on the other, must be seen as one tradition and not two, and that the genealogy of the modern age may be seen to conform to the antinomic configuration which *together* these lines represent. On the one hand, modern culture invokes a conception of reason that resembles that of the mathematical sciences; it begins, as in Galileo and Descartes, with a form of abstraction that brings about the geometrization of the world. As Lacan said, "the Freudian field was possible only a certain time after the emergence of the Cartesian subject, in so far as modern

---

36 Heidegger, "The Age of the World Picture," p. 132.

35

science began only after Descartes made his inaugural step."[37] Yet "science" concludes in a movement that leaves inaccessible to judgment the entire range of phenomena associated with values, desires, and the will.

As Roy Bhaskar has argued, the need for a critical assessment of subjectivity can be understood from within modernity as a reaction to the empiricist conceptions of science set in place by the followers of Descartes. Like the notion of knowledge as a representation of the world to the mind, the empiricist conception of facts as immediately apprehended in sense-perception generates the prevailing ideologies of science. These rationalize what Thomas Kuhn has called "normal science," or what we might describe as "uncritical" knowledge. At the same time, these ideologies sustain a mystique of expertise, which, coupled with a belief in the value of "common sense," has produced a series of mystifications equal in every respect to the priestly swindles the Enlightenment originally decried. Similarly, descriptivist and instrumentalist interpretations of the *relationships* among facts mask the possibility of any critical account of value and thereby reduce the speculative power of reason to that of a self-validating reflection on the world that exists. It goes almost without saying that the project of a rational social science is disabled as a result.[38]

In a well-known essay, "Against Dryness," Iris Murdoch made the related assessment that philosophical currents as apparently diverse as French existentialism and logical positivism actually shared a model of value judgment, that of reason supplying the mind with value-neutral "facts" on the basis of which the will can exercise only arbitrary designs.[39] Murdoch has in addition argued that modern thought derives from the assumption that the world possesses no inherent qualities but is essentially a quantity of matter, while the individual in it is a free-floating will: "From Hume through Bertrand Russell, with friendly help from mathematical logic and science, we

37 Jacques Lacan, *The Four Fundamental Concepts of Psychoanalysis*, trans. Alan Sheridan (New York: Norton, 1981), p. 47.

38 Kuhn, *The Structure of Scientific Revolutions* (Chicago: University of Chicago Press, 1970). See also Roy Bhaskar, "Realism in the Natural Sciences," in *Reclaiming Reality* (London: Verso, 1989), p. 23; and also Bhaskar's critique of Rorty ("Rorty, Realism, and the Idea of Freedom"), pp. 146–79 in that same volume.

39 For a related argument concerning contemporary analytical philosophy and (Heideggerean) fundamental ontology, see Stanley Rosen, *The Limits of Analysis* (1980; rpt. New Haven: Yale University Press, 1985).

derive the idea that reality is finally a quantity of material atoms and that significant discourse must relate itself directly or indirectly to reality so conceived ... This is one side of the picture, the Humean and post-Humean side. On the other side, we derive from Kant, and also from Hobbes and Bentham through John Stuart Mill, a picture of the individual as a free rational will."[40] Insofar as the "free rational will" satisfies the formal requirements of rational method and embodies objective, "third-person" perspectives, it is devoid of content or, at best, is unable to speak to the individual life.[41] Thus I would argue more strongly than Murdoch that the modern project of self-criticism is compromised by the particular conception of reason with which it is aligned, and that the model of reason as a form of quasi-mathematical representation is only one side of a coin that also projects a vision of desires and of the will as beyond all rational control. For if reason is conceived as the capacity to see the world and human actions in it as objective "representations," to view it in the abstract, then the individual will, and the first-person desires that it pursues, are bound to fall outside of reason's bounds.[42] Thus where reason is thought to consist in the power to make judgments from a wholly detached perspective, individual desires and the operations of the will may seem arbitrary at best: "reason," so conceived, may be able to tell us what is the case, but it is powerless to tell us what to want; it stands mute with regard to ends. Thus the modern self, while in principle open to revision, is bound to become a vehicle of the will to power directed ultimately at overcoming itself. The project to assert the priority of the "subject" over the claims of the empirical or historical self may well be counted as a form of transcendence – as Pascal said, "man infinitely transcends man" – but it risks being transcendence to nothing.[43]

Pace Habermas, who has placed Nietzsche among the opponents of the enlightened modern age, these arguments would confirm

---

40 "Against Dryness," reprinted from *Encounter* (1961), in Stanley Hauerwas and Alasdair MacIntyre, eds., *Revisions* (Notre Dame: University of Notre Dame Press, 1983), p. 44.

41 See Kurt Baier, *The Moral Point of View* (Ithaca: Cornell University Press, 1958), and Thomas Nagel, *The View from Nowhere* (New York: Oxford University Press, 1986).

42 See the discussion of related problems in A. J. Cascardi, *The Bounds of Reason: Cervantes, Dostoevsky, Flaubert* (New York: Columbia University Press, 1986).

43 Pascal, *Pensées*, trans. A. J. Krailsheimer (Harmondsworth: Penguin Books, 1966), fr. 131, p. 65.

Nietzsche's place within the self-contradictory culture of the Enlightenment and would secure Nietzsche's role in the "unfinished" project of modernity and its self-overcoming.[44] Whereas modernity begins with the efforts of philosophers like Descartes and Hobbes to overcome history, Nietzsche discovers that history is a circle which must seek continuously to transcend (more accurately, to overcome) itself. According to Nietzsche, this "transcendence" takes place through a process of "active forgetting" that even more powerfully rearticulates modernity's claims to be new:

the origin of historical culture – its quite radical conflict with the spirit of any "new age," any "modern awareness" – this origin *must* itself be known historically, history *must* turn its sting against itself – this threefold *must* is the imperative of the "new age," supposing this age really does contain anything new, powerful, original and promising more life.[45]

Insofar as modernity begins with the historical self-assertion of reason but ultimately places reason itself at risk, the present interpretation of modernity may be further related to Heidegger's reading of Descartes and to his critique of subjectivity as forming the groundwork of the modern age. Heidegger describes subjectivity as a form of self-assertion that culminates in the will to power, transcending only to itself. In Heidegger's view, as in Hegel's, modernity is an historical expression of subjectivity and as such may be considered as an expression of human freedom and autonomy, for in it claims about truth and the ends of man are secured by man's powers of perception and reflection alone. The autonomy that is gained in subjective self-consciousness carries with it an obligation to transcend nature and overcome the passions, and to transform both in accordance with human reason. Accordingly, the task set for modernity is to fulfill the purpose of self-consciousness by subordinating a fundamentally brutish nature to reason's laws. But since the reasoning subject recognizes only mathematized representations, the natural world will inevitably be transformed, as Heidegger says, into a "standing reserve," while the passions and desires are left unmediated and can only be repressed or directed violently against themselves.

44 For related arguments see Stanley Rosen, *Hermeneutics as Politics* (New York: Oxford University Press, 1988).
45 Nietzsche, "On the Uses and Disadvantages of History for Life," in *Untimely Meditations*, trans. R. J. Hollingdale (Cambridge: Cambridge University Press, 1983), pp. 102–03.

The modern conception of reason, which is closely aligned with the rise of modern science, may well be credited with the "disenchantment" of the world, but is in turn the source of a new range of gods and demons associated with values, desires, and the will. While the modern self is defined in terms of its freedom to choose from among a plurality of values, it is at the same time dependent on a conception of reason that proves powerless to make meaningful distinctions among values or to mediate between the will and the possible objects of its choice. The challenge of modern moral theory has been to provide a non-arbitrary basis for making judgments about values while recognizing the fact that reason is powerless to dictate specific ends; the difficulties it encounters are evident in the prevailing moralities of "subjectivism" and "relativism," and in the moral phenomenon that Alasdair MacIntyre has characterized as "emotivism," viz., the belief that "all judgments and specifically all moral judgments are *nothing but* expressions of preference, expressions of attitude or feeling, insofar as they are moral or evaluative in character."[46] Thus while the modern self (more accurately, the "subject") must be in principle open to those forms of criticism and self-revision that are consistent with the project of an enlightened critique, this same self is likely to be found at sea among its various desires, not knowing how to choose appropriate ends. And while modern society offers the self the potentially liberating experience of choosing from among a variety of different roles, the modern psyche is reflected in the image of a scattered, fragmented, or "disseminated" whole.

In its most radical form, the modern conception of the self as subject becomes the expression of a pure possibility with no content; in this dimension of its existence, the subject is centered in the experience of itself as will; as Descartes says in the *Passions of the Soul*, "I see only one thing in us which could give us good reason for esteeming ourselves, namely, the exercise of our free will and the control we have over our volitions" (III, 152, p. 384). Descartes goes on to describe one of the highest virtues, *générosité*, as "knowing that nothing belongs to [a person] but this freedom to dispose his volitions" (III, 153, p. 384). In the *Meditations* Descartes explains that

---

46 See *After Virtue* (Notre Dame: University of Notre Dame Press, 1981), p. 11. The term "emotivism" gained prominence on the basis of C. L. Stevenson's *Ethics and Language* (New Haven: Yale University Press, 1944).

he is incommensurable to God in all respects except this one: "If I examine the faculties of memory or imagination, or any others, I discover that in my case each one of these faculties is weak and limited, while in the case of God it is immeasurable. It is only the will, or freedom of choice, which I experience within me to be so great that the idea of any greater faculty is beyond my grasp; so much so that it is above all in virtue of the will that I understand myself to bear in some way the image and likeness of God" (*Meditations*, IV, p. 40). The experience of the willing subject in turn becomes a central theme of Kantian morality as formulated in the second Critique and in the *Foundations of the Metaphysics of Morals*; the claims are explicit at the beginning of the latter work, where Kant says that "nothing in the world...can possibly be conceived which could be called good without qualification except a *good will*."[47] Indeed, the fact of the moral law – of freedom – precedes the notion of God, understood as the idea of the infinite will. In this way, moral autonomy is distinguished from mere obedience to an alien will (heteronomy), whether the other is God or finite beings. Religion is thus kept "within the limits of reason alone"; revelation can only be thought as lying beyond its bounds. In Heidegger's terms, "knowing that remains a willing, and willing remains a knowing, is the existing human being's entrance into and compliance with the unconcealedness of Being."[48] Yet the price of such an entrance into the realm of Being is that rationality becomes inexplicable and God or the infinite will becomes unknowable. The subject is thus *reduced* to its freedom of will. And as becomes immediately apparent in examples ranging from Pascalian "anxiety" to Sartrean "choice," it is impossible to determine whether the exercise of this freedom will be abject or sublime.[49]

47 Kant, *Foundations of the Metaphysics of Morals*, trans. Lewis White Beck, with critical essays, ed. Robert Paul Wolff (Indianapolis: Bobbs Merrill, 1969), p. 11. On the relationship between the will and Cartesian "generosity," see Jean-François Lyotard, *Just Gaming*, trans. Wlad Godzich (Minneapolis: University of Minnesota Press, 1985), p. 18.

48 Heidegger, "The Origin of the Work of Art," trans. Albert Hofstadter, in *Poetry, Language, Thought* (New York: Harper Torchbooks, 1971), p. 67.

49 Pascal writes: "Man's greatness and wretchedness are so evident that the true religion must necessarily teach us that there is in man some great principle of greatness and some great principle of wretchedness"; and "There is no doctrine better suited to man than that which teaches him his dual capacity for receiving and losing grace, on account of the dual danger to which he is always exposed of despair or pride." *Pensées*, frs. 149, 354, pp. 76, 133. As the example of Pascal makes clear, a certain fruitfulness may be derived from philosophical reflections

Modes of rationalization

Schematically viewed, Weber's interpretation of the "disenchant-ment" of the world in terms of the increasing rationalization of society rests on a contrast between two modes of rationality, the substantive and the formal. This juxtaposition in turn supports Weber's understanding of the fundamental differences between the traditional and modern worlds. We shall over the course of what follows see that Weber's contrasts are, in a very specific sense, both abstract and false, and serve mainly to obscure the problematic relationship between reason and value around which the culture of modernity was shaped. Likewise, the idea of a linear narrative describing a direct and unmediated transition from substantive to formal modes of social rationality could not realistically expect to account for the emergence of new modes of consciousness and the social structures they came to inhabit. Yet for the very reason that contrasts like these were internal to modernity's original under-standing of itself, it is important to recapitulate them here. In the case of societies organized according to the principles of substantive rationality, it may be said that the commanding power of values, their authority as both valid and true, derives from the belief that nature constitutes a realm of essences, reference to which is deemed sufficient to supply the ends of action and desire and to justify the division of labor in the form of social roles. Insofar as the values of such a society are taken to reflect a fixed natural order, they are seen as independent of the particular choices that we as individuals might make. A society grounded in substantive notions of rationality may thus be relatively secure in its values, which are regarded as matters of fact, but inevitably demonstrates a resistance to the possibility of its reinvention in history, for its ideals are regarded as untransformable reflections of nature itself.

As Roberto Mangabeira Unger has argued, the naturalistic premise is anti-modern insofar as it attempts to deny the contingencies of value and the conditionality of social worlds:

It takes a particular form of social life as the context of all contexts – the true and undistorted form of social existence .... The natural context of social life

on the condition of anxiety itself. See, for example, Paul Ricoeur, "Vraie et fausse angoisse," *Histoire et vérité* (Paris: Seuil, 1955), pp. 317–35. Ricoeur's remarks on Kant are especially illuminating.

may pass through decay or renascence, but it cannot be remade. Nor is there, in this view, any sense in which the defining context of social life can become less contextual – less arbitrary and confining. It is already the real thing .... This authentic pattern of social life can undergo corruption and regeneration. But it can never be rearranged.[50]

As Unger goes on to say, the naturalistic thesis is attached to a compelling ideology insofar as it holds up the ideal of a social order immune to the pressures of deception and fraud. And yet it must at the same time be said that most versions of the naturalistic thesis narrowly circumscribe the possibilities of what the self may be. The self is regarded as expressing a proper range of emotions and as enmeshed in a stable scheme of virtues and vices, so that each individual's participation in the division of labor, as expressed in the variety of roles, may be taken as an occasion to reaffirm the essential order of society as a whole.

The development of modernity is tied to the shift from substantive to formal modes of rationality insofar as historical changes rendered reference to a pre-existing order of nature impossible. In the *Lectures on the Philosophy of History*, Hegel located these principally in the effects of the Reformation, which in his analysis claimed a direct part in confirming the destiny of man as a free and rational being by liberating spiritual consciousness from the mystifications of religious traditions; and secondarily in the increasing power of an autonomous State, which the Reformation helped promote. We may add to these factors the discovery of the New World, the creation for the first time in history of something approaching a global marketplace, the inflation and consequent devaluation of honorific titles, and the redistribution of the European population toward urban centers, all of which served to destabilize an existing social order. These may collectively be regarded as the historical "conditions of possibility" to which the recentering of selfhood in the form of subjectivity was a response. The modern social order is founded on a rejection of the naturalistic thesis insofar as values, beliefs, and indeed society itself came to be seen as open to change, hence as requiring new forms of legitimation. The problem that immediately presented itself in this

---

50 Unger, *Social Theory: Its Situation and Its Task* (Cambridge: Cambridge University Press, 1987), pp. 23–24. For a critical discussion of the "naturalistic fallacy" rooted in twentieth-century linguistic (i.e. "modernist") philosophy and its ban on definitions of goodness, see Bernard Williams, *Ethics and the Limits of Philosophy* (Cambridge, MA: Harvard University Press, 1985), pp. 121–24.

light was how ethical agents could pursue values where recourse to the order of nature as a legitimizing framework was no longer possible. The early modern philosophers understood their achievement as having come to an appraisal of man "as he really is," an appraisal that was informed by the "disenchanted" assumption that there are no intelligible essences, and no natural order inherent in the world. In the absence of nature as a fixed and stable standard, how was the subject to evaluate and choose appropriate ends? How would the "I" dispose the will in such a context, and how could the will in turn gain a grip on the world? As we have already begun to see, the historical task of the subject was to discover, and if not to discover then to create, a center of value in the absence of any natural or original value-ground. This was accomplished through the articulation of a program of reason and shaped through the subject's "transcendental" stance. By claiming to picture the world and objects in it from a purely objective, "third-person," point of view, the subject claimed access to a framework of comprehensive and generalized beliefs that could serve as the basis for true and valid descriptions of actions and events. It was (falsely) assumed that an order of desires or ends could be deduced therefrom. "Modernization" may thus be described as a process by which the legitimation of ethical and political action came to proceed not by the invocation of a natural order or a prescribed set of social roles, but rather by the recourse to a "transcendental" position from which to assess the world. The consequence is a social order in which the subject may be imagined as the agent of a series of universal (which is also to say, moral) propositions, and also in which moral agency is rendered schematic and abstract.[51]

As we shall see in connection with the problem of secularization in chapter 3 below, the shift from substantive to formal modes of rationality that Weber describes is complicated by a consideration of charismatic authority, which opposes both of these. For now, it is enough to observe that for Weber the shift from substantive to formal modes of rationality parallels a contrast in the types of social structure and visions of personal identity mentioned above. On the one hand Weber pictures traditional societies comprised primarily of religious believers who live according to a prescribed set of values and rules.

51 Maurice Natanson makes a cogent case for the role of literature in reducing this schematism. See "The Schematism of Moral Agency," *New Literary History*, 15 (1983), 13–23.

In this case, the obligatory nature of the social order, and the authoritative principles underlying its norms, are interpreted by the person in terms of his or her social role. On the other hand he describes a world of relatively autonomous and mobile individuals who make decisions in an objective way and so seek to maximize their self-chosen individual or collective ends. While the modern individual tends to be mistrustful of role-playing, and often fails to recognize its capacity to reduce the schematism of moral agency mentioned above, it must at the same time be said that the notion of a direct and immediate contrast between traditional and modern societies only originated once the latter became aware of the need for legitimation in the face of the social changes that initially gave it shape.

In Habermas's interpretation, this is a consequence of the increasing specialization of modern life:

there appear the structures of cognitive-instrumental, moral-practical, and of aesthetic-expressive rationality, each of these under the control of specialists who seem more adept at being logical in these particular ways than other people are. As a result, the distance has grown between the culture of the experts and that of the larger public.[52]

And yet the argument from specialization seems to take an effect for a cause. It does not adequately explain the contradictions among normative principles that social differentiation reflects. The separation of political science from the principles of prudence, for instance, embodies the central belief that desires may be regarded either as facts, drives, and needs, or as objects of choice, but not as both, since there is no bridge between facts and values, or conversely between values and facts. Hume formulated the principle that divides morality from science in the *Treatise on Human Understanding* when he said that no statements of obligation could be derived from premises of fact. Similarly, there is no transition between the descriptive and prescriptive aspects of modern law – the one describing a realm of nature, the other a realm of obligation. Hence the recourse, in theorists from Hobbes and Locke to Rousseau, to the idea that society is raised out of the state of nature by some "contract" that we make.

In the Hobbesian or Lockean State, the aristocratic criteria of privilege, prestige, status, and caste – and the vision of natural order

---

52 Habermas, "Modernity versus Postmodernity," *New German Critique*,
22 (1981), 8.

on which they rely – are seen as in principle irrelevant to considerations of moral, legal, or political personhood, which are founded on the right to represent and to be represented and freely to make contracts of association in the open marketplace. Insofar as civil society is embedded in the economic relations of the market, it recognizes no prior substantive restrictions on the terms of the agreements we may make: "modern persons recognize one another as individuals who can make choices and have needs: first the need to exist and make choices and have a hold in the world through property, then the natural needs connected with self-maintenance, then socially developed needs. Even the natural needs exist as involved in a social structure of mutual recognition."[53] Similarly, the nature of political personhood is understood to be independent of any antecedent conceptions about the hierarchy or relative value of social roles. As a set of relations expressing what Weber calls "formal rationality," the structure of civil society is independent of the particular content that individuals may bring to it; in this way, those "substantive" conceptions of rationality founded on the all-embracing orders of nature, social hierarchy, and role are eclipsed by the liberalism of the modern State. Yet it may also be said that the formalism (as opposed to the substantive quality) of the structures of recognition and association in such a State define a correspondingly formal and schematic individuality, a subjectivity that is both theorized and exercised as abstract. Hobbes, for example, draws on a mathematized conception of reason that parallels the pure formality of modern political relations. Yet in order to maintain a neutral stance concerning values, and so to assure the contentment of individuals and the "rational" functioning of such a society as a whole (for example, the protection of those rights which are said to accrue to all), he must imagine a state of nature in which the passions are unmediated and provoke the war of all against all: "nature" is no longer a realm of fixed and stable essences but rather defines a condition in which everyone fears death and therefore seeks to assert him, or herself by any available means. This condition can be terminated only when the overriding passion of fear induces all men to invest a single authority with a monopoly of force, thus compelling them to keep the peace. In this way, the rational justification of liberal

53 David Kolb, *The Critique of Pure Modernity: Hegel, Heidegger, and After* (Chicago: University of Chicago Press, 1986), p. 27.

society is contradicted by the potentially devouring Absolutism of the modern State.[54]

As we can see in the case of Hobbes, the experience of history itself becomes evidence in confirmation of the proposition that there is no natural or pre-established order by which any existing political regime might be measured. Legitimation within the context of modernity must ultimately be *self*-legitimation, the achievement of which requires reason to adopt an ideological stance with respect to the past and to cast the "traditional" world as the locus of unenlightened or "superstitious" beliefs:

From this ignorance of how to distinguish Dreams, and other strong Fancies, from Vision and Sense, did arise the greatest part of the Religion of the Gentiles in time past, that worshipped Satyres, Fawnes, Nymphs, and the like; and now adayes the opinion that rude people have of Fayries, Ghosts, and Goblins; and of the power of Witches. For as for Witches, I think not that their witchcraft is any reall power; but yet that they are justly punished, for the false belief they have, that they can do such mischiefe, joyned with their purpose to do it if they can: their trade being nearer to a new Religion, than to a Craft or Science. And for Fayries and walking Ghosts, the opinion of them has I think been on purpose, either taught, or not confuted, to keep in credit the use of Exorcisms, of Crosses, of holy Water, and other such inventions of Ghostly men. Neverthelesse, there is no doubt but God can make unnatural Apparitions; but that he does it so often, as men need to feare such things, more than they feare the stay, or change, of the course of Nature, which he can also stay, and change, is no point of Christian faith.
(*Leviathan*, I, 2, p. 92)

In this and other ways, Hobbes presents a fully "disenchanted" understanding of the world. But this is not to say that the secularization process was, or ever could be made, complete. Indeed, the modern emphasis on self-improvement and progress may actually enhance the power of the past by demonizing it. According to Hobbes, religion draws on man's chronic vulnerability to anxiety and fear. Specifically, religion is generated out of the fear that ensues when the mind's ability to imagine what is likely or adverse exceeds its capacity to calculate a successful course of action. In Hobbes's words, "this Feare of things invisible, is the naturall seed of that, which every one in himself calleth Religion" (*Leviathan*, I, 11, p. 168). Having observed this "seed of religion," some men cultivate it; they

54 See Habermas's commentary on Hobbes in "The Classical Doctrine of Politics," in *Theory and Practice* (Boston: Beacon Press, 1973), pp. 41–81.

give anxiety over the future a legitimate form and use it to rule over others. They constitute the "kingdom of darknesse," otherwise described as "a Confederacy of Deceivers, that to obtain dominion over men in this present world, endeavour by dark, and erroneous Doctrines, to extinguish in them the Light, both of Nature, and of the Gospell; and so to dis-prepare them for the Kingdome of God to come" (*Leviathan*, IV, 44, pp. 627–28). The greatest error preached by such deceivers is that the Kingdom of God is not "to come" but already in place in the form of the Church to which they belong. These and similar passages from the *Leviathan* serve also to demonstrate that the process of rationalization, which we may provisionally interpret with Weber as a form of secularization, was neither all-embracing nor, in those spheres where it did occur, complete. Indeed, the contrast between "substantive" and "formal" rationality is rendered significantly complex by virtue of the fact that the phenomenon described as "rationalization" is neither uniquely modern nor exclusively historical. Despite the fact that formalized, bureaucratic modes of organization are for Weber the quintessential expressions of the modern State,[55] some striking instances of rationalization may be observed in pre-modern communities. For instance, the medieval monastery stands as an enclave of rationalization within a tradition-oriented world; the monk, not the entrepreneur or the political subject, is in Weber's words "the first human being who lives rationally, who works methodically and by rational means toward a goal, namely the future life. Only for him did the clock strike, only for him were the hours of the day divided – for prayer. The economic life of the monastic communities was also rational."[56] Indeed, Hobbes's own account of the emergence of ecclesiastical power in *Leviathan* IV ("Of the Kingdome of Darknesse")

55 "Bureaucracy...is fully developed in political and ecclesiastical communities only in the modern state, and in the private economy only in the most advanced institutions of capitalism" (*Economy and Society*, ed. Guenther Roth and Claus Wittich [Berkeley: University of California Press, 1978], II, p. 956).

56 Weber, *General Economic History*, trans. Frank H. Knight (New York: Collier Books, 1961), p. 267. See also Weber's discussion in *The Protestant Ethic and the Spirit of Capitalism*, trans. Talcott Parsons (New York: Scribner's, 1958), pp. 118–22. There, Weber explains how modern Christian asceticism is anticipated in medieval monasticism, which "had developed *a systematic method of rational conduct* with the purpose of overcoming the *status naturae*, to free man from the power of irrational impulses and his dependence on the world and on nature.... It trained the monk, objectively, as a worker in the service of the kingdom of God" (pp. 118–19; emphasis added).

presents a striking, if somewhat more complex, example of the rationalization thesis in the form of an argument that Christianity was itself transformed from small communities of believers led by charismatic individuals into a hierarchical edifice whose institutionalized power came paradoxically to rely on the *increased* susceptibility of men to various forms of coercive "enchantment" within a rationalized world.

If we go on to consider the differentiation of society in ethical terms, it then becomes clear that the notion of "substantive rationality," with principles rooted in the order of nature, will appear as the expression of an ethos based on a series of qualitative distinctions that set such categories as good and evil, truth and falsehood, right and wrong, in line with an equally categorical division of society into two constitutive value-groups, the noble and the base.[57] The self-scrutinizing tendencies within enlightened modernity undertook to criticize the naturalistic thesis, along with the hierarchical social structure it was used to support, in favor of an ethics grounded in principles acceptable to all rational beings. Beginning the "morale provisoire" set forth in Descartes's *Discourse on Method* (III), and continuing most importantly in Kant, ethics came to be seen as a function of the knowledge that could be framed and expressed in the form of universal maxims or rules, the truth of which is guaranteed from a "transcendental" point of view. And yet the socio-ethical distinctions of power, status, lineage, and caste were carried forward into modernity, where they were reincorporated into market-sanctioned distinctions of class. In the absence of rigid social hierarchies, or of a teleology founded on "nature," however, the purpose of these residual distinctions did not always remain clear. Indeed, the contradictions resulting from such a misalignment are visible already within the courtly world, where the continued association of goodness with high status generated a series of protocols that were no longer able to command the respect of society

---

57 As the most complex example of the Enlightenment's self-contradictions, Nietzsche continued to insist on the need for rank ordering. Thus while Nietzsche launched a trenchant critique of "metaphysics," he fought tirelessly against the notion of "liberal" society in favor of a "higher culture": "A higher culture can come into existence only where there are two different castes in society: that of the workers and that of the idle, of those capable of true leisure; or, expressed more vigorously: the caste compelled to work and the caste that works if it wants to." *Human, All Too Human*, trans. R. J. Hollingdale (Cambridge: Cambridge University Press, 1986), p. 162, para. 439.

as a whole: "the interaction of high society, still representing the 'good society' within the societal system, became an island of rationality, isolated from all serious business."[58] It was in situations like this, where the substantive ideals proper to an older type of ethical selfhood had been eroded while the discursive structures needed to accommodate the emergent values of modernity had not yet been formed, that the invention of subjectivity played a crucial role, for the individual's self-assertion as subject, founded on the belief that the self as constituted in pure reflection, could transcend all merely historical and social differences; thus it proved powerful enough to legitimize a series of social and ethical relations that had been fashioned along essentially new lines.

For the majority of Weber's commentators, however, the difference between rational modes of legitimation on the one hand and traditional, religious, and affectual modes on the other remains a purely thematic concern within a linear narrative. And yet no such set of contrasts could possibly explain the scope and peculiar ambivalence that the concept of rationalization attains within the corpus of Weber's own work. Weber may have been unable to comprehend the degree to which the intellectual content of modern culture failed to find a total embodiment in these newly secularized moral and social forms of life.[59] Similarly, Weber may have been unable to see that a position such as that of the subject may have reinhabited or, in Blumenberg's terminology, "reoccupied," positions that were in fact carried forward into modernity in a newly secularized form. And while his analyses may hinge on the contrast between modes of rationalization described above, Weber has a somewhat more complex explanatory pattern to offer than many of his commentators have allowed: that increasing rationalization has exerted a constant, if contradictory, pressure on the this-worldly orientation of social life, increasing rather than decreasing the irrationalism of action.

In one form or another, most contrastive accounts of "substantive" and "formal" types of rationality can be traced to Hegel's analysis of

---

58 Niklas Luhmann, "The Individuality of the Individual," in *Reconstructing Individualism*, ed. Thomas C. Heller, Morton Sosna, and David E. Wellbery (Stanford: Stanford University Press, 1986), p. 319.

59 See Alasdair MacIntyre, "The Fate of Theism," in Alasdair MacIntyre and Paul Ricoeur, *The Religious Significance of Atheism* (New York: Columbia University Press, 1966), p. 17.

the breakdown of social relations in Ancient Greece and to his account of the "alienation" of consciousness in the modern world. In Hegel's view, Greek society was founded on modes of acknowledgment and recognition that exemplify the principles of substantive rationality discussed above; in the words of one recent commentator, "each member is aware of himself as recognizing and recognized by the others according to particular roles fitting into a social whole that is immediately present in the acts of all."[60] Yet at the same time Hegel recognized an inherent tension in the "immediate" (i.e. unreflective) identification of one's particular role with the whole of society or with the universal good: any particular role may be authorized by society at large, but it will inevitably come into conflict with other, similarly sanctioned roles. With the discovery of this conflict, consciousness withdraws and begins to conceive of itself as autonomous, as existing independently of and in opposition to the whole:

The single, individual consciousness as it exists in the real ethical order, or in the nation, is a solid unshaken trust in which Spirit has not, for the individual, resolved itself into its *abstract* moments, and therefore he is not aware of himself as being a pure individuality on his own account. But once he has arrived at this idea, as he must, then this *immediate* unity with Spirit, his trust, is lost. In thus establishing himself ... the individual has thereby placed himself in opposition to the laws and customs. They are regarded as mere ideas having no absolute essentiality, as abstract theory without any reality, while he as this particular "I" is his own living truth.

(*PhS*, 259, sec. 355)

For Hegel, the immediate unity of Greek society marks it as a primitive stage in human history. It follows that the differentiation of social relations in the modern world is also a demonstration of its maturity. Indeed, the *Philosophy of Right* allows us to see the differentiation of society not only as disintegrative and oppositional but also as beneficial to the full flowering of *Geist*. More specifically, the differentiation of society into classes or groups (which Hegel calls *Stände*) is predicated on the division of labor. These groups and the needs they articulate – the need for ethical immediacy in the agricultural class, for self-expression through rationalized work in the business class, and for community in the class of civil servants – cannot be synthesized in any individual, but must nonetheless be represented within the State as a whole. Otherwise phrased, the complexity of modern society is too great for the modern individual

60 Kolb, *The Critique of Pure Modernity*, p. 25.

to comprehend or embrace; but the differentiation of society presents an opportunity for the subject to express the principle of freedom by choosing his walk of life. Hence Hegel concludes that subjects *must* differentiate themselves; but since a synthesis is not available immediately, as in the Ancient world, the differentiated subject must also recognize himself as an individual within a larger community.[61]

Hegel's critique of the abstraction of consciousness through the conflict of self-chosen values with the totality of substantive social relations and his allied discussion of the differentiation of modern society have been carried forward in more concrete terms in recent accounts of the changing social structure of early modern Europe. In an interpretation of modernity that emphasizes the (dis)placement of the subject within society, for instance, Niklas Luhmann has suggested that the transformation from substantive to formal modes of rationality was coextensive with the increased differentiation of functions within society itself – functions which may no longer properly be described as traditional "roles." Luhmann's theory of social differentiation is in many ways implicated in the contradictions of social science discussed in connection with Weber above, but this does not invalidate some of the more specific socio-historical claims he has been able to make. Building on Durkheim's crucial insight that individuals in the modern world regularly have dealings of significance with persons whom they do not know (and, we might add, might never see face to face), Luhmann argued that these same individuals are no longer able to identify themselves with a single role whose place in the whole is secure, but must act instead as members of several different functional groups, each one of which, we might add, myopically regards itself as the center of a world.[62] In Luhmann's

---

61 Charles Taylor provides an excellent discussion of the necessary differentiation of modern society in *Hegel* (Cambridge: Cambridge University Press, 1975), pp. 433–36, 487–88. See also Laurence Dickey's discussion of the division of labor in Hegel in *Hegel: Religion, Economics, and the Politics of Spirit 1770–1807* (Cambridge: Cambridge University Press, 1987), pp. 253–77.

62 Freud made a related observation in the context of a general anthropological investigation: "Each individual is a component part of numerous groups, he is bound by ties of identification in many directions, and he has built up his ego ideal upon the most various models. Each individual therefore has a share in numerous group minds – those of his race, of his class, of his creed, of his nationality, etc. – and he can also raise himself above them to the extent of having a scrap of independence and originality." Freud, *Group Psychology and the Analysis of the Ego*, trans. James Strachey (New York: Boni and Liveright, 1921), p. 101.

analysis, every individual in modern society belongs to a large number of significant groups, but each of these affects only a limited part of his existence. As a result, the substantive aspects of selfhood are carved up into separate spheres and can be unified only at the level of a formally abstract and substantively empty subject:

The evolution of this highly improbable social order required replacing stratification with functional differentiation as the main principle of forming subsystems within the overall system of society. In stratified societies, the human individual was regularly placed only in one subsystem. Social status (*condition, qualité, état*) was the most stable characteristic of an individual's personality. This is no longer possible for a society differentiated with respect to functions such as politics, economy, intimate relations, religion, sciences, and education. Nobody can live in only one of these systems.

There is ... a hidden relation between the functional differentiation of the societal system and the individual's self-proclamation as subject. Given the traditional connotations of *hypokeimenon/subiectum* – something "lying under" and supporting attributes – "subject" means something that underlies and carries the world, and, therefore, something that exists in its own right as a transcendental and not as an empirical phenomenon. ... The individual leaves the world in order to look at it. I interpret this extramundane position of the transcendental subject as a symbol for the new position of the empirical individual in relation to a system of functional subsystems. He does not belong to any one of them in particular but depends on their interdependence.[63]

Similarly, the work of social historians like Norbert Elias allows us to see that the transition from the hierarchical social and political arrangements of the premodern world to the market- and contract-oriented individualism of liberal society was mediated by the court societies and city-states of the Renaissance, both of which attempted to embrace a set of rapidly changing social values.[64] Likewise, the

---

63 Luhmann, "Individuality," pp. 318, 319. See also Luhmann, *The Differentiation of Society* (New York: Columbia University Press, 1982). This is not the place to attempt a full-scale critique of Luhmann's methodology; still it must be noted that a purely functional analysis of society suffers many of the same limitations with regard to values as does Weber's "value-free" inquiry.

64 Elias, *The Court Society*, trans. Edmund Jephcott (New York: Pantheon, 1983). See also Elias, *Power and Civility*, trans. Jephcott (New York: Pantheon, 1982). As we will see in greater detail in chapter 3 below, it is Hegel's analysis of the origins of the modern state in rhetoric that are crucial for an understanding of the relationship between rhetoric and power in the Renaissance: "The heroism of silent service becomes the heroism of flattery. This vocal reflection of service constitutes the spiritual self-separating middle term and reflects back into itself

work of historians of rhetoric like Nancy Struever and Thomas Sloane has helped us to see that in their discursive orientation, these city-states responded to the conditions of social change by attempting to secure a sense of ethical selfhood and *communitas* for the subject when faced with the erosion of an existing value-ground.[65] We can in retrospect see that the attempt to embrace the contradictory aspects of history and human nature by recourse to the arts of dialogue and controversial argumentation was an unstable solution to the problems posed by historical change; as the rhetorical principles of this controversial, perspectivist, and "dialogic" ethos were superseded by the model of subjective self-consciousness described above a more powerful way was found to secure the position of the self, in part by positing selfhood as the subject of a transcendental stance and a newly "foundational" discourse. These and other mediating conjunctures nonetheless provide indispensable routes of access into the shifting discursive orientations of modern society during its formative period. First, they serve to make comprehensible the transformation of those values that otherwise could be juxtaposed only in schematic and contrastive terms; in this they resemble the "bridge structures" that Talcott Parsons described.[66] And second, in producing "solutions" to the problem of historical change, they generate distinct expressive possibilities, through which subjects may tran-

not only its own extreme, but also reflects into this self the extreme of universal power, making that power, which is at first only implicit, into a power that is explicit with an existence of its own, makes itself into a self-conscious individuality. The result is that the Spirit of this power is now an unlimited monarch: unlimited, because the language of flattery raises this power into its purified universality" (*PhS*, sec. 511, p. 310).

65 Nancy Struever, *The Language of History in the Renaissance* (Princeton: Princeton University Press, 1970); Thomas Sloane, *Donne, Milton, and the End of Humanist Rhetoric* (Berkeley: University of California Press, 1985). See also David Marsh, *The Quattrocento Dialogue: Classical Tradition and Humanist Innovation* (Cambridge, MA: Harvard University Press, 1980), and Jerrold Siegel, *Rhetoric and Philosophy in Renaissance Humanism* (Princeton: Princeton University Press, 1968).

66 See Talcott Parsons, *The System of Modern Society* (Englewood Cliffs: Prentice Hall, 1971), and Schluchter's discussion in *The Rise of Western Rationalism*, p. 153. Jameson offers a general theory of mediation in conjunction with Weber's work in his essay "The Vanishing Mediator," in *The Ideologies of Theory, II* (Minneapolis: University of Minnesota Press, 1988), pp. 3–34. Jameson's theory raises at least as many questions as it answers: first, the notion that world-historical conjunctures are indeed "vanishing"; and second, that they serve a purely functional rather than an expressive potential. As we will see in the concluding pages of this chapter, Hegel's analysis represents a powerful attempt to reconcile the differences between these two types of historical analysis.

scend the merely functional roles that social science may assign to them. In this way we may distinguish the process of social differentiation into classes, functions, or "estates" on the one hand from the differentiation of a series of autonomous "discourses" on the other. If the first constitutes an order of social facts, the second may be thought of as a second-order range of responses that are implicated but never fully determined by those facts.

It can in this light be said that what is most significant about the emergence of the subject can be uncovered not from the history of events but from the modes of discourse and consciousness that were evolved in response to the process of social change. Some of the implications of this claim may become clear if we consider briefly the shift in the early modern period from the aesthetics of wonder and awe (*admiratio*) visible in the late romances of Shakespeare and Cervantes in contrast to the eighteenth-century aesthetics of the sublime, which was likewise designed to stir and move the passions of the spectator-subject. Recent studies have for instance shown that both aesthetic theory and practice came in the eighteenth century to be dominated by the figural juxtaposition of various states of deprivation, alienation, isolation, and division with some absent and longed-for state of communal solidarity.[67] As we shall see in connection with Lukács's *Theory of the Novel* below, this constitutes one of the ways in which the ceaseless, internal tension within society between the parts and the whole is projected in the form of a distinction between a degraded or inferior present and a utopian future or ideal past. The fact that effects of sympathy, pity, and other strong "passions" came to be prized does not of course go to say that these same effects had not previously been experienced or that the needs underlying them had not previously existed in society. But whereas in the Renaissance romances the subject is successfully reincorporated into the stable structures of family and state, the subject position in the eighteenth century remains strongly indicated as the locus of utopian desires, but in practice often unoccupied. Thus

67 The relevant studies are Michael Fried, *Absorption and Thetatricality: Painting and Beholder in the Age of Diderot* (Berkeley: University of California Press, 1980); Jay Caplan, *Framed Narratives: Diderot's Genealogy of the Beholder* (Minneapolis: University of Minnesota Press, 1985); and David Marshall, *The Surprising Effects of Sympathy: Marivaux, Diderot, Rousseau, and Mary Shelley* (Chicago: University of Chicago Press, 1988).

while a lack of unity or loss of totality may have been part of the felt experience in the early modern age, they do not in themselves say anything about the preceding state of affairs or the actual dissolution of a pre-existing social bond. Rather, the claim is that an increasing degree of societal differentiation transformed a social lack into a sense of historical loss that required increasingly utopian projections in order to be met.[68]

A variety of accounts, however, including Descartes's own, decline to consider the invention of subjectivity in social or historical terms at all. The subject is seen as emerging from a prior moment of enchantment, from mythical consciousness, or from a "mimetic" union with the natural world. Because of a failure to distinguish the "natural" motions of consciousness – as witnessed, for example, in the anti-skeptical arguments of the Cartesian texts – from the cultural history of subjectivity as embodied in social institutions, the phenomenon that Weber referred to as the "disenchantment" of the world has often been interpreted as a psychological process of objectification and ego-formation rather than as the establishment of a legitimizing framework for new values. To be sure, the idea of an original union with nature suggests the reassuring possibility of deriving an ethics from a knowledge of first principles. But as Horkheimer and Adorno warned, to begin from the premise of an original union with nature leads to an ultimately self-deceptive understanding of the process of enlightenment and leaves no line of defense against the self-destructive consequences of rationalization. Although the subject may be seen as empowered to gain distance from and to master a natural world rendered correspondingly "disenchanted" or "desouled," the goal of reason must consist in the avoidance of a "fall" out of consciousness back into enchantment; indeed, its primary task is to resist reabsorption into nature itself.

In so saying, Horkheimer and Adorno preempt the Hegelian critique of subjectivity, which attempts to reconcile spirit and nature and to supply the overarching *telos* that the rational subject in its divorce from nature admittedly lacks. We will return to consider Hegel's totalizing critique of subjectivity in the pages that follow. In closing this section it may be sufficient to remind ourselves of Adorno's central claim, which is that the logic of subjectivity induces

68 See Jochen Schulte-Sasse, "Art and the Sacrificial Structure of Modernity," "Afterword" to Caplan, *Framed Narratives*, pp. 103–4.

a forgetfulness of the process through which the subject becomes subject to the barbarism of its own self-assertion over against nature:

That reason is something different from nature and yet a moment within it – this is its prehistory, which has become part of its immanent determination. As the psychic force branching out for the purposes of self-preservation, it is natural; however, once it has been split off and contrasted with nature, it also becomes the other of nature. Reason, cutting nature down to size in an ephemeral way, is identical and nonidentical with nature, dialectical in accord with its own concept. Yet the more unrestrainedly reason is made into an absolute over against nature within that dialectic and becomes oblivious of itself in this, the more it regresses, as self-assertion gone wild, into nature; only as nature's reflection would it be supernature.[69]

For Adorno, consciousness is shaped by the need to resist the seductions of the naturalistic thesis described above; this requires a rational if strategic opposition to those institutions that would enforce a connection between the overwhelming powers of nature and a mimetic, labile, but as yet unformed and unsocialized self. To refer the origins of subjectivity back to the moment of an original union with nature, or to conceive of existence in an enchanted world, may indeed provide the "metaphysical comfort" of an ethics derivable from first principles; but it will force us subsequently to choose between the projects to recuperate a lost and original unity with nature and the desire to subordinate the authority of nature to the demands of a fully rational critique. As Hegel's example will help us see, none of these courses can remain open for long once the subject has gained an awareness of the historical nature of its stance.

Selfhood and subjectivity

As we have begun to see above, claims for the "historical absolutism" of the modern age constitute attempts to supply reason with a presuppositionless starting-point or "ungrounded ground" and so to derive the *telos* of man from the powers of self-reflection rather than from reference to nature itself. I have at the same time argued that this attempt is accompanied by a paradigmatic social change, in which a hierarchical society that derived its legitimizing principles by reference to a natural order was replaced by one of functionally differentiated but "equal" individuals, subjects who were free in principle to make contracts of association, to represent themselves

69 Adorno, *Negative Dialectics*, cited in Habermas, *Philosophical-Political Profiles*, trans. Frederick Lawrence (Cambridge, MA: MIT Press, 1983), p. 100.

politically, and to participate in a system of free-market exchanges. Whether or not the procedures of subjective self-reflection were sufficient to legitimize this new social order is a question that remains to be addressed. For present purposes it is sufficient to say that the goal of radical self-assertion through subjective self-reflection fails as a form of foundationalism as soon as it becomes clear that subjective reason is unable fully to comprehend the process through which its own historical emergence takes place: insofar as its "founding" is based on the "overcoming" of history, the subject remains radically incomplete just where it purports to stand on a self-sufficient ground. Yet as we also shall see a totalizing critique of subjectivity in the manner that Hegel undertook runs additional risks; the Hegelian Absolute is predicated on the end of history, the closure of contexts, and the full conceptualization of the world.

Given the antinomies characteristic of the modern age, some of which have been made all the more apparent still in certain aspects of "postmodern" discourse, it might be better to begin the task of reinterpreting subjectivity by recognizing the contradiction between the discursive claims of reason's radical emergence from nature and history and the story-like forms through which its origins are expressed. On the one hand the "disenchantment" of the world by reason is registered at the point where reason, the *cogito*, breaks from the discursive structures of the past; yet on the other hand, we may recover the discursivity of reason even from a thinker like Descartes. This much may become clear if we look at the narrative mode rather than isolate the logical claims of the *Meditations* and the *Discourse on Method*, for the mathematical ideals of reason prove in the final analysis unable to suppress the story-like forms through which they are expressed. The rhetorical mode of the *Meditations* and the *Discourse* is that of a narrative in which claims for the origins of subjectivity in pure reflection are refashioned as the account of a crisis in which the subject emerges from the deceptions of its own autobiographical past.[70] Recall the beginning of *Meditations* I and II and the opening of the *Discourse on Method* in this regard:

70 On subjectivity and autobiography in Descartes, see John D. Lyons, "Subjectivity and Imitation in the *Discours de la méthode*," *Neophilologus*, 66 (1982), 508–24, and Dalia Judovitz, "Autobiographical Discourse and Critical Praxis in Descartes," *Philosophy and Literature*, 5 (1981), 91–107, and *Subjectivity and Representation: The Origins of Modern Thought in Descartes* (Cambridge: Cambridge University Press, 1988).

Some years ago I was struck by the large number of falsehoods that I had accepted as true in my childhood, and by the highly doubtful nature of the whole edifice that I had subsequently based on them.

(*Meditations*, I, p. 12)

So serious are the doubts into which I have been thrown as a result of yesterday's meditation that I can neither put them out of my mind nor see any way of resolving them. (*Meditations*, II, p. 16)

From my childhood I have been nourished upon letters and because I was persuaded that by their means one could acquire a clear and certain knowledge of all that is useful in life, I was extremely eager to learn them. But as soon as I had completed the course of study at the end of which one is normally admitted to the ranks of the learned, I completely changed my opinion. For I found myself beset by so many doubts and errors that I came to think I had gained nothing from my attempts to become educated but increasing recognition of my ignorance. (*Discourse*, I, pp. 112–13)

More specifically, the problem of origination results in a narrative of crisis whose principal topic is that of skeptical doubt; as Descartes says graphically in a crucial moment of the *Meditations*, "it feels as if I have fallen unexpectedly into a deep whirlpool which tumbles me around so that I can neither stand on the bottom nor swim up to the top."[71]. Indeed, whether the history of modernity is seen to commence with the historical priority claimed for reason by Descartes, or whether that occurs only with the Kantian division of empirical and transcendental worlds, as both Habermas and Foucault have claimed, it must be said that the ideal that human rationality should model itself on mathematics never was able fully to displace the discursive means through which subjectivity initially was expressed. Moreover, if we probe behind conventional interpretations of Descartes to uncover the plot of skepticism and reason played out in the Cartesian texts, we can see that the disorienting experience provoked by the loss of natural forms precipitates the narrative search for a "transcendental" position from which to evaluate competing points of view. As the anti-skeptical narrative of the Cartesian texts reveal, and as our discussions of Cervantes in the chapter to follow will show, the disconcerting multiplicity of perspectives may be stabilized through the formation of a narrative subject and a

71 Descartes, *Meditations*, II; in *The Philosophical Works of Descartes*, trans. John Cottingham, Robert Stoothoff, and Dugald Murdoch (Cambridge: Cambridge University Press, 1984), II, p. 16.

corresponding "world view." But while it may be possible to stabilize the diversity of perspectives within the world, through a narrative of reason, it could also be said that the problem of reason is thus reduced to that form that is fundamentally congruous with the methods of modern science, for such a narrative requires a (reading) subject who can stand in a position of true knowledge *above* the world. Similarly, the investigation of perspectivism or of difference becomes not an inquiry into the transcendent grounding of speech but rather an investigation of the differences among individuals interested in reducing their differences in the image of a coherent narrative about shareable truths. Through the experiences of doubt and self-alienation figured in the Cartesian narrative, Descartes also articulates the assumptions that will be taken up by modern politics; these are that difference may be located within the interpersonal space that separates the subject-self from a community of others, rather than in the relationship between the space of beings and the Logos.

In order to understand the importance of approaching the subject of modernity in terms of the ways in which agents both conceptualize and legitimate the values they hold, it may be useful to contrast the analysis of subjectivity outlined above with the account of modern individualism presented in some of Charles Taylor's work.[72] Since Taylor's critique of the model of a disengaged and disembodied self and his emphasis on the relationship between valuing agents and contextual or background practices are in many respects compatible with the critique of subjectivity presented here, I should clarify that the purpose of this contrast is to reveal what is additionally at stake in attempting to define the subject as having provided the legitimizing framework for the values of a new age. One dimension of Taylor's critique is based on the fact that the knowledge that may be gained through transcendental arguments and formulated in purely conceptual terms is the fruit of an illusory search for the "fundamental" representations that our practices are thought to conceal. The foundationalism that we customarily associate with subjectivity is on his account undermined once we come to realize that there are no such deeper or more basic representations and that our relationship to

72 See, for example, Taylor's "Overcoming Epistemology," in Kenneth Baynes, James Bohman, and Thomas McCarthy, eds., *After Philosophy: End or Transformation* (Cambridge: MIT Press, 1987), pp. 464–88, and his recently published *Sources of the Self* (Cambridge, MA: Harvard University Press, 1989).

the world is more accurately described in terms of our "dealings" with it, which fall largely outside the bounds of our conceptualized practices and explicit beliefs. On this view, there can be no question of ever fully articulating the grasp that we as agents have on the world because any project of conceptual articulation would itself depend on a prior background of tacit engagement with the world. The standard interpretation of subjectivity may accordingly be taken as operating under the illusion of complete self-objectification,[73] the price of which is paid in a form of abstraction that debars the subject from addressing values in any concrete or substantive way.

We may with Taylor identify three principal elements of the conventional account. First, the modern subject is seen as both free and rational to the extent that the power claimed by reason confirms its autonomy from the natural and social worlds. The achievements of rationality and freedom are guaranteed by the subject's position as an "ideal spectator" on the world, which is to say as one whose identity is constituted as independent of what lies outside it. In representing the world from such a position, the subject may be seen as one who has freed himself from thralldom to the "enchantments" of nature as well as from the need for obedience to external authority or control. Second, and closely allied to the position of the subject as "ideal spectator," is a view of the self as an agent of change in the external world. As a free and rational being and autonomous individual, the subject is inclined to manipulate the world in order to secure his own happiness or the satisfaction of his aims. The third element of this account expresses the social consequences of the first two: a State comprised of subjects will be regarded as a free association of equal individuals whose corporate identity is confirmed by the success of individual social and economic aims.

If we look more closely at this account, we can see that each element in it provides a partial interpretation of what we have described, with Weber, as the "disenchantment" of the world, and that each helps clarify the value within the culture of modernity that is attached to gaining freedom from nature through the assertion of rational control. Yet we can also see that the achievement of this freedom entails substantial costs and that this account does not fully

---

73 Taylor's critique may in this respect be compared to that of Thomas Kuhn's claim that paradigms cannot fully be rationalized. See *The Structure of Scientific Revolutions*, especially pp. 43–51, "The Priority of Paradigms."

take these into consideration. For instance, the vision of the self as an "ideal spectator" is closely bound up with the classical forms of dualism, so that the subject *qua* "thinking thing" must be withdrawn even from its own body, which in turn is regarded as an object of quasi-scientific manipulation and control. The view of personal identity that originates in Humanist ideals of prudent self-governance, as taken up for instance by Montaigne, are with Descartes transformed into instrumental forms of behavior that generate instrumental and therapeutic approaches to social policy, medicine, psychology, and public health. Finally, it can be seen that a society comprised of subjects will tend to be an atomistic association of individuals whose efforts at achieving collective ends will come into conflict with the purposes and aims of individual members of the group.

Since the analysis of subjectivity I am presenting here differs from the conventional one, it is necessary to augment certain dimensions of Taylor's critique. Whereas Taylor stresses the illusion involved in seeking to provide "deep" foundations for our practices, and so strives to level the distinction between background practices and foreground concepts, the account I have proposed would stress the potential emptiness or abstraction involved in positing the subject as *hypokeimenon* or underlying ground, and the contradictions that may follow from this, while continuing to emphasize the entrenchment of subjectivity as providing the dominant framework for the culture of modernity. The philosophical discourse established by Descartes may be regarded as a practice, but it is not just one practice among many. Rather, the case to be made about Descartes as the "inventor" of subjectivity is closer to the one that Alasdair MacIntyre has made for Luther, viz., that he is able to grasp the moral experience of his public and in so doing leads to the acceptance of a discourse in which their experience may be comprehended in stock "Lutheran" ways.[74] And yet it must be said that the concerns just mentioned encompass and do not exclude the ones that Taylor has expressed. For to think of the subject as providing an abstract foundation or underlying ground for our practices inevitably jeopardizes the grasp that we as agents may have on any particular, practical world: on the one hand the world is transformed into a picture of the same categories through which the subject's universal, rational nature is expressed, while on the other hand the subject's values and the objects of its desires are idealized

74 MacIntyre, *A Short History of Ethics* (New York: Macmillan, 1966), p. 125.

beyond the bounds of its own reason or are subordinated to the powers of an unmasterable will. Similarly, the complaint against the classical dualism of mind and body may be restated in terms of the discursive conflict between a reflective psychology that asks the subject to free itself from all states of dependence, and a "scientific" psychology that seeks to control the organism as part of objectified natural processes.[75] But since the subject in some sense inhabits both sides of these divisions, the subject is divided as if from within: on the one side is a transcendental self or "thinking thing" who exerts its strongest hold precisely where our relationship to "external" nature is framed objectively and in the abstract; and on the other side is the socially constituted, individuated, and physically embodied subject, who abides by the belief that value-goals can be pursued, if at all, by forceful exertions of the will.

The contrast between the Cartesian *Meditations* and *Discourse on Method* on the one hand, and Montaigne's *Essais* on the other, provides an illuminating example of the increasing abstraction that accompanies this historical shift. For, unlike the writings of Descartes, the *Essais* resist the transformation of historically contingent modes of discourse into objectified structures or "positivities" and demonstrate that these have no real validity independent of the agents by whom they are articulated and expressed. Whereas some critics have taken Montaigne's self-examination as anticipating Descartes's self-reflection, and have seen Montaigne as fully involved in the possessive individualism and appropriative ideology of the modern age, and whereas others have come to project onto Montaigne the nostalgic hope for an older, pre-subjective form of ethical selfhood, it can be seen that a series of historical and discursive differences separate the Cartesian subject from the Montaignian self in a more or less categorical way. Seen from the point of view of Descartes, a thinker like Blumenberg is of course right: the very possibility of "witnessing" history is ruled out by the requirements of the Cartesian

75 I have found the following accounts to be of interest: Roberto Mangabeira Unger, "A Program for Late Twentieth-Century Psychiatry," Appendix to *Passion: An Essay on Personality* (New York: Free Press, 1984), pp. 275–300; and Jürgen Habermas, "The Scientistic Self-Misunderstanding of Metapsychology: On the Logic of General Interpretation," in *Knowledge and Human Interests*, trans. Jeremy J. Shapiro (Boston: Beacon Press, 1971), pp. 246–73. See also Paul Ricoeur, *Freud and Philosophy: An Essay on Interpretation*, trans. Denis Savage (New Haven: Yale University Press, 1970), especially the section on "Energetics and Hermeneutics," pp. 65–151.

critique.[76] But whereas Descartes responds to historical change through a series of self-assertive gestures – thus preparing the ground for a "presuppositionless"philosophical critique – Montaigne takes the diversity of historical experience and cultural practices as reason to renounce the possibility that transcendental arguments might ever serve to "ground" the self. He registers the experience of an "unruly age" ("un siècle desbordé," III, 9) in the disparity between his desire for a stable form of self-governance and an essentially unmasterable past. In contrast to the vision of the self as subject, as ideally disengaged from the processes of nature and history, and as standing over both of these in a posture of confident self-possession, the *Essais* present a self immersed in, and sometimes absorbed by, historical change. If the Cartesian subject assumes a stance in which reason asserts its independence even from the rhetoric of its own discourse, the Montaignian self claims to be consubstantial with the discursive modes of its self-presentation while at the same time questioning the degree to which such modes can ever be fully appropriated or "owned."[77]

According to Jean Starobinski's account, the *Essais* may be situated within the spectrum of the subjective individualism of modernity insofar as they demonstrate the appropriation of all "external" aspects of form, including nature, as features of the self. According to the arguments put forward in *Montaigne in Motion*, the semantic opposition between internal and external, as between "proper" and "alien" modes of discourse, governs a process of individuation in which the positive term is said always to be that which is "mine," "internal," or "intrinsic." Insofar as it remains opposed to and uncontrollable by the self, for instance, nature is an aspect of external form. Similarly, custom is a limiting, "external" constraint and so constitutes the object of a negative critique. Montaigne's

---

76 Cf. Montaigne, who registers this transformation in personal terms: "I do not portray being: I portray passing. Not the passing from one age to another, or, as the people say, from seven years to seven years, but from day to day, from minute to minute." *The Complete Essays of Montaigne*, trans. Donald Frame (Stanford: Stanford University Press, 1958), III, 2, "Of Repentance."

77 The question that naturally arises in this connection is to what extent Montaigne *speaks*, and to what extent he *quotes* in the *Essais*. On quotation in Montaigne see Antoine Compagnon, *La Seconde Main ou le travail de la citation* (Paris: Seuil, 1979), and Marc Fumaroli, *L'Age de l'éloquence: rhétorique et 'res literaria' de la Renaissance au seuil de l'époque classique* (Geneva: Droz, 1980), especially pp. 464–66.

propensity to quote would on this account be the sign of a natural weakness and is in fact associated with the self-denigration of the melancholic. And yet Starobinski finds that Montaigne ultimately exhorts us to obey that nature which exerts its control from within. He claims that only when custom and the other external forces that shape us can be appropriated by the self may they be considered as "proper" attributes or effects of the subject; as soon as they can be called "my own," Starobinski argues, they may be exonerated of all charges and made legitimate. Montaigne's desire for autonomy ("je veux estre maistre de moy, a tout sens" III, 5) is dependent on his rejection of the dominance of *autrui* over the self.

Following this argument, however, appropriation is legitimation. The process of individuation Starobinski sees in Montaigne is a form of discursive self-"possession" that serves to confirm the more general pattern by which the writer of the *Essais* evolves from dependency on nature to the final achievement of selfhood through the acceptance of a world of appearances. In this way, Montaigne is seen to experience the liberating force of modern individualism without suffering any of its deleterious consequences. Montaigne constructs a reply to skeptical doubts about the existence and stability of an order of nature while at the same time avoiding the reifying movement through which subjective experience is refashioned into the ground of absolute truths. Instead, the writer's initial anxiety about his "alienation" from nature in a world of appearances is brought to an end when the constraints imposed by external forms are freely assimilated and suitably appropriated as part of the self: "form is then imposed from within; it is the result of individual effort and labor. However docile the individual may be in accepting social custom, he will be obliged to no one but himself for what constitutes him *qua* individual. At the same time, he will have internalized that which was initially alien or hostile...'By long usage this form of mine has turned into substance, and fortune into nature' [III, 10]. At this moment custom has ceased to be external and become entirely *my own*. It belongs to me; it is a *human accomplishment*. Far from altering my true nature, it makes me what I am."[78]

Since I have suggested above that the emergence of subjectivity must be understood as a self-legitimizing attempt to "ground" the values of a new age, in part by rejecting the naturalistic thesis about

78 Starobinski, *Montaigne in Movement*, trans. Arthur Goldhammer (Chicago: University of Chicago Press, 1985), p. 217.

society as it stands, I would dispute these claims and argue that there is no "subject" – self-conscious, appropriative, or otherwise – governing the discourse of the *Essais*. Indeed, Montaigne has difficulty in imagining any stable future context for the self. It may instead be seen that the "formlessness" of Montaigne's writing, the characteristic waywardness of the *Essais* and the errant nature of the self whose "passing" is portrayed therein, mark an historical transformation, and so constitute an inherited source of questions to which the modern subject may be viewed as providing a critical response.[79] This is one implication of Timothy Reiss's analysis of the "discourse of modernism," which refashions a generally Foucaultian perspective on the breaks between epistemes into a statement of the emergence of the new within the old.[80] But as we have already begun to see, that response is itself the source of a series of contradictions of which the antinomy between history and theory is but one. While the subject comes to imagine itself as standing outside of history in order abstractly to govern a "detotalized" world, its concrete experience is shaped by a series of related splits between fact and theory, reason and desire, value and rule. Some comprehension of these antinomies must figure as part of any theoretical approach to the subject, yet they remain unacknowledged by thinkers on both sides of the debate over modernity and postmodernism, including Habermas and Lyotard. My equal dissatisfaction with Habermas and with post-structuralist thought remains in important ways indebted to a series of Hegelian perspectives on modernity, yet my approach differs from Hegel's in ways that warrant further explanation here.

From a purely retrospective point of view, Hegel saw the philosophy of subjectivity, as first formulated by Descartes and as refined by Kant, as having provided the initial orientation and self-interpretation

79 Insofar as the "possessive" nature of this individualism is concerned, let us note that Montaigne says that he would rather *jouir*: "It is the enjoying, not the possessing, that makes us happy" (I, 42, "Of the Inequality that is Between Us," p. 192: "C'est le jouir, non le posséder, qui nous rend heureux"); also: "when a man has mortgaged his work to the world, it seems to me that he has no further right to it" (III, 9, "Of Vanity," p. 736).

80 See Reiss, *The Discourse of Modernism* (Ithaca: Cornell University Press, 1982), and also his essay "Montaigne and the Subject of Polity," in *Literary Theory/Renaissance Texts*, ed. Patricia Parker and David Quint (Baltimore: Johns Hopkins University Press, 1986), pp. 115–49.

of the modern age. Yet Hegel claimed also to have understood what remained concealed and uncomprehended by their thought:

Consciousness, therefore, through the experience in which its truth ought to have come to light, has instead become to itself a dark riddle; the consequences of its deeds are to it not really its own deeds. What happens to it is found to be not the experience of what it *inherently* is; the transition is not a mere alteration in form of the same content and essential nature, presented now as content and true reality of consciousness, thereafter as object or *intuitively perceived* essence of itself. The *abstract necessity* thus gets the significance of the merely negative uncomprehended *power of universality*, on which individuality is broken in pieces.[81]

On Hegel's account, the self-enlightened subjectivity that defines modern rational consciousness had not yet begun to comprehend the fact that different modes of discourse, like the institutional divisions of culture itself, were in fact divisions within a whole. Yet whereas Hegel thought it possible to comprehend this whole and to reconcile its divided terms through a progressive and totalizing dialectic, it can also be seen that Hegel's attempt, through the philosophy of Spirit, to recover the consciousness of history that the subject was presumed to have "overcome," is possible only given the closure of contexts, the end of discourse, and the completion of history itself. For Hegel, knowledge of the design of history, although not immediately visible at any particular moment within time, could be gleaned from an examination of the movement of history as a whole, and in Hegel's view that design must demonstrate the inner necessity of reason itself. Thus Hegel said of the belief that there is reason in history that "It is not simply a presupposition of study; it is a result which happens to be known to myself because I already know the whole. Therefore, only the study of the world history itself can show that it has proceeded rationally, that it represents the rationally necessary course of the World Spirit."[82]

Hegel's conception of the totality was meant to repair the separation of reason and history within the context of a still higher form of speculative thought. In this way he hoped also to overcome the loss of a natural *telos* for reason. Hegel's *Geist* thus resolves the problem of modernity by "transcending" subjectivity, but in order

81 I owe this reference to Georg Lukács, *The Young Hegel*, trans. Rodney Livingstone (London: Merlin, 1975), p. 479.

82 Hegel, *Reason in History*, trans. Robert S. Hartman (New York, 1953), p. 30; cited in Taylor, *Hegel and Modern Society* (Cambridge: Cambridge University Press, 1979), p. 65.

for this transcendence to take place within the framework of enlightened historical discourse, Hegel was forced to speak with the voice of the Absolute. Quite apart from the purely theoretical difficulties that inhere in gaining access to the Absolute, Hegel's attempt to recover the totality of reason (spirit) and nature provides further evidence that the process of "disenchantment" – understood in this context as a form of secularization – was never in fact complete. Indeed, there continued to remain within modernity the displaced and vacated forms of traditional and sacred beliefs, and it is these that Hegel attempted to redeem as part of his program to make the process of enlightenment complete. As the following observations from the section of the *Phenomenology of Spirit* entitled "The Struggle of Enlightenment with Superstition" indicate, this project began with Hegel's recovery of the hidden unity of reason and faith: "what Enlightenment declares to be an error and a fiction is the very same thing as Enlightenment itself is. Enlightenment that wants to teach faith the new wisdom does not tell it anything new" (*PhS*, p. 334, sec. 549).

Hegel's attempt, in the *Phenomenology of Spirit* and elsewhere, to reconcile his conception of the sacred and ultimately salvational pattern of history with his modernist faith in the powers of a self-enlightened critique, are representative of his efforts to recover a natural context for reason by binding all the spheres of culture together as moments of a spiritual whole. In order to do so, however, he found it necessary to transform modernity's historical loss of a natural context into a positive expression of the movement of Spirit or *Geist*. In Habermas's reading of Hegel, such a need is thrust upon consciousness as a necessity the very moment the subject comes to conceive itself historically,[83] which is to say that it becomes an imperative as soon as the subject confronts and attempts to comprehend its own will to constitute itself as autonomous and mark a new beginning in time. Yet Habermas does not see the other side of the dialectical coin, viz., that the confrontation of established institutions and beliefs with a series of destabilizing historical conditions produced a shift in values that only an invention such as the subject, with claims to radical novelty and metaphysical certainty, could possibly have grasped; insofar as he does not recognize this fact, Habermas can only answer Hegel in the abstract. Rather, what

83 See *The Philosophical Discourse of Modernity*, p. 19.

appears as the historical absolutism of the modern age and as the positive dimension of its task – viz., the heroic effort to generate all that is normative out of itself – must be seen as an attempt to legitimize values that had been produced by historical change.

Hegel's analysis of modernity is historical insofar as it is occasioned by changes in the nature of society. Yet at the same time it aspires to be self-surpassing in a way that is distinctive of theoretical discourse. It is a form of articulation that claims to provide a coherent interpretation of history and at the same time to justify its own interpretation as complete.[84] However, if we accept the fact that history has no end and that the process of enlightenment can never be made complete in the rigorous sense that Hegel required, we must reinterpret Hegel's absolute perspective on modernity not as an ideal for the ultimate unity of history and theory but rather as the pivotal moment in the interpretation of self-consciousness, the totalizing elements of which may, like Wittgenstein's ladder, be cast aside once their initial work is done. It might then be possible to shift the critique of modernity from the analysis of what Hegel called a "positivity" or Foucault an "episteme" toward what Marx called a "simple" or "rational" abstraction, i.e., a conjuncture that reflects the ways in which values are not so much falsified as negated in their internal structure simply in order to be grasped.[85] Insofar as "vulgar" Marxist analyses remain content with summary allusion to such ready-made concepts as "feudalism," "capitalism," "the rise of the bourgeoisie," and the like, their interpretive force will be blunted by the need to contain the discourse about process within the very narrow bounds of a categorizing mode of thought. Yet it may be possible to free Marx's analysis from the false necessities generated by a "deep-structure" view of history while preserving his insights into the function of the concept as a fulcrum or lever of history. In a comment

---

84 See the discussion in Barry Cooper, *The End of History, passim,* and in Stanley Rosen, *G. W. F. Hegel: An Introduction to the Science of Wisdom* (New Haven: Yale University Press, 1974), especially pp. 29–46 ("The Completion of World History").

85 The analysis of Daniel Little in *The Scientific Marx* (Minnesota: University of Minnesota Press, 1986), pp. 92–126 (on "Essentialism, Abstraction, and Dialectics") makes a *prima facie* case that Marx is himself a proponent of a method of scientific abstraction, but surely this misses the argument against the various forms of abstraction that Marx himself makes. I have found the account of "simple" and "rational" abstraction in Marx in Michael McKeon's *The Origins of the English Novel, 1600–1740* (Baltimore: Johns Hopkins University Press, 1987) far more illuminating.

on Descartes's metaphysics, Hegel wrote that "pure being is not something concretely real, but a pure abstraction,"[86] yet we would miss the fundamental point of this comment if we did not also see that conceptual abstractions, while necessarily false, reveal an important dimension of truth. What is false in them lies precisely in the assumptions they make about the nature of conceptual categories (e.g. that of the "subject"), and especially about the adequacy of any category to the historical reality it attempts to describe. Thus Marx can say that "as a rule, the most general abstractions arise only in the midst of the richest possible concrete development, where one thing appears as common to many, to all. Then it ceases to be thinkable in a particular form alone"; and also that "The simplest abstraction ['labor,' 'labor as such,' 'labor pure and simple']... which modern economics places at the head of its discussions, and which expresses an immeasurably ancient relation valid in all forms of society, nevertheless achieves particular truth as an abstraction only as a category of the most modern society."[87]

Taken in tandem with the claim that abstractions may reach their most powerful level precisely where the nature of historical relations is most complex, Hegel's assertions may well serve as a reminder of how Marx's critical and historical methods might be salvaged for the purposes of reconstructing the relationship between history and theory in the modern age. Marx's understanding of abstraction, counterbalanced by his interpretation of the category of the contradiction, points to the irreducible character of a symptomatic forgetfulness – a forgetfulness that is essential to the discourse of rational "self-assertion" – that enables the subject to deny the process by which it comes to be empowered to think and speak. In retrospect, we can see that insofar as the invention of subjectivity marks the beginning of the modern age by laying claim to an absolute break within time it is aligned to a concept of modernity that is equally abstract and false; for, strictly speaking, there is neither a temporal nor an absolute break, only what amounts to the consciousness of such a break, combined in the case of Descartes with the attempt to subordinate it to "rational" ends; yet it is this very

86 Hegel, *PhS*, sec. 578, p. 352.
87 Marx, *Grundrisse*, trans. Martin Nicolaus (Harmondsworth: Penguin, 1973), pp. 104, 105. See also "Introduction to a Critique of Political Economy," in *The German Ideology*, ed. C. J. Arthur (New York: International Publishers, 1970), pp. 124–51.

attempt that points up the gap between history and subjectivity and that subsequently allows us to grasp the abstraction's "truth." Once the truth of this abstraction is made plain – and on the account that Hegel advanced, modernity becomes visible *as* an abstraction the very moment the subject attempts to comprehend itself historically or otherwise acquires an awareness of itself – it becomes possible to see that the invention of subjectivity based on the concept and practice of representation provided a way in which a series of social and historical conditions could conveniently be framed. *Pace* Blumenberg, who has said that "there are no witnesses to changes of historical epochs," that "the epochal turning is an imperceptible frontier" (*Legitimacy of the Modern Age*, p. 469), I would argue that subjective reason provided an instrument through which the transformations of historical experience could be legitimized and grasped, if not exactly "viewed," in the process of its self-formation. Phrased in other terms, it could be said that the metaphysical position of the subject was itself invented in order to grasp the process through which its own historical origination took place. Once institutionalized, this invention provided a legitimizing context for a number of terms – nature, history, society, desire, the State, the self – that over the course of history had been substantially transformed.

As we have already begun to see, however, the formation of subjective reason, as regularized in the culture of modernity, proved to be a contradictory and self-limiting response to the values that had gained ascendancy in the modern world. Hence the urgency felt by postmodern critics to locate the limits of "subjective" forms of foundational thought. The critique of subjectivity that begins in Heidegger and is continued in Foucault and Derrida may be situated within this sphere; it constitutes an attempt to displace the absolute nature of the origin, and with it a crucial part of the legacy of the modern age, substituting for the "absolute beginning" the notion of an "originary trace" (Derrida). But this is a successful attempt only insofar as it allows us to comprehend the truth that the abstraction of the origin both contains and conceals. As our subsequent discussions will reveal, the modern subject not only legitimizes itself but "rationalizes" the status of its own beginning by transforming the difference between history and theory into the self-justifying, homogeneous, and ostensibly coherent narratives of human progress, self-improvement, and growth. For now, it may be enough to see that if no explanation can be given of the absolute origins of subjective self-consciousness, this is because self-consciousness "originates" absolutely only in the abstract. An investigation into the invention of the subject as the key to an understanding and critique of the modern age depends on the prior recognition that each of these terms – "history," "theory," "subjectivity," "modernity" – is an immensely powerful abstraction and that none alone provides an adequate framework in which the problems of modern culture can be framed.[88]

88 Cf. Habermas, who argues that "as the principle of modernity, subjectivity was supposed to determine its normative content as well; at the same time, subject-centered reason led to abstractions that fragmented the ethical totality" (*PDM*, p. 347). As this passage reveals, Habermas is cognizant of the abstractions to which the subject is led, but he remains unaware of the nature of subjectivity and modernity as themselves the (perhaps central) abstractions. The discussions in Alfred Schmidt, *History and Structure: An Essay on Hegelian-Marxist and Structuralist Theories of History*, trans. Jeffrey Herf (Cambridge MA: MIT Press, 1981), provide a stimulating exploration of some of the problems involved here. See also Perry Anderson, "Structure and Subject," *In the Tracks of Historical Materialism* (London: Verso, 1983), pp. 32–55.

❖❖❖

2

The theory of the novel and the autonomy of art

❖❖❖

The theory of the novel

We have invented the productivity of the spirit: that is why the primaeval images have irrevocably lost their objective self-evidence for us ... We have invented the creation of forms: and that is why everything that falls from our weary and despairing hands must always be incomplete.

Lukács, *Theory of the Novel*

At several points in *The Theory of the Novel*, Georg Lukács advanced the claim that the novel is a form of epic literature characteristic of "disintegrated" civilizations or of what Weber called the "disenchanted" world. "The novel," Lukács says, "is the epic of an age in which the extensive totality of life is no longer directly given, yet which still thinks in terms of totality."[1] If the epic world is "rounded from within," so that, as Hegel said in his *Aesthetics*, each individual action and each object in it is the reflection of a totality complete in itself, then the novel reflects the "transcendental homelessness" characteristic of the subject in the modern world;[2] this is a world in which man is "unsheltered," deprived of the metaphysical comfort provided by the gods or of access to a natural context of desire, yet hard-pressed to derive any ultimate meaning from the world itself. Lukács places the origins of the novel in Cervantes' *Don Quixote* on the edge of a great upheaval of values. On the one hand, Cervantes appears as the faithful Christian and loyal patriot, a steadfast believer in the values of traditional society; yet on the other hand his protagonist is set in a world that no longer recognizes the purpose of heroic action and that has come to doubt the value of literature as

1 Lukács, *The Theory of the Novel* (henceforward *TN*), trans. Anna Bostock (Cambridge, MA: MIT Press, 1977), p. 56.
2 Hegel already described the novel as the "modern popular [middle-class] epic" in the *Aesthetics*, trans. T. M. Knox (Oxford: Oxford University Press, 1975), II, p. 1,092.

a source of ethical instruction and cultural renewal. According to Lukács, "the first great novel of world literature stands at the beginning of the time when the Christian god began to forsake the world; when man became lonely and could find meaning and substance only in his own soul, whose home was nowhere; when the world, released from its paradoxical anchorage in a beyond that is truly present, was abandoned to its immanent meaninglessness" (*TN*, p. 103).

Yet Lukács also saw that the fate of the novel was inseparable from that of philosophical discourse. It is not only the novel, where the inward and reflective turn of heroic adventuring confirms the risks involved in seeking value and the anxiety involved in form-giving in the modern world, but the philosophy of subjectivity as well which, Lukács says, "as a form of life or as that which determines the form and supplies the content of literary creation, is always a symptom of the rift between 'inside' and 'outside,' a sign of the essential difference between the self and the world, the incongruence of soul and deed" (*TN*, p. 29). In Lukács's view, forms that may be conceived as whole and accepted as natural cannot be found in the modern world. Since Lukács understands the ethical implications of aesthetic "form," this means that the ends of action must be secured from the abstract position of the transcendental subject. And yet the attempt to form ethical judgments from a wholly detached, third-person point of view puts us at a loss to find a corresponding *telos* for action within the world; indeed, the subject will tend to elevate its own claims to noumenal freedom beyond any purely rational bounds to the status of an Absolute. Hence the altogether ethical but nonetheless quixotic "idealism" of Cervantes' knight. The contradictions that ensue for aesthetics are no less striking than these: while in principle rejecting the claims of art to serve as a vehicle for the transmission of values or the legitimation of truth, the subject continues to look in art for the authentication of an experience that has otherwise been degraded, divided, or rendered corrupt. Hence the notion that art may serve to "compensate" for the disenchantment of the world.

In contrast to the implicit claim that the novel rejects totalities, Lukács argued that the novel is a form of literature that "thinks" in terms of totality even in a disenchanted world. Since Lukács defines the novel as the outward reflection of a cultural totality whose substance has been lost but whose forms have remained more or less intact, he sees the problem posed by disenchantment as the reintegration of the internal and external aspects of experience, of substance and form, of *Wesen* and *Leben*. The concern for the heroic ethics of virtue and for the exemplary function of literature visible in *Don Quixote* derive from the fact that these represent distinct alternatives to the dualisms of experience and the schematism of moral agency dominant in the modern world. Seen in this light, the irony of Don Quixote's project to imitate the heroes of great books may be taken to represent the waning of what was an historical possibility within the framework of the epic world; henceforward, the attempt to reconcile the ethical and aesthetic aspects of experience risks entrapment in an aesthetic ideology that reverses rather than reconciles the aspects of subjectivity that Lukács calls "form" and "life."[3] But a solution to the problem of modernity as diagnosed by Lukács remains impossible from inside the novel, which struggles to maintain a balance between the ethics of conviction and that of compromise. In contrast to the epic hero, who is drawn toward superhuman feats, the hero of the novel must be instructed in the art of what remains possible within the bounds of a "dis-enchanted"world. Yet at the same time the novelistic hero remains convinced of the intrinsic value of his acts and resists accommodation to a reality perceived as "degraded" or corrupt. Indeed, if a reconciliation between the self and the world were to be brought about simply by a process of accommodation it would seriously jeopardize the novel's critical powers, and would undermine the ethical negativity implicit in the novel's distance from the social and historical realities at hand. While the ethics of compromise and accommodation may provide the only means by which "form" and "life" may be reintegrated, the passivity that ensues may well reduce the very tensions from which novelistic narration derives. Thus the novel "remembers" the ethic of conviction of the epic while compromise remains a constant temptation and a risk. The need for an accommodation between the self and the world must be attested if the demands of society are to be met; but resentment, deception, and what Hegel calls "affliction" may follow where accommodation requires a compromise of the convictions and desires of the self:

The subject sows his wild oats, builds himself with his wishes and opinions into harmony with subsisting relationships and their rationality, enters the

3 Cf. Habermas's critique of the "aesthetic ideology" of Surrealists and Dadaists in *The Philosophical Discourse of Modernity* (henceforward *PDM*), trans. Frederick Lawrence (Cambridge, MA: MIT Press, 1987), p. 49.

concatenation of the world, and acquires for himself an appropriate attitude toward it. However much he may have quarrelled with the world, or been pushed about in it, in most cases at last he gets his girl and some sort of position, marries her, and becomes as good a Philistine as others. The woman takes charge of the household management, children arrive, the adored wife, at first unique, an angel, behaves pretty much as all other wives do; the man's profession provides work and vexations, marriage brings domestic affliction.[4]

One might contemplate reconciliation with the world through the fulfillment of a wholly devout form of love, of the kind that is imaged in Don Quixote's devotion to Dulcinea, but virtue is novelistic only insofar as it represents an idea that has become an unattainable ideal. As Stendhal said in *De L'amour*, virtue and love are incompatible with the nature of the novel as a genre: "the canon of the novel demands that virtuous love be depicted as essentially tedious and uninteresting," adding in a footnote that "if for the spectator's benefit one depicts the sentiment of virtue in conjunction with the sentiment of love, one finds one has portrayed a heart torn between the two. Virtue in a novel is only there to be sacrificed."[5]

In considering the possibility of a reconciliation between the "problematic individual," guided by his commitment to virtuous ideals, and a recalcitrant social reality, Lukács takes the example of *Wilhelm Meister* to represent a new type of community, one that is neither the reflection of an identity that is "naively and naturally rooted in a specific social structure, [or] of any natural solidarity of kinship (as in the ancient epics), nor ... a mystical experience of community, a sudden illumination which rejects the lonely individuality as something sinful." Rather, Goethe's novel is taken as a model of community according to what Habermas might call a communicative ideal; in Lukács's terms, it provides a vision of the social as "achieved by personalities, previously lonely and confined within their own selves, adapting and accustoming themselves to one another" (*TN*, p. 133).[6] We will consider Habermas's model of an

---

4 Hegel, *Aesthetics*, I, p. 593. Hegel's description of what I term the "domestication of romance" in the *Aesthetics* provides the basis for an analysis of the relationship between the novel and other popular modern forms, such as the soap-opera.

5 Stendhal, *Love*, trans. Gilbert and Suzanne Sale (1957; rpt. Harmondsworth: Penguin Books, 1982), p. 207.

6 Franco Moretti makes the convincing claim that such a community is established in Jane Austen's novels: "If Lukács had known English literature there is no doubt that *Pride and Prejudice* would have stood alongside *Wilhelm Meister's*

"aesthetic state" as a society based on the ideal of freely communicating rational subjects in somewhat greater detail below. For now it is enough to see that the reconciliation between the self and the world in *Wilhelm Meister* is made possible only by the introduction of a masonic hierarchy of professions, classes, and ranks. The full comprehension of their meaning depends on an esoteric wisdom that remains the privilege of initiates and so is unavailable for scrutiny according to the general principles (i.e. "common sense") consistent with modernizing ideals.[7]

Given the fact of our condition as moderns – given, that is, our displacement from the real or imagined authenticity of the communities of the past and the impossibility of a complete reintegration of substance and form – Lukács posits irony as the highest category of expression available to us. Thus whereas Lukács may invoke the concept of totality as an absolute horizon for the evaluation of all discourse, it is irony that corresponds to the "normative mentality" of the novel (*TN*, p. 84). Similarly, it is irony that keeps the novel from lapsing into the kind of soap-opera romance that Hegel described in the passage cited above. Conceived primarily in terms of ethical and aesthetic form, and only secondarily in terms of tone, Lukács reads the irony of the novel as a reflection of the difficulty of form-giving in the modern age. As such, the novel's irony provides a means to resist the "unconditional affirmation" of the world and its objectified social structures "even," Lukács says, "when describing the eventual homecoming" of the hero (*TN*, p. 138).[8] Irony comes to afford a critical perspective on the

Apprenticeship as an unparalleled example of the *Bildungsroman*. In reading it we witness the complete success of a 'compromise' as Lukács understood it in the *Theory of the Novel*: the founding of a relationship, a community, which neither exhausts nor radically modifies reality, and yet is invested with an intersubjective sense: the family, formed on the basis of the eighteenth-century sense of complimentariness [*sic*], of sympathy." *Signs Taken for Wonders* (London: NLB, 1988), pp. 171–72.

7 The presence of esoteric wisdom in modernity is a subject that bears more attention than it has received. The best philosophical discussion that I know is Stanley Rosen's essay on Leo Strauss and Alexandre Kojève, "Hermeneutics as Politics," in his volume of that title (New York: Oxford University Press, 1988), pp. 87–140.

8 The passage is worth quoting in full: "the author must not abandon his ironic attitude, replacing it by unconditional affirmation, even when describing the eventual homecoming. This objectivation of social life is merely the occasion for something which lies outside and beyond it to become visible, fruitful and active" (*TN*, p. 138).

distance that separates the claims of representation as a measure of the real from our tendency to project a realm of essences, a sphere of noumenal freedom, or an absolute *telos* of desire that would transcend the empirical world. Insofar as irony allows us to comprehend the displacement of the subject between these two worlds, the novel may be considered an aesthetic expression, although not a sublimation, of the characteristic dualisms of the modern age. As an expression of the antinomic relation between these dualistic terms, the irony of the novel is for Lukács paradigmatic of a coming to terms with value in a world without "spirit"; it is at once an aesthetic "correction" of the process of disenchantment and an ethical response to a world said to be without essential forms. Irony is an act of form-making that transcends the hero's quest for meaning in a formless world and stands as a momentary reconciliation of substance and form:

irony consists in this freedom of the writer in his relationship to God, the transcendental condition of the objectivity of form-giving. Irony, with intuitive double vision, can see where God is to be found in a world abandoned by God; irony sees the lost, utopian home of the idea that has become an ideal, and yet at the same time it understands that the ideal is subjectively and psychologically conditioned, because that is its only possible form of existence ... Irony, the self-surmounting of a subjectivity that has gone as far as it is possible to go, is the highest freedom that can be achieved in a world without God.   (*TN*, pp. 92–93)[9]

In making these and similar claims about freedom, irony, and form, Lukács's *Theory* declines to provide a sociological theory that would explore the connections between the morphology of the novel on the one hand and the structure of society on the other. Instead, Lukács speaks in terms of the most general available categories – about "soul," "being," "gods," and "demons." As Paul de Man observed in his well-known essay on *The Theory of the Novel*, "Lukács is not offering us, in this essay, a sociological theory that would explore relationships between the structure and development of the novel and those of society, nor is he proposing a psychological theory explaining the novel in terms of human relationships. Least of all do we find him conferring an autonomy on formal categories that would

---

9 Thus Paul de Man could write in his essay on Lukács that "the ironic language of the novel mediates between experience and desire, and unites ideal and real within the complex paradox of form." De Man, "Georg Lukács's *Theory of the Novel*," in *Blindness and Insight* (1971; rpt. Minneapolis: University of Minnesota Press, 1983), p. 56.

give them a life of their own, independent of the more general intent
that produces them" (*Blindness and Insight*, p. 53). The sometimes
elusive quality of Lukács's prose in *The Theory of the Novel* may
initially be read as the reflection of an overly abstract rendering of the
speculative language in which Hegel wrote. Indeed, Lukács himself
denounced *The Theory of the Novel* in a 1962 Preface as hopelessly
idealist and unforgivably abstract. It has nonetheless been argued that
the powerful historicism exemplified in the essays of the later *History
and Class Consciousness* (especially "Class Consciousness" and the
seminal "Reification and the Consciousness of the Proletariat") is not
incompatible with Lukács's earliest works, so that even if *The Theory
of the Novel* is nostalgic in tone and avowedly speculative in intent,
an historical account of the novel could be reconstructed from the
framework it provides.[10] Recent critics and theorists of the novel
like Fredric Jameson, Michael McKeon, and J. M. Bernstein have
attempted to recover some of the historical implications of Lukács's
insistence on the question of totality through a critique of the
category of genre. In arguing for the social construction of literary
categories, for instance, McKeon's work on the origins of the English
novel has sought to explain how the relationship between genre as
a "conceptual"category and a series of quasi-objective social facts can
"dialectically" explain the origins of the novel as a category that both
pre-exists and is precipitated by its own objective conceptual
formulation.[11] Bernstein has gone so far as to re-cast *The Theory of the
Novel* as a dialectical-materialist text, claiming in effect that Marxism
provides the only terms in which its categories can make sense
("whatever remnants of idealism *The Theory of the Novel* contains ... its
essential strategy is anti-Cartesian and anti-dualistic; its dialectical
history relating changes in the development of narrative, in epic
production and consumption, to changes elsewhere in the social
totality"[12]). And Jameson has said that "if Lukács became a
Communist, it was precisely because the problems of narration raised
in *The Theory of the Novel* required a Marxist framework to be thought

10 See for example J. M. Bernstein, *The Philosophy of the Novel: Lukács, Marxism and
the Dialectics of Form* (Minneapolis: University of Minnesota Press, 1984).
Jameson's writings in *The Political Unconscious* (Ithaca: Cornell University Press,
1981) may also be understood in this way.
11 Michael McKeon, *The Origins of the English Novel 1600–1740* (Baltimore: Johns
Hopkins University Press, 1987). McKeon argues, correctly it seems to me, for
the persistence of literary romance and of a social aristocracy within the scope
of the novel.
12 Bernstein, *Philosophy of the Novel*, p. 230.

through."[13] The details of their arguments are in fact very different, and yet these critics share certain central assumptions that are important to retrace. These are that the early Lukács conceives the operative principles of novelistic form along the lines of a Cartesian dualism of mind and world and a Kantian antinomy of inner-worldly experience and transcendental value and, moreover, that these philosophies give expression on a purely conceptual plane to the circumstances of the modern world, in which the nature of the real is seen philosophically as a function of its objective representation and materially in terms of the transformation by the market system of human labor into a series of almost mechanically hardened effects. By reading the problem of rationalization as one of reification,[14] the antinomies of the modern age, which begin with the transformation of selfhood into subjectivity in the philosophy of Descartes and culminate in Kant's vision of human existence as divided between two worlds – one in which we are determined and another in which we are free – become, as for the later Lukács, the "antinomies of bourgeois thought," and novelistic narration in turn is seen as an adaptation of the idealist search for value to conditions in which the world has become reified and consciousness rendered contemplative and abstract.

As this work demonstrates, the concept of genre should allow us to situate literature between the terms of history and theory, just as the concept of legitimacy allows us to mediate between the categories of fact and value in the social and political spheres. And yet the attempts of some post-Lukácsean critics to historicize the dizzying, idealist idiom of *The Theory of the Novel* may leave some of the more pressing problems of subjectivity still very much intact. Indeed, *merely* to historicize *The Theory of the Novel* would leave the demands that Lukács himself made of that work largely unmet. For the need to explain the social origins and subsequent historical transformations of the novel as a literary genre would simply have been transferred from a speculative philosophy of history that traces out some abstract and inscrutable process like the "disappearance of

---

13 Jameson, *Marxism and Form* (Princeton: Princeton University Press, 1971), p. 182.

14 Habermas discusses this shift in some detail in *The Theory of Communicative Action, 1: Reason and the Rationalization of Society*, trans. Thomas McCarthy (Boston: Beacon Press, 1981), especially pp. 355–65, "Lukács' Interpretation of Weber's Rationalization Thesis."

form" or the "disenchantment of the world" to one that is couched in class and materialist terms. It might well be said that the novel had thus been "historicized," but without some further, dialectical attempt to recover the role of the aesthetic categories in the transmission of values and, in the specific case at hand, to show how novelistic narratives attempt, in the absence of nature as a primary value-ground, to give shape to values, the antinomies characteristic of modernity would remain intact, even if their terms had been reversed.[15] In such an event, the further possibility of reconciling the power of literature to transmit values and beliefs with the claims of modern philosophy as a form of enlightened discourse centered in the subject would be precluded. The disjunction of literature and philosophy that Lukács took as central to his diagnosis of modernity in *The Theory of the Novel* would remain firmly entrenched and the condition of subjectivity would remain divided — simultaneously reified and abstract — even if its constitutive terms had been historically reinterpreted and its various codes "remapped."

According to Lukács, the emergence of the novel as an autonomous cultural object and "inessential" form reflects the impossibility of form-making given the condition of existence in a "disenchanted" world. But it is just as apparent that the novel is not itself a shapeless form.[16] Rather, the novel seeks to give form to experience in the only way that is possible within the culture of modernity, viz., from the position of the subject as the detached observer of an "objective" world. According to a series of standard arguments, the formal identity of the novel derives from a set of narrative procedures or mimetic techniques that reflect a faith in the experience of the individual, as confirmed by the correspondence of a series of literary/philosophical categories to a world of empirical facts. Thus the critic Ian Watt writes that "The various technical procedures of the novel ... all seem to contribute to the furthering of an aim which

15 I discuss the category of "aesthetic liberalism" in the final section of the present volume. Cf. the deconstructive critique of *The Theory of the Novel* by Paul de Man in "Georg Lukács' *Theory of the Novel*," *Blindness and Insight*, pp. 51–59; and also David Carroll, *The Subject in Question* (Chicago: University of Chicago Press, 1982).

16 In the words of Paul de Man, "this form can have nothing in common with the homogeneous, organic form of nature: it is founded on an act of consciousness, not the imitation of a natural object" (*Blindness and Insight*, p. 56).

the novelist shares with the philosopher – the production of what purports to be an authentic account of the actual experiences of individuals."[17] Beginning with Cervantes' project to legitimize fictions by bringing an end to the "illicit" fancies of romance, and continuing through the development of techniques of verisimilar narration, narrative closure, and the representation of social conventions that correspond to these, the novel is seen to ground a world of objective representations and purports to be the faithful and realistic portrayal of a world. But since the modern novel emerges, with Cervantes' *Don Quixote*, at a moment when the world has been carved up into a variety of independent discourses that are subject to no controlling authority or master code, it follows that neither the subject of the novel nor the novelistic world can be taken as given or simply reflected as whole. Indeed, the plurality of discourses in a work like *Don Quixote* shows us that the historical world can no longer be subsumed under the image of a social or aesthetic whole. Rather, the subject and the world must be fashioned by the synthesis of separate and sometimes incompatible parts. Thus while conventional histories of literature, including Lukács's *Theory*, point to *Don Quixote* as the founding novel of the genre, I would suggest that the novel is only anticipated, rather than truly founded, by it. As we have seen in our discussion of Montaigne's *Essais*, and as might also be shown for Rabelais, this is a text which projects at its limit, but does not itself contain, the position of "transcendental" reflection associated with the subject's absolute claims to truth. Rather, the reading subject of the novel – who we may provisionally identify as Alonso Quijano "el Bueno," the *post*-quixotic figure whose identity is recovered only as Don Quixote renounces the books of chivalry at the conclusion of Part II – stands at the limit of this novel, just as the transcendental subject stands at the limit of a world. In contrast to the "heroic reader" that Don Quixote imagines himself to be, this figure provides no essential content, but only the form in which the values of subjectivity can be framed.

Seen from one perspective, the presence of such a frame marks the novel as what Lukács calls an "inessential" form. And yet the necessity of the frame becomes clear if we consider the reader's temptation to become absorbed by the imitation of heroes and texts. A number of mimetically absorptive activities (e.g., sleeping,

17 Watt, *Rise of the Novel* (Berkeley: University of California Press, 1957), p. 27.

dreaming, watching the puppet-theatre) find a central place in *Don Quixote*, but perhaps none is as important as the scene of reading depicted in the opening pages of the book. At the beginning of the *Quixote* Cervantes describes the circumstances of a landed gentleman who spends so much time reading that he grows oblivious to the external world ("he gave himself up to the reading of books of knight errantry, which he loved and enjoyed so much that he almost entirely forgot his hunting and even the care of his estate"[18]). The hero of the novel, who at this point still goes by the indistinguishable names of Quijada, Quesada, and Quejana, exists in a state of absorption by reading, the consequence of which Descartes feared would lead to dementia or madness: "he so buried himself in his books that he spent the nights reading from twilight till daybreak and the days from dawn till dark; and so from little sleep and much reading his brain dried up and he lost his wits" (p. 32). We learn that this hero passed "sleepless nights trying to understand [these books] and disentangle their meaning, though Aristotle himself would never have unravelled or understood them, had he been resurrected for that sole purpose" (*ibid.*). Nonetheless, he greatly admired one of the authors "for ending his book with the promise to continue the interminable adventure, and often the desire seized him to take up the pen himself, and write the promised sequel; and no doubt he would have done so, and even would have brought it to light, if other more important and persistent thoughts had not kept him from it" (*ibid.*). Don Quixote becomes so thoroughly absorbed in his reading, so completely preoccupied by his books, that he is eventually distracted from reading itself. This distraction *by* reading *from* reading means that he has fallen into the text in such a way as to literalize the process of imitation, so that if the reading subject of the novel is to interpret this text he must somehow reverse this process and resist the quixotic "fall" into the text.[19]

Thus while it is customary to think that the novel and its ethos begin with the disappearance of imitative models, this is only partially the case. The example of *Don Quixote* suggests that the eclipse of

18 *Don Quixote de la Mancha*, trans. J. M. Cohen (Harmondsworth: Penguin Books, 1950), I, 1, p. 31. Further references will be incorporated into the text.

19 For an account of the aesthetic and moral problems of absorptive imitation in the Spanish context, see B. W. Ife, *Reading and Fiction in Golden-Age Spain* (Cambridge: Cambridge University Press, 1985), especially pp. 49–83, "Reading and Rapture."

imitation as a standard of reading in fact generates a *proliferation* of models, none of which can be determined as authentic according to existing standards of literary truth. Thus in response to a question concerning his identity, for instance, Don Quixote responds by claiming "I know that I am capable of being not only the characters I have named [e.g. the Cid, Baldovinos, and Abindarráez], but all the Twelve Peers of France and all the Nine Worthies as well, for my exploits are far greater than all the deeds they have done, all together and each by himself"(I, 5, p. 54). The formation of the novel as an autonomous object may be described as a result of the process by which this "mimetic" consciousness comes to divorce itself from the literary-ethical practice of imitations. Phrased in terms of the requirements of genre, it can be said that the proliferation of models demands the stabilizing of identity in a way that can become institutionalized, fixed, and incorporated as a requirement for the comprehension of texts. This demand – which indicates a discursive possibility standing at the limit of the pre-novelistic framework of the *Quixote*, as of the works of Rabelais and Montaigne as well – consists in the formation of a governing point of view, one that relies on the separation of values from facts.

The new, novelistic point of view is explicitly established by the construction of what would later be called the "subject." It corresponds to the position that Descartes constructs in the *Meditations* as exterior to the world, as standing steadfastly beyond all possibility of sensory error and also beyond all conceptual doubt. It is the self which reflects itself in its own silence and its own invisibility as a being of pure thought ("I shall now close my eyes, I shall call away all my senses, I shall efface even from my thoughts all the images of corporeal things...I shall try little by little to reach a better knowledge of and a more familiar relationship with myself"[20]). The transformation of the mimetic, quixotic self into the subject of modernity takes place in part because, in order to make its claims truly transcendental, the "I" of the *Meditations* must establish a place for itself that is not only above the possibility of sensory error, but beyond the deceits of imitation as well.[21] Apart from the technical

---

20 Descartes, *Meditations*, in *The Philosophical Works of Descartes*, trans. John Cottingham, Robert Stoothoff, and Dugald Murdoch (Cambridge: Cambridge University Press, 1984), II, p. 24.

21 See John D. Lyons' discussion of imitation and representation in relation to the *Discourse* in his "Subjectivity and Imitation in the *Discours de la méthode*,"

sense in which the term was later appropriated by Kant, to describe the Cartesian subject, or the reader of the *Quixote*, as "transcendental" is also to describe it as inimitable, or, from within the perspective of the novel itself, as necessary and real but empirically undefined. Yet by virtue of the fact that the transcendental subject thus constructed remains but a frame and is vacant, its position, in all its formal emptiness, becomes available for any reader who might come to read by resisting the absorptive power of the text. Reading is thus aligned in principle to freedom; formulated in "liberal"terms, the freedom of reading allows that we may "appreciate" texts whose beliefs we may nonetheless reject.

The *Quixote* is "modern" insofar as it shows us that the world cannot be understood through the principles of imitation and can no longer be subsumed under the image of any pre-existing social or aesthetic whole. The discursive heterogeneity of the novel, which Bakhtin described in terms of its "heteroglossia," corresponds to the discursive heterogeneity of the modern world.[22] In response to this heterogeneity, the activity of reading becomes the process by which we may synthesize a (coherent) world, in Cartesian terms by representing that world, picturing it; in Kantian terms by bringing that world into agreement with the categories of our understanding.[23] In the opinion of Wolfgang Iser, which may be taken as representative in this respect, the reading of works of modern fiction, which in general do not present totalities that can be taken in at a glance, confirms the productivity of the faculties of the understanding in synthesizing a world: "instead of finding out whether the text gives

Neophilologus, 66 (1982), 508–25. There, Lyons points to two opposing and interrelated dangers facing the reader of the Cartesian text: "The danger of reading, earlier mentioned by Descartes, was that the reader might lose himself in the text, might identify too completely with a figure that would estrange him from himself and finish like the *extravagant* hero of a romance. Here, in Part IV, the author expresses the opposite fear – that the reader may modify the text according to his own understanding. The reader who transforms opinions to suit himself has avoided the danger of surrender to a text, but now the author fears a loss. The reader's opinions are no longer those of the author."

22 See especially "Discourse in the Novel," in *The Dialogic Imagination: Four Essays by M. Bakhtin* ed. Michael Holquist, trans. Caryl Emerson and Michael Holquist (Austin: University of Texas Press, 1981), pp. 259–422.

23 I argue for the function of genre in this way in "Genre Definition and Multiplicity in *Don Quixote*," *Cervantes*, 6 (1986), 39–49. For a statement of the "conservative" case, see Alan Trueblood, "Sobre la selección artística en el *Quijote*, 'lo que he dejado de escribir' (II. 44)," *Nueva revista de filología hispánica*, 10 (1956), 44–50.

an accurate or inaccurate description of the object, [the reader] has to build up the object for himself."[24] The constitution of the novel as a genre depends on the dialectical (or "dialogical") implication of the reader in a process that drives him to construct a totality from the heterogeneity of the novel's discursive forms, thus validating Lukács's claim that the novel "remembers" the totality even in a disenchanted world. And yet we should note that Lukács goes on to say that "the relationships which create cohesion between the abstract components [of the novel] are abstractly pure and formal, and the ultimate unifying principle therefore has to be the ethic of creative subjectivity, *an ethic which the content reveals*" (*TN*, p. 84; emphasis added).

To understand the novel as a dialectical genre, and to comprehend the subject as positioned always at the limit of the novel's world, means that the novel's efforts at world-representation through the techniques of "formal realism," the establishment of an omniscient authorial voice, a stable third-person point of view, and the incorporation of aesthetic distance with regard to imitative models, can provide only a partial perspective on the central problem of how the subject and the world can be synthesized and made whole. The solution to that problem may be considered complete only when the "formal" version of subjectivity, understood in terms of objective world-representation or -construction, is aligned to an ethic of individual autonomy and freedom, and when that ethic in turn becomes substantively incorporated within the novel as a genre. Indeed, the procedures of representation, as revealed in details of characterization, and in the novel's claim to truth through the "particularization" of experience, naming, temporality, causation, and events, do not in themselves endow a specifically *novelistic* form, for they provide no essential content for the values that are thus given shape. Thus Lukács must claim in the passage cited above that the form of the novel, or more accurately the "productivity of spirit" as revealed in the making of novelistic form, requires an ethic of "creative subjectivity" which, he adds, is an ethic that the *content* reveals: the abstract "form" of the novel, which may be said to emerge in response to the requirements placed on reading *Don Quixote*, in reconstructing its discursive heterogeneity as a (whole)

---

24 Iser, *The Act of Reading* (Baltimore: Johns Hopkins University Press, 1978), p. 109. See also p. 108: "The reader's enjoyment begins when he himself becomes productive, i.e., when the text allows him to bring his own faculties into play."

text, acquires generic status and concrete narrative shape only when the quixotism of Cervantes' errant hero is regularized and, in this special sense, "redeemed" in figures like Daniel Defoe's individualist adventurer and mercantile knight, Robinson Crusoe. Insofar as quixotism is thus naturalized, adapted via the procedures of novelistic mimesis and verisimilar narration to the modernizing projects of "self-improvement" and "progress," the novel serves to legitimize the self-definition of the subject as a free and autonomous individual, who attempts to reestablish the origins of society and plumb the foundations of the self. Defoe's protagonist may inherit all the quirks, all the inconsistency and incoherence that contribute to Don Quixote's madness, and yet somehow this quixotic hero no longer appears mad; in the words of Marthe Robert, Robinson Crusoe is "better equipped for life, he is adaptable and amenable to development and improvement, all of which his model is obliged to reject…. Instead of coming back home as a failure forced to disown himself and admit defeat, as the sombre Knight has done, he returns as a successful, healthy, self-confident person prepared to settle down on 'this side' as a model for all self-made men."[25]

Robinson Crusoe's project and the values which he attempts to assert – the loosening of pre-established constraints on the structures of society and the self, the enhanced opportunities for self-revision made possible by a rejection of stable hierarchies and fixed social roles, and the will to give shape to values in the absence of an original value-ground – establish the basis of an alliance between the novel as an "inessential" form and the "productivity of spirit" that Lukács described as characteristic of the modern age. In ethical terms, Robinson Crusoe attempts to prove that man can exercise his freedom and live autonomously; he seeks to show that modern man can reinvent society and establish a productive world on his own. These efforts are given thematic shape in the project to cut the self loose from social and familial ties. What I have described above as the will to self-revision is characteristic of the endeavors to move beyond the bounds of a socially contained, time-bound, or otherwise centered self.[26] The narrative of individualism, which affords a new way of binding content and form, affords a resolution to the problems of

25 Robert, *Origins of the Novel*, trans. Sacha Rabinovich (Bloomington: Indiana University Press, 1980), pp. 110–11.
26 See Leo Bersani, *A Future for Astyanax* (New York: Columbia University Press, 1984) and *Baudelaire and Freud* (Berkeley: University of California Press, 1977).

personal identity and novelistic "formlessness," in this particular case by adapting the spiritual autobiography of the repentant sinner to the circumstances of what Lukács calls the "problematic individual" in the modern world.

At the same time Robinson Crusoe's experiences lead us to the more circumspect view that independent man is by nature neither free nor good. Thus while *Robinson Crusoe* may promise a return to origins, a recovery of the fullness of nature, and the re-enchantment of the world, Robinson's gaze remains destitute, "deprived and impoverished rather than naive."[27] Nature is lost, while there are no clear means for recovering the practices of civilized society as an originary reflection of the powers of the subject himself. Robinson Crusoe's island-world is characterized as a "tissue of wonders" reminiscent of the marvels of nature celebrated in romance. Read as pure romance, the novel would seem to contradict what Blumenberg has called the "new seriousness" of the age represented by thinkers like Bacon and Descartes, to whom nature's extraordinary playfulness would indicate a violation of the transcendent adherence to lawfulness, regularity, and rule.[28] Defoe's conceptual experiment of man on a deserted island may be taken as an attempt to reverse the process of rationalization by reimagining a oneness with nature and by rescuing the origins of subjective consciousness from historical time. As Lukács said in *The Theory of the Novel*, the desire to re-enchant the world is predicated on the belief that "this world is the same one which God had previously transformed into a dangerous but wonderful magic garden; now, turned into prose by evil demons, this world yearns to be transformed back again into a magic garden by faithful heroes"(*TN*, p. 103). And yet *Robinson Crusoe* is no romance. As Lukács went on to say, "that which, in the fairy-tale, had only to be guarded against so as to preserve the beneficent spell, here becomes positive action, becomes a struggle for the existing paradise of a fairy-tale reality which awaits the redeeming word" (*TN*, p. 103).

27 Pierre Macherey, *A Theory of Literary Production*, trans. Geoffrey Wall (London: Routledge & Kegan Paul, 1978), p. 242.

28 The concept of nature in terms of lawfulness and rule becomes a central principle for Kant in e.g. the *Prolegomena to Any Future Metaphysics*. Hans Blumenberg writes of Bacon: "Part of Bacon's program is to reduce the *miracula naturae* [marvels of nature] to the strictness of *forma* and *lex* [pattern and law], in that, in their oddness, they merely represent the uncommon coincidence (*concursus rara*) of regularities," *The Legitimacy of the Modern Age*, trans. Robert M. Wallace (Cambridge, MA: MIT Press, 1985), p. 475.

Defoe's novel reveals that there is no recovery of the "natural context" or "first nature" in terms of which the essence of man might be defined.

Otherwise put, the attempt to reverse the "disenchantment" of the world by reinterpreting it through personal and psychological categories, rather than in social, historical, and conceptual terms, may represent the desire to re-establish an original relationship between the subject and the natural world, but any attempt to fulfill this wish serves only to reproduce the social and economic relations of the world that Robinson Crusoe left behind. Indeed, the same circumstances that drive Robinson Crusoe to turn the threats of culture into the tools of self-improvement force him to repeat the "civilizing" process in the context of his island world. Insofar as Robinson Crusoe is torn from society by shipwreck but is also bound to refashion society from the tools that are salvaged from his ship, we are led to the view that culture is a web from which we cannot break free, even if we realize that it rests on no absolute or original grounds. On the contrary, values in the novel, including those of freedom, must be established in the absence of origins and without reference to nature as a primary value-ground. Thus in chapter 1 of the *Serious Reflections of Robinson Crusoe* (1790), Defoe has his hero look back over his life of solitude and conclude that "The world is ... nothing to us, but as it is more or less to our relish: all reflection is carried home, and our dear self is, in one respect, the end of living."[29]

Some of the reasons why Robinson Crusoe's freedom may appear abstract and empty, if not also debased, may become clear if we look at the genealogy of novelistic freedom in relation to modern philosophical discourse, with special reference to Kant and to the Hegelian critique of Kant. According to Kant, the idea of a duality of worlds is necessary in order to guarantee the subject's transcendental freedom in light of the reign of causality over empirical events. If we follow Kant's discussion of the antinomies of pure reason, every change that occurs within nature has a cause and may as such be

29 From this, Crusoe argues that life on the island was not solitude at all, and that he can enjoy "much more solitude in the middle of the greatest collection of mankind in the world, I mean at London, that ever I could say I enjoyed in eight and twenty years of confinement to a desert island." Defoe, *Serious Reflections of Robinson Crusoe with His Vision of the Angelic World* (London, 1790), ch. 1 ("Of Solitude").

determined as a "necessary"aspect of reality.[30] Transforming the "seriousness"of nature in Bacon and Descartes into metaphysical principles, Kant claims that nature constitutes a realm of lawful experience as confirmed by its conformity to rules and by our ability to synthesize experience into a coherent whole. Thus in the *Prolegomena to Any Future Metaphysics* Kant asks:

How is nature possible in the *formal* sense, as the totality of rules under which all appearances must come in order to be thought of as connected in an experience? The answer must be this: it is only possible by means of the constitution of our understanding, according to which all those representations of sensibility are necessarily referred to a consciousness, and by which the peculiar way in which we think (viz., by rules) and hence also experience are possible.[31]

Yet this notion of causality and this understanding of the lawfulness of experience fly in the face of our conception of human agents as capable of originating actions free from external constraints, hence as giving rise to changes spontaneously. In order to resolve this antinomy Kant had to ascribe freedom the status of an a priori concept, claiming in effect that freedom is a transcendental idea and, indeed, "the only [one] whose possibility we know a priori. We do not understand it, but we know it as the condition of the moral law which we do know."[32] Indeed, all ideas which cannot be supported by speculative reason, including our ideas of immortality and of God, are seen by Kant to depend on it. Yet in making this claim, Kant was forced also to argue that freedom belongs not to nature itself but to a "transcendental" realm, to which categories like causality do not apply. On the one hand Kant views reason as productive of the categories through which we view the world, while on the other hand he regards freedom as necessary for the operations of reason, but not open to validation by it. The result is a recourse to freedom, or spontaneity, as the "ungrounded ground" of that form of reason through which the subject configures a world.[33]

30 Kant, *Critique of Pure Reason*, trans. Norman Kemp Smith (New York: St. Martin's Press, 1965), A 536, B 564.
31 Kant, *Prolegomena to Any Future Metaphysics*, trans. Paul Carus, rev. James W. Ellington (Indianapolis: Hackett, 1977), p. 60, sec. 36.
32 Kant, *Critique of Practical Reason*, trans. Lewis White Beck (Indianapolis: Bobbs-Merrill, 1956), pp. 3–4.
33 For a related critique of "spontaneity" in Kant, see Stanley Rosen, "Transcendental Ambiguity: The Rhetoric of the Enlightenment," in *Hermeneutics as Politics* (New York: Oxford University Press, 1988), pp. 19–49.

As *Robinson Crusoe* and *Don Quixote* reveal, the problem of form-giving in the modern (post-epic) world may be resolved in two different ways: through the representation of a world that is objective, rational, and real; and through the creation of a free and autonomous individual, an independent self. But in a deeper respect these solutions are versions of but one, for the represented world is the subject's world. If we take the philosophy of representation as formulated by Descartes and perfected by Kant as a paradigmatic example of the antinomies of the subject in the modern age, as the groundwork both of the ethic of freedom and of the novel's representational claims, then we may reinterpret the normative challenge of modernity in the following terms: not simply to secure the accurate representation of a world as objective, rational, and real, or to assert our roles as ethical agents through the exercise of an a priori, ungrounded, and willful freedom, but to mediate between these two, thus giving a coherent shape to the engagement of values, as pursued through the terms that Lukács refers to as "form" and "life." But since this project cannot possibly succeed if we continue to think of truth as the correspondence between a representational "frame" and a world of objective facts on the one hand, and of freedom as lying beyond the bounds of reason on the other, then we can see why an account of modernity that takes a critical stance with respect to the philosophies of Descartes and Kant might well seek its orientation in narrative understanding of reason. According to a line of thinkers that goes back to M. H. Abrams and, before Abrams, to Josiah Royce, the narrative of reason is epitomized in the story of spiritual progress, of *Bildung*, told in Hegel's *Phenomenology of Spirit*. However, if the novel is the genre of subjectivity and seeks through the procedures of representation to arrive at an accurate portrayal of the real while relegating questions of value to a realm beyond a world of appearances, then a work like the *Phenomenology of Spirit* must be seen not only as limit-case of the novel but also as a supremely anti-novelistic text. For insofar as the *Phenomenology of Spirit* offers a critical response to subjective thought, it subsumes the form-giving efforts of the novel within the movement of a dialectic that proposes to achieve the complete and satisfactory equation of consciousness and the real within the context of a totality where all mediation is internal (self-mediation) and where form is therefore complete. Whether Hegel is able to reconcile the freedom or "productivity of spirit" characteristic of the modern subject with the disappearance of natural forms remains an important question, one that can only be addressed fully within the context of Hegel's philosophy of religion, in which the activity of God is seen to be coextensive with human history and making, and which claims that nature is implicitly divine.[34] It may be enough for us now to see that the *Phenomenology of Spirit* overcomes the limits of representation and transcends the bounds of novelistic narration insofar as it reconciles the demand for an objective conception of the world and a confirmation of the lawfulness of experience within that world with a concept of freedom that represents the self-overcoming of the limited rationality of "subjective" thought.

Consider for example Hegel's response to the first objects of the philosophical "critique" in Descartes and Kant and their role in the project of novelistic mimesis, as seen in the relationship between the instruments of knowledge and novelistic frames. For Descartes and Kant these instruments mediate between (objective) representations and the (subjective) mind; in the novel, this process of mediation is taken over as a function of mimesis ("formal realism"), the framing powers of which in turn allow the ethical dimension of subjectivity to be given shape. In either case, the techniques of representation provide nothing more than the form in which the ethical values of subjectivity can appear, but according to Hegel's critique, the values thus asserted will inevitably be undermined insofar as they remain "external" to the frame through which they are expressed. Thus Hegel asks the human subject to reconstitute every external relation as internal in order to achieve adequacy to itself and its world. In discovering the limits of representation – or, more accurately, in allowing the limits of subjective thinking to reveal themselves – the *Phenomenology of Spirit* internalizes the process of mediation, so that no world external to consciousness is represented or "framed"; mediation in its fullest sense becomes revealed as a mode of production taking place *within* spirit as an expression of the (conscious, historical, rational) whole. And yet Hegel's critique of

34 Hegel's succinct explanation is that thus "the raising of [nature] to reconciliation is on the one hand what finite spirit implicitly is, while on the other hand it arrives at this reconciliation, or brings it forth, in world history. This reconciliation is the peace of God, which does not 'surpass all reason' but is rather the peace that *through* reason is first known and thought and is recognized as what is true." *Lectures on the Philosophy of Religion* (1827), ed. Peter C. Hodgson (Berkeley: University of California Press, 1988), p. 489.

subjectivity requires a logical rigor that can only be bought at the price of some of modernity's central goals. His system forces us to question the absolute spontaneity or freedom of self-assertion that is found in the self-confirming and -authenticating production of new ideas. Moreover, Hegel's vision of the totality, in which to think or to know one thing is to think or to know everything, proposes an unbearable model of knowledge.[35] If Hegel has claimed for himself the completion of discourse, what in turn explains the origins, and what the productivity of this discourse? Consciousness in the *Phenomenology of Spirit* becomes a further example of the generation of form by the self-producing powers of spirit or mind. In these and other ways, the *Phenomenology of Spirit* represents not only the limit-case of the novel, but also modern philosophy's "overcoming" of the representational claims of art. In confirming the famous assertion of the *Aesthetics* – that "art is and remains for us, from the side of its highest vocation, a thing of the past" – the *Phenomenology of Spirit* situates itself both as an antithesis to the novel and as a pivotal manifestation of modern thought.[36]

Hegel's concept of the whole is no longer expressed as the reconciliation of ethical and aesthetic form or as the immediacy of substantive relations in the ancient epic world; rather, it supersedes both ethics and aesthetics and declares itself to be the culmination of philosophical discourse. Thus Hegel envisions the course of the *Phenomenology* as that of a systematic and logical progression that presses beyond the bounds of narrative form; this progression conforms to the mutual accommodation of human rationality and the real, and provides for the gradual enrichment of consciousness as well. As we proceed through the *Phenomenology of Spirit* we pass from the impoverished beginnings of consciousness in immediate sense-certainty to an all-embracing spiritual Absolute. Yet at the same time

---

35 Thus Habermas argues that "if individuals are integrated and subordinated as parts to the higher-level subject of society as a whole, there arises a zero-sum game in which modern phenomena such as the expanding scope for movement and the increasing degrees of freedom cannot be adequately accommodated" (*PDM*, p. 376). I discuss Habermas's claim in relation to Hegel further in the final chapter of this study.

36 Hegel, *Aesthetics*, p. 10. Gillian Rose presents a cogent interpretation of this claim in her section on "The End of Art" in *Hegel Contra Sociology* (London: Athlone Press, 1981), pp. 121–23. For a further discussion of this claim with respect to the culture of modernity, see Karsten Harries, "Hegel on the Future of Art," *Review of Metaphysics*, 24 (June, 1974), 677–96.

the perspective adopted throughout the *Phenomenology* assumes the completion of history and the rigorous integration of all prior moments of knowledge – partial with respect to the whole – within the Absolute. For this reason, the *Phenomenology* embodies Hegel's claim to have produced a truly philosophical discourse: it is his example of a speech that is fully articulate and enlightened, which is to say, complete. Phrased in only slightly different terms, however, it could be said that Hegel is able to imagine a solution to the problems of subjectivity only by totalizing the scope of philosophical discourse. Thus, not unsurprisingly, Hegel's critics have often been led to wonder whether his "solution" to the problem of subjectivity could be imagined without the institution of a totalitarian regime of thought.[37]

In substituting the totalizing circle of consciousness for the partial and divided stance imposed by the subject of modernity, Hegel leaves us with a number of questions to which the *Phenomenology* itself provides no immediate response. For example, if the final goals of the *Phenomenology* in Absolute Knowing are already implicit in every prior stage of thought, so that the onward march of consciousness may be confirmed not simply according to the standards of literary verisimilitude or novelistic representation as possible or probable, but as rationally necessary, how can we begin the process that will take us from beginning to end? Soon it becomes apparent that the

---

37 Richard Rorty makes a related point when he contrasts Hegel and Proust. The concept of totality in force in Hegel's *Phenomenology* rules out contingency. World-historical agents like Spirit and Being are seen not just as accumulations of contingencies, but as the necessary players in versions of a narrative that might be called "The True Description of the World." In Rorty's view, this invention of a larger-than-self hero is what sets philosophers like Hegel and Heidegger apart from novelists such as Proust. There is in Hegel a ceaseless and finally unresolved tension between the demands of a contingent narrative of history and selfhood, with all the sense of discovery that this entails, and the awareness that this is all plotted in accordance with necessity, so that it can in turn be spoken with the authority of the Absolute. The narrator of *The Past Recaptured*, by contrast, would not be worried by the prospect of being *aufgehoben*, for as Rorty says "his job was done once he had put the events of his own life in his own order, made a pattern out of the little things – Gilberte among the hawthorns, the color of the windows in the Guermantes chapel, the sound of the name 'Guermantes,' the two walks, the shifting spires. He knows this pattern would have been different had he died earlier or later, for there would have been fewer or more little things which would have to be fitted into it." Rorty, *Contingency, Irony, and Solidarity* (Cambridge: Cambridge University Press, 1989), p. 105.

movement of the *Phenomenology* cannot be driven by any mechanism external to consciousness, but is a circle that must be explained by the natural workings of reason itself. In this way Hegel generates a succession of historical paradigms that express the self-producing powers of consciousness or mind. Hegel describes the different forms of consciousness as moments of a self-surpassing spiritual whole and, in addition, claims that consciousness is "something that goes beyond limits, and since these limits are its own, [as] something that goes beyond itself."[38] But this also means that Hegel has to make the scope of consciousness total; and since consciousness, or spirit, necessarily works by concepts, this also means that Hegelian wisdom is predicated on the complete conceptualization of the world. In these and other ways, Hegel's critique of modernity confirms the process of rationalization that Weber described as the "disenchantment" of the world.

Epic and novel

Before going on to give further consideration to the problem of the autonomy of art, and the implications of this autonomy for art-theoretical discourse, let us look at the relationship between the novel and the epic as understood by Hegel and Lukács. To be sure, one could reject an historical account of the novel out of hand and regard Lukács's "theory" as a purely hermeneutical construct or interpretive device. In this case, the idea of the unity of ethical and aesthetic form would constitute little more than a hypothetical construct, and Lukács's nostalgic invocation of the epic would provide nothing more than the horizon of interpretation for the workings of novelistic plot. As we shall see in greater detail below, however, this is not in fact the case; when suitably modified and refined to allow for the mediation of literary romance and the increasing abstraction of virtue in the modern world, the thesis of the novel's epic genealogy can provide a useful understanding of the way in which the novel responded to circumstances of social and historical change.

It cannot be denied that Lukács's thesis of the novel's indebtedness to the ancient epic past resembles a number of attempts to subordinate the novel to some prior literary genre, including Socratic dialogue, Menippean satire, picaresque fiction, and Byzantine

---

38 Hegel, *Phenomenology of Spirit* (henceforth *PhS*), trans. A. V. Miller (New York: Oxford University Press, 1977), p. 51, sec. 80.

romance. And Lukács does in fact claim that the novel adapts the epic *mythos* to the conditions of a world that has been abandoned by God. But it would in all of these instances be more accurate to say that Lukács understands the rise of the novel in relation to the decline of great epic literature as a form of secularization and, in this respect, as not unrelated to the secularization process that Weber described in terms of the "disenchantment" of the world. Indeed, the mature Lukács attributed some of the intellectual tendencies within *The Theory of the Novel* to his youthful enthusiasm for Weber's work,[39] even if in describing the origins of the novel he made no explicit mention of Weber or of the process of world-disenchantment as such. As we shall see in greater detail in chapter 3, what Weber means by "disenchantment" has often been interpreted as a process of secularization, wherein modern cultural forms are understood as having a meaning that is fundamentally indebted to the past. Thus Lukács regards the novel as a product of the secularization process insofar as it gives evidence that the cultural forms of belief may be preserved and their outward effects perpetuated even in the absence of authentic belief.[40] Accordingly, when Alasdair MacIntyre says of Jane Austen in *After Virtue* that "the restricted households of Highbury and Mansfield Park have to serve as surrogates for the Greek city-states and the medieval kingdom," he follows an essentially Lukácsean line; so too a critic like Fredric Jameson, who describes the novel in *The Political Unconscious* as "the end of genre ... a narrative ideologeme whose outer form, secreted like a shell or exoskeleton, continues to emit its ideological message long after the extinction of its host."[41] But whereas Weber's interpretation

---

39 "I was then in the process of turning from Kant to Hegel, without, however, changing any aspect of my attitude towards the so-called 'intellectual sciences' school, an attitude based essentially on my youthful enthusiasm for the work of Dilthey, Simmel and Max Weber" ("Preface," *TN*, p. 12). Alan Sica explores the Weber–Lukács connection further in *Weber, Irrationality, and Social Order* (Berkeley: University of California Press, 1988).

40 See Jean-Pierre Mileur, *Literary Revisionism and the Burden of Modernity* (Berkeley: University of California Press, 1985), p. 3.

41 MacIntyre, *After Virtue* (Notre Dame: University of Notre Dame Press, 1981), p. 224; Jameson, *The Political Unconscious*, p. 151. For a critic like Wolfgang Iser, this process stands at the root of the antithetical task of modern art: "if a modern work of art is to succeed in communicating even a partial reality, it must still carry with it all the old connotations of form, such as order, balance, harmony, integration, etc., and yet at the same time constantly invalidate these connotations. For without this process there would be the illusion of a false

of the secularization process issues in a form of "value-free" science, Lukács's position is symptomatic of the "disenchantment" of the world in a different way, for he seems to accept the premise that the novel cannot possibly recuperate, nor modernity fulfill, the legacy of the ancient epic past. When Lukács claims that the novel "thinks" in terms of totality while nonetheless recognizing the conditions of its own existence in a disenchanted world, he may be interpreted as saying that the novel repeats or "remembers" the totality of ethical and aesthetic form in circumstances where these conditions are no longer substantively or immediately given, and where the totality has been divided among a series of different value-spheres and rendered abstract. And yet as an example of what Lukács called the "productivity of spirit" in a world without essential forms, the novel's repetition of the epic does not constitute an act of bad faith. Indeed, the novel is not a "modern epic" at all, as is sometimes claimed; although genealogically related to the epic, demonstrating a "family resemblance" to it, the novel remains generically undefined; it is an essentially formless genre whose principles of construction, like the values it asserts, require constitution by the subject insofar as the world they reflect is lacking in essential forms.[42] As Lukács himself said, "the composition of the novel is the paradoxical fusion of heterogeneous and discrete components into an organic whole which is then abolished over and over again"(*TN*, p. 84).[43]

So seen, the formation of the novel may be related not only to the history of subjectivity but also to the process that Weber describes

totality such as the ideological art of today is once more trying to bring about"(*The Act of Reading*, p. 12).

42 Commenting on the formlessness of the novel, Marthe Robert observes that "if the genre is undefined and virtually undefinable, can it constitute a form recognizable as such? Should we not rather consider each work as an isolated case to be appreciated on its own terms according to the descriptive criteria it suggests? In other words, can a theory of the novel, based on a few indispensable, adequate and relatively stable principles, be formulated which would make it possible first to classify such works rationally, and then to analyse them from a standpoint that would be as free as possible from pre-conceptions?" *Origins of the Novel*, pp. 5–6. See also Mario Vargas Llosa, *The Perpetual Orgy: Flaubert and "Madame Bovary*," trans. Helen R. Lane (New York: Farrar, Strauss, Giroux, 1986), and A. J. Cascardi, "Genre Definition and Multiplicity in *Don Quixote*."

43 We might add that this whole is constantly resynthesized as part of the subject's self-sustaining work. On the relationship between literature, the subject, and (the) work see Philippe Lacoue-Labarthe and Jean-Luc Nancy, *L'Absolu littéraire* (Paris: Seuil, 1978).

in terms of the passing of "traditional" societies. In the modern world, society no longer prescribes in advance what the role of individuals, and what the truth of their lives, shall be. This meaning is no longer recognized as a pre-established norm or accepted as prior to the individual. Rather, it must be created and affirmed by acts of individual choice. The experience of subjective freedom is thus accompanied by an increased *need* for values, as well as for a period of personal value-formation and self-creation, an adolescence or apprenticeship in which the individual can realize the cultural ideal of *Bildung*. *Qua* "problematic individual," it would seem that the hero in the disenchanted world would be unable to complete this process: the full irony of Don Quixote's attempt to imitate the heroes of great books can only be measured against the impossibility of "successful" imitation, and a hero like Robinson Crusoe comes to reject models *tout court*. All the more reason, then, for the novelistic hero to assert himself as the *new model*, the self-made man, through a process of struggle and self-proving. In contrast to the epic, where the hero's trials consist of objective obstacles to be overcome and demonstrate collective values to be won, the novel dramatizes a process that Hegel described as "the education of the individual into the realities of the present" (*Aesthetics*, I, p. 593). Insofar as the novel resists resignation or compromise and remains faithful to the demands of both self and world, it remains divided from within. Set against a world that is objective, rational, and real, we find the novelistic subject-hero, whose truth is inward and who remains faithful above all to his heart's own laws.

When seen from the perspective of a work like Lukács's *Theory of the Novel*, of course, the idea of epic literature is likely to appear stunningly vague and abstract. In much the same way, the categories of criticism that Lukács brings to bear on the novel are likely to appear all but inapplicable to some of its most representative texts. Granted the abstraction of Lukács's conception of the epic, and granted also the schematism of Lukács's classification of the novel according to a typology of forms, the epic's apparent resistance to interpretation does not imply that there is no truth to be recovered from the epic world. For Hegel, and for Lukács insofar as he remains faithful to Hegel, the contrast between the epic and the novel can be measured according to two types of virtue and the corresponding possibilities of ethical selfhood that they represent. On the one hand we have virtue in the Ancient world, virtue understood as a form of practical reason that is a reflection of collective values ("Virtue in the ancient world had its own definite sure meaning, for it had in the *spiritual substance* of the nation a foundation full of meaning, and for its purpose an actual good already in existence. Consequently, too, it was not directed against the actual world as against something *generally perverted*, and against a 'way of the world'," *PhS*, sec. 390, p. 234.). This may be contrasted with the modern understanding of virtue, whose dominant shape is quixotism. Quixotism is virtue that has been secularized and rendered abstract. It "glories in this pompous talk about doing what is best for humanity, about the oppression of humanity, about making sacrifices for the sake of the good, and the misuse of gifts"; as Hegel goes on to say, "ideal entities and purposes of this kind are empty, ineffectual words which lift up the heart but leave reason unsatisfied, which edify, but raise no edifice; declamations which specifically declare merely this: that the individual who professes to act for such noble ends and who deals in such fine phrases is in his own eyes an excellent creature – a puffing-up which inflates him with a sense of his own importance in the eyes of others, whereas he is, in fact, inflated with his own conceit" (*PhS*, sec. 390, p. 234).

Hegel's contrastive reading of Ancient and modern virtue is in turn aligned to the more general process that lies at the heart of the *Phenomenology of Spirit*, viz., the dramatization of the limits of subjective self-consciousness. For both Hegel and Lukács, the epic marks a historico-philosophical moment in which individual consciousness has not yet been sundered from Spirit or its equivalent, society as a whole. This is a moment in which "the single, individual consciousness as it exists immediately in the real ethical order, or in the nation, is a solid unshaken trust in which Spirit has not, for the individual, resolved itself into its abstract moments, and therefore he is not aware of himself as being a pure individuality on his own account" (*PhS*, sec. 355, p. 214). As we have already begun to see in chapter 1, Hegel suggests that the whole cannot remain intact; the inevitable competition among roles will generate a series of pressures within it and these will result in a conflictive relationship between the individual and social customs and rules, which come to appear as objectified and alien forms of life:

once he has arrived at this idea [of individuality], as he must, then this immediate unity with Spirit, the [mere] being of himself in Spirit, his trust, is lost. Isolated and on his own, it is he who is now the essence, no longer universal Spirit ... In thus establishing himself, the individual has thereby placed himself in opposition to the laws and customs. These are regarded as mere ideas having no absolute essentiality, an abstract theory without any reality, while he as this particular 'I' is his own living truth.

(PhS, sec. 355, pp. 214–15)

This heart is confronted by a real world .... This reality is ... on the one hand a law by which the particular individuality is oppressed, a violent ordering of the world which contradicts the law of the heart, and, on the other hand, a humanity suffering under that ordering, a humanity that does not follow the law of the heart, but is subjected to an alien necessity.

(PhS, sec. 369, p. 221)

As the subjective "I" establishes its own "living truth," the individual tends to withdraw from society into a purely subjective world; the subject comes to abide by a "law of the heart," set in opposition to a world of inhospitable external rules. These external laws, which constitute an impartial or "disinterested" order arising out of the actions of countless individuals, represent the normative aspect of an "alien ordering" of social life, which Hegel calls the "way of the world."[44] Condemned from the standpoint of virtue, the "way of the world" nonetheless represents what virtue wants to encompass and annul. But since (modern, quixotic) virtue uproots the individuality and interest essential to its practical realization, it is eventually overwhelmed by the world's impartial laws. Whereas virtue once expressed a series of concrete possibilities for the self in society, the novelistic hero of "virtue" is now set grotesquely against the world and is nullified by it. As Hegel sees it, "the fatuousness of this rhetoric seems, too, in an unconscious way to have come to be a certainty for the culture of our time, since all interest in the whole mass of such rhetoric, and the way it is used to boost one's ego, has vanished – a loss of interest which is expressed in the fact that it produces only a feeling of boredom" *(PhS*, sec. 390, p. 234).

Seen in this light, the significance of a work like *Don Quixote* for the culture of modernity becomes increasingly clear. Cervantes' positive task is to criticize an abstract understanding of virtue, i.e. "an unreal virtue, a virtue in imagination and name only, which lacks that substantial content" *(ibid.)*, by laying bare the degraded quality of the

44 See *PhS*, sec. 381, pp. 228–29. Cf. Nietzsche and Freud, for whom the world, in its resistances, is *stronger*, not more moral or rational, than the delirium of the individual. See Franco Moretti, *Signs Taken for Wonders* (London: Verso, 1988), p. 177.

chivalric romances. The condition for his undertaking is neither the loss of virtue, as of a primary good, nor even the vanishing of an epic past, but rather the loss of virtue's ability to sustain practical interests, hence the loss of those interests themselves. Quixotism thus serves to mask a typically modern form of abstraction whose symptomology gravitates toward boredom rather than the highly charged if categorical distinctions between good and evil or noble and base that Don Quixote still remembers and strives to invoke. Supremely aware of this contrast, Cervantes begins his book with an appeal to the "idle reader" ("Desocupado lector ..."), i.e. to the reader who has ceased to consider reading as an ethical form of imitation and who has come to regard books as a refuge from the nullifying boredom of the world. Phrased in other terms, it can be said that when the pursuit of virtue (which Aristotle classified as a form of practical reason) becomes abstract, boredom sets in; reading, its antidote, is transformed from a means of ethical instruction into an autonomous practice whose objects are defined as works of "art."

Understood in these terms, the appearance of the novel represents less the absolute disappearance of virtue from the world than a representation of the process by which ethics becomes aligned to a normative position that is objective, universal, and abstract. To be sure, it may seem from the perspective of the novel and its privileging of individual autonomy and transcendental freedom that the achievement of epic totality is a form of absolute unfreedom or servitude. The upshot of Lyotard's arguments in *Just Gaming* is that this is not servitude at all but passivity, since it exists prior to and independent of the discourse of freedom. But it might be more accurate to say that the novel represents neither the absolute loss of ethical obligations nor the achievement of absolute freedom, but that a form of (post)epic literature in which the concept of totality as an immediate and undifferentiated relationship between the individual and society is brought to criticism of itself as self-limiting insofar as it relies on a system of social hierarchies, ranks, and castes. Epic society may well offer its members the security of a stable collective identity and the "metaphysical comfort" of values derived as if from first principles, but this society also limits the possibilities of what the self may be. Its controlling institutions remain closed to the majority of its members, who cannot aspire to the autonomy and freedom of liberal society, however problematical these values may be. Hegel may be right in his critique of virtue as quixotism; and Lukács may be correct in positing the novel as the locus of an "idea that has become an ideal" (*TN*, p. 92); but the example of the novel would in addition suggest that the epic version of "totality" constitutes an implausible goal. In terms of the comic, deflationary impulse of *Don Quixote*, it seems that epic society expects its heroes to carry out a series of extraordinary tasks whose social and historical origins it chooses also to ignore. The hero may thus be momentarily exalted, and the ordinary members of this society may find themselves temporarily ennobled and empowered by the hero's exemplary deeds; but the hero is bound eventually to be deflated, and the non-heroic individuals of this society may find themselves betrayed when they learn that he is not in fact an ultimate source of empowerment but a human artefact who expresses their own interests, desires, and fears. In the judgment of Roberto Unger, "they would have done better to seek this empowerment through the criticism and revision of their ordinary experience, beliefs, and institutions," rather than in the quixotic pursuit of heroic ideals.[45]

Insofar as we regard *Don Quixote* as itself that criticism, it becomes possible also to reverse Lukács's remaining complaint against literary romance, which performs a crucial mediating role in transforming the collective values of the epic into individually achievable desires and goals. According to Lukács, "the chivalrous novels against which *Don Quixote* was in the first place a polemic and which it parodied had lost the necessary transcendent relationship" (*TN*, p. 103). As long as the rise of the novel is seen to represent an absolute loss of totality rather than a critique of the epic forms through which totality was achieved, literary romance will continue to appear as a degraded form, one which turns to the pure thrill of adventure or grows preoccupied with the intricacies of plotting in order to mask the fact that a certain set of values has all but disappeared from sight. As Lukács in that passage went on to say, "their mysterious and fairy-tale like surfaces were bound to degenerate into banal superficiality." But it might be more accurate to conclude that romance represents a stage in the critique

---

45 Unger, *Passion: An Essay on Personality* (New York: The Free Press, 1984), p. 56. Cervantes' supreme awareness of this danger stands at the heart of his ambivalence towards the theatre of his day, especially that of Lope de Vega. See A. J. Cascardi, "The Old and the New: The Spanish *comedia* and the Resistance to Historical Change," *Renaissance Drama*, n.s., 17 (1986), 1–28.

of the epic, motivated not by the demands of society or the "law," but by the hero's unsatisfied need for personal love and individual fulfillment. As it later takes shape in what Lukács describes as the "novels of disillusionment," romance comes to reflect skepticism about the possibilities for the satisfaction of desire and the achievement of human virtue in the modern world. In novelists like Lawrence and Flaubert, its controlling anxiety is increased by a growing loss of faith in the existence of a natural context for desire.[46]

The precondition for the creation of a work like *Don Quixote* was by contrast a "pre-romantic" world in which the subject *qua* individual remained incompletely dissociated from the hierarchical order of epic society. Don Quixote "remembers" that society and its literature as places wherein it was still possible to invoke the principles of virtue and make judgments according to unambiguous ethical criteria; he "re-reads" the conflicts of the modern world in terms of the categorical oppositions between the noble and the base. Similarly, he remembers the once-historical possibility of existence in a world of unambiguous values in the form of the romances of chivalry, so that with the *Quixote* the novel itself becomes neither a naive and unquestioned repetition of the epic, nor a nostalgic attempt to relocate value in the past of romance, but a coming to self-consciousness of the modern subject as precipitated by the loss of faith in the existence of a natural context of thought and desire.

To say this much is also to say that Don Quixote's madness was not itself arbitrary, capricious, or yet quixotic, but corresponded to an historical possibility that in Cervantes' day had not yet been entirely lost from memory. As the twin processes of secularization and disenchantment come to dominate the modern world, however, the particular set of tensions that gave *Don Quixote* its peculiar ambivalence and vitality begin to lose their force. As Don Quixote's quixotism is increasingly naturalized, the heroes of "abstract idealism" are no longer able find their justification in any objective social order, but tend increasingly to become the creatures of an arbitrary desire, whose commanding idea is a product of the will, divorced from all objective truth. The quixotic hero is transformed into a figure like Lord Jim, who pursues autonomy like an *idée fixe* and in so doing is brought face to face with the anxiety involved in attempting to

---

46 See Unger, *Passion*, pp. 30–31.

provide the absolute grounding of a moral law. In an eighteenth-century novelist like Fielding, quixotism becomes naturalized as part of a compromising equation of madness with the "good natured soul." In the figure of Fielding's Parson Adams, for instance, madness becomes mere absentmindedness, and virtue no longer represents a commitment to transcendent ideals but rather becomes the expression of moral qualities that are accessible to all.[47] In Fredric Jameson's view, we find in later novelists a static opposition between the quixotic hero as an amusing eccentric or quaint romantic on the one hand, and a sentimentalized middle-class world on the other – sentimentalized, in Jameson's analysis, insofar as the novelist has come to accept it at face value, having begun from a preconception about the nature of that external reality which *Don Quixote* could not yet presuppose. If, as Jameson wishes to claim, the novel is a fully historical genre, then *Don Quixote* is no more free from "pre-conditions" than any later work. But, unlike many of those works, it was written during a period when the incessant, inner tensions between the individual and society, the ideal and the real – in Lukács's terms, the soul and the world – were reflected in society's awareness of its own modernity. Perhaps for this reason it has remained the genre's master text, its narrative possibilities continuously serving to foil efforts to define the novel as a genre.

The autonomy of art

I detest the novel insofar as it wants to be a separate genre.
Friedrich Schlegel, *Dialogue on Poetry*, "Letter on the Novel"

In going on to consider the problem of the autonomy of art, let us look further at the status of literature within the horizon of what we have so far been calling the "modern age" in order to enlarge that field beyond the scope of what may be visible by reference to *The Theory of the Novel*, the examples of Cervantes and Defoe, and the philosophies of Descartes and Kant. For, as I have suggested in chapter 1 above, while the culture of modernity may initially be grasped through a series of propositions regarding the mathematical

---

47 Cf. Lukács: "This is the artistic reason why Dickens' novels, so marvellously rich in comic characters, seem in the end so flat and moralistic. He had to make his heroes come to terms, without conflict, with the bourgeois society of his time and, for the sake of poetic effect, to surround the qualities needed for this purpose with a false, or anyway inadequate, poetic glow" (*TN*, p. 107).

nature of reason and the paradox of its radical emergence on an historical plane, what is ultimately at stake in modernity involves a much larger complex of cultural practices and institutionalized beliefs; indeed, according to the account that I have proposed, no one discursive formulation of their interrelationship may legitimately claim privilege over any other, and each is intelligible only in relation to the culture of modernity as a whole. By systematically ignoring the role of literature in the shaping of modern culture, critics like Habermas and Blumenberg fail to see how, in marking off an autonomous "aesthetic" sphere, a genre like the novel attempts to provide legitimate access to values that would seem archaic or potentially irrational when measured in relation to a purely representational concept of the real. When Lukács says in the passage quoted above that "the very disintegration and inadequacy of the world is the precondition for the existence of art and its becoming conscious"(*TN*, p. 38), he gives an accurate indication of the circumstances surrounding the autonomy of art. This autonomy is confirmed from philosophy's point of view when Descartes excludes fictions from the realm of philosophical truth; apparently thinking of Don Quixote he warns that "those who regulate their conduct by examples drawn from these works are liable to fall into the excesses of the knights-errant in our tales of chivalry, and conceive plans beyond their powers" (*Discourse*, I, p. 114). But Lukács fails to see that the novel, and the aesthetic ideology it projects, may come to enjoy the special privilege of a mimetic activity seen as dangerous, illicit, or archaic when judged against a paradigm of experience defined by rationalist conceptions of the truth. The techniques of representation provide a series of formal and rhetorical indications that the novel's world is like our own and, as such, able to sustain belief; phrased in other terms, they allow us to "naturalize" a world. And yet value in the novel is characteristically sought in other-worldly experiences or goals, which are romanticized and rendered correspondingly abstract. Since the inner-worldly subject can claim no legitimate relation to these values, the self-referential rhetoric of "sincerity" and "authenticity" – an expression of freedom as the subject's "ungrounded ground" – comes to underwrite the novel's supreme moments of value or novelistic "truth."[48]

48 In *Theorizing* (London: Heineman, 1974), Alan Blum explains how in Descartes authenticity in fact becomes the reason for speaking. See pp. 150–53. In *The Philosophy of the Novel* (pp. 173ff), J. M. Bernstein has argued that a rhetoric of

In these and other ways the novel risks reproducing even as it inverts a series of dichotomies that define the subject as divided between two worlds. For instance, it can be seen that the implied readers of the novel adapt a series of longstanding literary assumptions to the conditions of the modern work of art, ranging from the ancient prejudice against fiction as a form of imitation in comparison to philosophy and history as the discourses of truth, to similarly antique preconceptions about the need for variety and the impropriety of digressions within the scope of a unified plot. The novel shapes a further range of expectations about verisimilitude and taste, about the nature of moral examples and the transformative power of ideals, as well as about such social and political issues as the nature of justice, the radius of the will, and the autonomy of the individual in the modern world. The novel comes to assume a status that is exemplary of the alienated place of art within the divided culture of modernity, for in it the traditional promise of literature as a source of creative inspiration and moral instruction is pitted against the "dangers" of fictional or quixotic modes of readerly identification; in so doing the novel imposes a need to find ways of reading in resistance to or against the text. The reading subject of the novel, who may be seen as the genealogical ancestor of the modern intellectual or "secular clerk," is modeled after the sedentary gentleman, the woman of virtue, or the *honnête homme*, rather than the *caballero andante* or errant knight. This reader is attracted by the imaginative powers of literature but remains nonetheless committed to the claims of enlightened discourse and so must develop a series of highly complex strategies in order to read while resisting seduction by the text. Since as modern readers we experience the claims of reason and the power of the imagination as contradictory demands – indeed, as divided parts of ourselves – we are likely to be embarrassed when faced with the need to provide reasons to justify the choice of which texts to read and which ideals to pursue. On the one hand, the constraints of reason would require us to revoke the quixotic imperative to regard texts as sources of inspiration or vehicles for the transmission of values according to the modes of identification proper to the "traditional" world, but we nonetheless maintain an investment in reading and recognize the power of literature to command belief.

frankness and authenticity marks the discourse of subjectivity from Descartes to Rousseau and beyond.

If we think of characters like Cervantes' Don Quixote, Austen's Catherine Morland, and Flaubert's Emma Bovary, it becomes clear that the novel attempts to deal with the dangers of "mimetic" or "absorptive" fictions in two very different ways, sometimes within the confines of a single work. The first seeks to redeem fictions by pitting literature against itself in an attempt to resist or control the process of identification. And yet if we think of these characters, it becomes equally clear that modern fiction is powerless to redeem itself from within; at best, characters in the novel achieve an ambiguous *desengaño* that leads them to positions of extreme self-irony or to death. As we shall see in somewhat greater detail below, the fact of fiction's inability to redeem itself, to afford any ultimate justifications for its status as an inferior or degraded world, is the occasion for the invention of an independent theoretical discourse. Beginning with the efforts of the Barber, the Canon of Toledo, and the Priest in *Don Quixote*, Cervantes recognizes the temptation to legitimize fiction by passing aesthetic experience through the communicative grid of aesthetic judgment. In this approach the problem of the status of fictional objects is "resolved," rendered invisible by an appeal to discursive norms, while a "remainder" of unaccounted quixotic experience is left to threaten and demonize the achievements of enlightened reason.

As the reflection of a typically modern predicament, it may be said that fiction's failure to redeem itself by coming to full self-consciousness results in the appeal to an independent theoretical discourse that in turn leaves aesthetic experience as the marginalized "other" of reason. This predicament is in a sense "superseded" by the historicist methods of criticism and resistance practiced by writers like Walter Benjamin and Harold Bloom. For Benjamin and Bloom, literature is essentially historical, and modern literature is uniquely so insofar as it is unable to provide forms of representation adequate to the expression of our literary desires, which are themselves historically defined. Writing, as a progressive attempt at form-making, must on this view be subordinate to the procedures of "creative" or "strong" reading, which is iconoclastic, or form-breaking, in its struggles with the burdens of the past. According to this view, the claims of creative novelty in the face of the reported disappearance of form, like the characteristic "absolutism" of the modern age, must be seen as mere covers for a sense of catastrophic displacement that stems from a loss of the cultural authority of art. This loss generates a literally infinite but fragmentary desire, in response to which all "modern" efforts must be classified as "revisionary ratios" or tropes. The result is a conception of literary history as an overwhelming accretion of forms which renders the task of artistic self-assertion ever more difficult to achieve. Thus in the analysis of one recent Bloomian critic, it is the impossibility of fulfillment that distinguishes the modern, secular canon from its sacred analogue: "because the secular canon is never fixed and the 'religion' of humanism never fully revealed, salvation or the achievement of poetic desire remains a salvation for one in which the poets are in a direct and intensely personal competition – the achievement of one detracts from all the others, and the higher the canon elevates the greats of the past, the greater the burden on the poetic future."[49] As a result, the modern writer is hurled toward the future as if in flight from the stormy accumulation of works in the past. In Walter Benjamin's description it is the *angelus novus* who serves to emblematize this predicament:

This is how one pictures the angel of history. His face is turned toward the past. Where we perceive a chain of events, *he* sees one single catastrophe which keeps piling wreckage upon wreckage, and hurls it in front of his feet. The angel would like to stay, awaken the dead, and make whole what has been smashed. But a storm is blowing from Paradise; it has got caught in his wings with such violence that the angel can no longer close them. This storm irresistibly propels him into the future to which his back is turned, while the pile of debris before him grows skyward. This storm is what we call progress.[50]

Insofar as the revisionist thesis derives the possibility of "progress" from the impossibility of a return to the fullness of the past, it is itself a fully "disenchanted" product of the modern age. As Benjamin goes on to say, "the concept of the historical progress of mankind cannot be sundered from the conception of its progression through a homogeneous, empty time. A critique of the concept of such a progression must be the basis of any criticism of the concept of progress itself. History is the subject of a structure whose site is not homogeneous, empty time, but time filled by the presence of the now [*Jetztzeit*]" (p. 261).

Revisionism and other "strong forms" of historicism nonetheless enable us to recognize the deficiencies of conventional literary

49 Jean-Pierre Mileur, *Literary Revisionism*, p. 130.
50 Benjamin, "Theses on the Philosophy of History," trans. Harry Zohn, in *Illuminations* (New York: Schocken Books, 1969), pp. 257–58.

history, according to which the claim of the novel as the major modern genre derives from the simple rejection of the authority of the tradition in establishing aesthetic norms. Watt, for instance, claimed that "previous literary forms had reflected the general tendency of their cultures to make conformity to traditional practice the major test of truth: the plots of classical and renaissance epic, for example, were based on past history or fable, and the merits of the author's treatment were judged largely according to a view of literary decorum derived from the accepted models of the genre. This literary traditionalism was first and foremost challenged by the novel" (*Rise of the Novel*, p. 13). As a characterization of modernity, such an account might at best be accurate for Descartes, who resists the claims of history by claiming for himself the invention of a new philosophical method and a new mode of discourse. Indeed, Descartes fully expects that his method of rational self-assertion will serve as an anchor for progress against the storm of history and as an absolute defense against the past. But the novel will thematize rather than repress what Bloom calls the "anxiety of influence" and Walter Jackson Bate the "burden of the past." When confronted with the demand that a great work of art should imitate and pay homage to pre-existing forms, the narrator of *Don Quixote* is counseled to buttress his modernizing efforts by reproducing the modes of discourse that historically have licensed literature, even if these are outmoded and no longer constitute signs of authentic belief:

"Let us come now to references to authors, which other books contain and yours lacks. The remedy for this is very simple; for you have nothing else to do but look for a book which quotes them all from A to Z, as you say. Then you put this same alphabet into yours. For, granted that the very small need you have to employ them will make your deception transparent, it does not matter a bit; and perhaps there will even be someone silly enough to believe that you have made use of them all in your simple and straightforward story. And if it serves no other purpose, at least that long catalogue of authors will be useful to lend authority to your book at the outset. Besides, nobody will take the trouble to examine whether you follow your authorities or not."   (*Don Quixote*, "Prologue," Part I, p. 29)

In contrast to Descartes, who establishes philosophy as a self-legitimizing form of discourse meant to reflect the new foundations of knowledge, and in contrast also to Hegel, who seeks to make those foundations both historical and absolute, modern literature begins when the "catalogue of authors" mentioned by Cervantes above is wrenched free from its traditional context and becomes available to be cited and reproduced in order to legitimize an otherwise "formless" or "inessential" text.[51]

It is thus on the basis of a perceived marginality, which the novel at its inception represents with regard to the entire tradition, that modernity has been able to become manifest as that which already breaches tradition from within. Phrased in other terms, it can be said that Cervantes has come to realize that knowledge is historical and spirit productive, but that the course of literature is not necessarily progressive. As a result of the secularization process, or of what we have called, with Lukács and Weber, the "disenchantment" of the world, the novel must take shape in the spaces left vacant by pre-existing forms. Thus when the Cervantean narrator affirms his iconoclastic desire in the famous concluding passage of *Don Quixote*, Part II – "My sole object has been to arouse men's contempt for all fabulous and absurd stories of knight errantry, whose credit this tale of my genuine Don Quixote has already shaken, and which will, without a doubt, soon tumble to the ground" (ch. 74) – he takes it as an historical fact that the forms produced by the novel will not be radically new, if only because there are, strictly speaking, no radically new forms left for the modern poet to create. The claims to originality which are mingled with Fielding's diatribe against critics and precepts in *Tom Jones*, XI, 1 ("A Crust for the Critics"), are, like Cervantes' boast in the Prologue to the *Exemplary Novels* that he is the first in Spanish to "novelize," borne out through the repetition of forms that have become historically outmoded but not outwardly destroyed.[52]

At the same time, the novel reveals itself to be a genre that must continuously defend itself in the face of challenges that it lacks any established principles or generic identity at all. The *Quixote* profoundly influences a genre that contravenes the "literary" version of the naturalistic thesis described in chapter 1 above, viz., that nature is an order of self-engendering likeness, a standard for mimetic imitation, the essential idea of which the artist reproduces in his work.

---

51 The "formlessness" of the text is reproduced in the claim that this text is similarly authorless. I refer to the passage in the Prologue to Part I, "I, though in appearance Don Quixote's father, am really his step-father," p. 25.

52 Some of the ambiguities of originality in Cervantes have been discussed by John G. Weiger in *The Substance of Cervantes* (Cambridge: Cambridge University Press, 1985), especially pp. 41–83, and by E. T. Aylward in *Cervantes: Pioneer and Plagiarist* (London: Tamesis Books, 1982).

According to an older view, still widely prevalent among conservative ideologues in Cervantes' day, nature generates only likeness; the "natural" makes reference to the generative principle by which the world is a self-producing succession of sameness ("en ella [la Naturaleza] cada cosa engendra a su semejante," *Don Quixote*, "Prologue," Part I, p. 27[53]). If this is so, then *Don Quixote* would on all accounts have to be regarded as an *un*natural kind. It appears to break nature's law of generic similitude by mixing a vast diversity of kinds – pastoral, chivalresque, *novela morisca*, autoportraiture, theatre, lyric, narrative, and burlesque verse; an italianate novella, the picaresque, Ciceronian-styled dialogue, Erasmian adages, political prose, letters, epigrams, as well as adventures modeled on Classical epic and Byzantine romance. The *Quixote* might in this respect be thought of as the limit-case of what Rosalie Colie described as the Renaissance passion for "inclusionism" and what Friedrich Schlegel in the "Letter on the Novel" described as *Mischung*. According to the Renaissance view, the multiplicity of genres we find in the *Quixote* would be a challenge to the core idea of genre – that there is an order of *kindness* to things – and thus a threat to the order of nature, which might be thought of as a totality insofar as it represents the essential coherence or *kinship* of these kinds.[54] And yet the novel transcends the limits of Renaissance theory and strives to fulfill a fundamentally romantic ambition insofar as it transforms the heterogeneous modes of discourse into a (whole) work. According to the "Letter on the Novel" in Schlegel's *Dialogue on Poetry*, for instance, it is scarcely possible to conceive of the novel except as a mixture of story-telling, song, and other forms: "Cervantes always composed in this manner," Schlegel writes, "and even the otherwise so prosaic Boccaccio adorns his collections of stories by framing them with songs. If there is a novel in which this does not or cannot occur, it is only due to the individuality of the work and not the character of the genre; on the

53 Literally, "In Nature, each thing engenders its likeness"; for further discussion see A. J. Cascardi, "Genre Multiplicity and Definition in *Don Quixote*." The generative principle of nature remained in force at least until Pascal, who writes that "Nature copies itself. A seed cast on good ground bears fruit, a principle cast into a good mind bears fruit. Numbers copy space, though so different by nature. Everything is made and directed by the same master. Root, branches, fruit: principles, consequences." *Pensées*, trans. A. J. Krailsheimer (Harmondsworth: Penguin Books, 1966), fr. 698, p. 247.

54 Colie, *The Resources of Kind: Genre Theory in the Renaissance*, ed. Barbara K. Lewalski (Berkeley: University of California Press, 1973), p. 31.

contrary, it is already an exception."[55] The reason Schlegel gives to explain the generic principle of this *Mischung* is that the novel, as opposed to the epic, is the genre of subjective freedom or what amounts to the same thing for him, a "romantic" book. In historical terms this means that the novel is a *Roman*, a work whose models are to be found only "in that age of knights, love, and fairy tales in which the thing itself [*der Roman*] and the word for it [romantic] originated" (p. 101). More deeply it means that the novel is Literature itself, that it is the equal to romanticism, which the "Letter" defines as not so much a genre as that element of poetry "which may be more or less dominant or recessive, but never entirely absent" in literature. In Schlegel's view, "all poetry should be Romantic...I detest the novel insofar as it wants to be a separate genre" (p. 101).

When drawn to reflect on the ethical implications of the propositions outlined above – that pre-existing forms have been essentially ruined and no longer have the power to command the social or aesthetic whole – novelists have often been tempted to draw the painful conclusion that, as one critic ruefully said, "good books do not necessarily make good people."[56] Indeed, the idea that literature should serve an exemplary function by inducing us to imitate the virtuous actions of the heroes modeled in great books is throughout *Don Quixote* submitted to a remorseless critique as characters succumb to various forms of the quixotic impulse. In particular, those who would uphold the principles of enlightened modernity against the dangers of quixotic reading through a commitment to the ideals of reason and common sense – especially the Barber and the Priest – are infected by a form of quixotism that undermines their ability to resist the project of reading they initially set out to defeat. But since these characters never become entirely possessed by books, they experience the seductive power of fictions in a disenchanted world in the form of a division from within. If Don Quixote represents the transformation of historical forms of experience into unanchored modes of "discourse" – if he is, in Foucault's terms, "nothing but language, text, printed pages, stories already written down...made

---

55 Friedrich Schlegel, *Dialogue on Poetry*, trans. Ernst Behler and Roman Struc (University Park: Pennsylvania State University Press, 1968), p. 102. See also Lacoue-Labarthe and Nancy, *L'Absolu littéraire*.

56 Mileur, *Literary Revisionism*, p. 27.

up of interwoven words"[57] – then these other characters confront the need to define themselves by resisting absorption by "discourse" or the "text." And yet were we to accept their example we would be drawn to conclude that the complete disenchantment of the world would require that reading take its place within modern society as a form of self-repression or as an historical exertion of what we might call the will to power over texts.

This much said, it might seem better to concede that literature and modern society are inherently antithetical to one another; indeed, the arguments put forward above might tempt us to admit that the project to reestablish literature's role in the transmission of ethical values is bound for purely historical reasons to fail – in the first instance because we as moderns are permanently alienated from the historical sources of literary creativity and ethical value in the Ancient epic world, and in the second instance because the achievement of critical enlightenment is the product of a secularizing process that claims to have excluded fictions from a value-shaping role in the modern world. In *The Philosophical Discourse of Modernity* and related texts Habermas has argued against the creation of an "aesthetic ideology" as a privileged "other" of reason that we have seen embedded within the subject and reflected in the creation of novelistic discourse. But because Habermas's account of aesthetic modernity ignores the internal complexities of the novel in favor of the vague notion of "modern art" as an amalgam of Nietzschean aestheticism, Baudelairian symbolism, and Surrealism, he fails to see the ways in which the tensions of modern culture are enclosed within the novel itself.

On the one hand, narration in the novel displays a preoccupation with the nature of reality that is coincident with the goals of philosophical enlightenment in securing the rationality of the world. Yet on the other hand, the novel responds to the need for the (conscious, historical, social) mediation of experience and for the articulation of desires as the bases of a vision of personal identity that cannot always be centered with respect to a social whole. At the same time, novelistic narration must balance the coherence and continuity required of a story against a variety of threats to the integrity of the whole. These threats often take the form of details, digressions, and apparent distractions from the principal story-line or

57 Foucault, *The Order of Things* (New York: Vintage, 1970), p. 46.

plot, and may be likened to what Bataille described as the "heterogeneous" elements at work within culture as a whole. Beginning with Cervantes, and in a remarkable way in Sterne, the tensions between continuity and digression, between distractive incidents and the will to conclude, constitute the twin poles of narration, and the fundamental energies of the novel may be seen to derive from them. The characteristic "waywardness" of the novel is fueled by the unpredictability of desire and by the introduction of the agencies of passion, often configured as a disruption or lack; yet novelistic narrative is at the same time sustained by the project to eliminate distraction and to satisfy desire as is manifested in the will to conclude. The various closural patterns through which the formal totality of the novel is achieved may be seen to correspond to the different possible ends of desire in modernity; these may range from satisfaction and the achievement of reciprocal "happiness" in marriage to the death of the desiring subject, but in either case closure marks the annihilation of desire and the termination of what may properly speaking be termed the "narrative" aspect of novelistic discourse.[58] Whereas Hegel's response to modernity sought to demonstrate the complete accommodation of rationality and the real, in part by making desire the motive force of consciousness in its pursuit of the real, novelistic narration is dispossessed of the self-confidence of the epic but does not venture the self-assured certainty of the Hegelian whole. For these and allied reasons the novel tends to interpret desire as a primarily disruptive force and risks falling into "bad" (i.e. purely idealizing) forms of romance.

In his discussion of modernity, by contrast, Habermas sees in the aesthetic sphere a rejection of the standards of rational discourse in favor of a Nietzschean will to establish an aesthetic ideology based on pre-rational experience and a series of irrational claims of taste. On the one hand, Habermas's worry is that certain aspects of modern experience may be prized *because* they cannot be measured by a standard that sees truth as the exactitude of (objective) representations in the mind. Habermas makes this argument in connection with "bourgeois art" which, he says, "has become the refuge for a satisfaction, even if only virtual, of those needs that have become, as it were, illegal in the material life-process of bourgeois society ... Bour-

---

58 See Peter Brooks, "Freud's Masterplot: A Model for Narrative," in *Reading for the Plot* (New York: Vintage Books, 1984); and also Leo Bersani, *A Future for Astyanax*.

geois art, unlike privatized religion, scientistic philosophy, and strategic-utilitarian morality, did not take on tasks in the economic and political systems. Instead it collected residual needs that could find no satisfaction within the 'system of needs.'"[59] On the other hand, Habermas complains that Nietzsche's response to this problem simply enthrones a vision of taste as "'the Yes and No of the palate,' as the organ of a knowledge beyond true and false, beyond good and evil. But *he cannot legitimate the criteria of aesthetic judgment that he holds on to because he transposes aesthetic experience into the archaic*, because he does not recognize as a moment of reason the critical capacity for assessing value that was sharpened through dealing with modern art.... The aesthetic domain, as the gateway to the Dionysian, is hypostatized instead into the other of reason" (*PDM*, p. 96; emphasis added). He goes on to say that "Nietzsche owes his concept of modernity...to an unmasking critique of reason that sets itself outside the horizon of reason. This critique has a certain suggestiveness because it appeals, at least implicitly, to criteria borrowed from the basic experiences of aesthetic modernity" (*ibid.*). Habermas's account of the dominance of Nietzschean theories of "taste" might be accurate as a caricature of certain tendencies in contemporary literary discourse; Roland Barthes writes for instance in *The Pleasure of the Text* that

if I agree to judge a text according to pleasure, I cannot go on to say: this one good, that bad. No awards, no "critique," for this always implies a tactical aim, a social usage, and frequently an extenuating image-reservoir. I cannot apportion, imagine that the text is perfectible, ready to enter into a play of normative predicates: it is too much *this*, not enough *that*; the text (the same is true of the singing voice) can wring from me only this judgment, in no way adjectival: *that's it*! And further still: *that's it for me*!. This "for me" is neither subjective nor existential, but Nietzschean.[60]

But because Habermas finds it necessary to pass all aesthetic experience through the crucible of aesthetic judgment, he must not only resist the pleasures of the text but must also ignore the expressive potential and inner coherence demonstrated by aesthetic forms. But for Habermas, it is in aesthetic judgment, rather than aesthetic experience, that we are able to recognize a "moment of

59 *Legitimation Crisis*, trans. Thomas McCarthy (Boston: Beacon Press, 1975), p. 78.
60 *The Pleasure of the Text*, trans. Richard Miller (New York: Hill and Wang, 1975), p. 13. The criticism to be leveled here is not the Habermassian one against the creation of "aesthetic ideologies," but rather against the impoverishment of critical discourse.

reason ... that is still at least procedurally connected with objectifying knowledge and moral insight in the process of providing argumentative grounds."[61] Thus literature for Habermas constitutes the medium through which otherwise unavailable human impulses, desires, and anxieties may be allowed to enter into the public realm, where they can be discursively negotiated assessed.

By insisting on the sublimation of aesthetic experience through aesthetic judgment, Habermas chooses to follow only one of the two paths toward aesthetic modernity outlined by Kant in the *Critique of Judgment*. Kant viewed his efforts in that work as an attempt to overcome the division between the sensible and supersensible worlds implicit in the first two critiques by mobilizing rather than collapsing the terms involved, recognizing that

> between the realm of the natural concept, as the sensible, and the realm of the concept of freedom, as the supersensible, there is a gulf fixed, so that it is not possible to pass from the former to the latter (by means of the theoretical employment of reason), just as if they were so many separate worlds, the first of which is powerless to exercise influence on the second: still the latter is *meant* to influence the former – that is to say, the concept of freedom is meant to actualize in the sensible world the end proposed by its laws; and nature must consequently also be capable of being regarded in such a way that in the conformity to the law of its own form it at least harmonizes with the possibility of ends to be effectuated [*sic*] in it according to the laws of freedom.[62]

For Kant, it is aesthetic experience that, prior to and apart from aesthetic judgment, proves the unity of the supersensible realm with the concept of freedom, understood in practical terms:

> although the concept of this ground neither theoretically nor practically attains to a knowledge of it, and so has no peculiar realm of its own, still it renders possible the transition from the mode of thought according to principles of the one to that according to the principles of the other. (*Ibid.*)

Kant's reputed attempt to repair the divided world of the subject by recourse to aesthetic experience in the *Critique of Judgment* was

---

61 Habermas, *PDM*, p. 96. Peter Bürger makes a related criticism of Kant: "It is not the work of art but the aesthetic judgment (the judgment of taste) that Kant investigates. It is situated between the realm of the senses and that of reason, between the 'interest of inclination in the case of the agreeable' (*Critique of Judgment*, sec. 5) and the interest of practical reason in the realization of the moral law, and is defined as *disinterested*." *The Theory of the Avant-Garde*, trans. Michael Shaw (Minneapolis: University of Minnesota Press, 1984), p. 42.

62 Kant, *The Critique of Judgment*, trans. James Creed Meredith (1928; rpt. Oxford: Clarendon Press, 1986), p. 14.

influential on a number of his immediate successors, including Schiller, who saw it as offering a possible solution to the social disintegration and political divisions of the modern age. We will have occasion to propose a rereading of Kant's aesthetic judgment in connection with the concept of "aesthetic liberalism" developed in the concluding pages of this study. For now it is sufficient to see that, according to the standard interpretation, the *Critique of Judgment* provides evidence that Kant himself could not rest content with the differentiations between sense and understanding, necessity and freedom, nature and mind that were implicit in the earlier Critiques because he perceived these distinctions as themselves an expression of the dichotomies inherent in modern life. Schiller follows Kant's example insofar as he is able to think of art as a means to achieve community in society. At the same time, Schiller anticipates the diagnoses of modernity later put forward by Weber, Lukács, and Marx; he recognizes the plight of the abstract thinker as parallel to that of the social subject in a heartless, soulless, world of capital and commodities:

The business spirit, confirmed in a monotonous cycle of objects, and inside these still further restricted by formulas, was forced to see the freedom of the whole snatched from under its eyes ... The abstract thinker very often has a cold heart, since he analyzes the impressions that really affect the soul only as a whole; the man of business has very often a narrow heart, because his imagination, confined within the monotonous circle of his profession, cannot expand to unfamiliar modes of representation.[63]

In reaction to such circumstances, Schiller expects aesthetic experience to generate a total revolution, to reveal the hidden wholeness of life, and to present this wholeness in terms of aesthetic forms. And yet the desire to recover an immanent totality must necessarily remain unfulfilled insofar as the experiences that occur within the province of symbols, figures, and signs can for Schiller only be approached by means of intuition rather than critical analysis. The resulting concept of the "aesthetic" could thus be in jeopardy of being appropriated in the service of anti-liberal goals, rather than to enlarge the possibilities of community through rational inquiry and reasoned critical debate.

In response to the potentially mystifying claims made for art in this regard, Habermas has come to focus on the Kantian notion of taste as the moment in which aesthetic experience enters into the sphere

---

63 Schiller, *On the Aesthetic Education of Man in a Series of Letters*, trans. Reginald Snell (New Haven: Yale University Press, 1954), pp. 42–43.

of public discourse and becomes available for rational debate. To this end he attempts to rewrite Schiller's vision of the revolutionary Aesthetic State in terms of the theory of communicative action. An aesthetically reconciled society would on this account be a structure in which a communicatively based intersubjectivity would act as a foil to the divisiveness imposed by modern culture. In Schiller's Aesthetic State, the generic differences between philosophy and literature drop out in favor of the commanding power of forms and symbols. We read in images, language, and plot (*mythos*) the ciphers of freedom itself. But Habermas's attempt to reconstruct reason in the form of a theory of communicative action rejects the intuitive power of figural language in order to maintain the clear and necessary separations among the discursive spheres. Habermas argues that these divisions are necessary in order to avoid a fall "backward" into the archaic or the pre-rational world of magical phenomena. But since he proposes no means by which to mediate among the discursive spheres,[64] and no means by which to recuperate the power of aesthetic experience, he comes to resemble those critics within the *Quixote* – the Barber, and the Priest – who insist on the rigid separation of fictional and philosophical modes of speech. By conceiving the forms of communicative reason as necessary for the sublimation of the expressive and aesthetic contents of experience, Habermas reproduces the conditions of rationalization, abstraction, and detotalization that his theory of communicative action was designed to correct. Aesthetic experience remains a component of such a world only to the extent that, as Habermas has himself recognized, without the influx of its energies, a practical discourse would necessarily become sterile.[65] We are as a result left to see that communicative action is in itself formal and content-less in precisely the way that the Kantian or Cartesian discourse of subjectivity is.

In a similar way, rather than recognize that an historical analysis of the alienation of literature within the modern world constitutes a precondition for a recovery of the ethical potential of aesthetic experience, Habermas has chosen to displace the aesthetic origins of

---

64 This can be said in spite of the claims made in the essay "Philosophy as Stand-In and Interpreter," in Kenneth Baynes, James Bohman, and Thomas McCarthy, eds. *After Philosophy: End or Transformation* (Cambridge, MA: MIT Press, 1987), pp. 296–315.

65 See especially Habermas, "Consciousness-Raising or Redemptive Criticism: The Contemporaneity of Walter Benjamin," in *Philosophical-Political Profiles*, trans. Frederick Lawrence (Cambridge, MA: MIT Press, 1983).

modernity from the century of Cervantes and Descartes in order to rewrite literary history according to the "progressive" narrative of Enlightenment thought. But in order to do so he must also deny the contradictions inherent within the Enlightenment itself. According to his account, which closely follows that of Hans-Robert Jauss, the process of aesthetic modernization begins only once the self-declared "moderns" in the eighteenth-century *querelle des anciens et des modernes* came to invoke historical-critical arguments in order to question the value of imitating ancient models: "in opposition to the norms of an apparently timeless and absolute beauty," Habermas writes, "they elaborated the criteria of a relative or time-conditioned beauty and thus articulated the self-understanding of the French Enlightenment as an epochal new beginning" (*PDM*, p. 8). By arguing that when these "moderns" rebelled against Classical norms they assimilated aesthetics to an historicist concept of progress modeled after achievements in science, Habermas implies that the Enlightenment was essentially unbroken by contradiction from within. And yet even as central a figure as David Hume could conclude that the same conditions that enable advancement in the arts to take place imply that the course of progress will be far from insured. According to Hume's historicist and "Enlightenment" account in the *Rise and Progress of the Arts and Sciences*, the reservoir of available creative talent varies unpredictably from generation to generation; thus it is possible that the record of prior human achievements may limit the range of endeavors that can serve as vehicles of progress in any given age.[66] Indeed, the greatness of a preceding age may bring the productive imitation of the past to an end, obliging writers to recognize the disappearance of form by abandoning their creative labors or forcing them to pursue novelty or the productiveness of form for its own sake.[67]

66 See Walter Jackson Bate, *Burden of the Past and the English Poet* (New York: Norton, 1972), pp. 80–82; and Mileur, *Literary Revisionism*, p. 169.

67 For Barthes, novelty remains a criterion of textual "bliss"; through it, the new is elevated to the status of a value in and of itself: "bliss may come only with the *absolutely new*, for only the new disturbs (weakens) consciousness ... The New is not a fashion, it is a value, the basis of all criticism: our evaluation of the world no longer depends, at least not directly, as in Nietzsche, on the opposition between *noble* and *base*, but on that between Old and New (the erotics of the New began in the eighteenth century: a long transformational process)." *The Pleasure of the Text*, p. 40.

In order to mitigate the conditions brought about by the alienation of art, modern society has in practice taken a somewhat contradictory tack. Modern culture has organized an autonomous "aesthetic sphere" which offers something other than the reconciliation of the sensible and supersensible worlds indicated in Kant's third Critique or the total revolution of the "whole made perception" promised in Schiller's Aesthetic State. But insofar as it has become aware of the problematic externality of literature to culture as a whole, society has established an army of professional readers charged with the legitimation of fictions and the validation of their "truth." Cervantes' Canon of Toledo, who draws his principles from the Humanist commentaries on Aristotle's *Poetics*, is an early example of a reader of this type. These readers are inclined to accept the role of philosophy as the guardian of truth and would prefer not to confront the problems inherent in the ghettoization of fiction in the modern world. Anticipating the "science" of aesthetic judgment, these readers come prepared quietly to accept the philosophical project to "legitimize" fictions by subordinating literature to the standards of a formalized discourse of truth. But already for Descartes the power of the mind to project images of what might be the case has no direct bearing on the faculties of rational judgment, which alone adjudicate claims to existence and truth; according to the *Discourse on Method*, "we can distinctly imagine a lion's head on a goat's body without having to conclude from this that a chimera exists in the world, our reason does not insist that what we thus see or imagine is true."[68]

The incorporation of theoretical discourse within the body of the novel is symptomatic of the separation of aesthetic judgment from aesthetic experience, but also constitutes an attempt to overcome the institutional alienation of literature by bringing the accomplishments of critical enlightenment to bear on the autonomous aesthetic sphere and by so doing to legitimize the existence of fictions in a secularized world. So seen, the discourse of "theory" and the recourse to the concept of "aesthetic distance" are but formalized extensions of the elaborate "conciliations" that Don Quixote finds necessary in order

---

68 Descartes, *Discourse*, IV, p. 131. With these and related arguments, Descartes begins the modern analytical tradition of reflection on the status of fictional objects. He is followed, for example, by Spinoza's discussion of the difference of true ideas from fictions and from false ideas, in the fragmentary treatise "De Intellectus Emendatione" ("On the Improvement of the Understanding") in *Works*, II, trans. R. H. M. Elwes (London: George Bell and Sons, 1884), pp. 3–41.

to make sense of the disparity between the romances of chivalry and lived experience.[69] When faced with a world that has been disenchanted, secularized, rendered prose – with untransformed windmills, sheep, peasant women, and barber's basins – Don Quixote typically explains that these things are not in accordance with what the romances suggest because they have been cast under a spell or have been transformed by the power of some malicious enchanter.[70] For Don Quixote, existence in a disenchanted world is made tolerable by recourse to what amounts to the mediation of a "theory" of enchantment. Thus when Don Quixote confronts Master Pedro's Puppet Show in Part II, he invokes this theory in order to explain why the puppets are not alive and real:

these enchanters who persecute me are always placing before my eyes shapes like these, and then changing and transforming them to look like whatever they please. I assure you gentlemen that all that has passed here seemed to me a real occurrence. Melisendra was Melisendra; Sir Gaiferos, Sir Gaiferos; Marsilio, Marsilio; and Charlemagne, Charlemagne ... If things have turned out contrariwise the fault is not mine, but lies with my wicked persecutors.   (p. 643)

The claims of verisimilitude and truth announced at the opening of the episode ("This true story ... taken word for word from the French chronicles and the Spanish ballads," p. 638) are overwhelmed by the reactions of Don Quixote, whose presence among "enchanters" now requires a competing theory of "aesthetic distance" or "disinterested pleasure" if the status of fictional objects (as "fictional") is to be ensured at all.[71]

The "disenchantment" of the world is thus marked not only by a loss of the archaic power of fictions to command belief but by the *persistence* of fictions, which engenders the invention of aesthetic "theory" to fill the gap. Taken in this context, the Canon's lengthy arguments in *Don Quixote*, Part I, represent an attempt to find a middle

69 Cf. Michael McKeon's observation in *The Origins of the English Novel*: "Theory develops in dialectical relation to genre as a supplementary discourse of detached commentary that is yet inseparable, in its own development, from the corollary process of genre formation" (p. 118).

70 For a fuller exploration of the relationship with Descartes see A. J. Cascardi, *The Bounds of Reason* (New York: Columbia University Press, 1986).

71 Cervantes' concern for aesthetic distance may reflect an engagement with Aristotle's *Poetics*. See B. W. Ife, *Reading and Fiction in Golden-Age Spain*, pp. 49–64 ("Literature and Aesthetic Belief") and also Forcione, *Cervantes, Aristotle, and the Persiles* (Princeton: Princeton University Press, 1970), and McKeon, *The Origins of the English Novel*, pp. 273–94.

ground between the terms of "enchantment" and "disenchantment." Recognizing the palpable objection that the novels of chivalry are lacking in verisimilitude, that they are "extravagant tales, whose purpose is to amaze, and not to instruct" (I, 47, p. 424), the Canon proposes a series of criteria for the legitimation of fictions that would allow us to preserve their role in ethical instruction and the dissemination of truth:

Fictions have to match the minds of their readers, and to be written in such a way that, by tempering the impossibilities, moderating excesses, and keeping judgment in the balance, they may so astonish, hold, excite, and entertain, that wonder and pleasure go hand in hand. None of this can be achieved by anyone departing from verisimilitude or from that imitation of nature in which lies the perfection of all that is written ... If all this is done in a pleasant style and with an ingenious plot, as close as possible to the truth, there is no doubt at all that the author will weave a beautiful and variegated fabric, which, when finished, will be perfect enough to achieve the excellent purpose of such works, which is, as I have said, to instruct and delight at the same time. (I, 47, pp. 425–26)

The Canon's solution reflects the Humanist attempt to reconcile the power of aesthetic experience with the claims of rational judgment, but we can in retrospect see that the Humanist proposal to resolve the tensions between theory and fiction in the form of a purified aesthetic object (here, in a perfected form of romance) proved an unstable historical response. Just as Hegel was wrong to predict the overcoming of aesthetics by the full philosophical manifestation of the Idea, so too Cervantes' Canon was wrong to expect that the ambivalent quixotism of the *Quixote* could be overcome in the form of a "purified" aesthetic object such as the one described here.[72] It would in both cases be more accurate to say that the attempt to legitimize fictions by containing them within the bounds of rational discourse has served only to reinforce the separation between aesthetic experience and rational judgment – licensing fictions while claiming for theory the privilege associated with the discourse of truth.

To be sure, critics who have wished to assert literature's more anarchic potential in the face of rational discourse have claimed in support of a "quixotic" reading of the novel that the use of literature

---

72 It has long been assumed that Cervantes' own *Persiles* represents his conception of such a work. See Forcione, *Cervantes, Aristotle, and the Persiles.*

as a means of instruction and source of value may have an adverse effect on its role as a spring of creative expression. The conclusion they would have us draw is that any rational defense of literature's cultural value is bound for wholly internal reasons to fail. It would certainly seem doubtful that an attempt to preserve the role of literature in the transmission of values by a bald assertion of "literary value" as a cultural norm could ever succeed. As Barbara Herrenstein Smith has argued, "the recurrent impulse or effort to define aesthetic value by contradistinction to all forms of utility or as the negation of all other nameable sources of interest or forms of value – hedonic, practical, sentimental, ornamental, historical, ideological, and so forth – is, in effect, to define it out of existence; for when all such particular utilities, interests, and sources of value have been subtracted, nothing remains."[73] Indeed, Nietzsche's critique of "value," and, more directly, Unamuno's reading of the *Quixote* and his critique of the division of literature and philosophy within the culture of modernity derive from their recognition of this very fact. Like Nietzsche, Unamuno, attempted in the *Life of Don Quixote and Sancho* and the essays surrounding that text, to rebel against the cultural containment of literature by overturning the contradictions of the conventional humanist literary defense: valuing literature *because* of its alienated position within modern society tends to create an unexpected and ultimately adverse alliance between literature's self-proclaimed defenders and those who would believe that the true measure of our modernity lies in the achievements of science and technology.

As the example of Descartes has shown, the formation of philosophy as a specialized discourse with privileged claims to knowledge depends on the exclusion of fictions from the realm of truth; but in their "quixotic" efforts both Nietzsche and Unamuno express a will to bring fictions back. Their quixotic project may be understood as an attempt to reform our habits of reading and so to reintegrate "substance" and "form"; but in striving to accomplish these goals, both were driven to revise the modern idea that we must give form to values in the absence of essential or natural forms. Unamuno was forced to embrace an "aesthetic ideology" based on a faith in the healing power of illusions, and Nietzsche – whose aestheticism was no less complex than this – was led to argue that

73 Smith, "Contingencies of Value," *Critical Inquiry*, 10 (1983), 14. See also her longer study *Contingencies of Value* (Cambridge, MA: Harvard University Press, 1988).

nature is chaos, or a formless text, hence susceptible to the endless conflict of interpretations as a war that can only be decided by "strong"readings or, in historical terms, brought to an end by actively forgetting the past: "history can be borne only by strong personalities," Nietzsche writes; "weak ones are utterly extinguished by it."[74] In either case, the effort that Lukács described as the "form-giving" project of the novel in a world without essential forms is decided in favor of formlessness, so that the process of reading (and of self-interpretation as well, since the Nietzschean self is a text) demands an exercise of the will to power over the authority of pre-existing forms.

The persistence of quixotic modes of reading within the culture of enlightened modernity is but one among a number of signs that the projects of secularization and rationalization – including the banishing of archaism, the substitution of enlightened reason for fancy, the elimination of romance, and the definitive separation of the present from the past – remained internally incoherent and radically incomplete.[75] There remain a series of residual elements that the culture of modernity has failed to eradicate. As witnessed in the commanding authority that *Don Quixote* has exerted over the novel as a genre, the reading subject has continued to make substantial investments in fantasy and romance, albeit in their newly secularized, aesthetically "legitimate" guise. As a "secularized" form of romance, the novel reveals the ethical risks present in a world without essential forms – that the self may be transformed into a subject governed by the designs of an arbitrary will; that the effort to refashion the existing world may give way to the pressures of a purely iconoclastic desire with respect to society as it stands; and that inner-worldly places or things may assume the status of an ultimate, possibly transcendent value-ground – witness Dulcinea of *Don Quixote*, Conrad's silver and ivory, Henry James's golden bowl.[76] On the one hand we can see that as long as the problem of modernity remains that which Lukács

74 Nietzsche, "On the Uses and Disadvantages of History for Life," *Untimely Meditations*, trans. R. J. Hollingdale (Cambridge: Cambridge University Press, 1983), p. 86.

75 Cf. the arguments for the persistence of myth in Hans Blumenberg, *Work on Myth*, trans. Robert M. Wallace (Cambridge, MA: MIT Press, 1985).

76 René Girard provides an illuminating analysis of this phenomenon in his discussion of the process by which "men become gods in the eyes of one another." See *Deceit, Desire, and the Novel*, trans. Yvonne Freccero (Baltimore: Johns Hopkins University Press, 1965), pp. 53–82.

described in terms of the diremption of form and life, the culture of modernity will remain "inessential," the subject will continue to be divided, and our relationship to values will remain incoherent and abstract. But whereas Lukács would argue that irony, as a recognition of the inevitable antinomy of "substance" and "form," is the novel's highest achievable goal, I would express the normative challenge set for modernity by the novel in the following terms: given the process of "disenchantment," i.e. given the impossibility of the return to a pre-reflective or non-conceptual union with the natural world, and given as well the problems that ensue from Hegel's attempt to reconcile the divided terms of modernity through a discourse of the whole, to recover a world of experience in which our relationship to values is not rendered "quixotic" or abstract. As our discussion of liberalism in chapter 4 will suggest, this possibility has implications for politics that are all but direct; there we shall see that the political problem of modernity is to establish grounds for community in the absence of a belief in the immediate accessibility of the whole.

3

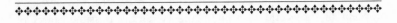

Secularization and modernization

Representation and secularization

The great Pan is dead.

We are equally incapable of truth and good.

Pascal, Pensées (frs. 343, 28)

In his essay on "The Age of the World Picture" cited in the Introduction above, Heidegger proposed a theory of representation that has since provided the accepted interpretation of the relationship between the subject and the modern age. In Heidegger's account, the position of transcendental reflection as established in the philosophy of Descartes marks the transformation of the world from an all-embracing cosmos into an objective representation, picture, or "view." When faced with the historical question of whether the origins of modernity may be explained with reference to any other age, Heidegger responds that the world picture does not change from an Ancient or medieval one into a modern one, but argues instead that the fact that the world becomes a picture at all is what defines subjectivity and distinguishes modernity as an historical paradigm. As a result of this process, Heidegger argues, the cosmos is seen as a world of represented objects, and truth, as well as the discourses that follow from claims to truth (e.g., morality), come to be measured in terms of their adequacy to a subject who stands over against the world. In Heidegger's view it is this, the self-proclaimed priority of the subject in its transcendental stance, that is characteristic of the historical self-assertion of the modern age.[1]

---

1 Heidegger writes that "The newness in this event by no means consists in the fact that now the position of man ... is an entirely different one in contrast to that of medieval and ancient man. What is decisive is that man himself expressly takes up this position as one constituted by himself, that he intentionally maintains it as that taken up by himself, and that he makes it secure as the solid footing for

To speak in terms of inner-worldly progress and self-improvement rather than the possibility of perfection, and therefore to invoke a concept of the world as a finite totality, as the possible object of transformation, presupposes the existence of a secular social and historical realm in a way that speech about the "cosmos" (for Antiquity, the Middle Ages, or the Renaissance) or the fate of Being (for the postmodern thinker who claims to have "overcome" secular history) does not.[2] This secular focus yields a world that is in principle open to transformation from within, but also raises fears that the world may be governed by no authoritative point of view. If we probe behind Heidegger's interpretation of subjectivity we can see that it is the disorienting experience provoked by the loss of belief in the existence of natural forms that in turn precipitates the search for a "transcendental" position from which to evaluate competing points of view. As the anti-skeptical arguments of the Cartesian texts reveal, the disconcerting multiplicity of perspectives may be stabilized through the formation of a transcendental subject and a corresponding "world view"; but this requires that we accept a division of reason, and a displacement of the subject, into two separate and sometimes conflictive domains, the empirical and transcendental. Thus while it may be possible for the subject to compensate for the disappearance of natural qualities from the world, and to stabilize the diversity of perspectives within the world, by placing itself in a position of true knowledge *above* the world, it could also be said that the problem of reason is thus necessarily reduced to that form which is amenable to the methods of modern science. While the "space" of belief may well

a possible development of humanity." "The Age of the World Picture," in *The Question Concerning Technology and Other Essays*, trans. William Lovitt (New York: Harper and Row, 1977), pp. 130, 132. See also Heidegger's *Nietzsche: IV*, "*Nihilism*": "Western history has now begun to enter into the completion of that period we call the *modern*, and which is defined by the fact that man becomes the measure and the center of beings. Man is what lies at the bottom of all objectification and responsibility." Trans. David Farrell Krell (San Francisco: Harper and Row, 1986). Heidegger's perspectives on the relationship between subjectivity and modernity are given ample critical treatment by David Kolb in *The Critique of Pure Modernity* (Chicago: University of Chicago Press, 1986). See especially pp. 121–27 and 137–50.

2 Cf. Alexandre Koyré, *From the Closed World to the Infinite Universe* (Baltimore: Johns Hopkins University Press, 1957). See also Hans Blumenberg's discussion of Pascal's sensibility to the new infinity in *The Legitimacy of the Modern Age*, trans. Robert M. Wallace (Cambridge, MA: MIT Press, 1985), pp. 83–85.

remain untouched by reason, the substance of belief stands literally outside reason's bounds.

❖ ❖ ❖

As I shall argue in the pages to follow, the emergence of a secular subject reflects the process by which the transcendent authority of religious ideals came to be replaced by a series of increasingly normative social practices, bound together by the newly formed "subject" of rational discourse. It may in this sense be said that the phenomenon Weber described as the "disenchantment of the world" takes shape in and through the secularization of culture. In his studies on the sociology of religion, for example, Weber was not so much interested in the substantive content of theological doctrines as in the social and psychological aspects of religious institutions.[3] As a consequence of the secularization process, the dualisms of the Judaeo-Christian tradition (the divisions, for instance, between the temporal and the eternal, the here and the hereafter, that had come to replace what Weber described as the original, "this-worldly" orientation of archaic religious beliefs) were refashioned into a division of the world along empirical and transcendental lines. Understood in terms of the transformation of the world into a representation, angled and framed by the subject, the secularization process became the source of a series of antinomies located within the subject-position itself. For instance, while the modern subject is committed to the denial of all pre-existent beliefs, so too is the subject committed rationally to transcending this condition, in an attempt to provide an inner-worldly grounding for practices and norms. And while the modernizing interests of the subject may rely on the rejection of all "auratic" presences in order to produce a world that would be open to the exercise of human freedom and control, the claims to truth of modern philosophical discourse depend on the subject's ability to transcend the potentially paralyzing doubts that the loss of such qualities would entail. The disappearance of a belief in intelligible essences and auratic presences

3 Weber himself acknowledges this much: "We are naturally not concerned with the question of what was theoretically and officially taught in the ethical compendia of the time, however much practical significance this may have had through the influence of Church discipline, pastoral work, and preaching. We are interested rather in something entirely different: the influence of those psychological sanctions which, originating in religious belief and the practice of religion, gave a direction to practical conduct and held the individual to it." *The Protestant Ethic* (henceforth *PE*), trans. Talcott Parsons (New York: Scribner's, 1958), p. 97.

may be regarded as a positive development insofar as it allows for the practical transformation of the world and for the openness of discursive contexts to endless reconfiguration from within. But whereas religion once provided a means to view the political and social transformations of the world either as motivated and willed by God, or as merely temporary and therefore as inconsequential, but in either case as not illegitimate, the modern subject's openness to inner-worldly transformation demands that the subject itself determine which contexts will enlarge its transformative capabilities and which are less likely to be open to transformation from within.

Beyond this, the shift from the theory of representation to a discussion of secularization can serve to show that the very concept of a unified "subject of representation" can be adequate only where the process of disenchantment is assumed to be complete. The process of "world disenchantment" – as witnessed for example in the overcoming of skepticism by rational discourse – has often been seen as predicated on the "death of God." But as Descartes's important Third Meditation suggests, it would more accurate to describe the process of disenchantment in terms of a division of the value-spheres of culture that separates reason from faith, rather than in the overcoming of religion or in the secularization of the theological problem of difference *tout court*:

It does not matter that I do not grasp the infinite, or that there are countless additional attributes of God which I cannot in any way grasp, and perhaps cannot even reach in my thought; for it is in the nature of the infinite not to be grasped by a finite being like myself. It is enough that I understand the infinite, and that I judge all the attributes which I clearly perceive and know to imply some perfection – and perhaps countless others of which I am ignorant – are present in God either formally or eminently. This is enough to make the idea that I have of God the truest and most clear and distinct of all my ideas. (*Meditation*, III, p. 32)

Moreover, if we look beyond Heidegger's interpretation of modernity in Descartes to figures like Milton and Pascal, and if we keep in mind the even more striking example of Kant, we can see that the invention of transcendental subjectivity does not in fact eliminate but rather *guarantees* the competing transcendence of faith.[4] Thus

4 With the proviso, of course, that this transcendence is *displaced*. Cf. Lacan, who attempts to interpret this displacement in terms of the transference, and who writes that "the true formula of atheism is not *God is dead* [but]... *God is unconscious.*" *The Four Fundamental Concepts of Psychoanalysis*, trans. Jacques-Alian Miller (New York: Norton, 1981), p. 59.

Pascal may recognize the dominance within modern culture of the rationalist and scientific conceptions of truth, but he denies that the mathematical analysis of nature can provide adequate grounds for belief. In the famous fragment of the *Pensées* on the wager, Pascal confronts an interlocutor who not only does not believe but whose position is in fact constituted so that he cannot believe. Alasdair MacIntyre could thus claim that Pascal represents something wholly new within the horizon of religious experience because of the unprejudicial nature of his encounter with skepticism. Whereas previous confrontations with unbelief – e.g., in the Medieval world – had been external to the culture of theism, Pascal treats atheism as itself a viable option. As MacIntyre explained, Pascal is unable to find any assumptions about the nature of the universe to invoke in disputing this man: "All he can confront him with is a choice, the choice elaborated in his doctrine of the wager ... Of course notions of choice are common enough in earlier theological writers, but there the choice is always between obedience – or allegiance – and disobedience to a given set of beliefs. What is new in Pascal is his exposition of the apparently paradoxical notion of 'choosing to believe.'"[5] As MacIntyre goes on to show, the notion that one could somehow choose to believe is an anomalous idea, because nothing that might be summoned up by an act of will could possibly qualify as a belief: "The essential truth about the nature of 'belief' is not really challenged by Pascal's advice that if only we will behave *as if* we believe, in time we shall come to believe. There is no moment of *choosing* to believe" (p. 23). Rather, it could be said that the transformation of belief into a simulacrum of faith will only exacerbate the subject's contradictory estimation of itself as both abject and sublime. (Cf. Milton: "reason is but choosing.")

Pascal claims that the mathematical analysis of nature can reveal nothing of consequence to the seeker of truth, because nature is itself "habit" (in a similar way that the position of the subject-self is for Pascal locatable only in a series of non-essential qualities or rhetorical "effects"[6]). Nature may be mathematizable, but if the "soul" is not

---

5 MacIntyre, in MacIntyre and Paul Ricoeur, *The Religious Significance of Atheism* (New York: Columbia University Press, 1969), p. 13.
6 Pascal raises the possibility that the self may be unlocatable to the extent that we identify it with some essential quality; rather, he concludes that the self is *only* qualities:

What is the self?
A man goes to the window to see the people passing by; if I pass by, can I say

itself to become reified or identified uniquely with the prototypical user of the method – the scientist – then it must lie beyond method. In Pascal's case, the division between faith and knowledge leads eventually to an historicist reinterpretation of nature itself: "Habit is a second nature that destroys the first. But what is nature? Why is habit not natural? I am very much afraid that nature itself is only a first habit, just as habit is a second nature" (*Pensées*, fr. 126, p. 61). If nature is "habit," or custom, then the claims to modernity registered by Pascal must be located not in the truth-assertions of his discourse, as in the case of Descartes or Hobbes, but rather in the self-conscious historicity of his rhetorical stance. Indeed, Pascal reinterprets Christianity as defined fundamentally by the problem of historicism. In the *Pensées*, that problem is explained in a myth according to which the fall from nature that generates the *saeculum* is said to have been recorded in a book placed in the safekeeping of the Jews. According to Pascal, the Jews are a privileged people because they wrote "the oldest book in the world; those of Homer, Hesiod, and others coming only six or seven hundred years later" (*Pensées*, fr. 451, p. 172):

When the creation of the world began to recede into the past, God provided a single contemporary historian, and charged an entire people with the custody of this book, so that this should be the most authentic history in the world and all men could learn from it something which it was so necessary for them to know and which could only be known from it.

(*Pensées*, fr. 474, p. 180)

As Stanley Rosen pointed out, the story of the Jews, as the annunciatory history of Christianity, may best be described as the

he went there to see me? No, for he is not thinking of me in particular. But what about a person who loves someone for the sake of her beauty; does he love *her*? No, for smallpox, which will destroy beauty without destroying the person, will put an end to his love for her.

And if someone loves me for my judgment or my memory, do they love *me*? No, for I could lose these qualities without losing my self. Where then is this self, if it is neither in the body nor the soul? And how can one love the body or the soul except for the sake of such qualities, which are not what makes up the self, since they are perishable? Would we love the substance of a person's soul, in the abstract, whatever qualities might be in it? That is not possible, and it would be wrong. Therefore we never love anyone, but only qualities.

I cite the *Pensées* according to the translation of A. J. Krailsheimer (Harmondsworth: Penguin Books, 1966); here, fr. 688, p. 245. This edition follows the text established by Louis Lafuma (Paris: Seuil, 1963), which in turn follows the order of Pascal's *Copy*, and includes cross-references to the Brunschvicg edition of the *Pensées* (Paris: Hachette, 1904).

quest for the hidden God, or at least for the Messiah. What particular burdens does this search impose on Christian hermeneutics? "As to the Christian," Rosen suggests, "the arrival of the day of judgment, or the fulfillment within eternity of his temporally conditioned faith, is postponed indefinitely by the (to him) barely comprehensible tenacity of the Jews...This obstinacy condemns the Christian to a continuation of historical existence, and the cleft opened within eternity by history casts a shadow of ambiguity over Holy Writ. *Theoria* is postponed indefinitely, to be represented for the time being...by interpretation."[7]

Phrased in other terms, it could be said that a consequence of the "hiding" of God described by Pascal is the production of the *saeculum*, or the realm of worldly signs. The result is an antinomy in which the subject is divided by the desire to escape the world of signs in order to locate a transcendent truth and by the realization that no attainable truth could possibly encompass the complete meaning of signs. On the one hand, Pascal writes that "we burn with desire to find a firm footing, an ultimate, lasting base on which to build a tower rising up to infinity"; while on the other hand he reminds us that there are always and everywhere "two contrary reasons. We must begin with that, otherwise we cannot understand anything and everything is heretical. And even at the end of each truth we must add that we are bearing the opposite truth in mind" (*Pensées*, fr. 72, p. 92; fr. 576, p. 224). Thus whereas the *Pensées* have sometimes been read as a series of moral pronouncements advising us on the problems that may follow from the loss of faith in a world dominated by scientific discourse, or even more generally as a series of "existential" meditations on such topics as the nothingness of man designed to induce "fear and trembling" before a distant God, it seems that the unity of whatever moral truth or "wisdom" the *Pensées* might offer

.

7 Rosen, "Theory and Interpretation," in *Hermeneutics as Politics* (New York: Oxford University Press, 1987), p. 162. As Rosen goes on to say, "In the absence of God and nature, the world is fractured into a multiplicity of 'worldviews,' a misleading expression in which the echo of vision is in fact a camouflaged reference to discourse. The divine *logos* becomes human language. The sign is detached from its referent; between them, in place of the hidden God, stands the concept, artifact of historicity"(pp. 162–63). As Paul Ricoeur pointed out, the modern modality of belief is expressed in its version of hermeneutics: we can believe only by interpreting. See Ricoeur, "The Hermeneutics of Symbols," in *The Philosophy of Paul Ricoeur*, ed. Charles E. Reagan and David Stewart (Boston: Beacon Press, 1978), p. 46.

will be undermined by the fissures that cut through the subject of their discourse. Indeed, the central dilemma of the *Pensées* is dramatized in terms of two incompatible actions or plots, one which is seen from the perspective of faith and of the glory of man, the other from the perspective of skepticism, uncertainty, and misery. Together, these dramas shape the contradictory nature of the culture within which the secular subject finds itself set. Seen from the perspective of faith, the drama of the subject is represented in terms of the fall from truth into language and of the desire to recapture a more integral truth. And yet seen from the perspective of uncertainty it appears that the drama of the Fall and redemption casts the subject into an incompatible plot, in which the subject's position is undecipherable because the only "fall" is the fall from the illusion of truth.[8]

Given these facts, it is not surprising to find that the rhetoric of the *Pensées* has been taken by critics like Paul de Man and Louis Marin as an allegory of its own unreadability, for it would seem that within its double framework the Fall can only be a fall from the illusion that human signs might correspond to truth.[9] Thus for Marin the *Pensées* represent the "counter-text" hidden within the Cartesian *Logique de Port-Royal*; when viewed on their own, they are an already deconstructed text, "governed by a virtual 'infraction,' prompting the reader to construct the text, without however authorizing him to enclose its meaning. The text constitutes a sort of transgression of the book or of the volume. It calls for its own discovery as a collection of signifying elements that are simultaneously, and with respect to one another, in a position of inter-referentiality and in a state of dispersion."[10] While it is clear that the task of constructing a unified meaning from the fragmentary *Pensées* may be blocked by the ultimately contradictory nature of the reading-subject projected *by* the *Pensées*, it remains nonetheless clear that Pascal is equally uncertain

8 See Sara Melzer, *Discourses of the Fall* (Berkeley: University of California Press, 1986), especially pp. 75–108 ("Two Stories of the Fall and Desire").
9 See Paul de Man, "Pascal's Allegory of Persuasion," in *Allegory and Representation*, ed. Stephen J. Greenblatt (Baltimore: Johns Hopkins University Press, 1981), pp. 1–25; and also Louis Marin, "Discourse of Power, Power of Discourse," in *Philosophy in France Today*, ed. Alan Montefiore (Cambridge: Cambridge University Press, 1983), pp. 155–74, and "On the Interpretation of Ordinary Language: A Parable of Pascal," in *Textual Strategies*, ed. Josué V. Harari (Ithaca: Cornell University Press, 1979), pp. 239–59.
10 Marin, "'Pascal': Text, Author, Discourse ...," *Yale French Studies*, 52 (1975), 130; and *Le Critique du discours* (Paris: Minuit, 1975).

about whether this is to be taken as cause for despair. With regard to the problem of interpretation, for instance, Pascal writes that "instead of complaining that God has hidden himself, you will give him thanks for revealing himself as much as he has" (*Pensées*, fr. 394, p. 145). Despite all the self-contradictions of the *Pensées* – or perhaps *because* of their contradictions – Pascal is remarkably apt in expressing both the losses and the gains that may accrue from the Fall of man and the "disenchantment" of the world: "First part: Nature is corrupt, proved by nature itself. Second part: There is a redeemer, proved by Scripture" (*Pensées*, fr. 6, p. 33). Insofar as the *Pensées* articulate the divided and contradictory nature of the subject, they transform the "loss" of nature into a form of human empowerment, while at the same time figuring the ground of any such empowerment as one of a prior loss: "Nature is such that it points at every turn to a God who has been lost, both within man and without, and to a corrupt nature" (*Pensées*, fr. 471, p. 180); "Since [man's] true nature has been lost, anything can become his nature: similarly, the true being lost, anything can become his true good" (*Pensées*, fr. 397, p. 145). As the following *pensée* and many examples from Hobbes will serve to make clear, the freedom that derives from the indeterminate nature of the subject carries with it the risk that social order and meaning may come simply to be imposed. For once Truth has been withdrawn, the subject is open to the fear that there may be nothing higher than a disenchanted world to ground discourse. If nature has been redefined by Pascal in terms of human isolation and by Hobbes in terms of the fundamental disgregation of men, then it follows that politics may be possible only through the imposition of an external force.

It is dangerous to tell the people that laws are not just, because they obey them only because they believe them to be just. That is why they must be told at the same time that laws are to be obeyed because they are laws, just as superiors must be obeyed because they are superior. That is how to forestall any sedition, if people can be made to understand that, and that is the proper definition of justice.   (*Pensées*, fr. 66, p. 48)

In this and other ways, the *Pensées* become an analogue or figure of the divided subject of modernity. They express the potential unity of the subject in terms of the incompatibility of its discursive "parts." In so doing, their oblique logic serves to contest the ground on which the unified subject of representations would claim to stand. Understood in Cartesian-Heideggerean terms, the unity of the subject is established by virtue of its ability to control a unified discursive field or "point of view." At the same time, representation serves to locate the subject in a position of authority with respect to the objects of its discourse. But Pascal sees representation likewise as providing an unreliable basis for moral assertions, which would claim as their ground a fixed and stable point of view, and he takes the insufficiency of representation as an expression of the potential unity between, e.g., faith and reason. On the subject of representation and morality, for instance, Pascal says that "It is like looking at pictures which are too near or too far away. There is just one indivisible point which is the right place. Others are too near, too far, or too low. In painting the rules of perspective decide it, but how will it be decided when it comes to truth and morality?" (*Pensées*, fr. 21, p. 35). Thus it becomes impossible to locate through Pascal the "universal subject" which a truly moral discourse would demand. Consequently, Pascal is drawn from the search for a universal morality to the development of an ethics appropriate to the conditions of a disenchanted world. Based on the assumption that all representations are misleading or incomplete, Pascal is led to assume a posture of world-refusal as the ethical response most appropriate to the disenchanted world.

The *Pensées* are known for their forceful indictment of vanity and of the quixotic effects of the imagination upon our lives. As the passage cited below will suggest, Pascal's critique of secular morality is not inconsistent with the critical use of reason as a source of enlightenment about the world. The imagination is for Pascal roughly what the "passions" are for Hobbes, i.e., sources of a constant striving of power after power that serve only the interests of human pride. In this sense, it is not just the imagination, but the passions themselves that act to deflect all claims of representational truth. Nonetheless, Pascal can, like Hobbes, see that the basis of social life lies in the passions and that it is expressed in the desire men have to be esteemed, acknowledged, or recognized by others: "We are not satisfied with the life we have in ourselves and our own being. We want to lead an imaginary life in the eyes of others, and so we try to make an impression. We strive constantly to embellish and preserve our imaginary being, and neglect the real one" (*Pensées*, fr. 806, p. 270). As Lucien Goldmann saw, Pascal thus articulates a first version of the concept of "recognition" developed in Hegel's thought.[11] And yet the world-be Pascalian dialectic is not completed through the

---

11 Lucien Goldmann, *Le Dieu caché* (Paris: Gallimard, 1959), pp. 307–8.

actions of an all-encompassing Spirit but rather is suspended in paradox.[12] The social corollary of Pascal's suspended dialectic is not an ethic of community, but a somewhat more contradictory posture in which the subject attempts to reject the world while remaining within it. To put the point in Goldmann's somewhat Lukácsean terms, we could say that while the subject's "soul" is inherently social, the subject cannot be reconciled with the world, which is society's home; meanwhile, the search for "recognition" inevitably draws the subject toward those forms of prideful behavior that reason would force us to reject.[13] This is, one might add, a precursor to the dilemma faced by Kant, in which moral virtue and happiness cannot be reconciled within the world but nonetheless are meaningless unless they make reference to it.

For Milton, not unlike Pascal, it is the Fall that separates all who inhabit history from those forms of truth and nature that we continuously but unsuccessfully struggle to find. But while Milton begins from a not unrelated account of the Fall from grace and of the processes of social and historical differentiation that ensue, he ultimately seeks to transcend paradox and to resolve the question of difference in the figure of a single, undifferentiated, transcendent truth. In *Aeropagitica*, Milton writes that

Truth indeed came once into the world with her divine Master, and was a perfect shape most glorious to look on: but when he ascended, and his Apostles after him were laid asleep, then strait arose a wicked race of

12 Louis Marin is perhaps clearer on the inability of the Pascalian "dialectic" to advance itself by means of reason: "When the common man says 'one must honor noblemen,' he says exactly what the clever man says. What he says is true, but he does not know what he is saying — he is not able to discern the 'reason of the effects' of meaning within his discourse. The clever man knows what he is saying. Nevertheless, his knowledge is ignorance. His ignorance is the same as that of the common man, but it is an ignorance that knows itself, for it is well aware that it is not 'because birth is an effective advantage' that the noble man must be honored. *The reason of the effect of meaning is purely a negative form of reason.* It is not 'une maladie naturelle à l'homme de croire qu'il possède la vérité directement'"(Marin, "'Pascal': Text, Author, Discourse," 145–46; emphasis added).

13 See Goldmann, *Le Dieu caché*, pp. 241, 244, and Alasdair MacIntyre's insightful review of Goldmann, "Pascal and Marx," in *Against the Self-Images of the Age* (1971; rpt. Notre Dame: University of Notre Dame, 1978), pp. 76–87.

deceivers, who...took the virgin Truth, hewed her lovely form into a thousand pieces, and scatter'd them to the four winds..[14]

For those who regard the Fall as a deprivation, the thankless task of human history will be to restore the form of Truth, "gathering up limb by limb her fragments" wherever they are found. "We have not yet found them all," continues Milton, "nor ever shall do, till her Master's second comming [sic]; he shall bring together every joynt and member, and shall mould them into an immortal feature of loveliness and perfection"(*ibid.*). Seen from this angle, it will appear that only a reintroduction of some principle of absolute Transcendence could provide for the recuperation of the form of Truth and all this would imply – the reconciliation of social differences, the achievement of happiness, and the overcoming of subjectivity itself. Seen from another point of view, however, the Fall may be regarded as a source of human empowerment precisely because it allows perspectives to proliferate and so prevents us from settling into forms of community that would unnecessarily blinker our perception. As Stanley Fish said, in the course of an argument against this very view, the consequences of the Fall may be fortunate insofar as they challenge us to enlarge rather than limit the horizons of our sight: "in order to see further we must always be in the process of unsettling and moving away from the ways of seeing that now offer themselves to us...The entire process is named by Milton 'knowledge in the making' and the 'constituting of human virtue,' and it will not be completed, he acknowledges, until our 'Masters second coming.' Meanwhile we must be ever on guard against the danger of freezing knowledge in its present form and making it into an idolatry."[15]

If, as Pascal writes, "we make an idol of truth itself, for truth apart from charity is not God, but his image and an idol that we must not love or worship" (*Pensées*, fr. 926, p. 318), then it would be a requirement of Christian charity to work toward an enlargement of our contexts, or at least toward increasing the accessibility of our contexts to change. In Milton's estimation, charity serves to broaden the space within which differences might tolerantly be expressed: "How many other things might be tolerated in peace, and left to conscience, had we but charity, and were it not the chief strong hold

14 Milton, *Aeropagitica*, in *The Complete Prose Works*, ii, ed. Douglas Bush *et al.* (New Haven: Yale University Press, 1959), p. 549. All further references are to this edition.
15 Fish, "Critical Legal Studies (I): Unger and Milton," *Raritan*, 7 (1987), 4–6.

of our hypocrisy to be ever judging one another" (*Aeropagitica*, p. 563). One would indeed expect a politics of liberal tolerance to emerge from Milton's skeptical epistemology. Thus with respect to the central question of the licensing and censorship of books raised in *Aeropagitica*, Milton argued that "if it come to prohibiting, there is not ought more likely to be prohibited than truth it self; whose first appearance to our eyes blear'd and dimm'd with prejudice and custom, is more unsightly and unplausible than many errors" (*Aeropagitica*, p. 565). Accordingly, it is incumbent upon us to make no exclusions at all but, "to welcome each and every voice which together, if in a different tone, will form so many 'brotherly dissimilitudes' and 'neighboring differences.'"[16] Seen in this light, worldly "difference" may itself become the source of the subject's connectedness with transcendent ideals and a form of human empowerment rather than a site for the struggle to locate acceptable norms. In a similar way, the social may become neither the sphere of what Pascal decried as "[an] open war between men, in which everyone is obliged to take sides" (*Pensées*, fr. 131, p. 63), nor the realm in which individual differences are subsumed under the image of an overarching whole, but rather the domain in which the limiting condition of difference can itself be perceived as the (partial) manifestation of a transcendent ideal. This, in the estimation of Fish, is why Milton's insistence "that we not pitch our tents *here*, on the campgrounds of any orthodoxy, is qualified by a future hope: 'till all visions will be one and indistinguishable from the vision of deity.' Difference then is only a temporary and regrettable condition, but one, paradoxically, that we must take advantage of if we are to transcend it."[17] And yet Milton's ultimate aim, like Descartes's, and also like Hobbes's, is to reintroduce a figure of transcendence in order to temporalize, relativize, and finally eradicate the condition of difference itself.[18]

Invoking "the temple of *Janus* with his two *controversal* faces" (p. 561), Milton extrapolates a rhetoric of controversy from his skeptical epistemology. In Thomas Sloane's reading of *Aeropagitica*, Milton's rhetoric indicates that controversy is itself a mode of knowledge, "the

16 *Ibid.*, 5.
17 *Ibid.* See also Unger, *Knowledge and Politics* (New York: The Free Press, 1975).
18 As Thomas Sloane has pointed out, the attempt to limit difference may be read as Milton's response to Humanist discourse. See Sloane, *Donne, Milton, and the End of Humanist Rhetoric* (Berkeley: University of California Press, 1985).

controversy of turning in two different directions and juxtaposing modes, manners, means, opinions."[19] And yet the rhetoric of controversy remains for Milton but a means toward a contrary end; for as Sloane shrewdly shows, Milton's ultimate belief is that an immutable Truth will indeed be revealed in the process. Thus it will be no surprise to find that in a preface to the second edition of his pamphlet entitled *The Doctrine and Discipline of Divorce* (1644) Milton would write that "Truth is as impossible to be soiled by any outward touch, as the Sun beam,"[20] or that in the body of the *Aeropagitica* he would argue that

There be who perpetually complain of schisms and sects, and make it such a calamity that any man dissents from their maxims...They are the troublers, they are the dividers of unity, who neglect and permit not others to unite those dissever'd pieces which are yet wanting to the body of Truth. To be still searching what we know not, by what we know, still closing up truth to truth as we find it (for all her body is *homogeneal*, and proportional), this is the golden rule in *Theology* as well as in Arithmetick, and makes up the best harmony in a Church. (pp. 550–51)

those neighboring differences, or rather indifferences, are what I speak of, whether in some point of doctrine or of discipline, which though they may be many, yet need not interrupt *the unity of Spirit*, if we could but find among us *the bond of peace*. (p. 565)

As we shall see below, the subject's resolution of the problem of difference through the assumption of a transcendental stance is the source for modernity of an unproductive conflict between our internal and ordinary practices or routines and our transcendent ideals. And although it could hardly be said that the Miltonic language of controversy and transcendence does not supply a very powerful basis for belief, we can better comprehend the genealogy of this conflict if we think in terms of the eclipse of the transcendent authority of religion or, more accurately, of the transformation of that authority into a series of rationally binding norms. To be sure, the loss of religion's authority was counterbalanced by the modern hope that we might be able to invent laws and institutions whose motives would be transparent to reason and accessible to us all. In this way, the process of secularization acts as a positive force in the breakdown of entrenched social hierarchies and may serve as a motive for the

19 *Ibid.,* p. 32.
20 Milton, *Prose Works,* II, p. 225. I owe this reference to Thomas Sloane.

differentiation of society from within. And yet it seems that the subject of the secularizing process of rationalization is bound to incur one of two fates: either the ideals that we associate with transcendent forms of authority become so fully rationalized that they no longer serve to exert any critical pressure on our ordinary contexts and routines; or else ideals become so dissociated from norms that they demand a Messianic power in order to break through our homogeneous perceptions and transform the continuum of normative, historical time. In either case, the goals of the subject in establishing modes of authority that would enable us to transform our ordinary contexts could not possibly be met. Indeed, in a fully rationalized world there would be no available ideals for authority to invoke, for all such ideals would have become internalized as norms or else would have been demonized as "values" and exiled to a realm that stands outside the sphere of rational debate. We will see the consequences of the second of these possibilities at greater length in the sections to follow. For now let us observe that the internalization of norms, which makes the success of a poem like *Paradise Lost* directly dependent on its effects in the reader's conscience, resulted in a condition not unlike the one that Milton described both in *The Christian Doctrine* and in *Aeropagitica* as "Christian Liberty," viz., a state in which we are (transcendentally) free, both from sin and from the "rule of the law of man," but bound to give ourselves over to a series of stringent internal demands. Arguing that the gospel offers a new dispensation, "far more excellent and perfect than the law," and defining Christian Liberty as "that whereby we are loosed as it were by enfranchisement, through Christ our deliverer, from the bondage of sin and consequently from the rule of the law of man," Milton explains that:

So far from a less degree of perfection being exacted from Christians, it is expected of them that they should be more perfect than those who were under the law, as the whole tenor of Christ's precepts evinces. The only difference is, that Moses imposed the letter, or external law, even on those who are not willing to receive it; whereas Christ writes the inward law of God by his Spirit on the hearts of his followers, and leads them as willing followers.[21]

21 Milton, *A Treatise on Christian Doctrine*, trans. Charles R. Sumner (Cambridge: Cambridge University Press, 1825); the citations are taken from pp. 407, 424, and 422–23. As Fish explains, "they will be willing followers not at this moment or at that moment but at every moment, since there will be no distance or tension between their own inclinations and the bidding of an *internalized* law." "Critical

Secularization stories: norms and ideals

As the above examples can help us see, an effective critique of modernity as a secularized realm would depend on our ability to imagine a coherent relationship between norms and ideals. This would in turn allow us to avoid those forms of false transcendence in which "value" is the result of a simple exclusion or the mere consequence of some prior restriction placed on truth, rationality, and objectivity. Let us look at Habermas's analysis of subjectivity once again in this light. When Habermas claims that "the deformations of a one-sidedly rationalized everyday practice" evoke the need for something like religion, he formulates the problem of modernity in such a way as to allow the theory of communicative action to confirm the very process of secularization required for its justification; by positioning "communicative action" as a wholly secular alternative to the philosophy of transcendental subjectivity, he insures the further rationalization of ideals and precludes the very processes of world-transformation he hopes to foment. In principle, communicative reason is meant to regulate the multiplicity of perspectives present within discourse by invoking a standard of intelligibility that must apply to discourse as a whole. To the extent that this standard is in turn derived from within the field of discourse, and not from a transcendent revelation or intuition that might break through and transform that field, the descriptive claims it has been used to support are manifestly true, but they are remarkably empty as well. Habermas seeks, for instance, to derive norms from what he describes as "the

Legal Studies (I)," 3. Cf. *Paradise Lost*: "... what the Spirit within / Shall on the heart engrave. What will they then / But force the Spirit of Grace it self, and bind / His consort Libertie" (ed. John T. Shawcross; Garden City: Anchor Books, 1971, XII, pp. 523–26). When Milton speaks in *Aeropagitica* against "the forc't and outward union of cold, and neutrall, and inwardly divided minds" (p. 551) he calls for the internalization of religious ideals in the form of a moral law as a means to make the subject and society whole. It must at the same time be added that no "inwardness" could possibly be inward enough to satisfy the demands of the (social) "law." Stephen Greenblatt provides some of the necessary corrections in his emphasis on the role of the body and of public institutions in his discussion of questions relating to secularization in the case of Tyndale in "The Word of God in the Age of Mechanical Reproduction," in *Renaissance Self-Fashioning* (Chicago: University of Chicago Press, 1980), pp. 74–114. In response it should be said that the problem lies not so much in characterizing these positions as "inward" or "outward," but rather, as Hegel would point out, in the breach between the inner and outer, or between self and society, that each of these positions is able only partially to characterize.

performative attitude of participants in interaction, who coordinate their plans for action by coming to an understanding about something in the world."[22] As Stanley Rosen pointed out, the proliferation of such "theories" is symptomatic of a decadent exuberance and of an overproductiveness that are themselves the products of a fully disenchanted world;[23] in the case of Habermas, I would say that the wish to theorize the obvious represents a symptomatic response to a reduction of ideals to discursive norms.

How may the stunning vacuity of Habermas's theory be explained? It is clear enough that the theory of communicative reason is thoroughly dependent on a diagnosis of the problem of modernity as one of societal rationalization and on a reading of the process of disenchantment from the perspective of the secular subject who has "overcome" the origins of its rational capacities in the "mystifications" of archaic religious beliefs.[24] Insofar as reification and rationalization require "liberal" solutions to the problem of modernity – solutions that can in principle be normalized and made accessible to all – they must not rely on the truths of revelation, which may be transmitted only to the chosen few. Indeed, enlightenment has frequently been seen as an inherently problematic concept precisely because of its exoteric dimension; the achievement of enlightenment is made possible by the processes of demystification and secularization, but in turn permits the indiscriminate dissemination of light, including into those regions that might better have been left to intuition or the powers of revelation.[25]

22 Habermas, *The Philosophical Discourse of Modernity* (henceforth *PDM*), trans. Frederick Lawrence (Cambridge, MA: MIT Press, 1987), p. 296.
23 In Rosen's wry view, "we do not need theories telling us how to cross the street or that the best way to communicate with people is by speaking to them." See *Hermeneutics as Politics*, p. 12. The introduction of the concept of "disenchantment" in this connection is mine; Rosen speaks instead of the "purely procedural, nonreligious, and nonmetaphysical nature of communicative reasoning." For Rosen's critique of "theory," see "Theory and Interpretation" in *ibid.*, pp. 141–74. There, he characterizes the exuberance of interpretation as "an exacerbation of the nervous sensibility" (p. 143).
24 Cf. Pascal, who writes that "other religions, like those of the heathens, are more popular, for they consist in externals ... A purely intellectual religion would be more appropriate to the clever, but would be no good for the people. The Christian religion alone is appropriate for all, being a blend of external and internal" (*Pensées*, fr. 219, p. 99).
25 See, for example, Leo Strauss, "The Crisis of Our Time," in *The Predicament of Modern Politics*, ed. Harold J. Spaeth (Detroit: University of Detroit Press, 1964), pp. 41–54.

It is in this context illuminating to note that Habermas's theory of communicative action was developed in part as a reaction to Walter Benjamin's more radical thesis of "secular illumination" as a response to the problem of the loss of "aura" in the modern world. As Habermas himself explains, the notion of "secular illumination" is bound to appear esoteric from an enlightenment point of view. It is antithetical to the process of enlightenment insofar as it does not seek to shed light upon what has been concealed or to liberate what has been repressed but depends, instead, on the lightning-like power of archaic meanings to break through and transform the homogeneous secular world. Secular illumination thus achieves its ends in ways that are antithetical to the methodical processes of critical reflection and rational debate: "it is gained in a manner other than reflection would be capable of, namely by taking up again a semantics that is pried piece by piece from the interior of myth and released messianically (that is, for the purposes of emancipation) into works of great art at the same time as it is preserved."[26] (One might in this respect think of Pascal, who wrote that "Reason works slowly, looking so often at so many principles, which must always be present ... Feeling does not work like that, but works instantly, and is always ready," *Pensées*, fr. 821, p. 274.) Insofar as the category of "secular illumination" is historical rather than transcendent but still does not posit the recuperation of the past, it represents for Benjamin both the "true, creative *overcoming* of religious illumination," and also a rejection of the enlightenment concept of progress through the "fulfillment" (in the strong, figural sense of that term) of the secular, materialist history of the world.[27] As such, it stands opposed to the progressive narratives of demystification that Habermas and others have told, all of which harken back to the paradigmatic instance of rational illumination in the modern age, viz., that of Descartes as recounted in Part II of the *Discourse*, as he conceived the Method in November of 1619.[28] But whereas Habermas would appear to believe that his own

26 Habermas, "Walter Benjamin: Consciousness-Raising or Rescuing Critique," in *Philosophical-Political Profiles*, trans. Frederick G. Lawrence (Cambridge, MA: MIT Press, 1983), p. 146.

27 Benjamin, *Reflections*, trans. Harry Zohn and ed. Hannah Arendt (New York: Schocken Books, 1969), p. 179.

28 It seems that on close inspection there is no method to the Method of a thinker like Descartes, only the chance occurrence of being caught by the onset of winter in the course of his travels in Germany ("At that time I was in Germany, where I had been called by the wars that are not yet ended there. While I was returning

discourse can be read as the product of the process of enlightenment or "demystification," Benjamin would seem to say that the image of rational enlightenment tropes the more radical religious illumination and blinds us to the fact that historical progress is in fact an illusion created out of the fragments of chance events. In Benjamin's anti-traditional, but still messianic conception of history, the primordial myths and images that the Cartesian philosopher rejects out of hand can be revived, but only in a *Jetztzeit* that breaks through the homogeneous continuum of "tradition" and "progress"; only thus can their semantic potential be made available for the sake of a more radical illumination than reason has to offer.

What remains anomalous about Benjamin's thesis is that the process of illumination is on his account bound to fail; redemption can never be reconciled with the course of progressive, historical time. Rather, the achievement of illumination produces limitless series of fragments that are for Benjamin best characterized in terms of allegory, exemplified in early modern culture in the German baroque drama of mourning ("disenchantment"), the *Trauerspiel*. But without the permanent exertion of a redemptive effort, which allegory both seeks to provide and fails to achieve, it seems that the accumulated testimony of our liberation from myth would fall silently into a void, like a world abandoned by its god. Indeed, the very concept and content of "tradition" would succumb to a quasi-Nietzschean forgetfulness without so much as leaving a trace.[29] But if Benjamin failed to resolve this aporia – if it is for him the limit to which all efforts at the production of cultural meaning must reach – and if he failed likewise to account for the origin of those "secular illuminations" that could shatter modernity's homogeneous face, consider the problems that the Habermassian theory must, for its part, face: the theory of communicative action must confront the possibility that the world of rational discourse might in fact be sterile, hence that the emancipation it might purchase may be wholly meaningless.

to the army from the coronation of the Emperor, the onset of winter detained me in quarters where, finding no conversation to divert me and fortunately having no cares or passions to trouble me, I stayed all day shut up alone in a stove-heated room, where I was completely free to converse with myself about my own thoughts." Descartes, *Discourse on the Method*, Part ii, in *The Philosophical Writings of Descartes*, ii, 116. For further discussion, see Christopher Braider, "The Denuded Muse: The Unmasking of Point of View in the Cartesian *Cogito* and Vermeer's *The Art of Painting*," *Poetics Today*, 10 (1989), 173–203.

29 See Habermas, "Consciousness-Raising," p. 146.

Hence it is Benjamin – and, to my knowledge, Benjamin alone – who prompts Habermas to worry that the victory of communicative action may be pyrrhic. "Can we preclude the possibility of a meaningless emancipation?" Habermas asks:

Is it possible that one day an emancipated human race could encounter itself within an expanded space of discursive formation of will and yet be robbed of the light in which it is capable of interpreting life as something good?...Right at the moment of overcoming age-old repressions, it would harbor no violence but it would have no content either. Without the influx of those semantic energies with which Benjamin's rescuing criticism was concerned, the structures of practical discourse – finally well-established – would necessarily become desolate. ("Consciousness-Raising," p. 158)

In developing his critique of modernity, Habermas turned away from the semantic possibilities revealed by his encounter with Benjamin in this 1972 text, in favor of a normative theory of reason. And yet, insofar as his is the most recent example of the attempt to complete the Enlightenment's project, Habermas's theory fails to generate any transformative ideals, for it will not allow us to discern which modes of discourse, or which communicative interactions, are likely to reduce the conditions of objectification, which may enlarge the contexts of speaker-subjects, or which may provide for a positive transformation of the reified conditions of the existing world. Indeed, since Habermas identifies the validity-sphere of communicative claims with the range of existing discourse, there is no reason to believe that he regards our present contexts as transformable at all. Thus while criticizing his anti-Enlightenment opponents for having abandoned the project to transform the world in accordance with the dictates of reason, Habermas invites the skeptical conclusion that the sphere of rational discourse can only be reconfigured, but never truly enlarged; by the same token, it would seem that an area of arbitrary and unexamined views, that Habermas elsewhere labels "values," will always escape the grasp of "rational" discourse. Hence in Habermas's later account of a thinker like Georges Bataille, the sacred is cast as the demonic "other" of reason; for Bataille would seem to say that the validity of norms is confirmed in the experience of transgression and that the authority of religion is affirmed in the experience of sacrilege: that which is prohibited becomes, for this very reason, an enticement to disobey.[30] Of course, if the phenomenon of

30 See, for example, "The Psychological Structure of Fascism," in *Visions of Excess: Selected Writings, 1927–1939*, trans. Alan Stoekl (Minneapolis: University of

"disenchantment" is read in ignorance of the process by which transcendent ideals or their counterparts, sacred prohibitions, were transformed into norms, then the sources of this residual irrationalism can largely be ignored. But only by telling the story of modernity from the disenchanted perspective of a fully secularized subject can Habermas produce a theory of an historical culture that could fail to recognize that the process of secularization left traces of religious authority hidden and repressed within the increasingly normalized content of its life. While Habermas has argued strenuously that the project of modernity still remains incomplete, he ignores the fact that the "subject" of modernity has in fact inherited a double fate: on the one hand, the subject tends to relate to the value-claims of religion through the ineradicable principles of tradition and charisma, while on the other hand the subject accepts the bureaucratic contexts of social action and the rational-legal methods of justifying knowledge in the secular public domain.

The examples of Habermas and Benjamin help reveal that the social conflict between norms and ideals visible in the process of secularization has implications for any account of modernity as both an historical and a theoretical paradigm. We can, for instance, see that a purely speculative interpretation of the secularization process is bound to deprive the subject of its powers in linking trans-historical ideals with the differences generated by historical contexts. By the same token, the emergence of a purely normative and historicist stance with regard to the rational ambitions of modernity may be seen as a reflex of conditions in which ideals have been thoroughly rationalized and their transformative powers correspondingly routinized and reduced. It may thus come as no surprise to find that in describing the process of secularization modern critics have on the one hand been inclined to regard the religious dimension of pre-

Minnesota Press, 1985), pp. 137–60. Here is the substance of Habermas's critique of Bataille: "If sovereignty and its source, the sacred, are related to the world of purposive-rational action in an absolutely heterogeneous fashion, if the subject and reason are constituted only by excluding all kinds of sacred power, if the other of reason is more than just the irrational or the unknown – namely, the *incommensurable*, which cannot be touched by reason except at the cost of an explosion of the rational subject – then there is no possibility of a theory that reaches beyond the horizon of what is accessible to reason and thematizes, let alone analyzes, the interaction of reason with a transcendent source of power. Bataille sensed this dilemma but did not resolve it"(*PDM*, pp. 235–6).

modern cultures as the locus of a nostalgic ideal, in the expectation that a reinstitution of religion might reverse the process of rationalization and save the secular subject from the effects of disenchantment and world-loss; while on the other hand critics have been drawn toward the rational and "progressive" view that the demystifying secularization of the world is *necessary* in order for the subject's claims to reason to be rendered valid and true. For, failing the possibility of a redemptive critique, one that is discontinuous with the history of modernity itself, it would seem that we are condemned to plot the continual allegorization of our fate as moderns in terms of privation and loss, or that we are bound to envision modernity as the result of a progressive history in which the overcoming of religion provides a wholly self-justifying basis for the emergence of reason and the final demystification of the world.

Hans Blumenberg has written one version of this story in his polemical interpretation of modernity as the result of cultural positions that were "reoccupied" as the Age of Reason gained supremacy over the Age of Faith. On Blumenberg's account in the *Legitimacy of the Modern Age*, to think of the modern culture not so much as secular but as *secularized* is dangerous because it threatens the integrity of an enlightened historiographical perspective of "self-understanding" with respect to the present age. More specifically, to posit the origins of modernity as the result of a process of secularization is to embrace a skeptical thesis with respect to the affirmative claim that the originating sources of value emanate from the historically enlightened subject itself. Thus Blumenberg argues against the secularization thesis insofar as it is the embodiment of an historiographical premise which, in its very content, would represent a threat to the legitimacy of the modern age. For if modernity were shown to be secularized, and if its modes of historical self-assertion were accordingly found to bear within them the hidden traces of pre-existing, sacred modes of belief, then the subject's claims to have achieved an unprecedented level of freedom and autonomy by having invented a new and rational context for itself would be drastically compromised. For Blumenberg, the idea of "secularization" is thus the source of an historical self-*mis*understanding from which we as moderns have been laboring to clear free.

On Blumenberg's account, a work like Max Weber's *The Protestant Ethic* presented a model of the secularization theorem, for in it a set of social practices and beliefs were explained as the transformation of other, more original ones preceding them. From Blumenberg's point of view, the problem with Weber's thesis lay neither in its sociological content – that inner-worldly asceticism may represent the de-originating transformation of an earlier saintliness – nor in the value-freedom of his social-science stance, but in the hidden threat that it, as an historiographical phenomenon, may pose to the autonomy of the modern age: "what is meant [by secularization] is not only the qualitative disappearance of features having a sacred or ecclesiastical derivation but also a type of transformation of this realm of derivation itself, that is, an 'alteration in the social form of religion' in the direction of a 'cultural religious' function, and thus a 'tendency towards the inner "secularization" of religious institutions them-selves.'"[31] In Weber, as in others, this process is said to occur "in such a way that the asserted transformation of the one into the other is neither an intensification nor a clarification but rather *an alienation from its original meaning and function*" (*Legitimacy of the Modern Age*, p. 10; emphasis added).

For Blumenberg, the secularization theorem places at risk modernity's crucial distinction between a language of belief, however tenuous, secondary, or remote, and a normalizing language of critical enlightenment, embodied not only in philosophy and science but in the historiographical modes through which the story of modernity is itself told. If the process of "secularization" somehow makes de-originating figures out of all historical transpositions from one realm to the other, then any instance of the rhetoric of "secularization" would threaten to reveal the inauthenticity of the connections between a secular, modern historical consciousness and the archaic paradigms of meaning informing it. In Blumenberg's terms, Protestant asceticism would be seen to "reoccupy" the position of an earlier, more authentic form of religious belief while remaining largely unaffected by the "content" with which that position had formerly been filled out. If, as Blumenberg posits, it is possible for totally heterogeneous contents to take on identical functions within the framework of man's changing interpretation of himself and of the world (see *Legitimacy of the Modern Age*, p. 64), then it is equally possible for apparently identical contents to inhabit vastly different functional positions within a similar social space. This leaves open the possibility that we shall explore in connection with Weber below,

31 Blumenberg, *Legitimacy of the Modern Age*, trans. Robert M. Wallace (Cambridge, MA: MIT Press, 1985), p. 9.

viz., that a tendency to "normalize" religious ideals may be endemic to all cultures, so that the ethics of Protestant asceticism may not in the end represent the transformation of a specifically *religious* substance at all.

For his part, Blumenberg took Karl Löwith's *Meaning in History* as the paradigmatic "misreading" of modern historical narrative, which Löwith claimed was modeled on the eschatological patterns of Christian and Jewish salvational history. We might cite a work like Jean Seznec's *La Survivance des dieux antiques* as a no less significant case, for Seznec absorbs the de-secularizing tendency visible in the Christian reinterpretation of myth within the more general inclination of the Renaissance to "reintegrate" pagan symbols with forms that had grown culturally inert. In Seznec's view, the Renaissance interpretation of pagan myth represents not the restoration or recovery of a hidden substance and meaning, but a reintegration of the (displaced) myths with their antique forms: "Not for a moment is there any question of 'resurrection,'" Seznec writes; "Hercules had never died, any more than Mars or Perseus. As concepts and as names, at least, they had survived tenaciously in the memory of man. It was their appearance alone which had vanished, Perseus living on in his Turkish disguise and Mars as a knight of chivalry ... In spite of long periods of eclipse, [the classical form of myth] survived during the Middle Ages – as a memory maintained and revived at certain privileged epochs."[32] The result of this process is the antithesis of the fragmentary secular illuminations that Benjamin proposed as the limit-case of cultural meaning – a confirmation of the continuity of the sacred and secular traditions that allows myth to be reincorporated into modernity through a recovery of its ancient forms. In either case, that of Löwith or of Seznec, an assertion of the continuity of traditions leads to a blurring of the distinctions between secular modernity and the mythical or religious traditions of the past.

Still more radically conceived, the secularization theorem is premised neither on the resurgence of the images and authority of the past, nor on their reintegration within the continuity of historical time, but rather on the failure of the secular fully to subsume the sacred. As the work of contemporary revisionists makes clear, those forms of modern (mis)reading that are available within the framework of historical time never become fully transumptive tropes of the

32 Seznec, *Survival of the Pagan Gods*, trans. Barbara F. Sessions (1940; rpt. Princeton: Princeton University Press, 1972), p. 211.

original; they remain always haunted, mysteriously possessed (and thus secretly energized) by various "demonized" forms of the precursor. The transformation of a failed secularization process into the dynamics of modern history thus represents for a critic like Harold Bloom a way to deflect the implications that the failure of secularization would otherwise have for modern culture as a whole. But because Bloom in effect adopts a negative version of the Enlightenment's secularization theorem, he must attempt to reverse the rhetoric of secularization by taking "misreading" not just as confirming evidence that no proper work remains for us as moderns to accomplish, but as an anti-idealist basis for the creation of the modern self; as one Bloomian critic, Jean-Pierre Mileur, explained, "the very notion of misreading argues the failure of secularization, suggesting also that precisely where secularization fails is in relation to our desire – our desire to envision a new end, appropriate to a secular age, for self and society. As long as the notion of secularization itself is not directly challenged ... this failure of desire to be satisfied necessarily appears either as a disordering of the process of desiring ... or as evidence that the modern, secular world is permanently divorced from human values."[33] Thus it must be said that for Bloom secularization is no longer the symptom of a pattern of misreading at all; rather, the very notions of trope and figure, and finally of misreading as such, demonstrate the demonic status of ideals within modernity itself.

Understood as a corrective to the Enlightenment's view, the secularization thesis leads us to a more complex formulation of the dynamics of the secularization process, historically conceived – that the "rational" institutions of modernity are not in fact autonomous, but represent the transformations of religious practices brought under the impossible (because unfulfillable) demand that the archaic sources of cultural authority be made regular and routine. For his part Blumenberg is loathe to see that the process of secularization thus remained radically incomplete, and chooses to interpret any historiographical recognition of this incompleteness as a threat to the legitimacy of the modern age. This is why Richard Rorty can read Blumenberg not as a philosopher or historian of ideas, but as a post-philosophical, post-historical demystifier of hoary views about the

---

33 Mileur, *Literary Revisionism and the Burden of Modernity* (Berkeley: University of California Press, 1985), p. 24.

nature of the Enlightenment and the origins of the modern age. Indeed, we might say that Blumenberg represents for Rorty what Plato and Aristotle were for Descartes – texts to be rewritten from a more fully demystified point of view. Thus Rorty radically foreshortens the story that Blumenberg has to tell and rewrites *The Legitimacy of the Modern Age* in fairy-tale fashion, saying that

> once upon a time we felt a need to worship something which lay beyond the visible world. Beginning in the seventeenth century we tried to substitute a love of truth for a love of God, treating the world described by science as a kind of divinity. Beginning at the end of the eighteenth century we tried to substitute a love of ourselves for a love of scientific truth ... [This line of thought] suggests that we try to get to the point where we no longer worship *anything*, where we treat *nothing* as a quasi-divinity, where we treat *everything* – our language, our conscience, our community – as a product of time and chance.[34]

So seen, the secularization of society would provide a confirmation of the thesis just announced, viz., that all "divinities" are the products of the illusion that there is something that may lie outside of time and chance. These beliefs in turn inhibit the process of self-creation made possible by the Nietzschean discovery that "God is dead." (Rorty: "To say, with Nietzsche, that God is dead, is to say that we serve no higher purposes," p. 20.) For much the same reasons, Rorty must in effect *recommend* the completion of the process that Blumenberg describes, since a fully secularized society would provide the conditions under which his pronouncements could best be rendered valid and true. From a critical point of view, it might be said that the modern concept of progress was invented for the sake of its own fulfillment by the rhetoric of disenchantment. A fully disenchanted world is modernity with a wholly secular face; it is however at the same time a world in which the Enlightenment transcends and cancels its ambitions to transform the world in accordance with the dictates of reason. For the thinker who has abandoned all redemptive hopes, religion no longer provides the source of authority or ideals but serves at best, in moments of nostalgia or despair, to provide "metaphysical comforts." It is, along with "philosophy," the source of those illusions that would prohibit us from recognizing the final Enlightenment truth – that all human practices, including religion itself, are the products of "time and chance."

34 Rorty, *Contingency, Irony, and Solidarity* (Cambridge: Cambridge University Press, 1989), p. 22.

In order to stabilize this assertion of contingency, Rorty has developed the category of the "interesting" as a term of secular aesthetics designed to provide some standard or measure for the discursive contexts which we will be expected to create.[35] Insofar as Rorty asks us to favor those modes of discourse that will allow us to produce "newer, more interesting" descriptions of ourselves, Rorty's intentions are fully consistent with the modernizing goal of the progressive liberation of culture from its bonds to the traditions of the past. But in order for such principles to work – in order for the set of possible discursive contexts and modes of self-creation to remain open in the way Rorty would require – there must be some way of recognizing which contexts are in fact more inventive, and which modes of discourse will provide the increased flexibility necessary for the self-invention he requires. Because Rorty implicitly rejects the possibility of a "secular illumination" of the kind that Benjamin hoped to find, he remains an epiphenomenon of the Enlightenment – a critic of "unexamined" prejudices (in this case, of all requests for "higher" or "deeper" criteria); he is committed to the transformation of society and the self but refuses to flesh out the category of "invention" with a description of the modes of agency and power that allow us to transform the continuities of tradition and historical time. Thus while Rorty rejects the transcendence of all ideals, he may be unwittingly committed to the untransformability of history and of the real.

Otherwise put, Rorty proposes in effect to complete the modernizing project begun by Descartes and Hobbes, for whom reflective thought was the principal ally in the process of demystification. His final and only "secular illumination" resides in the fully demystified belief that there are no longer any illuminations to be had. This is to say that Rorty takes philosophy in much the same way that Hobbes takes religion, viz., as the object of a reductive and demystifying critique.[36] As with the postmodern critique of metaphysics, this project declines to enter into philosophical argument with philosophy. Instead, it transforms philosophy and its history into a series of sketches, which Rosen has wryly described as "cartoons" (in much the same way that Descartes's picture of

---

35 Richard Shusterman fleshes out the concept of a "postmodern aestheticism" with respect to Rorty, Lyotard, and others in his essay "Postmodernist Aestheticism: A New Moral Philosophy?" *Theory, Culture and Society*, 5 (1988), 337–55.

36 Cf. Rorty's description of Hobbes as a "reductionist writer" in *Contingency, Irony, and Solidarity*, p. 31.

Aristotle may also be described as a cartoon).[37] One might thus say of Rorty something akin to what Leo Strauss said of Hobbes – that he finds himself compelled to uncover the origin from which the complex of fallacious thinking characteristic of philosophy and religion arises.[38]

The rationalization of religion

Religion is (subjectively regarded) the recognition of all duties as divine commands.   Kant, *Religion Within the Limits of Reason Alone* (p. 142)

What happens if we reject the view that Blumenberg and Rorty share with Habermas – that secularization describes the category of an historical misconception and poses a threat to the autonomy and "legitimacy" of the modern age? What happens if we accept, with the ultimate idea of demonstrating the political consequences of his stance in chapter 4, something like the Hobbesian distinction between a rational critique of religion and a cultural critique of religious institutions and ideals? Can the history of modernity then be written so as to reflect the incompleteness of the secularization process itself? Seen in Weberian terms, secular traditions have their archaic roots in charismatic forms of religious authority, i.e. in forms of authority that we ascribe to those endowed with extraordinary powers or virtues and whom we approach with the ambivalence characteristic of obedience and respect.[39] If the secularizing process of "disenchantment" is not taken so much as representing the destruction of

37 Rosen, "Rorty and Systematic Philosophy," in *The Ancients and the Moderns: Rethinking Modernity* (New Haven: Yale University Press, 1989), pp. 175–88; see especially p. 183.

38 See Strauss's essay on Hobbes in *Spinoza's Critique of Religion*, trans. E. M. Sinclair (New York: Schocken, 1965), pp. 86–104. It should be clear that Rorty's attack is directed at philosophy, not religion; yet his comments on Nietzsche suggest that the linkage to religion can be made without any fundamental distortion of his stance.

39 Weber: "The term 'charisma' will be applied to a certain quality of an individual personality by virtue of which he is considered extraordinary and treated as endowed with supernatural, superhuman, or at least specifically exceptional powers or qualities. These are such as are not accessible to the ordinary person, but are regarded as of divine origin or as exemplary, and on the basis of them the individual concerned is treated as a 'leader.'" *Economy and Society* (henceforth *ES*), ed. Guenther Roth and Claus Wittich (Berkeley: University of California Press, 1978), p. 241.

a natural "aura" and thereby shattering a mythical "oneness" with nature, or rather if "aura" is itself seen as deriving from the ambivalent response that charismatic forms of authority produce in us, then some compensation for the process of secularization may be sought among the benefits afforded by increasingly normalized procedures and routines. For Weber, the process of "secularization" reflects a struggle to contain the potentially disorienting effects of religious and charismatic ideals in an effort to normalize and extend their authority for society as a whole:

In radical contrast to bureaucratic organization, charisma knows no formal and regulated appointment or dismissal, no career, advancement or salary, no supervisory or appeals body, no local or purely technical jurisdiction, and no permanent institutions in the manner of bureaucratic agencies, which are independent of the incumbents and their personal charisma. Charisma is self-determined and sets its own limits. Its bearer seizes the task for which he is destined and demands that others obey and follow him by virtue of his mission. If those to whom he feels sent do not recognize him, his claim collapses; if they recognize him, he is their master as long as he "proves" himself. However, he does not derive his claims from the will of his followers, in the manner of an election; rather, it is their *duty* to recognize his charisma ... Charismatic authority is naturally unstable.

(*ES*, pp. 1112–14)

Since it is "extra-ordinary," charismatic authority is sharply opposed to rational, and particularly bureaucratic, authority, and to traditional authority, whether in its patriarchal, patrimonial, or estate variants, all of which are everyday forms of domination; while the charismatic type is the direct antithesis of this.   (*ES*, p. 244)

Again and again, Weber insists on the opposition of charisma to all forms of tradition and routine: "pure charisma is opposed to all systematic economic activities; in fact, it is *the* strongest anti-economic force, when it is after material possessions, as in the case of the charismatic warrior. For charisma is by nature not a continuous institution, but in its pure type the very opposite" (*ES*, p. 1,113). Thus if charisma is not to remain a purely transitory phenomenon, but is to take on the permanence embodied in any sort of political, social, religious, or economic order, it is necessary for that authority to become radically transformed: "In its pure form charismatic authority may be said to exist only *in statu nascendi*. It cannot remain stable, but becomes either traditionalized or rationalized, or a combination of both"(*ES*, p. 246). Otherwise put, it can be said that since charismatic authority exalts a standard of self-grounding speech and action as both authoritative and true, it will dissolve into the anarchy of perspectivism unless it is organized into some controlling system or contained by force (in, e.g., the form of traditional practices, rational subjectivity, or the bureaucratic–legal state).[40] Read against this background, secularization is the process by which the instability inherent in the charismatic authority of prophets and priests came to be regularized, contained, and in the end transformed into a normative force for society as a whole. Indeed, if the basic orientation of social systems, whether through organized religion or any other means, is toward the perpetuation of order in the interests of overcoming the utter contingency that would be human existence without them, then norms may best be understood as the internal means by which a society incorporates and regularizes the prohibitions and ideals of its charismatic leaders, in order to maintain itself against the possibility of atrophy, decadence, or decline.[41] In the mythical and religious societies that are said to have prevailed before the modern "disenchantment" of the world, norms could be validated by reference to an underlying scheme whose essence was symbolized

40 I have found useful Alan Blum's account of social theory, and of Weber in particular, in his chapter on "Unity and Difference" in his *Theorizing* (London: Heinemann, 1974), pp. 218–41. As Edward Shils points out, the routinization of charisma goes beyond the simple stabilization of authority but brings changes in the substance of social relations as well. See Shils, *Tradition* (Chicago: University of Chicago Press, 1981), especially pp. 230–31. And Weber himself reminds us of the possibility of shifts from traditional to charismatic forms of authority; these reveal the truly revolutionary potential of charismatic authority: "in a revolutionary and sovereign manner, charismatic domination transforms all values and breaks all traditional and rational norms: 'It has been written...but I say unto you....'" (*ES*, p. 1,115).

41 The contrast between the Habermassian concept of decadence as the disgregation of meaning-structures and the breakdown of overarching forms of interpretation (or "metanarratives"), with Ortega y Gasset's concept of decadence as decline, would repay further analysis. Ortega offers the following diagnostic guide and argument against the notion that modernity represents a decline: "There is only one view-point which is justifiable and natural; to take up one's position in life itself, to look at it from the inside, and to see if it feels itself decadent, that is to say, diminished, weakened, insipid. But even when we look at it from the inside, how can we know whether life feels itself on the decline or not? To my mind there can be no doubt as to the decisive symptom: a life which does not give the preference to any other life, of any previous period, which therefore prefers its own existence, cannot in any serious sense be called decadent." *The Revolt of the Masses* (New York: Norton, 1960), pp. 34–35. See also A. J. Cascardi, "Ortega's Critique of Modernity," *Hispanic Issues*, 5 (1989), 337–68.

in the very person of the charismatic individual; the tasks of constituting identities and of ordering the interests of groups were interwoven with a cognitive interpretation of the world and reinforced by the tribal chieftain, the poet, or the priest.[42] But the social transformations of modernity imposed conditions in which the system of charismatic authority necessary to establish order is itself resisted and, in a certain sense, overcome. The implications of Weber's thought are thus that the normalization of ideals characteristic of modernization in the West represents the outcome of a tendency inherent within charismatic authority itself.

So seen, the routinization of charisma becomes another way of expressing the social need to stabilize percepts through systematic knowledge, in effect by creating a world of practices appropriate to the regularization of its authoritative force. An examination of the primary vehicle of this process, the process of disenchantment understood as secularization, can thus help account for the increasing authority of collective practices in normalizing the force of prohibitions and ideals in a society of subject-selves. But while the contradictory effects of such normalization may be "rationalized" to the extent that they are seen by Weber to form the outlines of a linear developmental history, the very basis of which tends to naturalize the differences between charisma, tradition, and rationalism, the concept of secularization does not necessarily make reference either to the content of those practices or to the historical schema according to which changes from the sacred to the secular might be assumed to take place. The presence of a body of theological doctrine, along with the institutional organization of the medieval monastery, are for instance evidence of a certain routinization, in the attempt already to transform other-worldly ideals into a series of inner-worldly goals. In Weber's view, "the monk is the first human being who lives rationally, who works methodically and by rational means toward a goal, namely the future life. Only for him did the clock strike, only for him were the hours of the day divided."[43] Equally striking is the

---

42 See Habermas, *Legitimation Crisis*, trans. Thomas McCarthy (Boston: Beacon Press, 1975), p. 118, and Charles Taylor, "Legitimation Crisis?" in *Philosophy and the Human Sciences: Philosophical Papers, II* (Cambridge: Cambridge University Press, 1985), pp. 248–88.

43 Weber, *General Economic History* (New York: Collier Books, 1961), p. 267. In this case, as in several others, Pascal provides the necessary corrective to Weber's views: "What difference is there between a soldier and a Carthusian as regards obedience? For they are equally obedient and dependent and engaged in equally

fact that Weber regards the prophets as playing a crucial role in releasing the world from superstition by the rationalizing influence of their teachings. Weber writes:

In all times there has been but one means of breaking down the power of magic and establishing a rational conduct of life; this means is great rational prophecy. Not every prophecy by any means destroys the power of magic; but it is possible for a prophet who furnishes credentials in the shape of miracles and otherwise, to break down the traditional sacred rules. Prophecies have released the world from magic and in doing so have created the basis for our modern science and technology, and for capitalism.[44]

Conversely, one of the paradoxes of Weber's view is that the rationalized forms of modern religious expression brought with them not a decrease but a redoubled *intensity* of the religious dimension of life. On the one hand, this process makes apparent the inherently social function of religion. Hobbes's account of the emergence of ecclesiastical power in *Leviathan* IV ("Of the Kingdome of Darknesse") presents a striking, if somewhat more complex, example of this aspect of the rationalization thesis in the form of an argument that Christianity was itself transformed from small communities of believers led by charismatic individuals into a hierarchical edifice whose institutionalized power came paradoxically to rely on the *increased* susceptibility of men to various forms of coercive "enchantment" within a rationalized world. It must thus on the other hand be said that the resulting concept of religion had been significantly transformed, that religion's sovereign authority was aligned to a normative conception of duty, obligation, and law, and was coupled with the rise of an internalized moral authority of reason over individual life. Since a primary mechanism for this process was

---

arduous exercises. But the soldier always hopes to become his own master, and never does, for even captains and princes are always slaves and dependent, but he always hopes, and always strives to achieve his object, whereas the Carthusian vows never to be anything but dependent. Thus they do not differ in their perpetual servitude, which is always their common lot, but in the hope that one always and the other never entertains" (*Pensées*, fr. 356, p. 134).

44 Weber, *General Economic History*, p. 265. As a corrective, one should read Weber's claims against those of Walter Benjamin: "We know that the Jews were prohibited from investigating the future. This stripped the future of its magic, to which all those succumb who turn to the soothsayers for enlightenment. This does not imply, however, that for the Jews the future turned into homogeneous, empty time. For every second of time was the strait gate through which the Messiah might enter." Benjamin, *Illuminations*, ed. Hannah Arendt, trans. Harry Zohn (New York: Harcourt, Brace and World, 1968), p. 264.

the subjectification of ideals as moral and rational norms, the space over which religion could have control was in principle infinite, since it was identical to the "inward" space of conscience itself.

In the paradigmatic example of Kant, the displacement of religion to the "inward" space of conscience leaves the subject with a heightened sense of duty and obligation, yet without a clear sense of what it is that duty and obligation are to serve. Thus in *Religion Within the Limits of Reason Alone* Kant would write that "conscience is a state of consciousness which in itself is duty" and, more extensively, that

to excite in man this feeling of the sublimity of his moral destiny is especially commendable as a method of awakening moral sentiments. For to do so works directly against the innate propensity to invert the incentives in the maxims of our will and toward the re-establishment in the human heart, in the form of an unconditioned respect for the law as the ultimate condition upon which maxims are to be adopted, of the original moral order among the incentives, and so of the predisposition to good in all its purity.[45]

In a famous passage in the second section of the *Grundlegung*, Kant tells us that when confronted with the person of Christ we must examine the patterns of rationality inherent within us in order to decide whether or not he meets with our corresponding idea of moral perfection.

Kant's emphasis on freedom, duty, and what Hegel would term the rational "universality of form" in morality were made possible by Kant's almost Pascalian assessment of the mixed and indeterminate nature of man: "man as a species is neither good nor bad, or at all events he is as much the one as the other, partly good, partly bad" (*Religion Within the Limits of Reason Alone*, p. 16). This was Kant's point of departure for his understanding of human freedom and the basis for a critique of religion in which a series of potential illusions resulting from illegitimate, "morally transcendent" ideas are seen to issue in fanaticism, superstitions, false illuminations, and thaumaturgy – "sheer aberrations of a reason going beyond its proper limits and that too for a purpose fancied to be moral (pleasing to God)" (*Religion Within the Limits of Reason Alone*, p. 48). In this, the Kantian critique of religion shows itself to be wholly consistent with the goals and methods established in the first Critique. The conclusion that Kant

45 Kant, *Religion Within the Limits of Reason Alone*, trans. Theodore M. Greene and Hoyt H. Hudson (New York: Harper Torchbooks, 1960); the references are to p. 173 and pp. 46–47, respectively.

here draws is that the reliance on the power of grace is an aberration that cannot be reconciled with the workings of reason, "for the employment of this idea would presuppose a rule concerning the good which (for a particular end) we ourselves must *do* in order to accomplish something, whereas to await a work of grace means exactly the opposite" (pp. 48–49). Kant thus stabilizes the dualism inherited through Pascal's *Pensées*, according to which belief is guaranteed insofar as it is absurd, because nothing rational can be said about faith. At the same time Kant remains faithful to the Protestant traditions described by Weber, according to which the workings of grace as a means to salvation must remain unknown to us: "We remain wholly in the dark as to when, what, or how much, *grace* will accomplish in us, and reason is left, on this score, as with the supernatural in general (to which morality, if regarded as *holiness*, belongs), without any knowledge of the laws according to which it might occur" (*Religion Within the Limits of Reason Alone*, p. 179). In the forms of Protestant asceticism studied by Weber, the absence of any reason to believe in the workings of grace is absorbed in the form of a disciplinary imperative to obey the moral law. And yet the following Pascalian paradox remains present in Kant: insofar as moral rules must be obeyed categorically, they are independent of the world, and yet there would be no reason to obey such rules unless they do in fact have a specific bearing on the world.

How may the increasing emphasis on religion's authority over the individual moral life be explained? As the example of Kant can help us see, the moralization of sin and guilt occurs together with the homogenization of society and the universalization of norms. Through the routinization of religion's authority as law, the consciousness of sin loses its transgressive character and takes on a purely moral quality.[46] Thus Kant reinterprets the original prohibitions of religion in terms of the universalizable morality of freedom and will, as expressed in terms of the paradigmatically lawful "maxims." In Kant's rereading of Genesis, for instance, the genealogy of those prohibitions relating to sin are relocated within the sphere of human freedom itself:

The moral law became known to mankind, as it must to any being not pure but tempted by desires, in the form of a *prohibition* (Genesis II, 16–17). Now instead of straightaway following this law as an adequate incentive ... man looked about for other incentives (Genesis III, 6) such as can be good only

46 See Habermas, *PDM*, p. 232.

conditionally (namely, so far as they involve no infringement of the law). He then made it his maxim – if one thinks of his action as consciously springing from freedom – to follow the law of duty, not as duty, but, if need be, with regard to other aims. Thereupon he began to call into question the severity of the commandment which excludes the influence of all other incentives; then by sophistry he reduced obedience to the law to the merely conditional character of a means ...; and finally he adopted into his maxim of conduct the ascendancy of the sensuous impulse over the incentive which springs from the law – and thus occurred sin (Genesis III, 6).

(Religion Within the Limits of Reason Alone, p. 37)

Seen from Kant's point of view, the chief advantage of the distinction between radical, pre-existent evil and the evil that springs from the free will of man is that the latter allows human goodness to be reconstituted as part of a story of progress:

[Scripture] finds a place for evil at the creation of the world, yet not in man, but in a *spirit* of an originally loftier destiny. This is the *first* beginning of all evil represented as inconceivable by us (for whence came evil to that spirit?); but man is represented as having fallen into evil only *through seduction*, and hence as being *not basically* corrupt (even as regards his original predisposition to good) but rather as still capable of an improvement, in contrast to a seducing *spirit*, that is, a being for whom temptation of the flesh cannot be accounted as an alleviation of guilt. For man, therefore, who despite a corrupted heart yet possesses a good will, there remains hope of a return to the good from which he has strayed. (p. 39)

Phrased in other terms, it can be said that a precondition for the existence of an autonomous secular morality of the kind developed by Kant is the reduction of an original dialectic of transgression and norm. When this occurs in a pervasive way, transgression becomes normalized, religion ceases to act as the heterogeneous source of authoritative prohibitions, and itself becomes transformed into the form of moral imperatives of the kind we see in Milton and Kant. The rationalization process is thus reflected in the displacement of what Bataille would describe as "sovereign" forces by a series of moral imperatives that mark an increase in the homogenization and consequent potential for domination of social groups.[47] As one critic said of Milton's Eve, "the challenge she meets is fundamental to the human mind which to become civilized at all beyond a wild or

47 Thus Bataille writes that "The inability of *homogeneous* society to find in itself a reason for being and acting is what makes it dependent upon imperative forces, just as the sadistic hostility of sovereigns toward the impoverished population is what allies them with any formation seeking to maintain the latter in a state of oppression." "The Psychological Structure of Fascism," pp. 146–47.

vegetable state has had to break innumerable taboos, always risking failure to distinguish the one true prohibition among so many false."[48] Yet if it is true that with the rise of the moral subject the very status of religion's prohibitions becomes increasingly an object for rational dispute, it is also the case that these are disputes that no form of "reason" could possibly resolve.

For Kant, the concept of morality is lodged principally in the autonomous, willing subject. "The good will is not good because of what it effects or accomplishes or because of its adequacy to achieve some proposed end," writes Kant; "it is good only because of its willing, i.e., it is good of itself."[49] It was precisely because Kant's call for human autonomy (for man to "make himself into whatever he is or is to become") relied on a concept of the will as speciously sovereign – as answerable only to itself – and was but a veiled form of self-domination that Hegel criticized Kant and the religious "positivity" of modern times:

the difference [between the Mongols and the Puritans] is not that the former make themselves slaves, while the latter is free, but that the former have their lord outside themselves, while the latter carries his lord in himself, yet at the same time is his own slave. For the particular – impulses, inclinations, pathological love, sensuous experience, or whatever else it is called – the universal is necessarily and always something alien and objective. There remains a residuum of indestructible positivity which finally shocks us because the content which the universal command of duty requires, a specific duty, contains the contradiction of being restricted and universal at the same time and makes the most stubborn claims for its one-sidedness, i.e., on the strength of possessing universality of form. Woe to the human relations which are not unquestionably found in the concept of duty; for this concept (since it is not merely the empty thought of universality but is to manifest itself in an action) excludes or dominates all other relations.[50]

In the critique of modern religion undertaken in his *Faith and Knowledge* (1802), Hegel located and named the "positivity" in ethical

48 W. B. C. Watkins, *An Anatomy of Milton's Verse* (Baton Rouge: Louisiana State University Press, 1955), p. 132. I owe this reference to Stanley Fish, *Surprised by Sin: The Reader in Paradise Lost* (Berkeley: University of California Press, 1967).

49 Kant, *Foundations of the Metaphysics of Morals*, trans. Lewis White Beck, ed. Robert Paul Wolff (Indianapolis: Bobbs-Merrill, 1969), p. 23.

50 Hegel, "The Spirit of Christianity and its Fate," in *Early Theological Writings*, trans. T. M. Knox, ed. Richard Kroner (Philadelphia: University of Pennsylvania Press, 1971), pp. 211–12. See also Georg Lukács, *The Young Hegel*, trans. Rodney Livingstone (London: Merlin Press, 1975), especially ch. 4.

life that had come to achieve dominance as the standard of conduct for the modern age. Hegel found evidence of this positivity in a nearly quixotic yearning for moral perfection coupled with an ethical authoritarianism of the kind that we have just seen in Kant, according to which the subject is directed toward methodical labors, in the hope of earning compensation in the beyond. For Hegel, this "positivity" was in turn symptomatic of the development of a religion of private belief divorced from the public manifestations of Spirit and could only be overcome by recognizing the fundamental affinities between the sacred and secular realms of culture.

And yet it seems that Hegel could find no clear case of how such a reconciliation might be achieved. One of his predilect examples was the Greek *polis*, which he describes as a realm in which religious law and custom had not yet been split apart. The *polis* "has in religion the supreme consciousness of its life as state and as ethical life and is indebted to the Gods for the general arrangements connected with the state, such as agriculture, property, marriage."[51] As Gillian Rose pointed out, however, the problem with taking Athens as an exemplary case is that in such a society there is no subjectivity and no religious representation as such.[52] Since Hegel believes that the process of individuation is in fact necessary for the development of Spirit, there can be no simple return to the Ancient ideal. Moreover, since religion, like Spirit itself, manifests itself through the medium of representation (*Vorstellung*),[53] then it could also be said that the absence of subjectivity is not the solution to the problem of modernity but only indicates the absence of religion itself. Accordingly, the religion of Greece plays a nearly impossible role in Hegel's thought.

Perhaps this is the reason why Hegel sought in the example of modernity itself a reconciliation of the forms of secular activity founded on the principle of self-acting Spirit, or human freedom and creativity, with the religious belief that the Kingdom of God is already in history, because forever, at hand. Thus in the 1827 *Lectures on the Philosophy of Religion*, Hegel writes that "the raising of [nature]

51 Hegel, *Lectures on the Philosophy of Religion*, ed. E. B. Speirs and J. Burdon (1895; rpt. London: Routledge and Kegan Paul, 1963), III, p. 135.
52 "It is the only case in which the state and religion are one, in the sense that custom and law are united, but if the state and religion are one in this sense then there will be no religious representation." Gillian Rose, *Hegel Contra Sociology* (London: Athlone, 1981), p. 113.
53 *Lectures on the Philosophy of Religion*, I, p. 401.

itself to reconciliation is on the one hand what finite spirit implicitly is, while on the other hand it arrives at this reconciliation, or brings it forth, in world history. This reconciliation is the peace of God, which does not 'surpass all reason' but is rather the peace that through reason is first known and thought and is recognized as what is true" (III, p. 347). Hegel can claim to perceive this unity because he takes the existing world as *already* being one, though perhaps recognizable as such only from the perspective of the philosophical Absolute. As Emil Fackenheim pointed out in his study of the religious dimension of Hegel's thought, it is only on the basis of an actual and, in principle, final secular-Protestant synthesis that Hegel can both "venture that final synthesis which is his philosophic thought and yet maintain that it will not end the life which has made it possible."[54] This is a synthesis that preserves both philosophy and society, and it is founded on the principle of the difference-within-unity of religion and the secular world. Accordingly, Hegel must reject any "simple unity" of Christianity and secular activity. On the one hand, a "simple unity" of these terms would produce a theocratic State whose principles would be grossly out of step with secular modernity itself. That may have been possible in the medieval Catholic State, whose religious basis was other-worldly and authoritarian, and which could afford to recognize the secular principles of right and law; but a State ruled by the modern Protestant "heart," freed from external authorities, could not possibly do so. Alternatively, a "simple unity" would issue in a State which had so completely absorbed religion as to *produce* the death of God. In either case, the difference-within-unity of the sacred and secular realms would be reduced, and the "necessary" relationship between the (for Hegel) final philosophy and the secular–religious world would remain obscured. Rather, Hegel believed that the conditions of philosophy could be met only if the religious conscience evident in Protestantism ceased to remain inward and assumed self-active expression in the secular world; likewise, only if secular activity came to recognize its foundation in a religious inwardness which transcends the scope of all secular authority could the conditions for philosophy be brought about.[55]

In concluding this much, it must be said that Hegel challenges not only Kant's interpretation of modernity, but also the methodical

54 Fackenheim, *The Religious Dimension in Hegel's Thought* (Chicago: University of Chicago Press, 1967), p. 212.   55 See *ibid.*, pp. 212, 220–21.

presuppositions behind any separation of a cognitive critique of religion from a cultural critique of religious institutions and ideals. Hegel needs religion in order to make his philosophy complete, because religion is part of the historical world that philosophy cannot forsake. And yet in developing his rational reconstruction of religion, several problems arise that cannot be resolved within the framework of Hegel's own thought. Perhaps the greatest of these is that Hegel's emphasis on rational reconciliation and on Spirit as Concept leaves little or no room in religion for the workings of faith.[56] The meaning of prayer as petition and thanksgiving, or as Iris Murdoch's secular-aesthetic "loving attention," as well as the forms of meditation that Weber and modern critics such as Louis Martz have identified as the basis of modern devotion, are all alien to Hegel's thought.[57] Kierkegaard may thus have been right in his attempt to make the call of God neither the function of the inward, duty-bound conscience of the modern bourgeois subject, nor a product of the "irrational" will, but rather a continuation of the modern paradox of belief, and a re-articulation of the faith required in response to the sovereign commands of Abraham's God.[58] In so doing, Kierkegaard attempted to transform the contradictions inherent in Pascalian discourse into spiritually productive tensions for the self and, by so doing, to resist the rationalization of religion implicit in Hegel's response to Kant. For his part, Hegel interpreted the story of the Fall not in terms of free will and transgression, as did Kant, but rather as a grand drama about the limits of knowledge: "What it [the Fall] really means is that humanity has elevated itself to the knowledge of good and evil; and this cognition, this distinction, is the source of evil itself. Being evil

---

56 See Taylor, *Hegel* (Cambridge: Cambridge University Press, 1975), especially pp. 493–95.

57 Weber writes that for the Puritan-ascetic, "only a life guided by constant thought could achieve conquest over the state of nature. Descartes's *cogito ergo sum* was taken over by the contemporary Puritans with this ethical reinterpretation" (*PE*, p. 118). The reference to Louis Martz is to *The Poetry of Meditation* (New Haven: Yale University Press, 1962). For Iris Murdoch see *The Sovereignty of Good* (1970; rpt. London: Ark, 1985).

58 It is worthwhile in this context to note Hegel's fascinating pages on Abraham in his early essay "The Spirit of Christianity." There, he concentrates on the absolute difference between God and nature for Abraham as leading to Abraham's masterful stance with regard to nature. For Hegel's Abraham's God is a jealous God and Abraham regards himself, his family, and his nation as favored by God. Yet there is no moment of "fear and trembling," nor any leap of faith registered even in this early work.

is located in the act of cognition, in consciousness" (*Lectures on the Philosophy of Religion*, III, p. 301). Hegel's point is this: if we can construe sin as the absence of absolute knowledge, rather than as transgression, then it follows that man may save (i.e., infinitize) himself through the labors of conceptual thought.

All truth comes to people initially in the form of authority.

(Hegel, *Lectures on the Philosophy of Religion*, III, p. 335)

In reading Weber's analysis of secularization as the manifestation of a tendency toward "rational world mastery" against the light of Hegel and Kant, it must be kept in mind that *The Protestant Ethic* was conceived as a quasi-idealist text, whose methodological purpose was to counterpose an interpretation of capitalism as an ethical structure to the historical materialism of Marx. Weber is thus interested in capitalism as a system of ethical action and beliefs whose "spirit" may well be out of phase with the course of history, materially understood. Weber thus describes business practices which may *appear* capitalist in nature as still dominated by a "traditionalist ethos," and this ethos is for him more telling than the economic lines along which these practices were organized.[59] So seen, modern capitalism and the religious asceticism with which it was closely allied are the manifestations of an impulse toward normativity and order that took the shapes of discipline, self-mastery, and world-renunciation. Thus Weber explains that the "powerful tendency toward uniformity of life, which today so immensely aids the capitalistic interest in the standardization of production, had its ideal foundations in the repudiation of all idolatry of the flesh" (*PE*, p. 169).

At one level, the development of inner-worldly asceticism may be seen as the modern expression of an abiding effort, characteristic of all cultures, to reduce and control the "irrational" elements of reality by means of pragmatic or intellectual discipline. At this level, capitalism channels and controls what Weber, anticipating Bataille, describes as the residual "heterogeneity" of authority in the modern bourgeois world.[60] And yet it seems that in the case of Protestant asceticism this process of control in turn *produces* a certain irrationality in the form of unmasterable desires, values, and needs that are absorbed by the individual subject, and are subsequently reintroduced

59 See Weber's examples in *PE*, pp. 66–67.
60 See Weber, *ES*, p. 1,111.

within the system of society as a whole. How could such a contradictory arrangement have come about? What could explain the origins of what appears to be a fundamentally irrational social formation? When viewed within the broad scope of Weber's historical sociology of world religions, the self-contradiction of the capitalist-ascetic ethos is seen to originate within the context of an archaic division of the cosmos into a series of two competing and unreconcilable domains — spirit and matter, charisma and routine, ideals and norms, the noble and the base. To the degree that these components are never fully separated, the irrational elements contained within reality are as if transformed into magnets for all attempts at theorization and classification; they become, in Weber's terms, the "*loci* to which the irrepressible quest of intellectualism for the possession of supernatural values has been compelled to retreat."[61] Conversely, in his writings on the sociology of religion, Weber explains at some length that the retreat of values to the realm of an inaccessible "beyond" grows as the world is brought increasingly under rational control: while reality is rendered ever more "rational," values are displaced to an ever more distant realm. Thus while a rationalized world may in principle be more accessible to domination and control, the subject finds it increasingly difficult to assume a posture of conviction or otherwise to relate his beliefs and values to that world. As a result, the ethic of conviction, rooted in a belief in an act's intrinsic and self-justifying worth, is transformed into a species of quixotism or is forced to yield to a (value-neutral) ethic of responsibility, as that stance which is best able to meet the demands of enterprise, efficiency, and effectiveness dominant in the disenchanted world:

[This] is the more so the more denuded of irrationality the world appears to be. The unity of the primitive image of the world, in which everything was concrete magic, has tended to split into rational cognition and mastery of nature, on the one hand, and into "mystic" experiences, on the other. The inexpressible contents of such experiences remain the only possible "beyond," added to the mechanism of a world robbed of gods. In fact, the beyond remains an incorporeal and metaphysical realm in which individuals

---

61 "The Social Psychology of the World Religions," in *From Max Weber*, ed. and trans. H. H. Gerth and C. Wright Mills (New York: Oxford University Press, 1958), pp. 281–82. According to Gerth and Mills, this essay is a translation of the Introduction to a series of studies that Weber published as articles in the *Archiv für Sozialforschung* under the title "Die Wirtschaftsethik der Weltreligion" ("The Economic Ethic of the World Religions").

intimately possess the holy. Where this conclusion has been drawn without any residue, the individual can pursue his quest for salvation only as an individual. This phenomenon appears in some form, with progressive intellectualist rationalism, wherever men have ventured to rationalize the image of the world as being a cosmos governed by impersonal rules.

(Weber, "The Social Psychology of the World Religions," p. 282)

Kant's attempt to make a place for religion "within the limits of reason alone" may be interpreted as an effort to control and reduce this very tension, but the twofold displacement of religion – inward, into the dutiful conscience of the subject–believer, and outward, through a desire for world-mastery that can never be achieved – only further shows up the dominance of the rationalization process itself.

For Weber, all religious practices must be understood against the background of religion's "this-worldly"orientation.[62] Ascetic inner-worldliness is both a principal factor in the displacement of the this-worldly nature of magical and animistic beliefs and the source, through its other-worldliness, of an irrationalism all its own. The rise with Protestant asceticism of a subject who stands as an isolated individual before the "absolute transcendence" of God is for Weber evidence of the "irrational presuppositions" that have been incorporated in the form of a contradiction within modern religious life.[63] And yet Weber's own developmental history of religion may be viewed as an attempt to rationalize precisely those contingent factors that, by his own account, remained profoundly irrational within the sphere of secular modernity. In response to the "irrational presuppositions" said to underlie all religious systems of belief, for instance, Weber advances a scheme of social and historical development that would rationalize and explain the logic of the Reformation as a world-historical event, accounting for the role within the modern age of the peculiar brand of ascetic world-mastery that came into being with Protestantism. Weber thus succeeds in coercing the irrational into the rational by constructing an account according to which the irrational was induced to submit to the methodical discipline of rational control. Insofar as Weber's own intellectualism is itself an attempt to deal with those elements of culture, including values and ideals, that he perceived as ultimately irrational and unexplainable, the story of the rise of Western rationalism, and of its "irrational" effects, can be read as the products

---

62 Weber discusses this point in, among other places, *ES*, pp. 399–401.
63 See Weber, "The Social Psychology of the World Religions," especially p. 281.

of a series of more "rational" historical developments. These serve to make plausible, if not to resolve, the unequal distribution of faith and reason characteristic of modernity in the West and help to explain the displacement within the subject of an external realm of (religious) laws by an inner realm of conscience.

The first of Weber's explanatory contexts is the emergence, within the Hellenic world, of a "cognitive universalism," and the allied notion that there exists an intelligible natural order which both gods and human beings must respect. The second is the invention, with Ancient Judaism, of the idea of a transcendent creator god, who established a universal order and a binding law over the world. In Weber's somewhat schematic view, the Hellenic orientation laid the groundwork for the rise of Western science, while ethical monotheism provided a means to orient action toward the political and social transformation of the world, which processes could then be undertaken as an extension of God's command. Over the course of time, these orientations became powerful supports of the "naturalistic vision" of society – the vision that modernity displaced – because they were able to communicate a sense of the existence of an order, independent of man, as both knowable and good. For, in either case, secular or "inner-worldly" experience could be viewed against this background as the reflection of universal laws, or as a temporal phenomenon destined to be replaced by a divine order.[64]

Seen in the light of Weber's formidable attempts to rationalize the developmental history of secular modernity, then, the inner-worldly asceticism practiced by the followers of Luther and Calvin came to appear as the expression of a potential for rationalism and world-mastery *inherent* within the West. In Weber's view, these rationalizing tendencies lay latent, but were not altogether invisible, within a variety of institutions in the pre-modern world; they required only a series of social transformations in order for their effects fully to be felt. In particular, ascetic monasticism and the proliferation of medieval religious sects served to demonstrate the relatively high potential for inner-worldly action of the ethical dimension of the inherited Judaeo-

64 Like most statements about modernity, this one must be qualified by the assertion that the process of secularization remained incomplete. Hence, there was a remarkable Reformation effort to view religion as a political instrument and to attempt the transformation of the State. See Michael Walzer's *The Revolution of the Saints* (Cambridge, MA: Harvard University Press, 1965), and also Wolfgang Schluchter, *The Rise of Western Rationalism*, trans. Guenther Roth (Berkeley: University of California Press, 1981), p. 152.

Christian tradition. Monastic asceticism may be taken as an example
of rationalism insofar as asceticism is in it "emancipated" from pure
other-worldliness, irrational self-discipline, and torture, while it
remains nonetheless the source of a compulsion to transcend more
"natural" inclinations toward the flesh. The monasteries were the
sites of a "systematic method of rational conduct with the purpose of
overcoming the *status naturae*, to free man from the power of
irrational impulses and his dependence on nature." As Weber went on
to explain, monasticism trained the monk to behave as a worker in the
service of the Kingdom of God, thereby assuring that salvation could
be achieved by methodical means.[65] And while it subjected its
practitioners to the supremacy of an all-powerful will, it also allowed
the monk "to bring his actions under constant self-control with a
careful consideration of their ethical consequences" (*PE*, pp. 118–19).

At some level, all forms of religion may be ethical and, to that
degree, complicit with human purposes, with the justification of social
practices, and with "rationalizing" existence on earth. (These are
nonetheless considered insufficient by Kant, whose image of a
Christianity wholly congruent with the requirements of reason
demands higher motives of the moral subject: "As regards men's
very natural expectation of an allotment of happiness proportional to
a man's moral conduct," Kant writes, Christianity promises "a reward
for these sacrifices in a future world, but one in accordance with the
differences of disposition in this conduct between those who did their
duty *for the sake of the reward* (or from release from deserved
punishment) and the better men who performed it merely for its own
sake" (*Religion Within the Limits of Reason Alone*, p. 149). In Weber's
analysis, the need for an ethical interpretation of the "meaning" of
the distributions of fortunes among men is a function of an inherent
discrepancy between interests in "this world" and an order thought
to be intrinsically capable of providing an interpretation of those
interests in terms of some truly "ultimate" meaning. Thus suffering
and injustice may be rationalized "by reference to individual sin
committed in a former life (the migration of souls), to the guilt of
ancestors, which is avenged down to the third and fourth
generation ... As compensatory promises, one can refer to hopes of

65 Weber relates the *Spiritual Exercises* of Ignatius Loyola with this tendency: "This
   active self-control, which formed the end of the *exercitia* of St. Ignatius and of the
   rational monastic virtues everywhere, was also the most important practical ideal
   of Puritanism" (*PE*, p. 119).

the individual for a better life in the hereafter (paradise)" ("Social Psychology of the World Religions," p. 275). The "need" for salvation may be explained in analogous terms; it is a consequence of the disparity between these two worlds and supplies, in Talcott Parson's formulation, "the need for a basis of personal legitimation which is in accord with these ultimate standards, themselves conceived as standing in essential conflict with those of *any* institutionalized worldly effort."[66] Thus, seen from Weber's point of view, Kant's analysis of Christian virtue would be a further instance of "rationalization," understood in its fullest sense as a form of justification congruent with reason's demands. The point of such an observation is not further to demystify religion, but rather to make apparent the fact that whether in the speculative optic of Kant or in the sociological matrix of Weber, the moral authority claimed by the subject is seen to originate within the subject itself. For this reason, it is equally important to recognize that Weber never loses sight of the fact that the "rationalization" of the world is also an example of a certain *ir*rationality, and that many of the "rational" solutions to religious anxiety are themselves sources of the irrationalism characteristic of the subject itself. Taking the extreme example of Puritanism, Weber writes that

That great historic process in the development of religions, the elimination of magic from the world which had begun with the old Hebrew prophets and, in conjunction with Hellenistic scientific thought, had repudiated all magical means to salvation as superstition and sin, came here to its logical conclusion. The genuine Puritan even rejected all signs of religious ceremony at the grave and buried his nearest and dearest without song or ritual in order that no superstition, no trust in the effects of magical and sacramental forces on salvation, should creep in. Combined with the harsh doctrines of the absolute transcendentality of God and the corruption of everything pertaining to the flesh, the inner isolation of the individual contains, on the one hand, the reason for the entirely negative attitude of Puritanism to all the sensuous and emotional elements in culture and in religion, because they are of no use toward salvation and promote sentimental illusions and idolatrous superstitions.   (*PE*, p. 105)

It remains nonetheless clear that the emergence of ascetic Protestantism can only be understood within the framework of pre-existing social structures. This is to say that modern asceticism emerges within the horizon of possibilities fixed by the basic social

66 Parsons, "Introduction" to Weber, *The Sociology of Religion* (Boston: Beacon Press, 1963), p. xlix.

configuration of what Weber calls "traditionalism," a configuration marked by a theocentric world view and hierarchical social arrangements. Thus while it may in one sense seem purely accidental that ascetic Protestantism not only transformed the religious order of society but had more far-reaching effects and became a constitutive factor in the shaping of Western modernity, it would be more accurate to say that, for Weber, an underlying propensity for rationalization was redirected as it came to confront a series of specific anxieties about the accessibility of transcendent ideals and the workings of grace given the increasingly worldly (i.e., homogeneous, normative, and capitalist) context in which the modern subject was immersed.[67] Because of its critical regard for the entrenched institutions of patriarchy and filial obedience, ascetic Protestantism transformed the existing social stratification in a very specific way. To some extent, a reduction in social stratification is a consequence that Weber would attribute to the imposition of all forms of discipline and routine, as can perhaps best be seen in attempts to bring the power of personal charisma under control: "the force of discipline not only eradicates personal charisma but also stratification by status groups; at least one of its results is the rational transformation of status stratification."[68] But Protestant asceticism contested the values of "traditional" society by replacing one form of discipline with another, more "modern" form. In accepting as its model the ideal of the self-made man, who is the product of his labor and responsive to his "calling," and who is likewise free from any internal dependence on tradition or community, the call to labor became a moral imperative ("Labor must ... be performed as if it were an absolute end in itself, a calling," *PE*, p. 62). Through labor, the authority of norms is internalized; the self-made man is the precursor of Kant's autonomous subject, and may be identified by virtue of the fact that

---

67 The connection between the rationalized world and anxiety is made explicit by Hobbes, who argues as follows: "being assured that there be causes of all things that have arrived hitherto, or shall arrive hereafter; it is impossible for a man, who continually endeavoureth to secure himself against the evill he feares, and procure the good he desireth, not to be in a perpetuall solicitude of the time to come ... So that man, which looks too far before him, in the care of future time, hath his heart all the day long, gnawed on by feare of death, poverty, or other calamity; and has no repose, nor pause of his anxiety, but in sleep" (*Leviathan*, I, 12, p. 169).

68 *ES*, p. 1,149. In this instance I follow the translation of Gerth and Mills in *From Max Weber*, p. 253.

he is able to give himself the law. Thus Kant: "Man *himself* must make or have made himself into whatever, in a moral sense, whether good or evil, he is or is to become. Either condition must be an effect of his free choice" (*Religion Within the Limits of Reason Alone*, p. 40).

To be sure, it must be emphasized that the peculiar irrationalism of modern society can only be made plain against a thesis about the nature of "traditional" society that, in its categorical nature, must remain highly schematic and abstract. And while Weber may have been more responsive to the vast differences among pre-modern societies than many subsequent theorists of modernity, it must be said that conceptually, if not historically as well, Weber associates traditionalism with a falsely naturalistic view of the nature of society and the world. Insofar as it is aligned with the naturalistic thesis, "tradition" stands ideologically opposed in Weber's thought not only to the irrational aspects of modern capitalism (e.g., its overproductiveness and acquisitiveness) but also to those particularly modern forms of denial and repression that generate the need for their own further containment. In developing this contrast, the term "traditional" comes to describe a range of social and ethical phenomena so wide that Weber himself begins to despair of providing any definition for it at all ("Every attempt at a final definition [of traditionalism] must be held in abeyance," he says; *PE*, p. 59). This admission notwithstanding, Weber proceeds to recount the place of capitalistic enterprise within the structure of a society that is described in every one of its aspects as "traditional," claiming that

it was traditionalistic business, if one considers the spirit which animated the entrepreneur: the traditional manner of life, the traditional rate of profit, the traditional amount of work, the traditional manner of regulating the relationships with labour, and the essentially traditional circle of customers and the manner of attracting new ones. All these dominated the conduct of the business, were at the basis, one may say, of the *ethos* of this group of business men. (*PE*, p. 67)

The thesis of the displacement of traditionalism by modernity thus comes to express a contrast that is conceptual and ideological, rather than social or historical in nature. It acts in this way as a lever by which the special "irrationalism" of modern world-mastery – its simultaneous tendency toward abstraction *and* reification – may be brought into view. A "traditional" social structure for instance is described by Weber as normative to the extent that it is one in which "a man does not 'by nature' wish to earn more and more money, but simply to live and to earn as much as it is necessary for that purpose" (*PE*, p. 60). Within capitalism, by contrast, it became necessary to justify, make rational, or neutralize the profits of one's labors, since these were seen as the products of desires that could not be defended as "natural" in themselves. As Weber explains of the modern vocational ethic, for instance, "such an attitude is by no means a product of nature. It ... can only be the product of a long and arduous process of education" (*PE*, p. 62). The imperative expressed in the ethical "call" to conscience is both a prerequisite of rational world-mastery and an expression of the failure of modern culture to find an adequate embodiment in the forms of normalized and rational social behavior it had itself developed. As such, it is a paradigmatic expression of the contradictory nature of the secular-rational world.

For instance, there arose an ethos within the secularized institutions of capitalism that simultaneously called for the increase and repression of worldly desires. The Protestant-capitalist confronts an ethical dilemma in the production of worldly goods and in the acquisition of wealth; he succeeds simultaneously in recognizing and resisting their allure through capital, which allows for worldly profits that remain nonetheless abstract and purged of worldliness. For instance, capitalist reinvestment is a strategy that promotes, in Weber's words, "an amazingly good, we may even say a pharisaically good, conscience in the acquisition of money" (*PE*, p. 176). And yet at the same time reinvestment also enables capital to grow, and so is a source of renewed temptation to worldliness. As a result, it appears that even from within the perspective of capitalism no rationalization of the world can be rational enough (just as for Pascal no form of worldly negation can sufficiently remove us from the world). Indeed, capital may itself be seen as contributing equally to rationalist world-mastery and to the process by which the subject's relation to the world is rendered contradictory, not to say irrational and un-real. One recent critic of asceticism, Geoffrey Harpham, has argued that money is itself a recognition of the subject's contradictory immersion in and resistance to a secular world; in his analysis, money is the form of both consumption and denial.[69] But insofar as money is never identical with worldly objects, but is instead a representation of the

---

69 Geoffrey Harpham, *The Ascetic Imperative in Culture and Criticism* (Chicago: University of Chicago Press, 1987), p. 62. In Harpham's interpretation, "Money seems almost to resist and assent to itself, to enact an ascetic struggle even without the participation of a human subject" (pp. 62–63).

exchange-value placed on these, this argument must apply to capital, which is also a species of non-consumption; as an abstract measure of value, capital stands as confirming evidence of the transposition of value-ideals into norms. As such, capital plays a central role in inculcating the modern subject's divided sense of responsibility toward a world he must also deny. As Weber explained, "The greater the possessions the heavier, if the ascetic attitude toward life stands the test, the feeling of responsibility for them, for holding them undiminished for the glory of God and increasing them by restless effort" (*PE*, p. 176). Insofar as modernity thus depends on a new understanding of the nature and use of capital, it requires the ethical "reversal" of a perspective that may otherwise be described as "natural"; in Weber's analysis of capitalism,

man is dominated by the making of money, by acquisition as the ultimate purpose of his life. Economic acquisition is no longer subordinated to man as the means for the satisfaction of his material needs. This reversal of what we should call the natural relationship, so irrational from a naive point of view, is evidently as definitely a leading principle of capitalism as it is foreign to all peoples not under capitalistic influence.   (*PE*, p. 53)

As Bataille would recognize, the contradictions of capital are the undoing of any economic theory founded on the principles of classical utility (that is, on the denial of expenditure without return). No less clearly than Bataille, Weber could see that there continued to exist a series of values, desires, and needs – residual "enchantments" – within secular modernity that were drawn inward and came to manifest themselves in a series of secularized forms. For Weber these are to be found in, among other examples, the vocational "calling" and the work imperative. In these instances, the institutions of modernity themselves provide us with evidence that the project for the secularization of society and the rationalization of the world remained both internally incoherent and radically incomplete. As an example of rationalization, Protestant asceticism is bound up with capitalism as the expression of a tendency toward homogeneity that follows from the internalization of norms. But this would not in itself be a remarkable fact. The paradox of modernity lies rather in the fact that this normativity is at the same time the source both of profound personal reassurance and of great inner need. It is the crux of a religious experience in which the subject finds radicalized within itself the difference between a purely personal, inner sense of obligations that may be carried out within the world, and the "absolute transcendence" of God. As Weber pointed out, the result is an experience of world-shattering loneliness, in which the individual feels himself standing helpless and alone before God:

In what was for the man of the age of the Reformation the most important thing in life, his eternal salvation, he was forced to follow his path alone to meet a destiny which had been decreed for him from eternity. No one could help him. No priest, for the chosen one can understand the word of God only through his own heart. No sacraments, for though the sacraments had been ordained by God for the increase of His glory, and must be scrupulously observed, they are not a means to the attainment of grace ... Finally, even no God. (*PE*, p. 105)[70]

With the new Protestant culture as with subjectivity in general, the central feature of this experience is that of the individual who is at once abstract and alone, both in society and before God. (Thus Kant in the *Lectures on Ethics*: "The term outward religion is contradictory. Religion must be inward; actions may be outward, but they do not constitute religion and in no wise serve God."[71]) Thus while ascetic Protestantism generated a literally unsatisfiable need for a transformation of the secular world, the invention of the secular subject resulted in an intensification of the normative dimension of social life and in a reinforcement of the sense of duty and obligation as such.

It must in conclusion be said that to analyze the culture of modernity as Weber does in *The Protestant Ethic* is to reduce the problem of secularization to a Protestant-ascetic form that is congruent with the morality of Kant but that denies the alternative developed in Pascal's ethic of world-flight. In his elaboration of the ethic of world-flight,

70 Cf. MacIntyre, *A Short History of Ethics* (New York: Macmillan, 1966), pp. 125–26: "When Luther wants to explain what an individual is he does so by pointing out that when you die, it is you who die, and no one else can do this for you. It is as such, stripped of all social attributes, abstracted, as a dying man is abstracted, from all his social relations, that the individual is continually before God." Weber's analysis stands in the background of MacIntyre's interpretation, but he might equally have cited Kant: "It is not essential, and hence not necessary, for every one to know what God does or has done for his salvation; but it is essential to know *what man himself must do* in order to become worthy of this assistance" (*Religion Within the Limits of Reason Alone*, p. 47).

71 Kant, *Lectures on Ethics*, trans. Louis Infield (1930; rpt. Indianapolis: Hackett, 1979), p. 106. Kant's pronouncements are anticipated in the Hobbesian critique of religion. On the "inwardness" of religion, see Weber's discussion of the "Inner isolation" of the individual before the "absolute transcendentality" of God in his section on "The Religious Foundations of Worldly Asceticism" in *PE*, especially pp. 104–09.

Pascal anticipated Weber's critique of the Jesuits' conception of themselves as "monks in the world." To be sure, the Jesuit "Spiritual Exercises" represent a model of methodical prayer and their institutionalization a regularization of the principles of charismatic leadership that are perhaps even more striking than some of the monastic examples Weber cites. For Pascal, however, the Jesuit effort stands as testimony of the failure of every attempt to reduce the divisions within the subject or to combine inner- and other-worldliness:

The Jesuits have tried to combine God and the world, and have only earned the contempt of God and the world. For, as regards conscience, this is evident, and, as regards the world, they are no good at intrigue... Their position as monks in the world is a very silly one, on their own admission. Yet you give way beneath those more powerful than yourselves, and use what small credit you enjoy to oppress those who intrigue less than you in the world. *(Pensées*, fr. 989, p. 352)

For Weber, by contrast, the formation of a secularized subject, while no less contradictory, is itself a response to anxieties about how the individual might pursue a course of salvific reconciliation with an absolutely transcendent God, by transforming all forms of inner-worldly effort and work into methodical practices oriented toward the salvation of the soul.[72]

Although Weber wrote that the moral justification of worldly activity characteristic of Protestantism is "worlds removed from the deep hatred of Pascal, in his contemplative moods, for all worldly activity, which he was deeply convinced could only be understood in terms of vanity or low cunning,"[73] he decided nonetheless to privilege the asceticism of world-denial over the individualism of world-rejection. To be sure, we may say again for Pascal roughly what Weber has said for Protestant asceticism, namely that he makes visible the contradictions inherent in the secularization process itself. But if the Pascalian critique of worldliness is indeed central to the culture of modernity, then why does Weber privilege ascetic

72 Weber writes "that worldly activity should be considered capable of this achievement, that it could, so to speak, be considered the most suitable means of counteracting feelings of religious anxiety, finds its explanation in the fundamental peculiarities of the Reformed Church" (*PE*, p. 112).

73 Weber, *PE*, p. 81. Elsewhere Weber explains that "The deep pessimism of Pascal, which also rests on the doctrine of predestination, is, on the other hand, of Jansenist origin, and the resulting individualism of renunciation by no means agrees with the official Catholic position" (*PE*, p. 222).

Protestantism in his analysis of religion's effect on the transformation of the world?[74] Perhaps the most obvious answer lies in the fact that Pascal's response to the autonomy of the world may too closely thematize the conflict between science and faith that lay at the heart of Weber's own work. Pascal writes for instance that in the light of the discoveries of the new science, all forms of finitude, and therefore all modes of human discourse, are bound in indissoluble paradox: "In the perspective of these infinities, all finites are equal and I see no reason to settle our imagination on one rather than another. Merely comparing ourselves with the finite is painful" (*Pensées*, fr. 199, p. 93). The conflict among the value-spheres that we find symptomatically expressed in Weber's own attempt to explain the course of the world's religions, and the formulation by Weber of a "value-free" stance, may be found explicit in Pascal as the incompatibility of those dualisms that go to shape the subject. In the relationship between religion and science as thematized in Pascal, we encounter an example of the conflict among the value-spheres as it may more pervasively be found in the context of the disenchanted world. For Pascal, this conflict produces anxiety precisely because of the divided nature of subjectivity itself; the subject stands in between the finite and the infinite, wretchedness and glory, the noble and the base, and experiences the division of the value-spheres of culture in terms of its own inability to mediate or reconcile these extremes within its own discourse. As Weber's attempt at an analysis of modernity helps us see, it is indicative of a tension which roots in the disparity of the religious and the purely intellectual views of the world. As Wolfgang Schluchter pointed out, after Cartesian rationalism legitimated modern science as the rationalism of world-mastery, pure intellectualism was able to make its own world view absolute. It became the proponent of the dominant world view, diametrically opposed to that of religion.[75] To this we should add that whereas scientific rationalism

74 MacIntyre: "Pascal's notion that theistic belief is something to be chosen is quite new in the history of theism. His innovation makes him the precursor of both Kierkegaard and Karl Barth." In MacIntyre and Ricoeur, *The Religious Significance of Atheism*, p. 13. Pascal returns at crucial moments in MacIntyre's *After Virtue* (Notre Dame: University of Notre Dame Press, 1981). And yet Pascal is farther removed from the Protestant position that MacIntyre would indicate by his reference to the "Protestant-cum-Jansenist conception of reason" (p. 52).

75 Schluchter, "The Paradox of Western Rationalization," in Wolfgang Schluchter and Guenther Roth, *Max Weber's Vision of History* (Berkeley: University of California Press, 1979), pp. 49–50.

championed the rationalism of world-mastery in the name of the subject, ascetic Protestantism advocated a not unrelated world-mastery in the name of God.

In his analysis of the process of rationalization, Weber remits us to a series of ethical stances whose validity asks to be appraised internally in terms of the ways in which these attempt to balance a series of competing needs within a context in which religion has become, in Hegel's terms, "positive," and the world has become autonomous and abstract. In view of the world's autonomy, the subject must answer the question of what should determine an ethical stance – science, which is oriented toward an action's outcome, or belief, which is concerned with an act's intrinsic worth. These twin prospects, which despite their incompatibility are conjoined within the subject of the modern age, represent the possibilities that Lukács described in *The Theory of the Novel* as available to the subject – to "normative man," who has achieved "freedom in his relationship to God."[76] Whereas the ethic of responsibility adjusts to the secularizing logic of modernity and to its effects upon the world, the ethic of conviction rejects this process and remains committed to the principle of an act's intrinsic worth. And whereas the ethic of responsibility seeks to generalize the principle of inner freedom as the freedom of conscience for all, in an effort to transform the value-neutrality of the subject into value-pluralism for society as a whole, the ethic of conviction must remain quixotically committed to the irrationality of society and the world.[77]

Weber's interest in the language of conviction – however "disenchanted" this language may itself have become – was sustained by a desire to preserve the authoritative function that religion once supplied for social life. The secularized subject is nonetheless caught up in the oppositions of transcendental freedom and inner constraint, of capital accumulation and ascetic self-denial, of world-adjustment and world-flight. These divisions in turn lead Weber to seek in the ethic of responsibility an appropriate response to the conditions of existence in a disenchanted world. Weber's work may be seen as a

76 Lukács explains that this freedom is possible "because the lofty norms of his actions and of his substantial ethic are rooted in the existence of the all-perfecting God, are rooted in the idea of redemption, because they remain untouched in their innermost essence by whoever dominates the present, be he God or demon." *Theory of the Novel*, trans. Anna Bostock (Cambridge, MA: MIT Press, 1971), p. 91.

77 See Wolfgang Schluchter, "The Paradox of Western Rationalization," pp. 55–56.

product of the very process he was attempting to diagnose to the extent that his attempt to reconcile conviction and responsibility in essays like "Politics as a Vocation" and "Science as a Vocation" provides evidence of the instability of the rationalization process itself. In Weber, the relationship between belief and science mirrors the conflict among the value-spheres as it is found in the disenchanted world. As Wolfgang Schluchter explained, "In the disenchanted world you must reckon not only with the dualism between value and reality, but also with a value pluralism, with the fact that a person can find different 'gods' and be obedient to them. The ethic of responsibility can effect a reconciliation neither among the various value positions and reality nor among the different values themselves. It can only establish the preconditions for facing up to and for arranging a rational confrontation."[78] (Cf. Pascal: "There will always be Pelagians and always Catholics, and always strife," *Pensées*, fr. 662, p. 241.) Weber failed to justify the responsibility of value-freedom as that position most appropriate to the conditions of a disenchanted world and he failed likewise to reestablish a language of belief. For Weber, there is no possibility of a recuperative or redemptive critique of religion that would be compatible with a normative social-scientific stance and, conversely, no normative science able to reproduce in us the convictions of religious ideals. Weber may be thus cited as an example of someone who holds convictions that no longer follow from beliefs. In this sense, his ethical pronouncements read like the after-effects of convictions; they serve nonetheless to help us recall what it might be like to behave in concert with belief.

78 *Ibid.*, p. 58.

4

❖❖

The subject and the State

❖❖

Questions of legitimation

At several points in the previous chapters we have seen that the process Weber described as the "disenchantment" of the world manifests itself as a change in the internal structure of the beliefs of subjects as well as in the organization of subjects through social institutions and discourses, but that any account of the culture of modernity must somehow explain the relationship between these two. We may well describe "disenchantment" as the condition of rational enlightenment believed necessary for a true and "objective" grasp of nature; yet this understanding remains empty and abstract unless it also makes reference to changes in social relations and to a restructuring of the values expressed therein. Weber's Frankfurt School followers came to identify the "disenchantment" of the world directly with the process of increasing rationalization, a crucial consequence of which was a reification of social relationships,[1] but I would suggest that the culture of modernity is given shape as a divided whole that can only be unified through the powers of an abstract subject, or its political analogue, the autonomous State. Indeed, it can be said that the State gains power and scope precisely insofar as it provides a means through which the divided subjects of modernity can be made whole. Thus whereas Weber tended to approach the problem of social order from the perspective of its political organization and came to regard society in terms of the institutionalized norms and structures of authority dominant in it, I would suggest that a political analysis of the problem of modernity may more directly be pursued through a vision of the State as the

---

1 See, for example, Habermas, *The Theory of Communicative Action, I, Reason and the Rationalization of Society*, trans. Thomas McCarthy (Boston: Beacon Press, 1984), p. 144.

overarching context in which the possibilities for legitimizing expression on the part of the subjects are created and sustained. I would suggest that the State provided the means through which "private" subjects could be given political structure and shape.

As we shall see in relation to the political theory of modernity, and in particular that of Hobbes, however, the founding of the State along rational lines is inherently contradictory. On the one hand, the modern State embodies a series of positive goals; these are premised on the rejection of social hierarchies, a belief in the equality of all before the procedures of the law, and the accession to a realm of subjective freedom founded on reason. But on the other hand, the authoritarian structure of the State reflects the fact that the subjects are radically uncertain about the nature of virtue and values; as a result, it indicates their susceptibility to manipulation and control. In Hobbes, the modern State relies on a "scientific" understanding of politics that attempts to resolve the problem of social order by recourse to the fiction of man in a "natural" or pre-political state. Appeal to the "state of nature" is a necessary part of Hobbes's attempt to replace the hierarchical distinctions among persons according to the "traditional" criteria of status, virtue, rank, or caste with a true and accurate (which is to say, scientific) understanding of the nature of all men. More precisely, Hobbes proposes a series of "genetic" arguments that are meant to supersede aristocratic prudence by the introduction of a morality that is systematically applicable and that, in its rationality, appeals to "the greatest part of men." Thus Leo Strauss could argue that "Hobbes admits the natural inequality, the natural gradation of men, and 'only' contests that this inequality is of any practical importance ... he denies that from this hierarchy of things earthly and things eternal anything can be adduced as to the relative position of the holder of secular power and the holder of spiritual power ... With this Hobbes lets us see that even if there were an eternal order, he would take into consideration only the actual behaviour of men."[2]

Hobbes's political theory carries with it the promise of freedom from unwanted domination, the overcoming of the mystifications of the priests, and the safety of subjects within a regime whose motives should in principle be transparent to all. As Hegel observed, Hobbes

2 Strauss, *The Political Philosophy of Hobbes, Its Basis and Its Genesis*, trans. Elsa M. Sinclair (1936; rpt. Chicago: University of Chicago Press, 1984), p. 99.

sought to derive the bonds which hold the State together and give it power from principles of reason thought to be inherent in man himself. As such, the political organization Hobbes proposes is a consequence of the secularized conditions described in chapter 3 above. Indeed, Hobbes eschews the vague and potentially mystifying term "conscience" in favor of secular "opinion," insofar as the latter admits the possibility of a rational critique. In Hobbes, politics takes place within what Habermas has described as an autonomous "public sphere"; but the public interest, about which the sovereign alone has the right to decide, no longer falls under the purview of morality or conscience. Conscience is protected but also alienated from the State, and becomes the center of a purely private morality, and the State is thus transformed into an impersonal machine: its gears and levers are laws, moved by a sovereign will.[3] Thus it seems that Hobbesian theory serves only to reinforce the subjection of the individual to an all-powerful sovereign or to the institutional controls of an anonymous State. The result is a contradiction that takes the following shape. On the one hand, the origins of State power are said to lie in a form of reasoning wherein the subjects themselves are seen as rational agents; similarly, the principles of sovereign power are derived from "universal" descriptions which could be predicated of any subject of the realm. But on the other hand Hobbes needs to ensure the obedience of subjects by the invocation of an absolute power, whose will is law.[4] Inevitably, the citizen-subjects come into conflict with an autonomous State that narrowly circumscribes the

3 See Reinhart Koselleck, *Critique and Crisis* (Cambridge, MA: MIT Press, 1988), p. 31. Georges Bataille presents an important analysis of this particular aspect of sovereignty in "The Psychological Structure of Fascism" when he argues that although the king may act for reasons of State, he nonetheless maintains the separate character of divine supremacy: "He is exempt from the specific principle of homogeneity, the compensation of rights and duties constituting the formal law of the State: the king's rights are unconditional." *Visions of Excess: Selected Writings, 1927–1939*, ed. and trans. Allan Stoekl (Minneapolis: University of Minnesota Press, 1985), p. 148. It should be noted that in so saying Bataille develops Hegel's analysis of kingly sovereignty in the *Phenomenology of Spirit* in terms of the heterogeneity of the king from the State that nonetheless supplies his identity: "the monarch is absolutely separated off from everyone else, exclusive and solitary; as monarch, he is a unique atom that cannot impart any of its essential nature." *Phenomenology of Spirit* (henceforth *PhS*), trans. A. V. Miller (New York: Oxford University Press, 1981), sec. 511, p. 311.
4 See Hegel's *Lectures on the Philosophy of History*, trans. Elizabeth S. Haldane and Frances H. Simson (London: Kegan Paul, Trench, Trübner 1896), III, p. 316.

morality of conscience and the principles of virtue and that establishes an abstract understanding of the nature of legitimacy and law. The political subject is in turn divided against itself: outwardly, its actions must comply with a set of formally instituted rules, while inwardly its mind remains at liberty, "in secret free."[5]

In Hobbes, the power of the sovereign over the commonwealth expresses the need for self-preservation of subjects who would otherwise be consumed by fear and dread of a violent death at the hands of others, for these others, we must presume, are equally violent and fearful subjects as well. The interest in self-preservation constitutes the basis of a political program rooted in the conflict among men who have, through reason, "overcome" history and who have come to recognize their origins in the violent "state of nature." In Hobbes, we thus move directly from the "disenchanted" principle of self-preservation to the belief that the will to power constitutes a fundamental category underlying the existence of all things.[6] In either case, the premise that the world has a particular quality for man that might prescribe his mode of political association is eliminated, in favor of a gesture of radical "self-assertion" whose ultimate consequence is subjection to State power.

In suggesting that the rational subject is led politically to subjection to a sovereign or an institutional State, I mean nonetheless to challenge the prevailing assumptions about power and politics in the modern age, viz., that an analysis of the constitution of subjects in terms of subjection should yield the exact *opposite* of Hobbes's project in the *Leviathan* and, as Foucault said, "of all jurists for whom the problem is the distillation of a single will – or rather, the constitution of a unitary, singular body animated by the spirit of

5 Thus Hobbes writes in the *Elements of Law* that "No human law is intended to oblige the conscience of a man, but the actions only." *De Corpore Politico, or The Elements of Law*, in *English Works*, IV, ed. William Molesworth (London: J. Bohn, 1839–45), II, 6, p. 172. In the *Leviathan* he argues that "There is a *Publique*, and a *Private* Worship. Publique, is the Worship that a Common-wealth performeth, as one Person. Private, is that which a Private person exhibeteth. Publique, in respect of the whole Common-wealth, is Free; but in respect of Particular men it is not so. Private, is in secret Free; but in the sight of the multitude, it is never without some Restraint, either from the Lawes, or from the Opinion of men." Ed. C. B. MacPherson (Harmondsworth, Penguin Books, 1968) II, 31, p. 401; further references will be to this edition. See also Reinhart Koselleck, *Critique and Crisis*, p. 37.

6 Blumenberg, *The Legitimacy of the Modern Age*, trans. Robert M. Wallace (Cambridge, MA: MIT Press, 1985), p. 143.

sovereignty – from the particular wills of a multiplicity of individuals."[7] According to Foucault, the politics of modernity dangerously attempts to deduce a single unifying principle in order to generate a "central spirit" or "general will" out of the multitude of interests that compete for power on any given social or historical stage. Thus in his writings on knowledge and power Foucault specifically rejects the figure of the Leviathan insofar as it represents the amalgamation of divergent interests into the totalizing structure of a sovereign State: "we must eschew the model of the Leviathan,"[8] which he said must be replaced by an analysis that would reveal the constitution of subjects *by* the State. For Foucault, the condition of sovereignty in the modern age is illegitimate insofar as sovereign power rests on a "right of seizure," through which power is exercised "mainly as a means of deduction, a subtraction mechanism, a right to appropriate a portion of the wealth, a tax of products, goods, and services, labor and blood, levied on the subjects."[9] However in this instance Foucault fails to recognize precisely what elsewhere he takes great pains to show: that by virtue of the fiction of representation, the sovereign is the subjects themselves – the subjects willfully constituting themselves *as* sovereign – and that the representational relation of the subject to the State depends on the fiction of authorship as a means for the legitimation of authority. In Hobbes's understanding, this means that "every Subject is Author of every act the Soveraign doth ... the Consent of a Subject to Soveraign Power, is contained in these words, *I Authorise, or take upon me, all his actions*" (*Leviathan*, II, 21, pp. 265, 269). The commonwealth is formed when the multitude decides to appoint one man to "beare their Person," or "represent" them,

and every one to owne, and acknowledge himself to be Author of whatsoever he that so beareth their Person, shall Act, or cause to be Acted, in those things which concern the Common Peace and Saftie; and therein to submit their Wills, every one to his Will, and their Judgments, to his Judgment. This is more than Consent, or Concord; it is a real Unity of them all, in one and the same Person, made by Covenant of every man with every man, in such manner, as if every man should say to every man, I *Authorise and give up my Right of Governing my selfe, to this Man, or this Assembly of men,*

---

7 Foucault, "Two Lectures," in *Power/Knowledge: Selected Interviews and Other Writings, 1972–1977*, ed. Colin Gordon (New York: Pantheon, 1980), p. 97.

8 *Ibid.*, p. 102.

9 Foucault, *The History of Sexuality, I: An Introduction*, trans. Robert Hurley (New York: Vintage Books, 1980), p. 136.

on this condition, that thou give up thy Right to him, and Authorise all his Actions in like manner. (*Leviathan*, II, 17, p. 227)

Moreover, by reversing the (modern) belief that the legitimation of power depends upon the validity of underlying judgments, and claiming instead the power-dependency of truth, power becomes an inscrutable force bred deeply into the social body, while politics is freed from the demands that the need for legitimacy might make. By treating "knowledge" principally as a resource of power we are unable to distinguish between political theory as a mode of apprehension for which critical self-reflection is essential, and such bureaucratic or clinical practices as medicine or penal law.[10] Unlike Weber, for whom the commitment to the principles of value-freedom did not obscure the hope that social-scientific reflection might direct itself to the analysis of normative orders and the ways in which these are made legitimate, Foucault tended to collapse the historical and "technical" notion of authority as manipulation or control with the principle or order to be apprehended theoretically and lived expressively – in this case, legitimacy, as manifested in sovereignty and the State. As a result, the ambition to produce a theory of politics is replaced by a series of politicized theories, none of which can provide the legitimacy required by the subjects of the modern State.

In the concluding chapter of this study I will outline a theory of "aesthetic liberalism" that is implicitly critical of the notion of politics inherited from Hobbes, yet which seeks also to guard against the tendency of anti-liberal positions to identify or collapse private and State interests. The result is a theory of legitimation consistent with the aims of modernity insofar as it rejects all prior social and political descriptions of the subject in favor of a concept of the political in which the State becomes the framework in which we may assume and test the depth and coherence of the descriptions we may adopt for ourselves. This would help address the crucial issue of the subject's *stance* with regard to the State, a matter that is particularly problematic in modernity in at least the following ways: first, the relationship between the two is made "artificially" dependent on the existence of an enforcing body; and second, the State is the product of human artifice but comes to alienate its authors and to exert a control over them. By focusing here on the need of social orders to

10 Gillian Rose makes a related point in *Dialectic of Nihilism* (Oxford: Basil Blackwell, 1984), p. 178.

provide for the expressions of legitimation of their constituent members, and by calling on the ways in which those legitimizing expressions in turn allow for the creation of the identities of political subjects, we can understand why the modes of political organization characteristic of modernity, as formulated through the theory of natural law, contractual relations, and the principles of sovereignty and representation, generated a paradoxical and self-limiting set of tensions between private subjects and the institutional State. As I hope over the course of this chapter to suggest, the paradox of modernity makes itself apparent in the form of a "legitimation crisis" *within* the framework of what Weber calls "rational authority" that does not leave the alternate theory of communicative reason unscathed; it takes the form of a continuous deficit of authority on the part of the liberal State, which appears unable to supply a coherent definition of the good. Not surprisingly, these are the same tensions with which liberal theory has historically had to contend. Liberalism characteristically seeks to legitimize the State by limiting any institutionalized vision of the nature of the good and by maximizing the opportunities for individual expression; but in both its contractarian and utilitarian dimensions liberal theory must invoke the fiction of the subject as a sovereign Observer or Judge capable of reconciling disparate needs and resolving disputes from a detached, third-person point of view if it is also to produce a coherent image of the State and resolve the problems of order that arise in it. The contractarian invokes the fiction of subjects in a hypothetical "original position," free of any specific knowledge about the particular desires of the other members of the social group, while the utilitarian imagines an Ideal Spectator, a sympathetic subject who identifies with and experiences the desires of others as if these were his own.

Insofar as one is willing to recognize what is manifestly modern in Hobbes — that the need for self-preservation endows man with the will to set himself free from society and from the past, and that the liberal theory of the State is dependent upon a series of prior assumptions about the condition of man in a disenchanted world — it should come as no surprise that those inclined to accept modern political theory in its liberal guise have been reluctant to embrace Hobbes as the first of its theorists, for liberalism's contradictions are brought together with frightening force in Hobbes's writings. Ronald

Dworkin for instance cites Hobbes as the only major thinker included in the "liberal" group capable of expressing a genuine unwillingness to believe that one means of ethical conduct might be superior to another: "none of these 'liberals' except Hobbes (why should Hobbes be counted a liberal?) adopted any form of skepticism about the possibility that one way of leading one's life can be more valuable than another."[11] This may well be the case, were it not for the fact that Hobbes also believes that men will be rationally motivated when confronted with the fear of death to act in only one way. In an effort to save liberalism from its own contradictions, Dworkin argues that healthy, liberal pluralism cannot possibly be founded on skepticism of the fully disenchanted, Hobbesian sort. He argues instead that the crucial mistake enters when we confuse Hobbesian arguments about the absence of an "utmost ayme" with claims that the variability of desires precludes our finding acceptable justifications for regulative political decisions. If liberalism rests on a value-neutral stance and seeks thereby to limit the powers of the State, Dworkin suggests that this is not for lack of a principle of justice, or for a failure to understand what is wrong or right, but rather because the principles of liberalism are themselves the embodiment of what is right and just:

[liberalism] is a theory of equality that requires official neutrality amongst theories of what is valuable in life. That argument will provoke a variety of objections. It might be said that liberalism so conceived rests on skepticism about theories of the good, or that it is based on a mean view of human nature that assumes that human beings are atoms who can exist and find self-fulfillment apart from political community ... [But] liberalism cannot be based on skepticism. Its constitutive morality provides that human beings must be treated as equals by their government, not because there is no right or wrong in political morality, but because that is what is right. Liberalism does not rest on any special theory of personality ... Liberalism is not self-contradictory: the liberal conception of equality is a principle of political organization that is required by justice, not a way of life for individuals.[12]

And yet just as Hobbes cannot so easily be excluded from the liberal sphere, the effort to distinguish liberalism as a "principle of political organization" from a "way of life for individuals" places severe constraints on the notion of political community. In an effort to limit

11 Dworkin, *Law's Empire* (Cambridge, MA: The Belknap Press of Harvard University Press, 1986), p. 441.
12 Dworkin, *A Matter of Principle* (Cambridge, MA: Harvard University Press, 1985), p. 203.

the intrusive powers of the State over the affairs of "private citizens," liberal theorists must characteristically exclude from the political arena precisely those areas of concern that are most likely to be of importance to individuals, who cannot so easily divorce their public and private lives. Indeed, the attempt to separate the two can yield only a transformation of the political sphere into a realm of procedural rather than substantive justice, which will result in a drastic reduction of the quality of interests that can be brought to bear on political debate.

If the consequences of the liberalism that derives from Hobbes are indeed these, we may understand the "disenchantment" of the world as that process by which the political order came to be viewed as autonomous and in which the criteria for legitimizing expression came to be viewed as obtaining to a standard of reason that was public, universal, and abstract. At the same time, the process of rationalization manifests itself in the tendency to reduce the competing interests underlying the need for political community to the level of merely empirical differences and to count them, with Hobbes, as "perceptions," "sentiments," or "desires." Insofar as these terms are taken to refer exclusively to "private" experience and fail to challenge the limited value-neutrality of their own first-person point of view, they circumscribe the extent and coherence of any political order founded on the ideal of public conversation or debate. As Habermas argued, the consequence for modern politics is the discovery of a contradiction in the form of an irrationality of values, purposes, and goals at the heart of a rationalized world:

The subjectivistic reduction of the interests which are decisive in the orientation for action to "sentiments" or "perceptions" which cannot be rationalized beyond that is a precise expression for the...value freedom central to the technological concept of rationality...Competing interest perspectives, hypostatized to values, are excluded from discussion. Revealingly enough, according to the criteria of technological rationality agreement on a collective value system can never be achieved by means of enlightened discussion carried on in public politics, thus by way of consensus rationally arrived at, but only by summation or compromise – values are in principle beyond discussion.[13]

My suggestion is that the problems posed by contemporary theorists like Habermas have their roots in a thinker like Hobbes. The

13 Habermas, *Theory and Practice*, trans. John Viertel (Boston: Beacon Press, 1974), p. 271.

importance of the Hobbesian position, and also its deep incoherence, can be made clear if we recognize that while Hobbes denies the teleology of nature he simultaneously thinks that the collective ends of human nature can be calculated in mathematical terms, based on a vision of each individual as an opposing will. The Hobbesian vision amounts to a "perspectivism" that is inseparable from the emergence of the new, mathematically-based physics, which teaches that nature is intelligible not as a divinity, nor as a principle of life, but as matter that can be measured and, to that extent, mastered by man.[14] Not surprisingly in this light, the attempt to fashion a theory of politics from within the perspectives afforded by Hobbes proves to be a difficult task, for the "perspectival" interpretation of human nature (as will) naturally falls prey to a purely technical understanding of the task of politics; eventually, the substitution of the new "science" of politics for the principles of prudential judgment leads us to Weber's "iron cage" and to the substitution of politicized theories for a theory of politics. However, before proceeding to examine in greater detail the ripostes of Weber and Habermas (which are no less problematic than the position they seek to criticize) let us look further at the problem of legitimation in relation to the conditions of dis-enchantment as understood by Hobbes.

As described by Hobbes, the conditions requiring legitimation are those in which social and civil bonds, including those of contracts, derive their power "not from their own Nature (for nothing is more easily broken than a mans word,) but from Feare of some evill consequence upon [their] rupture" (*Leviathan*, I, 14, p. 192). Penal law sanctions the order of civil society, but is restricted to a purely instrumental significance. Formality of the law insures the citizens freedom in the sense of liberality or fairness but the laws themselves have the character of formal and general norms. Similarly, the laws guarantee an equal distribution of rights and duties and mandate an equal sharing in the burdens of taxation. In addition, they require the sovereign to see to it that he enables the citizens to live as comfortably as human nature permits. But at the same time the existence of formally rational law separates the legal order from the order of life and creates "private" areas of freedom – those which

14 See Stanley Rosen, *G.W.F. Hegel: An Introduction to the Science of Wisdom* (New Haven: Yale University Press, 1974), pp. 136–37.

liberal theory would at all costs protect – which are not in their content subject to legitimizing norms.

Hobbesian political science and the State it founds thus demonstrate that "rational" modes of legitimation constitute attempts to stabilize social structures through means that may be unstable, "irrational," or contradictory in themselves. Recall Hobbes's response to the problems of conflict, competition, and social justice in the modern age – that while some groups will inevitably have more power than others, no group may legitimately claim to dominate another. Hobbes's arguments justifying the principle of sovereignty in the State presuppose the existence of subjects who are motivated "rationally" by the fear of domination by those more powerful than themselves to form a social bond ("Feare of oppression, disposeth a man to anticipate, or to seek ayd by society: for there is no other way by which a man can secure his life and liberty," *Leviathan*, I, 11, p. 163). Similarly, laws develop in the "neutral" space between protection and obedience designed to limit the threat of unwanted domination or State interference, and yet in such a State only the formal legality of the laws may be considered rational, not their content; only in this sense may the commandment of modern political morality to obey the laws regardless of their substance be taken as a "reasonable" obligation.[15]

The political science of Hobbes furthermore allows us to see that reference to the State as an objective and autonomous ordering body is in itself insufficient to supply the justification that the State demands. Indeed, the modern State seems to labor under a constant legitimation deficit, for its formal procedures are continuously brought under the pressure to attain a type and degree of justification they cannot provide. Simple appeal to the State's monopoly on power and its control over the creation and application of laws cannot for instance suffice as legitimizing principles. The State can meet its obligations only if all men individually cede their rights to the sovereign who represents them collectively. As Reinhart Koselleck has said, "not until compliance with this commandment of reason has been guaranteed by the State will the morality of reason have the force of law. On its own, the subjective wish for peace is insufficient; in order to become 'moral', it requires the sanction of the State" (*Critique and Crisis*, pp. 31–32). Thus, a prior condition must be met

15 See Koselleck, *Critique and Crisis*, p. 33.

if legitimation is to take place; as indicated in Hobbes's claims for the scientific nature of politics, "grounds" must be sought; rational "foundations" for the State's formal procedures and its legitimizing force must be derived from free and equally reasonable subjects. It must for instance be shown that procedural authority lies with a representationally authorized body, or in what amounts to the same thing, with the sovereign himself: this authority can be constituted as legitimate and just only insofar as the Sovereign mirrors the subjects' authorizing Will.[16] Indeed, it is only in this way (as expressed, typically, in the form of a constitution) that the subjects can distinguish the rule of sovereignty from tyrannical oppression or abuse. As Hegel explained in the *Philosophy of Right,*

The fact that the sovereignty of the state is the ideality of all particular authorities within it gives rise to the easy and also very common misunderstanding that this ideality is only might and pure arbitrariness while "sovereignty" is a synonym for "despotism". But despotism means any state of affairs where law has disappeared and where the particular will as such, whether of a monarch or a mob (ochlocracy), counts as law or rather takes the place of law; while it is precisely in legal, constitutional, government that sovereignty is to be found as the moment of ideality..[17]

As we shall see in greater detail below, the establishment of the laws of reason in the socio-political realm allows for a "conclusive" demonstration of the principle of sovereignty. Such a demonstration is necessary, given the permanent inconstancy of public affairs on the one hand and the gradual disappearance of the ideal of personal service to the State as a duty on the other; a private conception of reason is thus replaced by a conception of universal laws that (in the form of a "contract" that binds the subjects' wills for the future) *produce* the civil society and the State. In this way, claims of "reason" become the foundations of the State.[18]

Strictly speaking, what men do when they agree to obey the sovereign's commands is voluntarily to bind their own wills for the

16 See Habermas, *Legitimation Crisis*, trans. Thomas McCarthy (Boston: Beacon Press, 1975), p. 98. On the question of the sovereign's body, see Louis Marin, *The Portrait of the King*, trans. Martha M. Houle (Minneapolis: University of Minnesota Press, 1988).
17 Hegel, *Philosophy of Right*, trans. T. M. Knox (New York: Oxford University Press, 1967), sec. 278, p. 180.
18 A related analysis of Montaigne is presented by Timothy Reiss, "Montaigne and the Subject of Polity," in *Literary Theory / Renaissance Texts*, ed. Patricia Parker and David Quint (Baltimore: Johns Hopkins University Press, 1986), pp. 115–49.

future. But insofar as the will is not itself the center of voluntary agency but is instead subject to circumstances, needs, and above all the passions, one cannot *rationally* bind the will; one cannot under any circumstances foresee what one may will tomorrow. As Hanna Pitkin argued, echoing Rousseau's complaint, it is absurd for the will to commit itself for the future; one cannot coherently will to will.[19] But while one cannot promise to will a certain thing tomorrow, one can establish certain circumstances today that may constrain or determine one's will. In particular, one can establish an enforcing power so strong that no one would rationally want to disobey it. One can, in other words, set the penalty for disobedience so stiff that disobedience loses all attraction. As Hobbes explains,

And though the will of man being not voluntary, but the beginning of voluntary actions, is not subject to deliberation and covenant; yet when a man covenanteth to subject his will to the command of another, he obligeth himself to this, that he resign his strength and means to him, whom he covenanteth to obey. And hereby he that is to command, may by the use of all their means and strength, be able by the terror thereof, to frame the will of them all to unity and concord, amongst themselves.[20]

As we can thus begin to see, the appeal to rational "foundations" fails to establish the conditions of community and obedience that society demands. Recourse to "reason" as the founding basis of the State leads the State to develop a body of laws external to ethics but necessary to its enforcement, while ethics remains itself confined within a "subjective" space. If, following Weber, law may be considered as "the authoritarian embodiment of those cultural traditions which are anchored both in world views and in the socialized individuals,"[21] then the specificity of modern law in its externality to ethics is revealed by its dependence on the existence of an enforcing body: the "disenchantment" of the world is in this case confirmed by the fact that law comes to exist as valid only when norms are externally guaranteed. As the example of Hobbes amply reveals, this distinguishes legal compulsion from the compulsion of conscience and insures the "liberal" principles of the State. But as we

---

19 Hanna Pitkin, "Hobbes's Concept of Representation – II," *American Political Science Review*, 58 (1964), 903.
20 Hobbes, *De Corpore Politico, or The Elements of Law*, 1, 6, in *English Works*, ed. William Molesworth (London: 1839–45), IV, p. 122.
21 Schluchter, *The Rise of Western Rationalism*, trans. Guenther Roth (Berkeley: University of California Press, 1981), p. 86.

shall see further below it also serves to reinforce, against Hobbes, the Habermassian critique of Foucault: insofar as we remain content simply to describe the forces that police, control, and distribute social power and locate their roots in an anonymous and multitudinous subject, we will be unable to establish distinctions between social and juridical norms. Both will remain within the category of enforced collective practices or dominations, and both will be reduced to their common basis in power or violence.

Immediately, the foregoing observations raise a series of questions regarding the historical relationship between the individual as (political) subject and the modern State as a domain of public order and call for a critique of authority in terms of a concept of legitimacy that would provide not only for the validation of public authority but the *creation* of subjects whose identities could be derived from the potential for expressions of legitimation afforded them by the State. In pursuit of these issues, we will return to the example of Hobbes in our discussion of ethics in the following section. For now let us draw out some of the consequences of the fact that the problem of legitimation in the modern age – the need to establish order given the absence of teleologies in nature and to show why it is empowered with legitimate force – is irreducible either to a series of theoretical propositions or to claims about the nature of historical fact. Of course, every political theory may be submitted to logical evaluation, and a variety of writers on Hobbes have done just this.[22] By the same token, Habermas, Ernst Bloch, C. B. MacPherson, Perry Anderson, and a host of others have shown that every social order, however contingent, may be understood in terms of the deeply structured historical and material interests at work in it. The question that remains is whether these can be the source of legitimizing principles for the modern State. Habermas has, for instance, advanced theses regarding the "crisis of legitimation" in late capitalist (i.e., modern)

---

22 Among recent examples are Gregory S. Kavka, *Hobbesian Moral and Political Theory* (Princeton: Princeton University Press, 1986), and Jean Hampton, *Hobbes and the Social Contract Tradition* (Cambridge: Cambridge University Press, 1986). Victoria Kahn raises some fundamental questions about such procedures in light of the rhetorical status of Hobbes's text in her *Rhetoric, Prudence, and Skepticism in the Renaissance* (Ithaca: Cornell University Press, 1985); for a response, see Jeffrey Barnouw, "Persuasion in Hobbes's *Leviathan*," *Hobbes Studies*, 1 (1988), 3–25.

society that attempt to address the problem of legitimation by transposing the Marxist theory of the economic origins of the State into the language of "communicative action," which makes an implicit claim to legitimacy based on the possibility of intersubjective agreement. Habermas begins from an analysis in which legitimation claims are seen as masks for a series of "deep-structure" interests rooted in class or economic factors which may obstruct full and equal participation in political life. For the Habermas of *Legitimation Crisis*, all legitimation problems are rooted in unresolved problems in the underlying mode of organization or "steering mechanism" of society. Although subjects are presumed not to be directly aware of them, these steering problems have consequences that endanger social cohesion in significant ways. Following a host of thinkers from Locke to Marx, Habermas locates the underlying steering mechanism of modern society in property and in economic exchange; its privileged political institution is the liberal State, insofar as the State, beginning with Hobbes, regulates and is itself regulated by citizens who are antecedently subject to the market's laws of competition and contract. The crises of societies organized around economic lines are thus transposed from their natural situation in the political sphere, which presumes in its outward dimension to be organized as a forum for public discussion, legitimation, and consensus-building, to that realm which most closely mimics the "state of nature," viz., the economic market. The advantage of such an arrangement is that legitimation no longer comes primarily "from above" – i.e., from the authority of virtuous individuals or charismatic leaders – but rather is produced "from below," i.e. from the theoretically "open communication" and inherent "justice" of freely competing individuals in a market environment.

There can be no doubt that the historical portion of Habermas's analysis is correct in point of fact, regardless of the notorious difficulty of locating a moment of origin for the emergence of propertied individuals and of the State in historical time. Christopher Hill has for instance argued that the legal institution of a modern economic order anticipates the publication of *Leviathan* by as little as five years; according to this argument, only with the formal abolition of feudal tenures and the Court of Wards did the ownership of property in England become autonomous, and not a condition of fealty and service. Only then could landowners manage, exploit, consolidate, and otherwise "improve" their estates, free of obligations to the king. Yet it has also been said that the origins of contract did not mark the end of feudal relations, and that as long as aristocratic agrarian property blocked the establishment of a truly free market in land and constrained the mobility of manpower (in Perry Anderson's terms, "as long as labour was not separated from the social conditions of its existence to become 'labour-power'") then rural relations of production remained essentially feudal.[23] In either case, the emergence of the modern State and its legitimizing principles could hardly be imagined without the ascension to power of a new class of individuals, whose productive capital and ideas came into conflict with a society that had been organized around a network of feudal hierarchies and kinship ties. Thus Ernst Bloch could argue in *Natural Law and Human Dignity* that "classical natural law is the ideology of an individual economy and of the capitalist relationships of merchants, who require that everything should be calculable, and who therefore replace the variegated rights of privilege found in the Middle Ages with the formal equality and universality of the laws."[24]

The new class of individuals naturally sought to consolidate the bases of their social and economic freedom through the juridical confirmation of personal rights and in the theories of rational natural law. As the dominant legal relation between those who own property, contract was assumed to guarantee bourgeois security or "self-preservation"; indeed, the idea that a legal contract could secure economic relations was extended to society as a whole, through the notion of a social compact. And yet recourse to the fictions of natural rights and a social contract failed adequately to link politics and economics, or to establish the connection between the political subject to the *polis* as an economic whole. To be sure, the idea of the modern State is that it is instituted for the sake of peace, and peace is pursued for the general (political) good; but the general good is no

23 Perry Anderson, *Lineages of the Absolutist State* (London: NLB, 1974), p. 17 and *passim*. It has also been argued that the beginnings of individual ownership were in existence since the thirteenth century, and that the concept of "individualism" itself represents a category by which the proponents of a modernizing ideology sought to legitimize conditions that had antecedently been in existence. See Alan Macfarlane, *The Origins of English Individualism: The Family, Property, and Social Transition* (Cambridge: Cambridge University Press, 1979), especially pp. 184, 203. For a related discussion, see McKeon, *The Origins of the English Novel* (Baltimore: Johns Hopkins University Press, 1987), pp. 176–78.

24 Ernst Bloch, *Natural Law and Human Dignity*, trans. Dennis J. Schmidt (Cambridge, MA: MIT Press, 1986), p. 54.

longer understood in terms of the principles of virtue, as is the "good life" of the classical tradition, or the "virtue" of the medieval hero; on the contrary, it is born from the absence of any such grounds, as revealed in the radical need for self-preservation of individuals in a competitive environment. The modern understanding of natural rights is, for instance, a corollary of the fundamental right of self-preservation, premised on the enjoyment of freely disposable property. But as it takes shape in Hobbes and Locke this argument is contradictory in itself; it offered a legitimizing principle, but it failed to guarantee the rights over property in a political sense; as Leo Strauss explained, "property is an institution of natural law; natural law defines the manner and the limitations of just appropriation. Men own property prior to civil society; they enter civil society in order to preserve or protect the property which they acquired in the state of nature. But, once civil society is formed, if not before, the natural law regarding property ceases to be valid; what we may call 'conventional' or 'civil' property – the property which is owned within civil society – is based on positive law alone."[25]

As this analysis suggests, an historical analysis of the problem of legitimation cannot avoid the material conditions of the society it addresses; but neither is such an analysis sufficient to generate the condition or possibility of legitimation. As Weber will help us see, any analysis of legitimation must also address the symbolic nature of social relations and the modes of authority embodied in them. For Habermas, by contrast, the objectivity of a given order, its claim to validity *as an order*, is in the final analysis contingent neither upon the material order of society nor on its symbolic status but rather on a principle of normativity underlying these. Thus he argues that "when ... one admits only the model of processes of subjugation, of confrontations mediated by the body, of contexts of more or less consciously strategic action; when one excludes any stabilizing of domains of action in terms of values, norms, and processes of mutual understanding ... then one is hardly able to explain just how persistent local struggles could get consolidated into institutionalized power."[26] The question nonetheless remains why Habermas continues to believe that legitimation must lead to participation in a rationally

---

25 Strauss, *Natural Right and History* (Chicago: University of Chicago Press, 1953), pp. 234–35.

26 Habermas, *The Philosophical Discourse of Modernity* (henceforth *PDM*), trans. Frederick Lawrence (Cambridge MA: MIT Press, 1987), p. 287.

constructed "universal community of mankind." Indeed, it seems that any attempt to rescue political theory from its anti-Enlightenment detractors that concentrates on the conditions of universal reason over and above the legitimizing expressions of political actors will lead only to new forms of opposition between the individual as subject and the principles of the autonomous State.

To be sure, Habermas means to provide an alternative to the theory of the socio-economic origins of legitimation problems in the modern State; but his alternative theory of communicative reason is better seen as a consequence of, rather than as a solution to, the very problems he is attempting to resolve. The notion of communicative action is meant to provide Habermas with a place from which to begin the process of a reconstructive critique of the modern State by appeal to the conditions of legitimizing expression that must be met by all participant-actors in political debate. In transposing the "depth-grammar" of a materialist form of ideology-criticism into the terms of communicative action, Habermas attempts to gain an understanding of the historical conditions underlying modern society while salvaging the possibility of a normative political critique. In his view, the ideal of a rational organization of society as modeled in the form of a liberal State – one which would be based on an open, non-coercive agreement among its members – is already contained, if in a distorted form, in those democratic institutions which embody the ethical principles of subjectivity: freedom and reason. According to Habermas, we simply need to transpose these principles into an intersubjective context, or reframe them in communicative terms, in order to realize that liberal institutions express a potential for rationality that may redeem the pervasive rationalization whose roots lie in the social and economic formations discussed above. It is only on this basis that Habermas can conceive of communicative action not solely as a technical "mechanism of coordination" for the actions of individuals in society, but as a theoretical achievement that is meant to have a heightening effect on the level of reason and speech. Once the obscurantist dogmatism of traditional world views has been shattered and the reifying potential of the Enlightenment's claims has been exposed, the concept of communicative action is poised to emerge as the benign master of an "intersubjective" universe which demands no justifications for validity claims outside the shared expectation that the principles of rational argumentation will be met. As a means of compensating for the negative effects of rationalization, communicative reason is positioned to assume a central role in those spheres of culture where religion or tradition once provided a stable foundation of common practices and beliefs. And yet it is just as clear that the theory of communicative action leaves the contradictions of the subject and the State largely intact insofar as the antinomy of freedom and reason is merely transposed to the "intersubjective" sphere. For instance, after attempting to meet Kant's formal requirements for the discursive justification of basic norms, Habermas finds it necessary, but nearly impossible, to reintroduce the individualizing questions of inclination, inner nature, and happiness into political discourse.[27] Accordingly, he is left with a division between inner nature (passion) and the State that is as least as troubling as Hobbes's. Similarly, it has been said that when Habermas asserts the secularized – i.e., purely procedural, non-religious, and non-metaphysical – nature of communicative action as a means for grounding all rational claims, including those of legitimation, he is not offering a program for social action, but is in fact proposing a theoretical account of society that, if valid, would serve merely to have displaced the claims of enlightenment from the realm of reason to the domain of speech.[28] As the remarks of one Habermassian critic unwittingly reveal, the possibility of social and political transformation is thereby reduced: "there are no possible external sources of validity, since the sphere of validity is – conceptually – identical with the sphere of human speech."[29]

For Weber, by contrast, the basis for the legitimacy or "validity" of any given order reflects both the order of fact – "the probability that to a relevant degree the appropriate attitudes will exist"[30] – and also the obligatory and exemplary character of the order itself. These are what determine "the ultimate grounds of the validity of a domination"(II, p. 953), including those upon which the claims of law and the demands for obedience rest. The claim to legitimacy that orders inevitably make is initially revealed in the obligatoriness of

---

27 See Joel Whitebook, "Reason and Happiness: Some Psychoanalytic Themes in Critical Theory," in Richard J. Bernstein, ed., *Habermas and Modernity* (Cambridge, MA: MIT Press, 1985), pp. 140–60.

28 See Stanley Rosen, *Hermeneutics as Politics* (New York: Oxford University Press, 1987), pp. 11–15.

29 Albrecht Wellmer, "Reason, Utopia, and the *Dialectic of Enlightenment*," in Bernstein, ed., *Habermas and Modernity*, p. 53.

30 *Economy and Society* (hereafter *ES*), ed. Guenther Roth and Claus Wittich (Berkeley: University of California Press, 1978), I, p. 214; see also I, p. 31.

certain social actions. "Custom," "convention," and "usage," as well as the motives of self-interest may be sufficient to generate regular patterns of behavior, but these must be distinguished from the obligatory nature of actions in accordance with the norms of an established order:

> The validity of an order means more than the mere existence of a uniformity of social action determined by custom or self-interest. If furniture movers regularly advertise at the time many leases expire, this uniformity is determined by self-interest ... However, when a civil servant appears in his office daily at a fixed time, he does not act only on the basis of custom or self-interest which he could disregard if he wanted to; as a rule, his action is also determined by the validity of an order (viz., the civil service rules), which he fulfills partly because disobedience would be disadvantageous to him but also because its violation would be abhorrent to his sense of duty. The content of a social relationship may be called an order only when the conduct is, approximately or on the average, oriented toward determinable "maxims." An order may be called "valid" only when the orientation toward these maxims occurs, among other reasons, because it is in some appreciable way regarded by the actor as in some way obligatory or exemplary for him.[31]

If we accept the principle that the legitimizing basis of a given social order may be understood in terms of the expressions it demands of its participant-actors, we may then ask, what grounds the need for legitimation itself? What drives the establishment of the norms or "maxims" described above? Weber begins by accepting the premise that society constitutes a normative community which exerts a coercive force over the individual in the form of obligations, dispositions, and predispositions. Practices and usages constitute the embedded traces of this social force.[32] As Luciano Pellicani observed in a recent essay, two corollaries follow from this view: (1) "'uses' are *constitutive social factors*, and the social is only a gigantic symbolic building block, whose 'bricks' are the uses"; and (2) that "since a use is not a simple habit, but rather an impersonal order or prohibition which, like all orders and prohibitions, is compulsory, it is called an *enforced collective use*."[33] The "social" actions thus defined are not,

---

31 *Ibid.*, I, p. 31. In this instance I have modified the translation for the sake of clarity.
32 Cf. Ortega y Gasset, *En Torno al pacifismo*, in *Obras completas* (hereafter *OC*), 2nd edn (Madrid: Revista de Occidente, 1965), IV, p. 297.
33 Pellicani, "Ortega's Theory of Social Action," *Telos*, 70 (1986–87), 118. See also his "Storia e sociologia secondo Ortega y Gasset," in Lorenzo Infantino and Luciano Pellicani, eds., *Attualit di Ortega y Gasset* (Firenze: Le Monnier, 1984), pp. 115–33.

strictly speaking, the actions of actors. Rather, they are the actions of the society of which the actors partake. Insofar as social actions are thus organized as "orders," they have the potential of assuming an objectified and alien existence: they are external to individuals, exercise a certain pressure on them, and are able to resist their will. The social order thus transcends the ethical grounds of subjectivity in freedom insofar as it is not simply a function of the life-projects of individuals; and yet neither is the social order bound by the precincts of the moral, for it assumes no totalizing, God's-eye point of view. Rather, it demonstrates the anonymous, impersonal, and potentially coercive nature of norms.

And yet Weber also suggests that it would be impossible to speak of an order which is enforced but which makes no claims to legitimacy at all.[34] Weber thus radicalizes Hegel's idea that the social relations of a given epoch provide internal criteria for the moral imperatives in force in it, while tempering Hobbes's claim that there is no law that can, strictly speaking, be considered unjust.[35] For Hegel, the "content" of any moral judgment is fully revealed only in the network of the social determinations of any given period of history.[36] As we have already begun to see, individuals who inhabit societies of the "traditional" or pre-modern world accept a principle of human excellence or "virtue" that allows the demand for legitimation to be satisfied and the problem of social order to be resolved through the leadership of outstanding individuals, who in their example summarize and give expression to the moral force inherent in norms. The binding power of law in such societies – its ability to exact respect and command obedience – depends in turn on an unswerving faith in the goodness and power of the exemplar. It is in this way that theoretical ideals acquire social force. Indeed, the exemplar's status

---

34 See Paul Ricoeur, *Lectures on Ideology and Utopia*, ed. George H. Taylor (New York: Columbia University Press, 1986), p. 188. Cf. Wolfgang Schluchter, *The Rise of Western Rationalism*.

35 Hobbes argument is as follows: "The Law is made by the Soveraign Power, and all that is done by such Power, is warranted, and owned by every one of the people; and that which every man will have so, no man can say is unjust. It is in the Lawes of a Commonwealth, as in the Lawes of Gaming: whatsoever the Gamesters all agree on, is Injustice to none of them" (*Leviathan*, II, 30, p. 388).

36 As Lukács explained, "the claim of the particular moment to absolute validity forms the focal point of Hegel's later appreciative critique of the so-called philosophy of reflection." *The Young Hegel*, trans. Rodney Livingstone (London: Merlin Press, 1975), p. 163.

would remain both abstract and ineffective if it did not also generate a social aura or "charisma"; it is thus that exemplary actions are invested with normative social force.

For Weber, the demand for legitimation – which, we must hasten to add, may or may not be met[37] – may ultimately be understood as one of the multifarious effects of power. Like Nietzsche, Weber believes that the existence of power as a constant "striving" and "subduing" stands at the root of all social orders and drives the process of legitimation as a form of self-justification from above. (Recall that for Nietzsche, "all events in the organic world are a subduing, a *becoming master*, and all subduing and becoming master involves a fresh interpretation, an adaptation through which any previous 'meaning' and 'purpose' are necessarily obscured or even obliterated."[38]) But according to Weber there exists in addition the "observable need of any power, or even *of any advantage of life*," to justify itself:

The fates of human beings are not equal. Men differ in their states of health or wealth or social status or what not … Simple observation shows that in every such situation he who is more favored feels the never ceasing need to look upon his position as in some way "legitimate," upon his advantage as "deserved," and the other's disadvantage as being brought about by the latter's "fault." That the purely accidental causes of the difference may be ever so obvious makes no difference.   (*ES*, II, p. 953)

The different means by which norms are institutionalized, enacted, and invested with force may be linked to an historical critique of modernity that takes shape around a contrast between various types of social structure and the modes of authority implicit in them. In his discussion of the bases of legitimate authority, for instance, Weber described the tendency for legitimation to proceed by reference to some version of the "naturalistic" thesis described in chapter 1 above. We may on this basis explain the first of Weber's distinctions, viz., that between rational modes of legitimation, in which every operative belief is assumed to have a basis in or immanent relation to truth-

---

37 Whereas Marx spoke of the ways in which contradictions lead to economic crisis, Weber implies the possibility of a "legitimation crisis." See Charles Taylor, "Legitimation Crisis?" in *Philosophy and the Human Sciences: Philosophical Papers* (Cambridge: Cambridge University Press, 1985), II, pp. 248–88, and Habermas, *Legitimation Crisis*.

38 *Genealogy of Morals*, trans. Walter Kaufmann (New York: Random House, 1969), II, p. 12.

claims, and traditional, affectual, or religious modes of legitimation. As for Nietzsche, reference to nature as a legitimizing principle does not imply the existence of an objective, external state of affairs; "nature" possesses no intrinsic order or end but rather constitutes a point of appeal established by those in power to justify their position before those less privileged. Weber suggests that as long as the uneven distribution of power in society yields a stable social structure, the naturalistic thesis will remain unassailed as a legitimizing principle. Indeed, he seems to accept the view that this thesis can be challenged by no higher ideal of community, only threatened or upset by radical social change:

Every highly privileged group develops the myth of its natural, especially its blood superiority. Under conditions of stable distribution of power and, consequently, of status order, that myth is accepted by the negatively privileged strata. Such a situation exists as long as the masses continue in that natural state of theirs in which thought about the order of domination remains but little developed, which means, as long as no urgent needs render the state of affairs "problematical." But in times in which the class situation has become unambiguously and openly visible to everyone as the factor determining every man's individual fate, that very myth of the highly privileged about everyone having deserved his particular lot has often become one of the most passionately hated objects of attack.

(*ES*, ɪɪ, pp. 953–54)

Given the tendency for groups in power to claim legitimacy in the name of such "naturalistic" criteria as race, geography, or blood, the emergence of rational modes of legitimation would seem anomalous indeed. Whereas the legitimation of power on the basis of naturalistic criteria appears inherently to supply the exemplarity and obligatoriness essential to the establishment of a valid order, it is not immediately apparent how a rationalized structure can provide these qualities. Insofar as rational modes of legitimation tend toward a formal rather than a substantive interpretation of the nature of obligations, they tend to dissolve into purely legalistic forms of authority. The promise of the modern, bureaucratic State is embodied in its legal system as a principle of fairness, in its economic system as one of efficiency, and in its administrative procedures as one of effectiveness. Indeed, in a fully rationalized world, the belief in legitimacy would collapse to a belief in formal legality; an appeal to the procedures through which an obligation comes about would suffice as its sole warranty. Already Christopher Hill suggested that the secularizing tendencies of the early modern age were reinforced by a shift from oaths of fealty to legal contracts as the dominant mode for the expression of loyalty, obligation, and consent.[39] And yet legality as such – as "enactments which are formally correct and which have been made in the accustomed manner ... independently of the highest legal principles and of the ideal interests of the ruled"[40] – cannot establish the motivations without which the very existence of the social bond would be endangered. Indeed, social orders that are sustained by instrumentally rational reasons alone are in Weber's view the most unstable structures imaginable, for they cannot produce the authority of exemplariness presumed necessary for every valid social order.

Reorientation in ethics

In *After Virtue* and in his *Short History of Ethics*, Alasdair MacIntyre described the ethical context for the emergence of the modern State as one in which authority was displaced from a web of closely related obligations to one in which the principal relationships came to take place among freely acting but dissociated subjects. MacIntyre and others have distinguished the principles of a "virtuous" society as one whose members share a substantive conception of the ends of man, hence of the qualities and dispositions people should strive to exhibit. They share this conception of virtue not only privately, as individuals, but publicly, and hold that their community, in its social and political activity, exhibits qualities, which they, as citizens, have a responsibility to promote. In that sense they treat the lives of other members of their own community as part of their lives.[41]

The model of a "virtuous society" would be compelling indeed were it not also the case that such an ideal has tended to take shape

39 Hill, "From Oaths to Interest," in *Society and Puritanism in Pre-Revolutionary England* (New York: Schocken Books, 1964), pp. 382–419.
40 See Schluchter, *The Rise of Western Rationalism*, p. 85.
41 MacIntyre, *After Virtue* (Notre Dame: University of Notre Dame Press, 1981); *A Short History of Ethics* (New York: Macmillan, 1966). This understanding of virtue may be distinguished from some versions of political conservatism, which hold that present society, with its existing institutions, is itself a representation of the virtuous ideal for the special reason that its history and experience are privileged examples of goodness and represent better guides than any non-historical and therefore abstract deduction of virtue from first principles could provide. See, for instance, Ronald Dworkin, *A Matter of Principle*, 198–99.

along fiercely conservative and indeed anti-modern lines. It would thus be better to describe the political nature of modernity in terms of a shift from a hierarchical society to a functionally differentiated society organized around a liberal conception of the good. The result of this shift was a demand for legitimation which Hobbes and others attempted to meet by recourse to the theory of natural law, the notion of political representation, and the fiction of a social contract. These principles in turn allow modern political theorists to distinguish the claims of sovereignty made by medieval rulers from the creation in the modern sovereign of an "Artificial Man":

In the Middle Ages the legitimacy of the final authority, the sovereign prince, was bound up with all the other ties of obligation and duty binding superiors and inferiors. These ties are by the seventeenth century fatally loosened. Man and man confront one another in an arena where the cash nexus of the free-market economy and the power of the centralizing state have together helped to destroy the social bonds on which traditional claims to legitimacy were founded. But how to legitimate the new order and especially the sovereign power? Claims to divine right and scriptural authority founder on arbitrariness. So the state must fall back on appeal, implicit or explicit, to social contract.[42]

In light of the rational appeal of the notion of a social contract, however, how can we account for the fact that the Hobbesian theory of the State turns away from the need to consider its beginnings in historical terms? As we have already seen in the case of Descartes, the genealogy of the subject conforms to the patterns of rational self-assertion characteristic of a specifically modern consciousness. It takes place in analytical rather than historical terms. The historical need for legitimacy is in this case met through claims about the *scientific* nature of politics, which is taken to represent a definitive form of human self-assertion. Indeed, Descartes articulates the assumptions that will be taken up by modern politics through the experiences of doubt and self-alienation figured in the drama of skepticism; these are that difference may be located within the interpersonal space that separates the subject-self from a community of others, rather than in

42 MacIntyre, *A Short History of Ethics* p. 156. It must also be said that a complex process of secularization is involved here, insofar as the notion of the "Artificial Man" represents an extension of one of the king's "two bodies" theorized in the Middle Ages. For a full elaboration of this topic, see Ernst Kantorowicz, *The King's Two Bodies* (Princeton: Princeton University Press, 1957), and Hegel, *Philosophy of Right*, sec. 275–86.

the relationship between the space of beings and the Logos. No less than Descartes, Hobbes's understanding of the nature of reason is an expression of the historical consciousness or ideology of a "new age" insofar as this remains consistent with the goal of attaining peace among subjects in the State: "When Novelty can breed no trouble, nor disorder in a State, men are not generally so much inclined to the reverence of Antiquity, as to preferre Ancient Errors, before New and well proved Truth"(*Leviathan*, "A Review and Conclusion," p. 726). Hobbes proposes to sweep away the "filth and fraud" of Ancient Greek philosophy[43] that encouraged men to look at the universe as endowed in an animistic way with near-magical essences:

The Philosophy-schooles, through all the Universities of Christendome, grounded upon certain Texts of *Aristotle*, teach another doctrine; and say, For the cause of *Vision*, that the thing seen, sendeth forth on every side a *visible species* (in English) a *visible shew, apparition*, or *aspect*, or *a being seen*; the receiving whereof into the Eye, is *Seeing*. And for the cause of *Hearing*, that the thing heard, sendeth forth an *Audible species*, that is, an *Audible aspect*, or *Audible being seen*; which entering at the Eare, maketh Hearing. Nay for the cause of *Understanding* also, they say the thing Understood sendeth forth *intelligible species* that is, an *intelligible being seen*; which comming into the Understanding, makes us Understand.   (*Leviathan*, I, 1, pp. 86–87)

Hobbes's disputes with Descartes notwithstanding, he accepts the principles of the "new mathesis" which, unlike the Platonic understanding of mathematics, is expected to apply directly to the motions of bodies in the sublunary world. Hobbes is motivated by the will to locate a natural principle, foundation, or ground by which one can produce, with scientific precision, political institutions which will regulate the affairs of men with the certitude and reliability of a clock.[44] In order to achieve this goal, Hobbes initiates a "genetic" form of argument, free from the constraints of actual history, that is meant to apply across all domains of knowledge. According to the first chapters of *De Corpore*, for instance, knowledge consists in the inquiry into first principles, or, as Hobbes says, into "first causes." Once a thing has been "defined" in this way, all of its properties can be derived in a strictly deductive fashion. But a definition remains inadequate insofar as it presupposes that the world possesses any

43 *De corpore*, in *English Works*, ed. William Molesworth (London, 1839–45), I, Ep. Ded., ix.
44 See Hannah Arendt's discussion of the transformation of reason in *The Human Condition* (Chicago: University of Chicago Press, 1958).

special "qualities" for the subject, including those established by history, religion, and tradition. Hence, as in Descartes, the production of valid knowledge is contingent on the elimination of any "secondary" qualities and in this sense on the "disenchantment" of the world: "Seeing there are no signes, nor fruit of *Religion*, but in Man onley; there is no cause to doubt, but that the seed of *Religion*, is also onley in Man; and consisteth in some peculiar quality, or at least in some eminent degree thereof, not to be found in other Living creatures" (*Leviathan*, I, 12, p. 168). If true definitions must be "genetic" or "causal" in nature, this means that knowledge not only has to answer the question of *what* a thing is, but of its derivation or generation. In the case of the State, this "generation" is not understood as a physical or historical process; on the contrary, Hobbes's argument acts to conceal the historical genesis of the Absolutist State in civil war through legitimizing arguments that claim their basis in the procedures of pure rational construction. As Ernst Cassirer pointed out, Hobbes demands genetic or causal definitions even in the field of geometry: like the State, the objects of geometry must be constructed in order to be made fully intelligible.[45] Thus when Hobbes describes the transition from the natural to the social state, he is not interested in the empirical origin of the *polis*. The point at issue is not the history but the *validity* of the social and political order. Once the chain of cause and effect and the manner of generation have been discovered – which it is Hobbes's claim to have done – it is bound to appear that the old moral philosophers grossly exaggerated the importance of prudence (see *Leviathan*, IV, ch. 46). For Hobbes, prudence consists in the ability to determine the consequences or effects of one's actions; it does not, as for Aristotle,

45 As Leo Strauss points out in his outline of Hobbes's theoretical critique of religion, this helps explain why any intelligible idea of God is impossible, for God is not "generated." The argument anticipates Kant in the following way. If the pursuit of genetic explanations leads men to believe that there is a First Cause, such a notion remains nonetheless inadmissible to reason: we are incapable of imagining anything we have not already perceived through our senses, or which is not composed of elements known through the senses. Knowledge of the infinite is not accessible to finite thought. Thus while Hobbes also anticipates Kant's attempt to construct a place for religion "within the limits of reason alone," the idea of God must remain only a vague premonition, not an object of true knowledge. See Strauss, *Spinoza's Critique of Religion*, trans. E. M. Sinclair (New York: Schocken Books, 1965), pp. 98–99. On the larger issue of Hobbes's "genetic" argument see Cassirer, *The Myth of the State* (New Haven: Yale University Press, 1973), pp. 173–74.

involve the judgment of appropriate actions. As a result, the task of political science becomes essentially technical, its practitioners political technicians (bureaucrats) or professional "ideologists."[46]

Hobbes's effort at demystification is carried out through the rejection of all traditional assumptions about the existence of a *summum bonum* or *telos* in favor of a frank appraisal of the nature of man: "there is no such *Finis ultimis*, (utmost ayme) nor *Summum bonum*, (greatest Good) as is spoken of in the books of the old Morrall Philosophers" (*Leviathan*, I, 11, p. 160). He sees the search for satisfaction as motivated by a "continuall progresse of desire, from one object to another" and by a quest for power after power: "I put for a general inclination of all mankind, a perpetuall and restlesse desire of Power after power, that ceaseth only in Death" (*ibid.*). Hobbesian political science rests on a series of ethical premises that are characteristically modern insofar as they define the good in terms of impressions, sentiments, perceptions, and desires, rather than as inherent in the cosmos or as an intuitable ideal. In contrast to Aristotle, who conceives of a natural context and ethical purpose for man – who argues that we desire what is good and hate what is evil – Hobbes believes that the good is what we desire and that the bad is that to which we are averse:

> But whatsoever is the object of any mans Appetite or Desire; that is it, which he for his part calleth *Good*: And the object of his Hate, and Aversion, *Evill*; And of his contempt, *Vile* and *Inconsiderable*. For these words of Good, Evill, and Contemptible, are ever used with relation to the person that useth them: There being nothing simply and absolutely so; nor any common Rule of Good and Evill, to be taken from the nature of the objects themselves.
>
> (*Leviathan*, I, 6, p. 120)

Indeed, it is only through language that men can formulate truly universal propositions at all, "there being nothing in the world Universall but Names" (*Leviathan*, I, 4, p. 102). The moral world is a product of human convention or custom; it is, no less than the Kantian world, a construction:

> we ourselves *make* the principles – that is, the causes of justice (namely laws and covenants) – whereby it is known what *justice* or what *equity*, and their

---

46 See Jürgen Habermas, "The Classical Doctrine of Politics," in *Theory and Practice*, trans. John Viertel (Boston: Beacon Press, 1974), pp. 41–81, and Barry Cooper, *The End of History: An Essay on Modern Hegelianism* (Toronto: University of Toronto Press, 1984), p. 40.

opposites *injustice* and *inequality*, are. For before covenants and laws were drawn up, neither justice nor injustice, neither public good nor public evil, was natural among men.[47]

And yet while the principle of constructivism, witnessed in the formation of agreements in language, is an expression of human freedom, these no longer carry the weight of oaths of fealty. Conventional agreements establish "merely moral"obligations that require the existence of an enforcement body:

The force of Words, being ... too weak to hold men to the performance of their Covenants; there are in mans [sic] nature, but two imaginable helps to strengthen it. And those are either a Feare of the consequences of breaking their word; or a Glory, or Pride in appearing not to need to break it. This latter is a generosity too rarely found to be presumed on ... The passion to be reckoned upon, is Fear.   (*Leviathan*, I, 14, p. 200)

Hobbes thus stands at the beginning of a reorientation in ethics that regards the administration and enforcement of law as central to its power. The law may in some respects always be taken to refer to the power of the sword, but with Hobbes we see that a power whose task is the self-preservation of citizens from their own self-destruction requires a continuous regulatory mechanism. The result is a condition which Foucault accurately diagnosed as one in which legal relations come to be more and more the norm, and in which judicial institutions are increasingly incorporated into a continuum of apparatuses (medical, administrative, and so on) whose functions are for the most part those of enforcement, compliance, and regulation.[48] But whereas Foucault argued the thesis that a "normalizing" society is the historical outcome of a technology of power directed toward the control of life, the arguments presented above would suggest that the technology of power is the consequence rather than the cause of a transformation in the nature of norms.

As we have begun to see, the beginning of modern political philosophy is marked by a reorientation in ethics characterized by

47 Hobbes, *De Homine*, in *Man and Citizen*, trans. and ed. Bernard Gert, T. S. K. Scott-Craig, and Charles T. Wood (New York: Anchor Books, 1972), 10.5. Lawrence Manley discusses this passage in connection with Hobbes's nominalism in *Convention 1500–1750* (Cambridge MA: Harvard University Press, 1980), p. 284.

48 See for instance Foucault, *History of Sexuality I: An Introduction*, p. 144.

two principal features. On the one hand, an interest in self-preservation replaces aristocratic virtue as the basis of political life; and on the other hand, politics is transformed from a variable and self-reflective praxis dependent on prudence into a technical science. Together, these factors produce a dramatic rise in the importance of rhetoric in political life. This is evident in Hobbes's *Brief* of Aristotle's *Rhetoric* (1637) and in the prefatory essay to his translation of Thucydides' *History of the Peloponnesian War* (1629), in which he takes up the problematic relationship between truth and elocution.[49] In Hegel's analysis of modernity, the demand for political rhetoric first arises when men become unsure of how to certify honor. Instead of confronting the danger of death and, perhaps, sacrificing himself in battle, the nobleman is transformed into a courtier, who can express his honor only through discourse. But in contrast to the discourse of the "noble soul," which terminates in the dignified silence of death, the court is marked by a fundamental heterogeneity with respect to the forms and styles of speech. This means that in order to gain recognition and command respect, the modern nobleman replaces heroic actions by discrete and calculated forms of speech. In Hegel's reading of modernity the result is a dialectical inversion in which the good man must become "bad" in order to provide a foundation for political discourse; the noble individual must become base, and precisely for the sake of the State.[50]

For Hegel, the modern nobility remembers the heroism of service; the advantage of service, as a form of duty, lies in its rejection of self-interest and its commitment to the interests of the State; in Hegel's words, it "sacrifices the single individual to the universal, thereby

---

49 Concerning Hobbes's relationship to Humanist rhetoric, see the contrasting positions of Strauss, *The Political Philosophy of Hobbes*; Kahn, *Rhetoric, Prudence, and Skepticism in the Renaissance*; and Miriam Reik, *The Golden Lands of Thomas Hobbes* (Detroit: Wayne State University Press, 1977).

50 See Stanley Rosen, *Hegel*, pp. 188–89. Frank Whigham provides a useful discussion of some of the literary ramifications in his chapter on "Tropes of Social Hierarchy: Gentle and Base," in *Ambition and Privilege: The Social Tropes of Elizabethan Courtesy Theory* (Berkeley: University of California Press, 1984), pp. 63–87. Whigham suggests that the goal of such tropes was to provide an absolute distinction between the ruling class and its subjects; of course, such a project makes sense only where such distinctions were in doubt. As Gary Schmidgall has shown, this has notable aesthetic consequences; see his *Shakespeare and the Courtly Aesthetic* (Berkeley: University of California Press, 1981), especially ch. 4, "The Courtly Aesthetic: Form and Expression," and ch. 5, "The Polarities of Courtly Art."

bringing this into existence – the *person*, one who voluntarily renounces possessions and enjoyment and acts and is effective in the interests of the ruling power" (*PhS*, sec. 503). But at the same time Hegel recognizes that this type of heroism easily loses any critical edge and quickly reveals the emptiness of its stance; it manifests itself as a mere "vocal reflection" of the ideal of duty and simply feeds the ruling monarch's absolutizing identification with the State: "The heroism of silent service becomes the heroism of flattery. This vocal reflection of service ... back into this self the extreme of universal power, making that power, which is at first only implicit, into a power that is explicit with an existence of its own ... The result is ... now an *unlimited monarch*: *unlimited*, because the language of flattery raises this power into its purified *universality*." The absolutism of the monarch can only be limited by his own awareness that his identity proceeds from the flattery of the court: "[He] knows that the nobles not only are ready and prepared for the service of the state power, but that they group themselves round the throne as an *ornamental setting*, and that they are continually *telling* him who sits on it what he *is*" (*PhS*, sec. 511, pp. 310–11).[51]

As numerous scholars have recognized, these conditions are anticipated in the literature of courtliness, and in particular in Machiavelli, who warns against flattery, but who nonetheless advises the Prince to surround himself with trusted counsellors.[52] Machiavelli's interest in the quality of *virtù* as a source of personal power and verbal energy represents a transformation of the heroic ideal of excellence (*arete*) in light of the fact that the conditions for nobility have grown uncertain. As formulated in *The Prince*, *virtù* is not to be identified with any or all of the classical virtues; rather, it represents a form of self-reliance and names those areas of action wherein men

51 Pascal offers a related analysis: "The fact that kings are habitually seen in the company of guards, drums, officers and all the things which prompt automatic responses of respect and fear has the result that, when they are sometimes alone and unaccompanied, their features are enough to strike respect and fear into their subjects, because we make no mental distinctions between their person and the retinue with which they are normally seen to be associated. And the world, which does not know that this is the effect of habit, believes it to derive from some natural force, hence such sayings as 'The character of divinity is stamped on his features.'" Pascal, *Pensées*, trans. A. J. Krailsheimer (Harmondsworth: Penguin Books, 1966), fr. 25, p. 36.
52 See *The Prince*, ch. 23, "Quomodo adulatores sint fugiendi" ("How to Avoid Flatterers"). For an analysis of historical cases see J. H. Elliott, *Richelieu and Olivares* (Cambridge: Cambridge University Press, 1984).

are free to exert their greatest abilities. As such, it stands opposed to *fortuna* and indeed to all those areas of contingency which must be submitted to human control. (In a famous passage, Machiavelli writes that "Fortune is a woman, and if you wish to master her, you must strike and beat her, and you will see that she allows herself to be more easily vanquished by the rash and the violent man than by those who proceed more slowly and coldly."[53]) In practical terms, *virtù* must be exercised if the Prince is to assert his control in newly acquired or non-hereditary states. Understood in this sense, *virtù* is a secularized term that has shed its Christian connotations of "virtue" as the obedience to natural laws or to conscience and has come instead to indicate the mixture of foresight, cunning, and opportunism necessary in order to achieve superiority in military and political affairs. Hence Machiavelli praises Ferdinand of Spain for his *reputed* "liberality" (i.e. for its effect on his subjects), but censures authentic liberality as a quality that readily undermines itself: "The very act of using [liberality] causes it to lose the faculty of being used, and will either impoverish you and make you despised, or it will make you rapacious and odious" (ch. 16, p. 71).

As these necessarily brief examples may help to suggest, the transition from hierarchical to differentiated societies was mediated by the existence of a social environment in which the conditions for virtue were uncertain and in which the procedures of rhetoric, including those of exemplary "imitation," were called upon to establish new precepts. However, if virtue is transformed into *virtù* or personal force, and if politics is seen simply as the province of self-assertion, the result may be a disintegration of the conditions necessary to sustain the *polis* itself. We can in this respect understand the need for a "transvaluation"of ethics that would take the conditions outlined in Machiavelli's *Prince* as given, but which would transform the freedom of *virtù* into a liberal theory of the good. This is the positive side of the project undertaken by Hobbes. The modern reorientation of ethics, and its eventual reorganization into a theory of sovereignty and subjectivity in the liberal State, is reinforced and its underlying principles are set forth in Hobbes's *De Homine*, which accepts the premise that neither virtue nor the good exists in itself: "one cannot speak of something as being *simply good*; since

53 I follow the translation of *The Prince* by Christian Detmold (New York: Washington Square Press, 1963), p. 114.

whatsoever is good, is good for someone or other ... Therefore good is said to be relative to person, place, and time."[54] These and similar ethical premises stake a claim for a specifically modern politics through the transformation of the uncertain conditions of virtue and the consequent need for legitimation into the grounds of political self-assertion: given the fact that all political orders rest on claims of legitimacy, and given as well the fact that the modern State is skeptical of all claims about the pre-existing nature of the good, its legitimacy must depend on the agreements that rational subjects make among themselves. For Aristotle, politics was a continuation of ethics and the ethical character of action was inseparable from custom and law. Beginning with Hobbes, and culminating in Kant, however, the ethical conduct of the individual who is rational and inwardly free is set apart from the legality of his external, political actions. Morality is divided from legality, and both are separated from political practice, which attains a dubious status as the technical expertise required for the efficient administration of the State. In this we see the negative side of Hobbes, who both transcends and reconfirms the Machiavellian interpretation of politics as technique.

Like Hobbes, the principal thinkers of the Enlightenment attempted to move from a "scientific" understanding of human nature to conclusions about the authority of moral rules and precepts. But, as Alasdair MacIntyre argued, any such project was bound to fail, because of an irrepressible discrepancy between their shared conception of moral rules and precepts on the one hand and what was shared in their conception of human nature on the other.[55] Since the purpose of both Classical and traditional Christian ethics was to enable man to progress from his present state to his true end, the elimination of any notion of essential human nature and with it the abandonment of any notion of a *telos* leaves behind a moral framework deprived of any substantive content. On the one hand there remains an empty "context" for morality, consisting of a set of injunctions; as expressions of human rationality and freedom, these are reduced to their purely formal dimension as Kantian "maxims" or rules. Yet at the same time there remains a view of untutored human nature rooted in the passions which the rules can only constrain: "The eighteenth-century moral philosophers engaged in what was an

---

54 Hobbes, *De Homine*, trans. Bernard Gert, in *Man and Citizen* (Atlantic Highlands, NJ: Humanities Press, 1968), XI, 4, p. 47.   55 *After Virtue*, p. 50.

inevitably unsuccessful project; for they did indeed attempt to find a rational basis for their moral beliefs in a particular understanding of human nature, while inheriting a set of moral injunctions on the one hand and a conception of human nature on the other which had been expressly designed to be discrepant with each other. This discrepancy was not removed by their revised beliefs about human nature" (*After Virtue*, pp. 52–53).

In this and other ways, the "scientific" claims of politics demonstrate their inability to establish the conditions of community or to instantiate the goal of happiness for the liberal State they are said to justify. Thus Habermas must reinsert the question of happiness back into an ethics that excludes its principles in favor of an "intersubjective" reading of what remains an essentially scientific account of speech. Aristotle accepted the fact that politics could not be compared in its claims to knowledge with a rigorous science because its subject-matter, the just and the excellent, is set within the context of a variable and contingent praxis and lacks the closure of ontological constancy and logical necessity.[56] But Hobbes wants to "perfect" the science of politics in order to secure knowledge of the essential nature of justice itself. And yet Hobbes can posit no means, aside from technique, by which to move from the knowledge of first principles to the realm of political practice exemplified in the laws and compacts of civil association. Indeed, the relations of cause and effect in the natural world allow nothing to be deduced as to the relationships among persons, for the former are completely independent of human will and are thus irrelevant to the use of means by men. At the same time, Hobbes embraces a notion of reason that is forced to "overcome" the "irrational" passions; his anthropology regards man in the state of nature as involved in a war of "all against all." Pre-political, "natural" man is consumed by the fear and dread of violent death, while the political subject must consent to live under formal rules. In other words, the need for a sovereign and for a social contract is premised on a belief that the condition of nature is one of conflict. The result is a never fully resolved tension between the "natural" condition of man and his political destiny in the State. As we have already begun to see, the legitimizing basis of the modern State rests on a theory that empowers subjects to "authorize" the actions of a sovereign; similarly, the social contract is taken as a

56 See Habermas, "The Classical Doctrine of Politics."

response to the mutuality of needs that impel the formation of the State.[57] To be sure, these and other concepts may be regarded as "fictions" used to describe man's political condition as it stands; but if this is so, then the State can only be justified as the suppression, by rational agreement or "contract," of an original violence that threatens always to return.

The conflict between the subject and the State is reinforced by Hobbes's attempt to generate the conditions of community by reasoning from the circumstances of autonomous individuals. Hobbes considers human nature in terms of the internal structure and powers of the individual man, both of which would be proper to him even if he were the sole example of the species. Hobbesian man is, Crusoe-like, a solitary individual.[58] And yet it would be inaccurate to say that Hobbesian man is *simply* solitary, for just as in the case of Robinson Crusoe, it is clear that Hobbesian man cannot for long exist alone. Rather, he stands at the center of a radical conflict between his own solitary and warlike nature and the natural destiny of mankind as a social species: "men have no pleasure, (but, on the contrary a great deal of griefe) in keeping company, where there is no power able to over-awe them all. For every man looketh that his companion should value him, at the same rate he sets upon himselfe: And upon all signes of contempt, or undervaluing, naturally endeavours, as far as he dares (which amongst them that have no common power, to keep them in quiet, is far enough to make them destroy each other,) to extort a greater value from his contemners, by dommage" (*Leviathan*, I, 13, p. 185).

Beginning from the "natural" equality of all men, Hobbes is impelled to deduce the principle of competition as the dominant motive force in political life:

Nature hath made men so equall, in the faculties of body, and mind; as that though there be found one man sometimes manifestly stronger in body, or

---

57 To be sure, related elements can be identified in Ancient law. See the venerable volume by Henry Sumner Maine, *Ancient Law; Its Connection with the Early History of Society and its Relation to Modern Ideas* (1897; rpt. Gloucester: P. Smith, 1970). The points to be emphasized in this regard are twofold: first, that the novelty lies in the particular conjuncture of these elements; and second, that modern political science, like modern philosophy generally, is indeed unintelligible without some reference to Ancient philosophy. To believe otherwise would be to accept complicity in the historical ideology of modernity.

58 See Michael Oakeshott, *Hobbes on Civil Association* (Berkeley: University of California Press, 1975), p. 32.

of quicker mind than another; yet when all is reckoned together, the difference between man, and man, is not so considerable, as that one man can thereupon claim to himself any benefit, to which another may not pretend, as well as he ... From this equality of ability, ariseth equality of hope in the attaining of our Ends. And therefore if any two men desire the same thing, which nevertheless they cannot both enjoy, they become enemies; and in the way to their End ... endeavor to destroy or subdue one another.

(*Leviathan.*, I, 13, pp. 183–84)

The thesis of the equality of all men – as Hegel said, an equality of weakness[59] – forms the groundwork for a concept of Natural Law that serves as a legitimizing principle for the derivation of the authority of the State. Consider the premise that reason is not the intuition or apprehension of pre-existing qualities or of a natural order, but rather the ability to see the connections between effects and causes, to "reckon upon consequences." The limit of one's rationality, the true measure of human greatness, but also the source of vanity and pride, is experienced in the adverse consequences that follow from the breakdown of one's powers of calculation. In particular, the threat of mortal danger shatters dreams of superiority and awakens natural man to his political destiny. Otherwise put, the priority of self-assertion expresses in existential terms the precedence of freedom over nature. This supersession of the natural leads to a political interest in self-assertion and to a demand for the acknowledgment of superiority among equals. While there may be no charismatic hero, no heroic exemplar to be found among the citizens of this disenchanted world, men continue nonetheless to imagine themselves superior. But they cannot find this superiority confirmed unless it is recognized by others. If it should be denied, they will be offended; and if they are acknowledged, then the other, in principle an equal, will be injured. In either case, one or the other member of the group is slighted and seeks revenge.

In the Hobbesian analysis, honor is the recognition of an excess or superiority of power by others. Its genesis and effects may be explained in the following terms: man is impelled not by the good, but by desire; he is driven by desire to overcome his natural condition, which is one of war. The means for the satisfaction of desire constitute the sources of human power. Since in any conflict between two human beings the surplus power of the one over the

59 Hegel, *Lectures on the Philosophy of History*, III, p. 317.

other will be decisive, that surplus is in effect absolute power. The recognition of this excess is the basis of honor and prestige; as Leo Strauss said, "what is at stake [in the Hobbesian analysis of desire] is not the enjoyment of the object desired at any time, but simply and solely the attainment of the object as a means to the recognition of one's power."[60] But the interest in honor does not lead to the cessation of desire, as the achievement of a final goal, because desire has no final goal; rather, honor and prestige themselves become the renewed objects of desire, so that life is the constantly refueled desire for recognition, driven by the excess of power.

Hobbes thus anticipates Hegel's belief that the human demand for acknowledgment, on which the possibility of community is based, is modeled after a fight to the death between interdependent parties who assumes the role of "master" and "slave." Both accept the belief that the natural condition of man is war rather than peace. For Hegel too the basic drive of the modern self is towards the reaffirmation of self-certitude in desire, and infinite desire serves only to frustrate itself by generating an intolerable dependence upon the object desired. But for Hegel the driving forces of subjectivity are not the preservation of the self or the search for peace, but the enrichment of Spirit. By claiming that self-expression can be gained through the recognition of another, in the context of human community, Hegel, unlike Hobbes, combines the principle of freedom as a higher manifestation of the will to self-assertion with the need for community. Phrased in other terms, it could be said that the structure of human self-consciousness for Hegel results from the collective internalization of the relationship between self and other.[61] As Richard Bernstein has shown, Hegel represents in this and many other ways a powerful alternative to the neo-Aristotelianism of MacIntyre and the linguistic intersubjectivity of Habermas.[62]

In the Hobbesian war of "each against each," however, every individual aims principally at the destruction of another: "a combatant

---

60 Strauss, *Spinoza's Critique of Religion*, p. 89.

61 See Seyla Benhabib, "Obligation, Contract and Exchange," in Z. A. Pelczynski, ed., *The State and Civil Society: Studies in Hegel's Political Philosophy* (Cambridge: Cambridge University Press, 1984), p. 169.

62 See especially Bernstein's review of MacIntyre, "Nietzsche or Aristotle?: Reflections on Alasdair MacIntyre's *After Virtue*," in Bernstein, *Philosophical Profiles* (Philadelphia: University of Pennsylvania Press, 1986), pp. 115–40, and also his "Why Hegel Now?" in that same volume, pp. 141–76.

in such a war does not fear any particular thing, or any particular moment, but fears for his entire being; what he feels is the fear of death, the absolute master."[63] For Hobbes, only an "artificial" state is able to overcome this "natural" condition of war. It is established when both combatants are terrified and "choose their sovereign ... for fear of one another" (*Leviathan*, II, 20, p. 252). Their pride and vanity thus "dialectically" overcome, the two find themselves predisposed to trust one another enough to satisfy their common need for self-preservation.[64] Each having seen in the other not simply an enemy to be killed, but the face of death itself, both are impelled to seek protection in the State. The basis of their relationship in fear and violence is thus "externalized" in the State, and they as subjects are "constrained" by the threat of their own violence to be free. The result is a "secularization" of political power that has its correlate in the sovereign himself. In fashioning the hypothetical agreement that founds the State, everyone covenants with everyone else "as if every man should say to every man, *I authorize and give up my right of Governing my selfe, to this Man, or to this Assembly of men, on this condition, that thou give up thy Right to him, and Authorize all his Actions in like manner.*" Having done so, thereby is created "that great Leviathan, or rather, to speak more reverently ... that *Mortall God*, to which we owe under the *Immortal God*, our peace and defence" (*Leviathan*, II, 17, p. 227). For the political subject, the prime cause of moral laws is no longer to be located in a transcendent God, but in the mortal power that puts an end to civil war.

More specifically, Hobbes anticipates Hegel's interpretation of modernity when he argues that the first stage in the "disenchantment" of the world was the demystification of religion; this took concrete shape in the Protestant Reformation, in which the yoke of papal power was thrown off. But it was not until the religious wars in France and, more importantly, the civil wars in England, that the bonds that had subjected the conscience of men to the decrees of formalized religions could be broken. Only then could man accede to a higher plane of reason; once the potential for mystification was recognized, then it was seen not only as rational but as *necessary* for

---

63 Koselleck, *Critique and Crisis*, p. 31.
64 For an excellent version of the "dialectical" interpretation, see Barry Cooper's interpretation of Hobbes in *The End of History* (Toronto: University of Toronto Press, 1984).

men to seek protection in the State. For an age that claimed to have
achieved the enlightenment of reason by banishing myth, fancy, and
superstitions, however, the decisive moment in the "disenchantment"
of the world is the explanation of religion as the product of anxiety
and dreams; it is the complement and culmination of the process of
enlightenment. Hobbes was, on this basis, able to link the critique of
religion as the source of mystifications (and, ultimately, of those
anxieties which obstruct the human search for peace) with the
Enlightenment's modernizing emphasis on self-assertion, autonomy,
progress, and the work of reason. Once this connection was made
complete, which it was Hobbes's claim to have begun (and Hume's to
have completed), it seems that there should be nothing to which the
"withdrawal of the gods" could coherently refer.

Hobbes's account of religion advances the goals of enlightenment
as founded on a paradigm of self-consciousness that distinguishes
between the "natural seed of religion," located in anxiety and dreams,
and the "culture" that religion took on within paganism and
subsequently revelation (see *Leviathan*, I, 12, pp. 168–83). This
distinction has served to orient the political critique of religion along
two divergent lines. Hobbes believes that religion arises initially from
an intellectual error or a failure in one's capacity to reckon. It springs
from the fear generated by the discrepancy between one's ability to
imagine adverse or favorable outcomes and one's inability to calculate
consequent courses of action. Conversely, an interest in prophecy and
prayer is the sign of a potential for mystification, and is easily
encouraged by feelings of grandeur or pride. One who claims to
speak on the basis of divine inspiration thus implies that he feels "an
ardent desire to speak, or some strong opinion of himself"; but since
he can produce "no naturall or sufficient reason" (*Leviathan*, III, 32, p.
411), the "supernatural inspiration" which any such religious virtuoso
might claim is nothing other than pride or *gloriatio* in thinly disguised
form.[65]

If religious belief is generated as Hobbes indicated, then to
recognize its principles is already to begin to overcome its seductions.
(Cf. Pascal, who writes that "Heathen religion has no foundations
today. It is said that it once had them in oracles that spoke. But what

---

65 Cf. Leo Strauss's gloss of Hobbes: "*Gloriatio* is the basis of prophecy, of the claim
    to revelation ... according to Hobbes' doctrine, *gloriatio* is the root of all evil"
    (*Spinoza's Critique of Religion*, p. 97).

are the books that assert this? Are they so reliable by virtue of their authors?" *Pensées*, fr. 242, p. 103.) But whereas the anxiety and fears from which religion stems might be "rationally" overcome, the culture of religion cannot so easily be suppressed, for its basis is not "natural" or even "psychological," but institutional; it takes as its aim what Hobbes would describe as "the education of mankind to obedience, peace, love, and ordered society." With this, Hobbes articulates the normative function of religion as articulated, albeit in vastly different connections, by figures like Weber and Durkheim. For his part, Hobbes attempted to pursue the normative critique of religion along rational lines and so was compelled to accept as binding and true the principle that the "culture" of religion must, despite the demands of conscience, never be incompatible with the interests of the State.[66] This was to be insured by reducing the purview of "conscience" to an inner sphere and by absorbing all "external" aspects of religion within the State. As Strauss said, "politics is to be a part of religion; religion can and never must contradict politics" (*Spinoza's Critique of Religion*, p. 96). If, on Hobbes's account, religion was for the pagans originally a part of politics – if at one time there was no distinction between (religious) custom and (civil) law – and if the pagan rulers thus contrived that the populace should never be inclined to rebel, then in the modern age religion has become antithetical to the State precisely because in it custom and law have been split apart. In Hobbes's view, subjects have come to obey a divided authority; on the one hand they respect the temporal authority of the State, which is a visible power, while on the other hand they feel commanded by a spiritual force, whose power is directly proportionate to their own capacity for fear. Only when the fear of spirits is expelled from men's minds can peace be assured. And yet the moment of fear, which may arise from an awareness of the breakdown of falsely "natural" hierarchies, may in turn lead to an awareness of one's immersion in the war of all against all, hence to a realization of one's dependence on others and need for recognition; fear itself is the beginning of reason insofar as it provides a knowledge of one's own weakness and of the need for the protections

66 Pascal provides a somewhat different understanding of the relationship between Church and State when he writes that "Just as the only object of peace within states is to safeguard people's property, so the only object of peace within the Church is to safeguard the truth, which is its property and the treasure wherein lies its heart" (*Pensées*, fr. 974, p. 346).

of the State.[67] On this basis, Hobbes attempts to outline and institute an ethics that would be appropriate to the conditions of a "disenchanted" world.

Arguing by reason from the "state of nature" to the Absolute State, Hobbes attempts to overcome the historical conditions of civil war and the religious conflicts underlying it. But while Hobbes's political philosophy may have satisfied an historical need for new modes of legitimation, it eventually came to nullify the philosophical significance of history itself. To be sure, it has been argued that Hobbes must have recognized that man's rationally derived destiny of self-emancipation was incompatible with his historical fate, because he had himself experienced history as the reality of civil and religious war and had come to interpret the need for the State in light of his own great fear of destruction. Yet it has also been said that Hobbes simply regarded the philosophical grounding of the principles of political judgment as more compelling than the most thoroughly grounded historical knowledge.[68] To be sure, Hobbes's argument provided a means to clear free of the partisan claims made by the combatants in the civil wars. By pacifying those devastated by the religious wars, the State provided a basis for the emergence of a new community; but this was but a temporary and at best unstable solution to the problem of order which the civil wars merely expressed, for just as soon as the religious basis of their obligations came to an end, the newly secularized individuals were bound to conflict with one another and indeed with the State itself:

Nor is it enough for the security, which men desire should last all the time of their life, that they be governed, and directed by one judgement, for a limited time; as in one Battell, or one Warre. For though they obtain a Victory by their unanimous endeavour against a forraign enemy; yet afterwards, when either they have no common enemy, or he that by one part is held for an enemy, is by another part held for a friend, they must needs by the difference of their interests dissolve, and fall again into Warre amongst themselves. (*Leviathan*, II, 17, p. 225)

Even though emancipating and guaranteeing the freedom of its subjects, the State was forced to deny them by restricting the purview

67 See Barry Cooper, *The End of History*, p. 39.
68 These are the arguments, respectively, of Reinhart Koselleck, in *Critique and Crisis*, and of Leo Strauss, in *The Political Philosophy of Hobbes* (see especially pp. 102–04).

of conscience to a purely private sphere: "Once implemented by the State the separation of morality and politics hence turns against the State itself: it is forced into standing a moral trial for having achieved something, i.e. to have created a space in which it was possible (for the individual) to survive" (Koselleck, *Critique and Crisis*, p. 11).

In this and other ways, the Hobbesian solution to the problem of political order results in a sharply divided, not to say disenchanted, world. If the rational motives guiding the formation of the State are impelled by the fear of death, which drives the commitment to civil laws and sovereignty, then carrying forward the task of enlightenment demands dispelling any of the residual fear that the priests might employ in order to undermine the sovereign power.[69] If Hobbes's initial advance lay in sweeping clear all pre-existing assumptions about the natural goodness of man, thus liberating politics from the mystifying bonds of "conscience," he recognizes that men are still prone to regard religion as a form of magic; they will for instance transform Eucharistic consecration into a form of conjuration or incantation (*Leviathan*, IV, 44). Accordingly, Hobbes must separate control over the "public" aspects of religion from what men in private may believe in order to insure that no object of belief can challenge the civil authority of the sovereign. Thus in the section of the *Leviathan* devoted to the "Kingdome of Darknesse" Hobbes condemns the belief that the Kingdom of God mentioned in scripture can be identified with the temporal Church (*Leviathan*, IV, 44, p. 629 and *passim*). Hobbes internalizes the split between conscience and politics and attempts to disengage the individual's concern with salvation from public expressions of worship to the point that it would no longer afford any opportunities for control to the Church: "A private man has alwaies the liberty (because thought is free), to beleeve, or not beleeve in his heart, those acts that have been given out for Miracles, according as he shall see, what benefit can accrew by means of belief... But when it comes to confession of that faith, the Private Reason must submit to the Publique; that is to say, to Gods Lieutenant" (*Leviathan*, III, 38, p. 478). In this and other ways, the *Leviathan* confirms the fact that the secularization of authority in the modern State remained both contradictory and incomplete. Just as

69 For an excellent discussion of these issues, see David Johnston, *The Rhetoric of "Leviathan": Thomas Hobbes and the Politics of Cultural Transformation* (Princeton: Princeton University Press, 1986), pp. 196–205 ("The History of Ecclesiastical Power") and, in response, Barnouw, "Persuasion in Hobbes's *Leviathan*."

the sovereign State must be defended against the potential mystifications of the priests, so too the inwardness of faith is required as a safeguard for the subjects and as a protection of belief.

Legitimation and representation

As we have seen in the pages above, Hobbes constructs sovereignty in accordance with the principles of a rationally based Natural Law and argues that the legitimizing reason for the existence of the sovereign is to make possible the "happiness" of subjects in the State. But in order to achieve a liberal State Hobbes must theorize sovereignty in the form of an absolute power. This contradiction is justified by means of the presupposition of a state of nature which is not only disenchanted but destructive, in which everyone fears death and seeks therefore to assert himself by all possible means. A rational interest in self-preservation requires that the potentially destructive passions be contained by the institution of a state of peace; absolute fear induces men to invest a single authority with a monopoly of physical force, empowered by them all to hold power. In other words, the liberal principles of the State are negated by its irrepressible absolutism. How may the emergence of such a contradiction be explained?

The rise of an antinomic relation between the (liberal) subject and the (absolutist) State, in which the subjects constitute the State but are in turn constituted by its power over them, may be understood as part of the larger transformation by which an order of society founded on a network of substantive beliefs came to adopt increasingly abstract and formalized modes of legitimation in response to the increasing differentiation of the self. In Weber's terms, the process of social differentiation, which we may understand in terms of the splintering of the self across a series of newly configured value-spheres, and ultimately its division into sharply divided "public" and "private" spheres, came to demand the consolidation of political power in a centralized State. On an institutional level, the existence of the State was brought about through the fusion of those organizations which had respectively engendered their own set of norms into a single compulsory association, claiming to be the sole source of all "legitimate" law (*ES*, ii, p. 666).

Hobbes provides the theoretical grounding for the existence of a centralized State when he argues that the State allows the citizens to overcome the conditions of dissociated spontaneity that would otherwise exist:

And be there never so great a Multitude; yet if their actions be directed according to the particular judgments, and particular appetites, they can expect thereby no defence, nor protection, neither against a common enemy, nor against the injuries of one another. For being in opinions concerning the best use and application of their strength, they do not help, but hinder one another; and reduce their strength by mutuall opposition to nothing; whereby they are easily, not only subdued by a very few who agree together; but also when there is no common enemy, they make war upon each other, for their particular interests.   (*Leviathan*, II, 17, pp. 224–25)

Critics conventionally locate Hobbes's response to the potentially destructive consequences of spontaneity in a theory of pure constraint.[70] And yet it also remains clear that such a theory would be unable to meet the conditions for legitimation that it would itself demand. The emergence of an autonomous State and of a professionally administered "public sphere" may for instance be understood to represent a contract or agreement fashioned by the members of society in order to impose order on otherwise contingent and random events; and yet it is equally clear that the notion of a social contract could never by itself fulfill the requirement of an obligation to the sovereign, since a contract is by nature bilateral in form.[71] Rather, the ordering mechanism of the State must be understood as an expression of the subjects' powers of representation and of authorship; these in turn are founded on a special understanding of the nature of artifice that is central to Hobbes's conception of the subject and that may explain both the freedom and autonomy of subjects and also their subjection to the structures that they themselves have made.

70 Dominick LaCapra makes a plausible argument for the "overcoming" of the Hobbesian vision of constraint in the form of a Durkheimian sociology that takes the need for discipline itself as normative and natural, rather than as imposed: "Theorists like Hobbes and Spencer opted for one horn of a dilemma. But the problem of legitimate social order could be resolved only by eliminating the dilemma itself: 'The principle which we espoused would create a sociology which sees in the spirit of discipline the essential condition of all common life, while at the same time founding it on reason and on truth' [Durkheim, *Règles de la méthode sociologique*]." LaCapra, *Emile Durkheim* (Ithaca: Cornell University Press, 1972), pp. 229–30.
71 Hanna Pitkin makes this argument in "Hobbes's Concept of Representation – II," 916.

In Book I of the *Leviathan*, Hobbes argues that persons are less agents than actors. In their capacity as actors, persons may be of two sorts – "natural" and "artificial" – depending on their relationship to the actions they perform:

A person, is he whose words or actions are considered, either as his own, or as representing the words of an other man, or of any other thing to whom they are attributed, whether Truly or by Fiction.

When they are considered as his owne, then is he called a *Naturall Person*: And when they are considered as representing the words and actions of an other, then is he a *Feigned* or *Artificiall person*.

Of Persons Artificiall, some have their words and actions Owned by those whom they represent. And then the Person is the *Actor*; and he that owneth his words and actions, is the AUTHOR: In which case the Actor acteth by Authority ... So that by Authority, is alwayes understood a Right of doing any act: and *done by Authority*, done by Commission, or Licence from him whose right it is. From hence it followeth, that when the Actor maketh a Covenant by Authority, he bindeth thereby the Author, no lesse than if he had made it himselfe; and no lesse subjecteth him to all the consequences of the same. (*Leviathan*, I, 16, pp. 217, 218)

The most accurate measure of full and mature personhood, according to Hobbes, lies in one's ability to assume the role of author in a representational relationship. Thus "Inanimate things, as a Church, a Bridge, may be Personated by a Rector, Master, or Overseer. But things Inanimate, cannot be Authors, nor therefore give authority to their Actors"; "Likewise Children, Fooles, and Mad-men that have no use of Reason, may be Personated by Guardians, or Curators; but can be no Authors (during that time) of any action done by them" (p. 219). Similarly, "An Idol, or meer Figment of the brain, may be personated; as were the Gods of the Heathen ... But idols cannot be Authors, for an idol is nothing" (p. 220). On this basis, Hobbes can argue that the legitimizing basis of the Body Politic, which stands as one person and is constituted by a common power, is that of the authorizing will of its constituent subjects:

A multitude of men, are made *one* person, when they are by one man, or one person, represented; so that it be done with the consent of every one of the multitude in particular. For it is the *unity* of the representer, not the *unity* of the represented, that maketh the person *one*. And it is the representer that beareth the person, and but one person: and *unity*, cannot otherwise be understood in multitude. (*Leviathan*, I, 16, p. 220)

Once in force, the fiction of authorship may be used to explain the legitimate basis of the authority of the State. For example, Hobbes argues that a criminal does not directly will his own punishment, but that he is nonetheless the author of it in this larger sense. Insofar as the principle of authorship remains intact, such a use of force remains within the bounds of legitimacy as established by the theory of representation. The contradictory nature of the powers of representation are brought to the fore only when the sovereign or the State obscures the source of its power in the authority of the subjects. Indeed, the creation of the Leviathan as an objectified entity or "Mortall God" reveals that this work of human artifice, this object that the subjects have themselves made, has acquired an autonomous existence and has in turn become something of which the subjects stand in awe. Once this situation has occurred, then the stage is set for the Foucaultian reversal by which power becomes grounded in its potential for mystification, manipulation, and control. Once the effect of power has been substituted for its cause, then men are held in thrall while at the same time they remain alienated from the State that they themselves have made.

Not surprisingly, these conditions are anticipated in the emergence of the Church as an autonomous institution, complete with its own hierarchy of powers and ranks.[72] In Hobbes's discussion "Of Power Ecclesiastical" in *Leviathan*, IV, 42, for instance, we read that in the beginning there was no unified Christian Church. Rather, the Christian faith was sustained by a network of independent and overlapping organizations. Ecclesiastical power had passed from Christ to the apostles, but had not yet been consolidated into an institutional hierarchy; the apostles held no power over congregations aside from that derived from their own personal charisma, and this was itself understood to be a manifestation of the absolute charisma of the prophets and of Christ ("All formed religion," Hobbes proclaims, "is founded at first, upon the faith which a multitude hath in some one person, whom they believe not only to be a wise man, and to labour to procure their happiness, but also to be a holy man, to whom God himselfe vouchsafeth to declare his will supernaturally," *Leviathan*, I, 12, p. 179). Indeed, the legitimation of power is at this stage purely "affective"; the apostles did not have the authority to impose their

---

72 I have drawn, in the following argument, on Johnston's discussion of ecclesiastical power in *The Rhetoric of "Leviathan"*, pp. 196–205.

own interpretations of Scripture, which had not itself been fixed or "rationalized" into a canon.

In practical terms, Hobbes describes the early Christians as living a communal existence, "upon a common stock of money, raised out of the voluntary contributions of the faithful"; "After our Saviours Ascension the Christians of every city lived in Common, upon the money which was made of the sale of their lands and possessions, and laid down at the feet of the Apostles" (*Leviathan*, IV, 42, pp. 555, 565). These conditions endured until the conversion of sovereigns to Christianity, which transformed Christianity in a fundamental way. With the conversion of the Emperor Constantine, a rationally ordered, ecclesiastical hierarchy came into existence. Then, in addition to their civil duties, Christian sovereigns became the pastoral rulers of their people. They assumed the right, previously non-existent, to establish authoritative interpretations of Scripture and to appoint other pastors. Whereas formerly Christian leaders had been empowered directly by their own congregations, now they became the subordinates of a supreme spiritual leader. The result was not simply a fusion of ecclesiastical and civil power. It established a new form of power by transforming the churches into something they may have had no intention of becoming, namely structures of authority.

The parallel histories of Church and State become clear when we recognize that these transformations have a direct bearing on the way in which men are led. If we accept the premise that everyone, including ecclesiastics, desires power, then it is no surprise to learn that the new character of the Churches led them to conceive structures of power. Though formally subordinate to their Christian sovereigns, ambitious ecclesiastics set out to create independent orderings of power. The corrupt, semi-pagan elements within Christianity provided much of the persuasive force needed to achieve this goal. As David Johnston argued in *The Rhetoric of "Leviathan,"* there could be nothing more useful than to encourage men to adopt the old Greek belief in an immortal soul, an immaterial self, subject to priestly influences but beyond the reach of any civil power. "What could be more effective than to convince men that priests are capable of literally making Christ and performing other magical marvels? What, finally, could be more valuable than to make men believe that they, the priests, are the magistrates of God's kingdom on earth, with a right to governance that supersedes mere civil sovereignty?" (p.

198). As we might well suspect, these and similar effects are part of an incomplete secularization process as a result of which the Church became a rival State, or as Hobbes put it, a "Kingdom of Fairies" existing alongside and in constant tension with the civil State, while its ultimate foundation rested on fantastic myths, superstitions, and above all on mens' susceptibility to enchantments:

> To this, and such like resemblances between the *Papacy*, and the Kingdome of *Fairies*, may be added this, that as the *Fairies* have no existence, but in the Fancies of ignorant people, rising from the Traditions of old Wives, or old Poets: so the Spirituall Power of the *Pope* ... consisteth onley in the Fear that Seduced people stand in, of their Excommunication; upon hearing of false Miracles, false Traditions, and false Interpretations of the Scripture.
>
> (*Leviathan*, IV, 47, p. 714)

Considered in this light, it becomes all the more striking that Hobbes fails to recognize that the same potential for "mystification" exists within the State itself. Indeed, it seems that, despite its "rational" basis, the State exhibits the same institutional and rhetorical tendencies as the Church, and that the process of modernization might best be understood in terms of their shift from one domain to the other. Recent studies of Hobbes's rhetoric by David Johnston and Victoria Kahn, for instance, have shown that the paradox of Hobbes's construal of sovereignty depends on such an effect; sovereignty in Hobbes derives from the fact that the sovereign as representative is created by a formal covenant, while the sovereign's coercive power in turn validates both the covenant and thus the legitimacy of his own power as representative.[73] In response it might be argued that if this were simply the case then the sovereign's power would be internally inconsistent and in fact *il*legitimate, that sovereignty would simply be a mask for the subliminal persuasions and tropes by which subjects ceaselessly delude themselves into subjection.[74] And yet is seems that the "rhetorical" structure in which the effect of the covenant is necessarily presupposed as its cause is itself the groundwork of the State. Indeed, Hobbes himself admits that the idea of a prior contract is not enough to legitimize power in the State:

> It is therefore vain to grant Soveraignty by way of precedent Covenant. The opinion that any Monarch receiveth his Power by Covenant, that is to say

---

73 Johnston, *The Rhetoric of "Leviathan"*; Kahn, *Rhetoric, Prudence, and Skepticism in the Renaissance*.
74 Barnouw makes a related argument in "Persuasion in Hobbes's *Leviathan*."

on Condition, proceedeth from want of understanding this easie truth, that
Covenants being but words, and breath, have no force to oblige, contain,
constrain, or protect any man, but what it has from *the publique Sword*.

(*Leviathan*, II, 18, p. 231)

Hobbes's claim to have established a "new science"of politics
notwithstanding, his argument in *Leviathan* reveals that the political
foundations of the Absolute State are the effects of a rhetoric of
alienation. In the specific instance at hand, fear of the effects of power
is necessary for the effective transfer of power, which explains the
creation of the "publique Sword." Accordingly, sovereignty in
Hobbes is described as "an irreducibly theatrical phenomenon," a
necessarily "visible Power."[75] It is based upon a theory that moves
from absolute fear to a structure of representation that is designed to
keep the subjects "in awe" (*Leviathan*, II, 17, p. 223). These claims
would not be so damaging were it not also for the fact that Hobbes
describes the State as both total and Absolute. To describe the State
in this way means that Hobbes can find no realm, outside the private
space of conscience, in which the subjects can be shielded from the
effects of its power. In overcoming their initial "disenchantment," it
seems that the subjects have in effect made themselves increasingly
susceptible to the mystifying effects of power in its rationalized and
institutionalized forms. In Hobbes, the achievement of order relies on
a special understanding of the powers of artifice, which in turn forms
the basis of the politics of representation and, indeed, of the fiction of
authorship itself (see *Leviathan*, I, 16, pp. 217–22). The Hobbesian
politics of representation depends on the power that is lodged in a
semblance or figure of order – in the sovereign as an Artificial Man
and in the State as a substitute order or second (political) nature (the
Commonwealth). In fashioning the State, the subjects create
something that comes to exert power over them, constrains their
wills, and may act independently of them, its subject-authors.
Understood in Hobbesian terms this comes as little or no surprise, for
despite its exemplary "rationality" the modern State is for Hobbes
but an example, writ large, of the coercive nature of political life.

75 See Christopher Pye, "The Sovereign, the Theatre, and the Kingdome of
   Darknesse: Hobbes and the Spectacle of Power," *Representations*, 8 (1984),
   85–106.

5

Subjective desire

Desire is that which transforms Being.
Alexandre Kojève, *Introduction to the Reading of Hegel*

Belief and desire

Seen from the perspective of the subject of the disenchanted world and its political analogue, the modern State, the prospect of restoring a context for belief would seem tempting indeed. If we take the divisions within the subject of transcendental ego and empirical self, together with the separation of public and private inherent in the modern State, as symptomatic of the antinomies of culture in the modern age, then the spirit that animates the psychology of belief would seem to say that the self is whole, that the domains of value and fact, ought and is, ideal and norm, are not at all divided but are in fact one. While the existence of the modern State is predicated on the secularization of society, the most radical implications of the psychology of belief would suggest that the ideal does not transcend the real but rather animates and moves it at every point. Similarly, values seen in the context of belief themselves appear as a species of fact and have a mode of existence independent of the subjects who posit and pursue them; facts so seen are correspondingly already what they ought to become. Phrased in other terms, the promise of belief is that of a context in which the intelligible essence of each thing in the world is of a piece with its ideal.[1]

Whether the psychology of belief is thought to be embodied in traditional societies, in societies organized around charismatic forms of authority, or as is more likely to be the case, in a mixture of these, the ideology it supports has consistently been used to buttress some version of the naturalistic thesis described above. Succinctly put, the

1 See Roberto Mangabeira Unger, *Knowledge and Politics* (New York: Free Press, 1975), p. 41.

ideology of belief forms the basis of the conviction that a given regime reflects the natural order and hierarchy of the world, and embodies in its principles a universally valid ideal of human life. But while both traditional and charismatic forms of authority may seem to negate the separateness of values and facts, and while both may offer the self a relatively secure position within the social environment, both are severely limited by the ways in which they are able to imagine social change. For they simultaneously depend on and produce a vision of authority as absolute and of society as closed to the possibility of reimagination and transformation from within. Thus, while traditional forms of authority may be marshalled in support of the theistic view that world-revolutionary actions are destined and willed by God, the very stability that tradition makes possible means that a society so organized is prone to the destabilizing threat of violent revolution or of change from without. To be sure, the charismatic leader may himself exert a revolutionary force on existing contexts and routines; his claim to power may rest on his attempt to "transvalue" all existing beliefs; as Weber noted, the charismatic leader may in a sovereign and revolutionary manner break all precedents and norms: "It has been written ... but *I* say unto you ..."[2] And, once in place, charismatic authority may likewise resist assimilation to any institutional form. But while the authority of charisma and the social order it governs are powerless unless they are also taken as absolute, it must also be said that, were it not for the absolute and categorical nature of its stance, charismatic authority would not be unstable in the particular way that it is.

Like the idea of existence in an "enchanted" world, the psychology of unrationalized belief is antithetical to the values of progress and self-improvement that predominate in the modern age. Unlike the psychology of belief, which posits that a prior acceptance of values is necessary for a true comprehension of the nature of things, the psychology of the subject depends on the separation of values and facts. Modern forms of foundational thought, and the liberal social order they have been used to support, thus stand opposed to the psychology of belief as embodied in traditional and charismatic societies; liberal psychology may be understood as standing in an antithetical relation to the psychology of belief. As we have seen in

2 Weber, *Economy and Society*, ed. Guenther Roth and Claus Wittich (Berkeley: University of California Press, 1978), p. 1,115.

chapter 3 above, the philosophical subject of modernity can more accurately be considered a product of the secularization of the psychology of belief, where secularization modulates the naturalistic thesis of society into the "foundational" claim that *cogito*, the subject *qua* "thinking thing," represents the universal essence of humanity itself. When philosophers like Descartes and Kant construct the position of the transcendental subject as the basis for philosophical truth, they begin from the premise, contrary to the psychology of belief, that there are no intelligible essences and no pre-existing hierarchies on which claims to authority might rest. For instance, Descartes takes pains to explain that residual claims of the form "Nature taught me to think this" mean nothing more than "that a spontaneous impulse leads me to believe it, not that its truth has been revealed to me by some natural light."[3] Where there are no natural ends or objects of desire, and where reason does not itself supply those ends, the result may be a form of empowerment, a freedom of self-creation, inaccessible from the Aristotelian position that a thinker like MacIntyre seeks to refashion for the modern age. And yet the liberation of desire from reason and from its attachment to any "natural" objects indicates the difficulty of directing desire toward a single coherent end. As we also have seen, the Hobbesian "naturalization" of passion inaugurates the reign of a pleasure principle in a newly secular and necessarily political form that depends on the institutionalized authority of the State.

The genealogy of subjective desire I would propose here takes its bearings by the Hegelian critique of the Cartesian version of subjectivity and proceeds from there to examine the grounding of desire in the search for recognition, as carried out in social and historical terms. As I hope in the second section of this chapter to show, the characteristic variability of modern desire, its shifting attachments to a sometimes bewildering variety of objects, is paradigmatically shaped in the myth of Don Juan, which represents desire as a labile force that constantly shifts its attention among a series of heterogeneous objects (Cf. Stendhal: "Love … is a craving for an activity which needs an incessant diversity of stimuli to challenge skill"; [Don Juan:] "*I must have novelty, be it the last thing on*

3 Descartes, *Meditations*, III, in *The Philosophical Works of Descartes*, trans. John Cottingham, Robert Stoothoff, and Dugald Murdoch (Cambridge: Cambridge University Press, 1984), II, p. 26.

earth"[4]). In the Mozart/Da Ponte version of the myth, the heterogeneity of desire is signalled in Don Giovanni's "catalogue" aria, in which he claims to have seduced "a thousand and three" women. While such a conception of desire may appear to be the source of nothing more than self-indulgence, we may also locate its transformative force insofar as it operates outside of a system of social ranks, and free from the constraints of belief. As we shall see in the historical portion of this analysis, the transformative power of subjective desire develops in the consciousness that attaches to the shift from a hierarchical society composed of relatively stable selves to a society of relatively disgregated and mobile individuals. Finally, the historical analysis of subjective desire may be brought to bear on a series of normative concerns. By reading desire as constitutive of subjectivity, rather than as posing an external threat to it, we may be able to recover the transformative or emancipatory potential of desire that is rooted in the very separation of desire from its "natural" ends. So understood, the task of modern desire is to locate a mode of empowerment for the self in the differences that heterogeneous desires create; similarly, the problem of society in the modern age is to recover the possibility of recognition from the heterogeneity of desiring selves.

In order to address these issues it is first necessary to clear free of the view that passion stands in fundamental opposition to social conventions, constraints, or rules. There is a tendency to view desire as the predecessor of madness, and to view madness as that which results when the passions are detached from their natural objects and are allowed to rage out of control.[5] Indeed, there is widespread acceptance of the view that madness is that which results when desire rises up against established forms of social life, and moves from adjustment toward antagonism or transgression. The Freudian critique of culture, and the Foucaultian critique of Freud, provide us with cases in point: desire is for Freud an expression of civilization's

---

4 Stendhal, *On Love*, trans. Gilbert and Suzanne Sale (Harmondsworth: Penguin Books, 1975), pp. 209, 211.

5 Thus Hobbes writes that "as to have no Desire, is to be Dead: so to have weak Passions, is Dulnesse; and to have Passions indifferently for every thing, Gidinesse, and *Distraction*; and to have stronger, and more vehement Passions for any thing, than is ordinarily seen in others, is that which men call madnesse." *Leviathan*, ed. C. B. MacPherson (Harmondsworth: Penguin Books, 1968), I, 8, p. 139.

"discontents" and can be stabilized, if at all, through a process of repression or social control. For Foucault, little is to be gained by those forms of control that make madness clinical; on the contrary, the "great confinement" of madness that began in the seventeenth century could succeed only in aligning the discourse about desire with the processes of social proscription and exclusion, thus reinforcing the authority of reason in the West.[6] For a thinker like Bataille the "heterogeneous" elements of culture are rooted in forms of desire and resist assimilation to all bourgeois forms of life. Barring a reinstitution of a principle of "sovereignty" (which Bataille makes clear is dependent on a desecularizing recovery of the transgressive potential of the erotic), it would seem that the therapeutic hope of normalcy is the best we can imagine for the desiring self. Similarly, the definition of desire as utility often begins with the conception of the passions as a manifestation of pre-social or "natural" predatory instincts in need of control, and carries through to a vision of desire as second-order social aggression in need of domination by various forms of rationalized behavior. We may examine the beginnings of both these understandings of desire in the seventeenth-century myth of Don Juan, which posits desire as a mobile force that virtually *demands* some form of social control, but it is not until the late eighteenth and early nineteenth centuries that the "disciplining" of passion, its transformation from aggression to utility, is complete. The point to be made here is that in either case the demand for recognition within society remains unmet and the transformative power of desire is lost. Rather than affirm desire as a form of empowerment that attempts to reconstitute a vision of society from the demand for recognition that modern subjectivity inherently creates, we are consigned to a vision of desire as a dark and inscrutable force, opposed to every constructive social aim.[7]

To locate the absolute "origins" of subjectivity in desire is, however, a fruitless task that fundamentally misinterprets the role of desire in

6 Foucault marks the moment of this "confinement" with the characteristically sovereign pronouncement that "the classical age was to reduce to silence the madness whose voices the Renaissance had just liberated, but whose violence it had already tamed." He takes the decree of 1656 establishing the Hôpital Générale as a landmark date. See *Madness and Civilization*, trans. Richard Howard (New York: Vintage Books, 1973), especially ch. 2, pp. 38–64 ("The Great Confinement").

7 See Unger, *Passion: An Essay on Personality* (New York: Free Press, 1984), p. 286.

the formation of the subject-self. As we can see in the case of Descartes, this is because the movement toward self-consciousness is itself inextricable from the complications that desire brings. In the *Meditations*, for instance, the coming to self-consciousness signalled by the *cogito* is precipitated by a process of affective self-seduction, i.e., by the thinker's self-inducement into a state of dreamlike absorption in the external world. This process begins as Descartes describes himself "seated by the fire, attired in a dressing gown, having this paper in my hands" (I, p. 145), wondering whether thinking and reading – the very activities in which he is presently engaged – might not absorb him to the point of dreamlike oblivion of the objective world:

How often it has happened to me that in the night I dreamt I found myself in this particular place, that I was dressed and seated near the fire, whilst in reality I was lying undressed in bed! At this moment it does indeed seem to me that it is with eyes awake that I am looking at this paper; that this head which I move is not asleep, that it is deliberately and of set purpose that I extend my hand and perceive it; what happens in sleep does not appear so clear nor so distinct as does all this. But in thinking over this I remind myself that on many occasions I have in sleep been deceived by similar illusions, and in dwelling carefully on this reflection I see so manifestly that there are no certain indications by which we may clearly distinguish wakefulness from sleep that I am lost in astonishment. And my astonishment is such that it is almost capable of persuading me that I now dream.   (I, pp. 146–47)

The experience of "astonishment" here anticipates a moment of illumination when consciousness is stunned by its accession to *self-*consciousness, a moment that is proved, as Hegel said, by the supercession of certainty by truth.[8] But because the accession to self-consciousness is also figured as the possible loss of consciousness *in* objects, the subject seems to be made vulnerable by the very means by which enlightenment is achieved.[9] If the avowed project of the *Meditations* is to demolish all existing beliefs in order to arrive at certainty, then Descartes's concealed or implicit task is to reduce the ambiguity of self-consciousness, and thereby to resist absorption by the objects of his own discourse. In a contradictory effort that reveals

8 See the analysis of self-consciousness in the *Phenomenology of Spirit* (*PhS*), trans. A. V. Miller (New York: Oxford University Press, 1981), sec. 166–67, pp. 104–05.

9 Hegel takes up the theme of self-consciousness as a form of loss in his crucial interpretation of acknowledgment and recognition in the *PhS*, sec. 179. For Hegel, consciousness experiences a loss insofar as it finds itself in/as another.

the fundamentally ambiguous nature of enlightenment itself, Descartes attempts to neutralize the risks of self-consciousness and to generalize the process of disenchantment by *assuming* "that we are asleep and that all these particulars, e.g. that we open our eyes, shake our head, extend our hand, and so on, are but false delusions, and let us reflect that possibly neither our hands nor our whole body are such as they appear to us to be?"(I, p. 147). This effort to score a preemptive strike is carried forward in *Meditation* III. There, Descartes begins with a statement of the seductions of self-consciousness and proceeds to certify the truth with his own self-inducement into a dreamlike, absorptive state:

I shall now close my eyes, I shall stop my ears, I shall call away all my senses, I shall efface even from my thoughts all the images of corporeal things, or (for the former is hardly possible) I shall at least esteem them as vain and false; and thus holding converse only with myself and considering my own nature, I shall try little by little to reach a better knowledge of and a more familiar acquaintanceship with myself.   (I, p. 157)

That the subject might self-induce such a state and still come to a clear judgment about the nature of consciousness suggests that there is a complication *within* the Cartesian subject, a tension or division inherent to the process of its formation, that statements about the nature of reason as truth and representation, or similarly formal pronouncements about the antinomy of reason and desire, cannot easily comprehend.

In the *Meditations*, the idea of an epistemological method couched in an "order of reasons"[10] is meant to provide resistance to the seductions of the subject's own consciousness and to secure the stable image of an objective world. In the *Discourse*, the burden of proof that there is a mind independent of the world, capable of constituting itself through self-reflection, is carried by the work's autobiographical form.[11] In either case, it becomes clear that although subjective self-consciousness may originate in the desire to achieve certainty where the grounds for belief are absent, or in the need to resist the residual desire for a reabsorption into nature, the drama played out in the

10 See Martial Guéroult, *Descartes selon l'ordre des raisons*, 2 vols. (Paris: Aubier, 1953).
11 See Dalia Judovitz, *Subjectivity and Representation in Descartes: The Origins of Modernity* (Cambridge: Cambridge University Press, 1988), and John Lyons, "Subjectivity and Imitation in the *Discours de la méthode*," *Neophilologus*, 66 (1982), 508–24.

Cartesian texts would seem to suggest that consciousness (as of objects) precipitates subjective *self*-consciousness, and that self-consciousness is in turn unsatisfied by the world of objects it constructs.

To say this much is to locate the concealed dialectic of desire that lies within the Cartesian texts. It is this dialectic that Hegel seeks to make explicit in his reformulation of the principles of self-consciousness in the *Phenomenology of Spirit*. According to Hegel, Spirit first comes to know itself as subjective feeling. When feeling is localized in a world of objects, spirit is split between the inner and outer world. As a result, we become alienated from ourselves and come to regard our true self as contained in the objects outside us, which we desire to assimilate. "The desire that springs from this division is thus the desire for myself, or for my interior essence, from which I have become detached. The struggle to satisfy my desires thus leads to the development of individual self-consciousness."[12] But, as Alexandre Kojève emphasized in his *Introduction to the Reading of Hegel*, self-consciousness is by nature unstable and incomplete and seeks recognition in the consciousness of another. Thus Hegel's theory of recognition posits subjectivity as a form of desiring consciousness to which only the desire of another can speak. The search for recognition is what remains tacit in the drama of consciousness in Descartes, and yet acknowledgment is what self-consciousness demands. More precisely, it is the need for recognition that Descartes seeks to suppress when he writes in his proof of the existence of God that "As far as concerns the ideas which represent other men, or animals, or angels, I have no difficulty in understanding that they could be put together from the ideas I have of myself, of corporeal things and of God, *even if the world contained no men besides me, no animals and no angels*" (*Meditation* III; 1, p. 29; emphasis mine). The substratum of the Cartesian ego, as confirmed by its preoccupation with doubt and distrust, is the fear of not finding another similar self; but since Descartes cannot seem to reconcile the desire for self-certainty with the demand for recognition, he projects an Other as one who lies beyond all possibility of doubt and deceit. Hence Lacan, who speaks of the "handing back of truth into the hands of the Other, in this instance the perfect God, whose truth is the nub of the matter, since, whatever he might have meant, would always be

12 Stanley Rosen, *G. W. F. Hegel* (New Haven: Yale University Press, 1974).

the truth."[13] The Cartesian recourse to an Other who reoccupies the space of belief is thus not the result, as has been thought historically to be the case, of Descartes's failure to eliminate all the old Scholastic truths. Rather, it is the result of the subject's wish for metaphysical comfort, to be found, as Lacan says, in the idea of "an Other that is not deceptive, and which shall, into the bargain, guarantee by its very existence the bases of truth, guarantee him that there are in his own objective reason the necessary foundations for the very real, about whose existence he has just re-assured himself, to find the dimension of truth" ("Of the Subject of Certainty," p. 36).

As we shall see in connection with our further discussion of Hegel below, it is necessary in order to recuperate desire's socializing potential, as well as its transformative force, to think of subjectivity as driven not by the search for certainty, but by a desire for recognition or acknowledgment, which are the infinite tasks of desiring selves. In Kojève's reinterpretation of the dialectic of self-consciousness (to which a thinker like Lacan owes significant debts), the "truth" of subjectivity is to be found neither in a world of objects nor in an all-perfect and infinite God, but in a form of human desire that represents something more than the subjective "good" of clear and undeceptive speech, for it is only through desire that a consciousness trapped or alienated in objects or the objective (i.e., disenchanted) world can be recognized and thereby "returned" to itself:

the analysis of "thought," "reason," "understanding," and so on – in general, of the cognitive, contemplative, passive behavior of a being or a "knowing subject" – never reveals the why or the how of the birth of the word "I," and consequently of self-consciousness – that is, of the human reality. The man who contemplates is "absorbed" by what he contemplates; the "knowing subject" "loses" himself in the object that is known. Contemplation reveals the object, not the subject. The object, and not the subject, is what shows itself to him in and by – or better, as – the act of knowing. The man who is "absorbed" by the object that he is contemplating can be "brought back to himself" [*rappelé a lui*] only by a Desire; by the desire to eat, for example. The (conscious) Desire of a being is what constitutes that being as I and reveals it as such by moving it to say "I..."[14]

13 Lacan, "Of the Subject of Certainty," in *The Four Fundamental Concepts of Psychoanalysis*, ed. Jacques-Alain Miller, trans. Alan Sheridan (New York: Norton, 1981), p. 36.

14 Kojève, *Introduction à la lecture de Hegel*, ed. Raymond Queneau (Paris: Gallimard, 1947); trans. as *Introduction to the Reading of Hegel* by James H. Nichols, Jr., and ed. Allan Bloom (Ithaca: Cornell University Press, 1980), p. 3.

This is to say that the psychology of subjectivity cannot be explained if we think exclusively either in terms of a direct recourse to belief or, alternatively, in terms of the desire for objects. A discourse that seeks to express the desire for God becomes the expression of what in psychoanalytic terms would be called a "transference," i.e., the projective *supposition* that some other subject knows what we cannot. On the other hand, a desire that seeks satisfaction in objects alone is bound to reduce and reify consciousness. Rather, human desire reflects the "intermediate" nature of the subject (cf. Descartes: "I am, as it were, something intermediate between God and nothingness, or between supreme being and non-being," *Meditation* IV; 1, p. 38). Subjective self-consciousness conceived as desire is defined by the fact that it is directed toward another desire; and insofar as subjectivity is a form of desire that desires another (desire), and demands recognition in return, it can never be complete.[15] Thus Kojève likened the complete satisfaction of human desire to the end of history: once desire is satisfied, the search for recognition comes to an end; either discourse is absorbed within an undifferentiated whole (as in the case of the totalitarian State), or, what amounts to the same thing, the subject reverts to its animal self.[16]

The attempt to complete desire has been taken by Kojève as the source of the inessential "chatter" that results when history comes to an end and we are left with nothing to say.[17] Thus it is no surprise to find that a post-historical thinker like Lacan takes belief as but an expression of the wish to force an endless chain of signifiers toward a premature closure, to alight upon a center, and thereby to deny the fact that human desire is driven by an all-pervasive lack. What remains nonetheless anomalous is that, as a form of discourse whose

15 This is a crucial point for Lacan, who elaborates it into a more generalized principle of alienation: "If it is merely at the level of the Desire of the Other that man can recognize his desire, as the desire of the Other, is there not something here that must appear to him to be an obstacle to his fading, which is a point at which his desire can never be recognized? This obstacle is never lifted, nor ever to be lifted, for analytic experience shows us that it is in seeing a whole chain come into play at the level of the desire of the Other that the subject's desire is constituted." "Of the Subject Who is Supposed to Know," in *The Four Fundamental Concepts of Psychoanalysis*, p. 235.

16 See Rosen, *Hermeneutics as Politics* (New York: Oxford University Press, 1987), p. 93. Kojève has been taken to exemplify the dialectical principle that every rational construction, whether mathematical or rhetorical, contradicts itself when carried through to its "logical" conclusion (Rosen, p. 94).

17 See Rosen, "Hermeneutics as Politics," in *ibid.*, pp. 96–97.

modes of articulation bear an uncanny resemblance to the causality of fate, psychoanalysis claims for its part to know that "There is no meaning; there is only *the causality of the scriptural signifier, to which man is consigned for the wandering of his desire and thought*, having for its object only something which is nothing."[18] As we shall see in connection with the psychoanalytic critique of the symbolic order of society below, the assignation of a causal power to a "scriptural signifier" places the subject in a universe where the law is always prior to and oftentimes incompatible with desire, hence where the demand for recognition is transposed into a law that has recognized us always and in advance. To be sure, it is necessary to acknowledge that the power of the social order over subjects derives from something more than the mere sum of individual desires; to persist in a denial of its symbolic force can only render any theory of desire founded on the need for recognition hopelessly abstract. But the slippage from an analysis of subjectivity to a theory of inescapable subjection weakens the otherwise trenchant critique of modernity that psychoanalytic critics writing in the wake of Lacan have attempted to make.

In Lacanian theory, desire is born of the difference between need and demand – for example, the child's need for nourishment (for the breast), and his demand for recognition from the Other (from the mother). As Laplanche and Pontalis point out, in this gap desire comes into being as a perpetual want for a satisfaction that cannot be offered in reality.[19] But whereas this analysis of desire might be taken as a warrant for the rereading of subjectivity as a form of ceaseless displacement, viz., as that form of consciousness which denies recognition and so cannot bring desire back home, I would suggest that it is through the creation of desire in the gap between need and demand that makes the search for recognition an opportunity for transformation, an occasion whereby the objects of our desire may come to have a shaping power over us. To expand only briefly on the example cited above, it is in desire that we see the transformation from "breast" – with its relatively limited range of possible

18 Antoine Vergotte, "From Freud's 'Other Scene'..." in *Interpreting Lacan*, ed. William Kerrigan and Joseph H. Smith (New Haven: Yale University Press, 1983), p. 214; emphasis added. On the concept of a "scriptural signifier," see especially Lacan, "The Agency of the Letter in the Unconscious or Reason Since Freud," in *Ecrits*, trans. Alan Sheridan (New York: Norton, 1977), pp. 146–78.
19 Jean Laplanche and J.-B. Pontalis, *Vocabulaire de la psychanalyse* (Paris: Presses Universitaires de France, 1971), "Désir," p. 122.

predications, and its inability for recognition – to "mother," a term whose possible predications are developed and enlarged as the work of recognition proceeds.

Seen from the perspective of psychoanalysis, however, the "truth" of subjectivity resides in the realization that the relation of desire to consciousness is fundamentally elusive and opaque, and that recognition is therefore impossible to achieve. For Lacan, the correlative of the subject is not the *malin génie*, the deceiving Other, but rather the deceived Other.[20] But if this is so, if the Other is at best the locus of my deception, then the demand for recognition is not only an infinite, but a destructive and illusory task. In Lacan's formulation, "I love you, but, because inexplicably I love in you something more than you – the *petit objet a* – I mutilate you" (*The Four Fundamental Concepts of Psychoanalysis*, p. 268). The demand of self-consciousness in the disenchanted world as formulated by Descartes – that desire, in the absence of belief, be recognized by a finite other – takes on the shape of a transference, one that stems from our tendency to presuppose a "subject who is opposed to know." According to Lacan, the analysis of this projection can lead us to see that as a "specular mirage," as a result of the projection of an illusory Ideal, "love is essentially deception. It is situated in the field established at the level of the pleasure reference, of that sole signifier necessary to introduce a perspective centered on the Ideal point, capital I, placed somewhere in the Other, from which the Other sees me, in the form I like to be seen" (p. 268). In response to this transferential projection, and in view of what it takes as the deceptive nature of love, psychoanalysis asks not for a desecularization of society or the reenchantment of the world, but rather for resistance, for the relentless denial of this projection. And yet as long as the infinite need for recognition is taken as a ceaseless demand for resistance, rather than as a motive for the transformation of society and the enlargement of the capacities for recognition, psychoanalysis will fail to provide a basis on which the critique of subjectivity can be aligned to a positive program for the transformation of social and personal relations in the postmodern age.

20 See Lacan, "On the Subject of Certainty," in *The Four Fundamental Concepts of Psychoanalysis*, p. 37.

Subjective desire and social change

Desire is death
Shakespeare, Sonnet 147

In Kojève's reinterpretation of Hegel, we are led to see that the transformative potential of the subject (and therefore the motive force of history) resides in desire; this is because in order for there to be self-consciousness, desire must be directed toward a non-natural object, toward something that goes beyond the reality of the given world. The problem of recognition is crucial within secular society insofar as the only thing that can reach beyond the given reality in such a world is the desire of another finite individual. By the same token, when desire is taken outside the space in which human acknowledgment is possible it becomes either the expression of the wish to desecularize the world or a veiled expression of mourning, a sign of the absence of God – in Kojève's terms "a revealed nothingness, an unreal emptiness" (p. 5).

As I hope in the present and concluding sections of this chapter to show, the demand for recognition has implications that reach in historical and speculative directions at once. A consideration of the demand for recognition may for instance allow us to address the normative questions involved in the problems of domination, order, and control with which any social theory must deal. To incorporate the demand for recognition as part of a social task would, for instance, curb the temptation to read modern desire exclusively as a drama of vulnerability and victimization perpetrated by male aggression, as might easily be possible in the case of the myth of Don Juan. And this in turn has consequences for the development of a thesis with respect to desire that would lead not to a facile idealization of the oppressed, but that would enable us to see that the problem with victimization is that it closes off almost every possibility for recognition, making recognition possible only through the total renunciation of the desiring self.[21] Otherwise put, the demand for recognition allows us to regard the finite social subject as potentially infinite, while nonetheless grounded in the concrete world. Furthermore, if we regard desire as constitutive of the subject rather than as antithetical to subjective self-consciousness, we may be able to explain the

21 See Jessica Benjamin, *The Bonds of Love: Psychoanalysis, Feminism, and the Problem of Domination* (New York: Pantheon, 1988), pp. 9–10.

genealogy of the subject more clearly in social and historical terms: history may be read in terms of the shifting struggles for recognition, and society may be taken as providing the symbolic structure in which competing desires are ordered and expressed. In this connection, an investigation of the myth of Don Juan will allow us to modify Hegel's interpretation of desire in a fundamental respect. According to the *Phenomenology of Spirit*, desire is not simply transformative; it is, by its own self-surpassing nature, a progressive force. But an analysis of subjective desire might seem to suggest that the characteristic mobility of modern desire may generate a need for recognition that might be supplied by a return to the hierarchical principles of distinction of the past. Otherwise put, mobile desires may generate a repressive rather than a transformative force, one that may be the source of a reactionary ideology and conservative social stance. Hence the predominance of concealed (and not so concealed) "imperatives" within the structure of modern society; hence the desire for domination as described by thinkers like Bataille and Foucault. Indeed, this could well explain the libidinal economy of fascism in the modern world; in Bataille's analysis, "the inability of *homogeneous* society to find in itself a reason for being and acting is what makes it dependent upon imperative forces, just as the sadistic hostility of sovereigns toward the impoverished population is what allies them with any formation seeking to maintain the latter in a state of oppression."[22]

How does the struggle for recognition take shape? Hegel claims that "self-consciousness exists in and for itself only when, and by the fact that, it so exists for another; that is, it exists only in being acknowledged" (*PhS*, sec. 178, p. 111). In the process of seeking recognition, each becomes the means or "middle term." "They *recognize* themselves as *mutually recognizing* one another" (184, p. 112). At first, this process will exhibit the inequality of the two, or the splitting up of the middle term into the extremes which, as extremes, are fundamentally opposed, "one being *recognized*, the other only *recognizing*" (185, 112–13). The outcome of the dialectic of lordship and bondage is for instance a form of recognition that is one-sided

---

22 Bataille, "The Psychological Structure of Fascism," in *Visions of Excess: Selected Writings, 1927–1939*, ed. and trans. Allan Stoekl (Minneapolis: University of Minnesota Press, 1985), pp. 146–47.

and unstable and goes to indicate the inherent instability of a society organized according to hierarchies or ranks. It is superseded by a more "rationalized" form of social existence, one in which the bondsman becomes truly conscious of what he is, and in which self-consciousness is "improved" through the enjoyment of work. Indeed, if the modes of recognition implicit in these two types of societies were not fundamentally distinct, then it would be possible to read the distinction between the noble and the base as simply carried forward in the (modern) distinction between rich and poor. In the world of rationalized work, the struggle for recognition is no less intense; but it is undertaken within the context of the material and psychological distinctions of social class, which reproduce daily and in a banalized form the trial by death essential to the confrontation of master and slave.[23]

When viewed in its historical context, the myth of Don Juan may be seen to reflect a shift in the patterns in which recognition has been sought and, similarly, a transformation of the modes in which the power to grant recognition has been controlled. In its original Spanish version by Tirso de Molina, the drama of Don Juan is projected along the axis defined by the features of "traditional" and "modern" societies and their respective modes of recognition: on the one hand, a culture of virtue and duty, in which interpersonal relations are determined by kinship ties and by bloodlines, in which actions are evaluated according to an archaic heroic ethos, and in which social functions and roles are sedimented into near static hierarchies; on the other hand, a culture in which the categories that determine personal worth are based largely on the standards of a psychologizing "individualism," as they came to be elaborated in the later writings of Gracián, Hobbes, and Locke; in which the central cultural myths are those of personal improvement and social progress (the latter to be achieved largely through self-cultivation and -individuation); and in which the self as desiring subject is displaced in fundamentally mobile ways.[24]

23 For a sociological analysis of the bourgeois principles of distinction, see Pierre Bourdieu, *Distinction: A Social Critique of the Judgement of Taste*, trans. Richard Nice (Cambridge, MA: Harvard University Press, 1984).
24 For a thinker like Bataille, the nature of "primitive" society is aligned to a thesis about the nature of societal rationalization as seen in the contrast between a bivalent archaic "sovereignty" and the bourgeois attachment to objects: "In archaic society, rank is tied to the consecrated presence of a subject whose

To be sure, it would be easy to read the story of Don Juan as a Manichaean drama of male aggression and female victimization, or as a display of phallic power and its assaults. In the most reactionary of these readings, critics have tended to construct the desire of the women in Mozart's operatic version of the myth as entirely subordinate to masculine power; the women surrounding Don Giovanni, and above all Donna Anna, are seen as hysterical figures *desiring* rape. But as Catherine Clément has shown, this is not only to misread female desire, it is to misinterpret the meaning of Don Juan as well. On her reading, Don Giovanni's central signifiers are "empty clothes"; the women are "entrapped by a figure, a cloak, a hat."[25] His desire is "good for seducing, good for identifying, good for locating oneself with empty images," but proves useless for providing the recognition that the desiring subject demands. For what are the possibilities of recognition where there is only "fear, threat, and the great, shadowy silhouette hiding in the dark" (*ibid.*)? Rather than assert masculine identity and power, Don Giovanni is in danger of losing himself through absorption with the women he seduces; but his absorption, unlike their hysteria, reveals the potential emptiness of an unrecognizable desire, the "emptiness of soul behind the cape and cloak" (p. 36).

The myth of Don Juan consistently appears to admit a vision of subjective desire, which seems to permit a heterogeneity of objects, and which is open to these risks of self-loss, while at the same time it seems to sacrifice that vision to the demand for cultural order and social control characteristic of the "traditional" world. In this case, I take the term "traditional" as indicating not only the hierarchical modes of recognition with which the morality of virtue was aligned, but also the gender distinctions supporting a patriarchal society. Whereas MacIntyre argued that the transition to modernity was the

sovereignty does not depend upon objects but integrates things into its movement. In bourgeois society, it still depends on ownership of objects that are neither sacral nor sovereign." I owe this reference to Habermas, in *The Philosophical Discourse of Modernity* (henceforth, *PDM*), trans. Frederick Lawrence (Cambridge, MA: MIT Press, 1987), p. 226. For a thinker like Lyotard, the difference between "modern" and "primitive" societies with respect to the question of desire is itself illusory. See *Economie libidinale* (Paris: Minuit, 1974), especially pp. 148–55.

25 Catherine Clément, *Opera or the Undoing of Women*, trans. Betsy Wing (Minneapolis: University of Minnesota Press, 1988), p. 35. See also Clément's discussion of the musicological interpretation of *Don Giovanni*, *ibid.*

product of a catastrophic "fall" in which the authentic meaning of virtue was lost to the memory of society as a whole, it may instead be seen that the principle of virtue was carried forward into modernity in the form of reactionary consciousness.

El burlador de Sevilla may further be seen as indicative of the problem of desire and recognition at the beginnings of the modern age insofar as Don Juan is the anti-type of the hero on whose behavior the values of traditional society so often are staked. If the traditional hero upholds the social order by remaining faithful to a series of pre-established values or codes, then Don Juan seeks by transgressing lines of distinction to undermine the social forms through which the values of traditional society are expressed. This possibility is opened up by a functional disposition of the ego which in its mobility is characteristic of modern, subjective desire, and it is reinforced by the promises offered both to the women whom Don Juan seduces and to an audience that had developed an expectation for values of a highly different sort. Don Juan is very much unlike the typical heroes of the Spanish stage, who seek to assert themselves through unswerving allegiance to the principles of heroic virtue, the formulation of which is given in the near talismanic slogan of epic derivation, "I am who I am" ("soy quien soy"). Don Juan splits the unity of self-consciousness emblematized in the quasi-epic integrity of word and deed. The seductions carried out by Don Juan are a direct function of the mobility he is able to achieve through his capacity for imitation and disguise and by his ability to anticipate (and thus pretend to "recognize") the desires of others. Indeed, the closural strength of this play and the social stability achieved at its conclusion must both be measured in proportion to the broken promises that precede them, and notwithstanding the fact that the promised pleasures must finally be repressed. As we will have occasion further to note, the play meets these demands through what is in essence a double ending: the first, adapted from classical tragedy, provides for the sublimation of those "illicit" desires that have been invested with Don Juan, while the second conforms to the patterns established by romantic comedy, and specifically to what is known as "new comedy,"[26] where the elimination of some central obstruction permits mutual recognition and the proper ordering of social relations in the

26 See Northrop Frye's early "The Argument of Comedy," *English Institute Essays*, 1948, ed. D. A. Robertson, Jr. (New York: Columbia University Press, 1949).

form of institutional marriages, or in the case of Isabela in this play, in what amounts to a remarriage:

> KING: Just punishment from Heaven has been dealt.
> Now let them all be married, since the cause
> Of all their harm is dead.
> OCTAVIO: Since Isabela has been widowed now, I wish to marry her.[27]

The conclusion of *El burlador de Sevilla* may thus be read as an example of the desire to reestablish social order, through a reassertion of the principles of recognition in terms of honor, within the modern age. The psychological mobility of Don Juan, which disrupts the possibilities for recognition in the traditional sense, is perceived as a threat to the ethical foundations of traditional society, but is overcome once it is discovered that within it lies an extreme concern for honor and virtue, the very bases of self-consciousness in a "traditional" world. Consider for instance the following exchange between Don Juan and the "Stone Guest":

> GONZALO: Will you keep your word as a gentleman?
> DON JUAN: I am a man of honor, and I keep my word, because I am a knight.
> GONZALO: Then give me your hand on it. Don't be afraid!
> DON JUAN: What! *Me* afraid? I'd give you my hand if you were Hell itself.

$$(\text{V. } 2435\text{–}41)$$

If the heroes of the fixed or stable self of traditional society are characteristically the bearers of a conservative ideology, then Don Juan is modern, mobile, and subversive in relation to them. As the inversion of the prototypical epic hero – the hero who sustains his identity through an inflexible selfhood and an unswerving honor – Don Juan is able to join Shakespeare's Iago and those other modern subjects who fashion a subversive identity through a series of disguises and feints. As "a man with no name" ("un hombre sin nombre") Don Juan matches Iago's claim of self-displacement, "I am not I": "It is as sure as you are Roderigo, / Were I the Moor, I would not be Iago; / In following him, I follow but myself" (*Othello*, I. i. 57–59). Don Juan's principle effort is to come into contact with a reservoir of energy which he discharges in typically modern fashion,

---

27 Except for slight modifications, I follow the translation of Eric Bently, in *The Classic Theatre*, III (Garden City: Doubleday, 1959). I follow the Spanish text of Joaquín Casalduero (Madrid: Cátedra, 1977), here v. 2852–56.

that is, in the form of discontinuous flows. The fragmentary nature of his experience is marked by his rapid flight after each encounter and is summed up in the refrain "¡Ensilla, Catalinón!" ("Saddle up, Catalinón!"). It has been said in this regard that Don Juan is one of the first dramatic heroes to be conscious of time, but it would be more accurate to say that time in *El burlador* is transformed into motion and that the essence of Don Juan's activity is elaborated in the moment of delay that is won in defiance. Hence the importance of his rejoinder, "¡Qué largo me lo fiáis!" ("Trust me a while longer!").

Insofar as Don Juan attempts to free himself from the social structurations of power of traditional society, he may also be seen as the subversive or revolutionary whose task is to produce a new, post-Oedipal model of desire, according to which the need for recognition would no longer exist. Read according to the model presented by Gilles Deleuze and Felix Guattari in *Anti-Oedipus: Capitalism and Schizophrenia*, he would represent the emancipatory potential of a desire freed from all constraints, one whose task is "to learn from the psychic flow how to shake off the Oedipal yoke and the effects of power, in order to initiate a radical politics of *desire freed from all beliefs*." Such an emancipatory desire "dissolves the mystifications of power through the kindling, on all levels, of anti-Oedipal forces – the schizzes-flows – forces that escape all coding, scramble all the codes, and fall in all directions: orphans (no daddy-mommy-me), atheists (no beliefs), and nomads (no habits, no territories)."[28] But if the transformative power of desire is characteristically regulated and contained by a series of narrative structures that embody and reinforce the values dominant within the social sphere, then *El burlador* is an anti-narrative that Tirso encloses within a framework of divine justice and retributive punishment, thereby subsuming Don Juan within the most orthodox of theocentric and Absolutist paradigms. In this way, the transformative potential inherent in the emancipatory vision of a "fatherless society" is forcefully restrained. The variability of subjective desire is embraced while its emancipatory potential is excluded, or perhaps more soberly viewed, that variability is embraced *in order to be* excluded; exclusion is the way in which society regulates itself, insulating itself against historical change by

28 *Anti-Oedipus: Capitalism and Schizophrenia*, trans. Robert Hurley, Mark Seem, and Helen R. Lane (1977; rpt. Minneapolis: University of Minnesota Press, 1983); from the Introduction by Mark Seem, p. xxi, emphasis mine.

effectively resisting the modes of recognition that new forms of desire might bring.

The fact that Don Juan is throughout the play an orphaned or nameless man ("un hombre sin nombre") is thrown into bold relief by his situation within a society that otherwise takes its bearings from figures of absolute self-possession and self-mastery, the King and the noble *caballero*, the knight. By contrast with these figures, Don Juan introduces us into the world of free circulation and exchange that has been often associated with the emergent consciousness of modernity. Indeed, it would not be difficult to press this point further and imagine a relationship between the "free circulation" of capital and the false promises offered by Don Juan. Like Ruiz de Alarcón's Don García in *La verdad sospechosa*, or Dorante of Corneille's *Le Menteur*, for whom the contractual promise becomes a veritable parody of the knight's sacred vow, Don Juan promises what he cannot deliver and gives what he does not own. In this way he disrupts the principles of mutual recognition founded on the ideal of direct exchange and thrusts us toward the endless alienation characteristic of the commodity production and exchange-value of the modern world.[29] He is, in other words, the underlying form of capital itself.

Consider in this light Marx's description of the disorienting effects of capital. According to Marx, when we buy in order to sell we enter a relationship in which a great leap (*salto mortale*) immediately takes place in the transformation of a commodity into that particular form of money known as capital; the circuit is rendered "complete" at the moment of purchase, when capital is again transformed into a commodity. As the mechanism of alienated relationships, money *qua* capital is "the absolutely alienable commodity, because it is all other commodities divested of their shape, the product of their universal alienation. It reads all prices backwards, and thus as it were mirrors itself in the bodies of all other commodities" (p. 205). In other words, the cycle of commodity exchange makes recognition impossible – by rendering things unrecognizable. Moreover, unlike the direct

29 I am thinking of the sections on the commodity, money, and exchange in Marx, *Capital*, I, trans. Ben Fowkes (New York: Vintage Books, 1977). See also Michel Serres's analysis of Molière's *Dom Juan*, "The Apparition of Hermes: *Dom Juan*," in *Hermes: Literature, Science, Philosophy*, ed. Josué Harari and David F. Bell (Baltimore: Johns Hopkins University Press, 1982), pp. 3–14; and also Shoshana Felman, *Le Scandale du corps parlant* (Paris: Seuil, 1980). In *Economie libidinale* Lyotard raises the interesting question of whether, from the perspective of desire, the concept of "traditional society" has any force.

exchange of products, the effects of alienation do not disappear once the commodities have themselves been exchanged. Rather, the process allows capital to proliferate as "absolute alienation" throughout society as a whole. Insofar as "alienation" may be understood in terms of the denial of the very possibility for recognition, it allows us to interpret the deep-structure Marxist analysis of modes of production in ethical terms. Whereas the direct exchange of commodities may be regarded as a relationship in which beings are taken as ends in themselves, the circulation of money as capital becomes itself an end, one whose validity is impossible to measure according to an objective standard or good. In Stendhal's interpretation, Don Juan represents a chief example of the alienation of value inherent in such a system; he is "a dishonest merchant who takes all and pays nothing" (*On Love*, p. 207). In repeatedly transgressing his word of honor Don Juan becomes in essence a model of free circulation, one who generates a need for the recognition that it is up to the symbolic order of society to provide.

In what ways does the drama of Don Juan itself deal with these disturbing facts? The initiating tension in the myth of Don Juan may well be that between the morality of virtue as embedded in a hierarchical society on the one hand and the modes of recognition characteristic of "subjective" desire on the other, based largely on the differentiations of gender and social class.[30] But the appropriate model for the final configuration of the Don Juan myth, one that might explain the paradigmatic status that it has achieved, would be one in which the problem of desire is "resolved" by a form of resistance to the openness that recognition within the context of modernity demands.[31] Rather than simply reinforce the standards of virtue, honor, and rank in terms of which the (masculine) distinctions of status are read, the myth of Don Juan itself recognizes the subject's potential "emptiness of the soul," but closes this awareness off, thus advancing the values of traditional, patriarchal society within

30 In the specific case of Spain, this hierarchy takes the form of caste relations, with its preoccupations over cleanliness of blood and personal inviolability. For further discussion, see Américo Castro, *De la edad conflictiva* (Madrid: Taurus, 1961), and A. J. Cascardi, "Don Juan and the Discourse of Modernism," in *Tirso's Don Juan: The Metamorphoses of a Theme*, ed. J. Solà-Solé, (Washington, D.C.: Catholic University of America Press, 1988), pp. 151–59.

31 For further discussion, see A. J. Cascardi, "The Old and the New: The Spanish *comedia* and the Resistance to Historical Change," *Renaissance Drama*, 17, n.s. (1986), 1–28.

modernity as a reactionary device, as a means to reestablish the possibilities of recognition demanded by subjective desire but which it is itself unable to meet. For this reason, the myth may provide some deeper understanding of the phenomenon we have encountered on several occasions in the chapters above, namely the presence within modernity of "residual" (and in this case, potentially reactionary) practices and beliefs, for the Don Juan myth reveals the desires through which such positions of resistance are sustained. Moreover, if one considers seventeenth-century society as open to disparate modes of recognition, then the conservatism of the myth of Don Juan need not be seen as a function of those interests devoted to the maintenance of the *status quo* and to the assurance of the power of those in whose hands it had already come to rest. Rather, the ultimately stabilizing function of the myth, its reassertion of the power of the social order over the desiring self, may be attributed to the greater need for recognition created by the loosening of the constraints on the attachment of desires to pre-established objects and ends. Without a source such as this, it would be nearly impossible to account for those features of the play which critics like J. A. Maravall have described as particular to the theatre in seventeenth-century Spain, most notably its ability to control and direct those who were least likely to benefit from the politics of conservatism, the *vulgo*.[32] In Maravall's judgment, early modern society had developed an affinity for theatrical works of this sort because of its need to lend an appearance of legitimacy to a structure of social relations founded on the practical domination of one group by another and, in so doing, to avoid the ethical questions which such situations of domination are bound to raise.[33] Yet nearly the reverse would seem to be closer to the truth. As we shall see, it is in fact the openness to an ethical principle, that of recognition, that establishes the patterns of closure

32 On Maravall's reading, the "traditional" order of society is one which was imposed on it in the seventeenth century in the interests of maintaining the status quo, in much the same way, and through many of the same techniques, that an orthodox theology was "imposed" by the preachers and moralists of the Baroque. See Maravall, *La cultura del barroco* (Barcelona: Ariel, 1975).

33 Maravall writes: "Los españoles emplearon el teatro para, sirviéndose de instrumento popularmente eficaz, contribuir a socializar un sistema de convenciones, sobre las cuales en ese momento se estimó había de verse apoyado el orden social concreto vigente en el país, orden que había que conservar, en cualquier paso, sin plantear la cuestión de un posible contenido ético." *Teatro y literatura en la sociedad Barroca* (Madrid: Seminarios y Ediciones, 1972), pp. 32–33.

and organizes the historical "content" of the theatrical version of the Don Juan myth.

And yet it would be wrong to center the demand for recognition (which may or may not be met) in Don Juan alone. The ambiguities of desire are reflected as well in the vacillations of female desire, in the women who succumb while defending themselves (Cf. Mozart: "vorrei e no vorrei"; "I would like and I would not like"). Consider for example the episode with Tisbea the fisherwoman in the Tirso play, the only one of the four seductions in this version of the work that does not in some manifest way conform to the patterns of mobility and improvisation mentioned above. Tisbea claims immunity from Don Juan by appeal to the power of her own self-mastery:

Of all whose feet the fleeting waters kiss (as the breezes kiss the rose and jasmine), of the fishers' daughters and longshore maidens, of all those I am the only one exempt from Love, the only one who rules in sole, tyrannical contempt the prisons which He stocks with fools. (v. 375–382)

But as Tisbea's impassioned rhetoric of resistance and her subsequent seduction display, no desire is powerful enough to master itself; every desire seeks recognition (and in a certain sense, mastery) in another desire. In the specific case at hand, we see that the resistance to desire is tantamount to a denial of the need for recognition, and that this in turn is a form of self-deception that ends in enslavement or domination: "I was the one that ever made fun of men and cheated them, then came a knight to sever the thread, and by base stratagem destroy and kill my honor dead by swearing marriage as his bait, enjoy me and profane my bed" (v. 1,013–21).

Historically, the need for recognition becomes all the more acute where desire is fundamentally mobile and cannot be modeled according to the pattern of an exemplary figure (e.g., the prince, the king, or noble knight); for where the possibility of winning the recognition of another is no longer available within the order of society as it stands, desire may become less the source of transformation than the object of repression; this repressive force may be brought to bear either by the individual or, as we witness in the tragic and comic endings of the play, by the symbolic power of society as such. With regard to those conclusions it now can be seen that they represent two distinct possible outcomes for modern desire. The first seeks to reduce the mobility of desire by moving toward stillness (for example, of the Stone Guest) and ultimately towards death. The second seeks the containment of desire, through social institutions, rules, and codes (for example, of marriage). Together, these work through a process wherein desire must first be desexualized – "cooled off," in Paul Ricoeur's phrase – so that the process of socialization or civilization may take place. More specifically in regard to *El burlador*, the first, tragic-like conclusion enacts the near sacrificial sublimation of desire in the form of a banquet; indeed, it would not be excessive to read this banquet as a secularized version of the Eucharistic or totem meal. This ritual in turn permits accession to that form of life which we recognize as "culture," as emblematized in the marriages sanctioned by the King. Yet in spite of the double ending of the play, desire is never eliminated and the demand for recognition is never met by another desire and so fails to satisfy the demands of self-consciousness; desire is at best "managed" or contained, with greater or lesser success, just as the damaged honor of Isabela, Ana, Aminta, and Tisbea may be hidden from historical or social consciousness, but never repaired.

In Don Juan's meeting with the Stone Guest, he would seem to demonstrate the consciousness that Hegel ascribes to the superior individual or noble-spirited soul, that is, to the one who seeks above all the certification of his honor in the recognition of another. In light of Don Juan's display of honor, though, two important qualifications must be made. The first is that while Don Juan seems to possess a deep-seated nobility, he is not a knight but an aristocratic courtier, which is to say, a degenerate transformation of the warrior whose true nobility is confirmed in the trial by death. The eradication of aristocratic vice, emblematized in the play's first, tragic-like ending and in the "ennobling" transformation of Don Juan, reverses the progression of consciousness that Hegel saw as necessarily following from the nobleman's willingness to risk everything in the fight to the death. In Tirso's version, this reversal permits the comic-romantic closure of the play and the refounding of society in the institution of marriage. All the figures who appear in the play's "second ending" have suffered degradation or dishonor at the hands of Don Juan. They have themselves been rendered "base." Yet they are uniformly redeemed, provided of course they can themselves find their need for mutual recognition "satisfied" by the symbolic authority of a noble-spirited soul, which Tirso supplies in the figure of the King.

Considered in this light, Don Juan's encounter with the Stone Guest may be seen to have implications that reach well beyond the manifest irony of the simultaneous defeat and ennoblement of a mobile ego by a statue, a man made of stone, and also beyond the containment or immobilization of the modern ego through the devices of dramatic closure. This is because the final encounter reincorporates by reenactment the procedures through which social recognition in pre-modern societies is imagined as taking place. The order of traditional society is typically confirmed in moments of ritual and symbolic exchange, such as occur on the occasions of duels, banquets, and wedding feasts. On such occasions the knight seeks to reconfirm his self-mastery and self-possession through the recognition of another; but, if this achievement is not to degenerate into an unstable dialectic, and thus perpetuate the very desires it is meant to control, the exchanges accomplished and the recognitions achieved must be absolutely reciprocal. There must be no net gain or loss, which in Tirso's version of the play is insured by the principle of retributive justice. As Don Gonzalo de Ulloa repeatedly asserts, "You must pay for what you've done" ("Quien tal hace, que tal pague"). The banquet scene neatly inverts the occasion of Don Juan's seduction of Aminta at the wedding feast, magically transforming him into a noble and honorable (which is also to say, self-possessed) knight. As a result, the encounter with the Stone Guest, which stills and immobilizes subjective desire, may be said to generate the very phenomenon that MacIntyre has described in terms of the morality of virtue, or that Weber has called the consciousness of "traditional society." We may now go further and say that modernity does not simply exclude the principles of virtue characteristic of the traditional world, but rather that subjective desire generates a need for recognition that may be supplied in terms of a conservative social vision. Programs to reinstitute the morality of virtue are ultimately the expressions of such a stance. With reference to the myth of Don Juan, it is only as a result of the production of this apparently reactionary mode of recognition, itself a response to the increasing mobility of desire in the early modern age, that *El burlador* can move beyond the exclusionary moment of tragedy to what is its true and revealing conclusion, the ending in which society maintains a wholly comic demeanor as it goes about its daily business and seeks to perpetuate itself. In this version of the myth of Don Juan, as in Freudian psychology, it is the repression of desire that allows for a vision of "civilized" love.

In conclusion, we can say that the principle of subjective desire turns on a tension between the mobile self, which pretends to cross or transcend every principle of distinction, and the tendency of society to locate an internal principle of order capable of regulating desires and establishing laws. Don Juan seduces women of every rank, and in so doing he confirms his position outside this dichotomy, thus revealing the hidden "nobility" of his desire. As Stendhal wrote, "Don Juan disclaims all the obligations which link him to the rest of humanity ... The idea of equality is as maddening to him as water to a rabid dog; this is why pride of birthright becomes Don Juan's character so well. With the idea of equality of rights vanishes that of justice – or rather, if Don Juan comes of an illustrious stock, such vulgar notions would never have entered his head" (*On Love*, p. 207). The mere introduction of a pre-existing principle of order will appear to generate a purely reactionary demand for recognition, in which the potentially liberating mobility of modern desire is put to rest by harsh external law. And yet the problem posed by the comic dimension of the Tirsian play is considerably more complex than this, for the order imposed is accepted as internal, as forthcoming from the desiring subjects themselves. The ability of the King to sanction the happiness of his subjects is the signature of the power of society to inspire voluntary submission to its laws. In this way, the promise of the satisfaction of desire acts to conceal the system of order from the subjects who are controlled by it, and comes to appear as if it is willed by the subjects themselves.

The genealogy of the "psychological subject" as in principle free, but as in reality bound to a symbolic social order that they themselves create, may further be explained in relation to the historical claim that the Renaissance constitutes a moment of transition or historical transformation from a society organized around a principle of hierarchical distinctions to one that is differentiated along increasingly functional, psychological, and economic lines (the divisions of class). In chapter 1 I suggested that the transition from the hierarchical social order of the traditional world to the functionally differentiated society of the early modern age was made possible in part by the principles of rhetoric in evidence at court. We may now extend this analysis and say that the these mediating conjunctures make possible the formation of a "desiring subject"or "psychological self." More precisely, the origins of the modern ego can be found in the rejection of the notion that honor can be certified, as in the case of the noble warrior, in a fight to the death. Rather, the modern individual must seek to certify honor through the more refined avenue of speech. Whereas the fight to the death will establish an undisputed hierarchy of rank and prestige, discourse establishes characteristically variable or "inessential" distinctions and so resembles rhetoric in the pejorative sense of the term. Accordingly, we may trace the emergence of a "psychological subject" and the ethical roots of modernity to the rhetorical traditions and courtly culture of the Renaissance. Through instruction in the techniques of argumentation *in utramque partem* and through the development of a complex psychology that emphasized astute observation and a cultivated "naturalism" (*sprezzatura*), the essential self, the self willing to assume the risks of epic and Classical tragedy (ultimately, the risk of death), came gradually to be transformed into a less essential and more playful self. This is the self paradigmatically modeled in, among other places, Castiglione's courtier book. The modern subject is marked in the first instance by a division between the essential and the inessential self, or perhaps more accurately, by the division of personal identity into these two versions of the self. In Kierkegaard's interpretation of the myth of Don Juan in *Either/Or*, for instance, the seducer is bifurcated into two separate identities: the "essential self" stands in need of only a single love, and exemplifies what Kierkegaard elsewhere refers to as "purity of heart," while the other, "inessential" self, like Mozart's Don Giovanni, requires a thousand and three. And yet the greater fear attached to the problem of self-division, as witnessed in such places as Diderot's *Neveu de Rameau*, is principally that the rhetorical or performing self, the "inessential" self, the self of mobile desires and fluent speech, may eclipse the central self. Stated in slightly different terms, this is the fear of the absorption of the self by its roles.

As the (sham) sincerity of Don Juan's promises makes plain, however, the fear that the self may be eclipsed by its roles is negated by the promise of an alternative to the "essential" self, which we might describe as the subject *qua* "authentic" self. Due in part to Lionel Trilling's remarks on *Hamlet* in *Sincerity and Authenticity*, Shakespeare's Polonius is widely regarded as the most important spokesman for the principle of "sincerity," and sincerity is taken as a means to stabilize against a self that is, like Hamlet's, fully absorbed by its roles. But I would instead cite Baltasar Gracián, who reformulates and elevates the principle of authenticity into the basis for social rationality in the early modern world: "Believe your heart. Never contradict it, for it usually predicts what matters most about the future."[34]

Gracián's observations must be understood in the context of a world that is critical of, but nonetheless still dominated by, the society of the court. The model of social relations exemplified in courtly society carries forward the principles of absolute distinctions and "exemplary" relations characteristic of a hierarchical society into an environment where they are tested by the increasingly verbal, psychological, and individualizing nature of personal relations. According to the principles of hierarchical order, for instance, the prince would provide the example for the members of the court; the protocols of courtship mimic a hierarchical distinction between "lower" and "higher" classes or kinds. In one respect, the courtiers constitute a distinct class; yet while they serve as educators to the prince they maintain an interest in their own self-advancement. As a class of "specialists," they maintain, as Kenneth Burke said, "a purely professional interest in truth, not identical with the preference of the 'sovereign.'"[35] The increasing "psychologization"of rules of conduct at court, their gradual penetration by detailed observations drawn from social experience, would in their turn have been inconceivable without the increasing differentiation of society along functional lines. In order for such distinctions to be achieved, the subjects involved must be individualized to such an extent that their behavior can be "read" on the basis of psychological traits.[36] The arts of "psychological" observation arose in a context where the individual did not yet have the full autonomy of the modern subject; indeed, in a world of absolutely disgregated individuals, it would be neither necessary nor possible to investigate another's consciousness, motives, or affects. Unlike the empirical psychology that later took shape in the writings of Locke and Hume, and that assumed as its object the subject-as-formed, the courtly art of human observation sought to view the self-in-process. The courtly art of observation took as its object a self that had not yet come to conceive of itself in

---

34 Gracián, *Oráculo manual y arte de prudencia*, ed. Arturo del Hoyo (Barcelona: Plaza y Janés, 1986), no. 178, p. 431; my translation.

35 Burke, *A Rhetoric of Motives* (Berkeley: University of California Press, 1969), p. 230.

36 Cf. Niklas Luhmann, *Love as Passion*, trans. Jeremy Gaines and Doris L. Jones (Cambridge, MA: Harvard University Press, 1986), p. 34.

abstract terms as detachable from a social context in the manner of the Cartesian, Lockean, or Humean subject.

Because of the central role of courtly society in enforcing tacit rules of conduct, in regulating manners, and in controlling social aggression, the members of the court came to be identified according to an ethical norm; they perceived themselves on an exclusionary basis by the identification of "high society" with "good society." In the interpretation of Norbert Elias, the "courtization" of society, and in particular the courtly transformation of the warrior caste, mirrors the civilizing process itself; it springs from the ascription of an ethical value to the taming of social aggression or, what amounts to the same thing, the sublimation of "untamed" desires and the transformation of the self into an object of psychological differentiation and control:

> In the midst of a large populated area which by and large is free of physical violence, a "good society" is formed. But even if the use of physical violence now recedes from human intercourse, if even duelling is now forbidden, people now exert pressure and force on each other in a wide variety of different ways.[37]

As Elias goes on to explain, continuous calculations of worth form the basis of every "good society." These are not, as in Hegel's interpretation of wealth, conceived to be a concealed or partial manifestation of a general and transcending good, but something closer to Nietzsche's analysis of the pseudo-moral distinctions underlying gradations of class.[38] In the case of the late Renaissance courts, the result is the formation for the first time in history of a "psychological subject" as both the acute observer of the social behavior of others and as the object of a similarly intense scrutiny and social/ethical positioning. Elias's point is that the development of courtly rationality played a no less important part in the modernization of society than the urban-commercial rationality treated by Weber. The court is, if not the first, then certainly among the most important centers of societal rationalization. Insofar as rationalization brings an increase in discipline and self-control, a renunciation of physical violence, and the increased regulation of libidinal impulses, the rationalization of society and the "psycho-

37 Norbert Elias, *Power and Civility*, trans. Edmund Jephcott (New York: Pantheon, 1982), pp. 270–71.
38 Hegel: "Wealth...is the Good; it leads to the general enjoyment, is there to be made use of, and procures for everyone the consciousness of his particular self. It is *implicitly* universal beneficence." *PhS*, sec. 497, p. 303.

logization" of the self go hand in hand; "psychological" analysis and observation develop in this context as techniques of mastery and as means of self-control. Hence La Bruyère on the courtly self: "A man who knows the court is master of his gestures, of his eyes and his expression; he is deep, impenetrable; he dissimulates the bad turns he does, smiles at his enemies, suppresses his ill-temper, disguises his passions, disavows his heart, speaks and acts against his feelings."[39] Hence Gracián, who attempts to adopt the courtly ethos to the circumstances of an emergent bourgeoisie: "To play an open game is neither useful nor fun."[40] As Gracián allows us to see, "psychological" observation represents something more than a mechanism of control; it affords a means for self-reflection comparable to the more abstract operations of the Cartesian *cogito*. Its goal is a form of "wisdom" that bears comparison with Aristotle's prudential reasoning, notwithstanding the fact that it has lost the sense of an inherent connection between means and ends: "No puede uno ser señor de sí," writes Gracián, "si primero no se comprehende. Hay espejos del rostro, no los hay del ánimo: séalo la discreta reflexión sobre sí" ("One cannot be master of oneself if one does not first understand oneself. There are mirrors for the face, but not the soul; let prudent self-reflection serve this role") (no. 89).

And yet it would be wrong to identify the court, as Elias does, exclusively with the increasing rationalization of the world. The formation of the psychological self as modeled through the process of courtization reflects a more pervasive "crisis" in the nature of self-consciousness or, what amounts to the same thing, a large-scale transformation in the nature of recognition and in the means for the certification of nobility (worth) and truth. A writer like Gracián is faced with the task of finding a new standard of conduct, an ethos, for the self where two potential pathways have been closed off. The first is that of the common man, the *vulgo*, who is characterized in ethical terms as incapable of self-reflection and whose discourse is therefore labeled as "base" (Cf. *Oráculo manual*, no. 28: "En nada vulgar"[41]). The second is the model of the aristocratic individual or "noble soul," whose pursuit of honor has been rendered "inessential" or transformed into an aristocratic vice and whose chief appeal, as

39 La Bruyère, "De la Cour," *Caractères*, in *Oeuvres*, ed. Julien Benda (Paris: Gallimard, 1951), p. 215, no. 2.
40 Gracián, *Oráculo manual*, no. 3, p. 359 ("El jugar a juego descubierto ni es de utilidad, ni de gusto").   41 See also nos. 69, 206, 209.

Kenneth Burke said in his reading of *Le Neveu de Rameau*, has come to reside in his somewhat extravagant "style."[42] Insofar as the images of "noble" and "base" no longer represent historically available or ethically viable positions for the self, Gracián fashions the image of the "prudent" man, the *discreto*, a forerunner of the modern subject *qua* bourgeois self. The "prudent man's" ideals are characterized by his self-imposed moderation and restraint as well as by the control of desire required, for reasons we shall discuss further below, in the rationalized bourgeois world. In his pursuit of moderation and self-control, Gracián's *discreto* must above all refuse the example of Don Juan, who in a moment of historical transition represents a sublime mixing of the noble and the base. I take the following observations, written in the characteristically tempered style of Gracián's *Oráculo manual*, as indicative of the restrictions that are self-imposed on existence in the modern bourgeois world: "A wise man reduced all wisdom to moderation in all things" (82); "Never refer to oneself" (117); "Without lying, not to speak all the truths. There is nothing that requires more tact than truth, which is like a bloodletting from the heart. Just as much is required to know how to speak the truth as to know how to silence it" (181). In part because the *discreto* has been "educated" in life at court, he has grown accustomed to the self-control that existence in a rationalized society entails. His "modesty" incorporates a newly psychologized "second nature"; it is a civilizing product of artifice that is necessary for existence within the symbolic order of the modern world.[43]

As I hope in the following section to show, an awareness of the ways in which the subject is pre-positioned within the symbolic order of society is necessary to a reimagination of desire's social force. Insofar as the subject can be made aware that the particularizing differences among individuals are the products of a second (psychological) nature, and are not themselves inherent, natural, or innate, it may be possible to view the differentiation among individuals as a positive moment in the achievement of the social, rather than as an impediment to the reconstruction of society along

42 Burke, "Diderot on 'Pantomime,'" in *A Rhetoric of Motives*, p. 145.
43 Gracián writes: "Más se requiere hoy para un sabio que antiguamente para siete, y más es menester para tratar con un solo hombre en estos tiempos que con todo un pueblo en los pasados." ("It takes more nowadays to make a single wise man than seven in times gone by, and more is needed these days to deal with a single man than with an entire town in former times.") *Oráculo manual*, no. 1, p. 359.

communitarian lines. As Hegel wrote of the passage from nature to culture, "If ... individuality is erroneously supposed to be rooted in the particularity of nature and character, then in the actual world there are no individualities and no characters, but everyone is like everyone else; but this presumed individuality really only exists in someone's mind, an imaginary existence which has no abiding place in this world" (*PhS*, 489, p. 298).

Social norms: recognition and transformation

Our discussion of the myth of Don Juan enables us to recover a vision of modernity in which the hierarchical principles of social distinction are reincorporated, albeit in a newly transformed and "secularized" way, within the individualizing and "psychological" differentiations characteristic of the modern world. At the same time, our discussion of the court has enabled us to see that the problem of recognition is exacerbated as the modernization of society is more thoroughly achieved. Whereas in the traditional world the self might take the king's desires as a model of libidinal investment, courtly society begins to mimic hierarchical principles where strict distinctions of rank can no longer be taken as a reflection of the order of nature itself. Following Hobbes, one might say that the crucial object of "possession" is, and continues to be, prestige. And yet, exactly as is the case with the "inner law" of conscience, the subject willingly allows his or her desires to be positioned by these social principles, and is thereby more constrained than under the conditions of an absolute hierarchy of differences in social rank. Ironically, the principle of constraint hidden within subjective desire is named "freedom" by the modern subject.[44] As Kenneth Burke remarked in his reading of *Le Neveu de Rameau*, a bona fide hierarchy allows for the participation within society, as constituted around a framework of "vertical" distinctions, for all those whose lives it organizes. But the substitute for hierarchy developed in the modern world is founded upon an opposing idea, viz., that of participation based on a series of non-essential, individualizing, or "psychological" differences. In the idiom of a Shaftesbury, participation in society is based on differences

44 See Juliet Flower MacCannell, "Oedipus Wrecks: Lacan, Stendhal and the Narrative Form of the Real," in *Lacan and Narration: The Psychoanalytic Difference in Narrative Theory*, ed. Robert Con Davis (Baltimore: Johns Hopkins University Press, 1983), p. 919; and also her *Figuring Lacan: Criticism and the Cultural Unconscious* (Lincoln: University of Nebraska Press, 1986).

in "characteristics," or on the refinements of "qualities." Whatever the specific terms invoked, it is the internal differentiation of society, as seen in the individualizing "psychologization" of subjects, that makes its participants unaware of the degree to which they are pre-positioned by a "symbolic order" that they themselves create. As Stendhal wrote in *On Love*, citing the Duchesse de Chaulnes, "'a duchess is never more than thirty in the eyes of a bourgeois'" (p. 43).

To be sure, a desire freed from the principles of imitation that bind it to the order of nature as represented in the central, sovereign will provides a significant source of empowerment for the modern individual *qua* subjective self. And yet a desire that lacks the clear distinctions between, e.g., master and slave, noble and base, is in danger of losing its orientation within a network of functional differentiations where roles are continuously reversed. Hence Kenneth Burke reminds us that "the division of labor requires a society of specialists serving one another. The garage man is the dishwasher's servant, the dishwasher is the garage man's servant, an 'invidious' relation made 'democratic' by money and the constant reversal of roles" (*Rhetoric of Motives*, p. 224). Hence Lacan's forceful critique of the social violence that results from the "emancipation" of desire from established terms of order:

What we are faced with ... is the increasing absence of all those saturations of the superego and ego ideal that are realized in all kinds of organic forms in traditional societies, forms that extend from the rituals of everyday intimacy to the periodical festivals in which the community manifests itself. We no longer know them except in their most obviously degraded aspects. Futhermore, in abolishing the cosmic polarity of the male and female principles, our society undergoes all the psychological effects proper to the modern phenomenon known as the "battle between the sexes" – a vast community of such efforts, at the limit between the "democratic" anarchy of the passions and their desperate levelling down by the "great winged hornet" of narcissistic tyranny. It is clear that the promotion of the ego today culminates, in conformity with the utilitarian conception of man that reinforces it, in an ever more advanced realization of man as individual, that is to say, in an isolation of the soul ever more akin to its original dereliction.[45]

45 Lacan, "Aggresivity in Psychoanalysis," in *Ecrits*, trans. Alan Sheridan (New York: Norton, 1977), pp. 26–27. Lacan goes on to say that "In the 'emancipated' man of modern society, this splitting reveals, right down to the depths of his being, a neurosis of self-punishment ... It is this pitiful victim, this escaped, irresponsible outlaw, who is condemning modern man to the most formidable social hell" (pp. 28–29).

The point to be added to this analysis is that desire loses its bearings under the false impression that it is "free" to transcend social structures, free to position itself outside the symbolic order of society *tout court*, while in fact it remains bound by a series of established codes and social controls. While a theory of the subject that would focus exclusively on society as the locus of repression and constraint necessarily denies the transformative nature of desire, the contrary attempt to deny all constraints can only produce a conception of freedom that is empty and abstract. As we shall presently see, an understanding of the way in which the subject is positioned by the symbolic order of society is a necessary step to the recovery of recognition and to the establishment of desire as a transformative force.

How can a theory of the transformative potential of desire be reconciled with the demand for recognition implicit in the formation of social norms? How can this potential and this demand be brought to bear on our understanding of the modern subject-self? As we have seen in the previous section of this chapter, a crucial, historical transformation of desire takes place in the shift from the hierarchical divisions of an honor-bound society to the individualizing principles of psychological and class distinction dominant in the modern world. One might describe this as a process in which the nobility or "self-possession" characteristic of the knight is replaced by the "selfishness" of the modern subject, where selfishness is understood primarily as a manifestation of individualistic psychology and only secondarily as a form of materialistic possessiveness. The civilizing effort to limit the aggressivity of desire through the institution of rationalized social procedures of the kind analyzed by thinkers like Weber is made more subtly apparent in the attempt to establish individualizing distinctions and to satisfy the demand for recognition in a cultured and discursive fashion. If the search for recognition is prototypically carried out in the noble warrior's trial by death, then that struggle is overturned and supplanted by the discursive warfare of modern society, which begins in the court. Modern "individualism" is a principle by which the members of society are set fundamentally apart; and yet the process of social differentiation remains a concealed expression of normative needs, from which we may derive a means for the reconstruction of desire in social terms. In other words, the demand for recognition – which is fundamentally a social demand – remains present within modern society despite the fact that individuals are defined as fundamentally disgregated and that material existence is a struggle for differentiation in a world where rigid hierarchies have broken down. Indeed, it seems that there is no desire so "private" that it will not lead us to reconstruct the social basis of existence according to the demand for recognition and to recover therefrom the possibility of recasting subjective desire along social lines.[46] And yet the attempt to reclaim the socializing potential of desire, and to recover the transformative potential that the differences among desiring individuals create, will remain empty and abstract as long as we fail to understand the nature of the social as a symbolic force. For it is only through and against the symbolic order of society that individual desires, poised for the task of recognition, can have any bearing on the concrete world.

In Kojève's analysis of desire, which follows Hegel's through at least the dialectic of master and slave, the problem of social reality follows immediately from the fact of subjective self-consciousness. More specifically, the manifold nature of self-consciousness and the heterogeneity of desires lead us to posit the social on the ground of the ineradicable differences among selves:

In order that Self-Consciousness be born from the Sentiment of self, in order that the human reality come into being within the animal reality, this reality must be essentially manifold. Therefore, man can appear on earth only within a herd. That is why the human reality can only be social. But for the herd to become a society, multiplicity of Desires is not sufficient by itself; in addition, the Desires of each member of the herd must be directed – or potentially directed – toward the Desires of the other members. If the human reality is a social reality, society is human only as a set of Desires mutually desiring one another as Desires.

(*Introduction to the Reading of Hegel*, pp. 5–6)

In Kojève's view, the relation of the subject to society is the relation of one desire to another. So conceived, desire is a force that serves to differentiate rather than to bind individuals. If we begin by accepting the differences among subjects that desire creates, and if we seek to preserve this differentiating power as a basis for the transformation of society itself, then we must interpret the demand for recognition as

---

46 For related arguments concerning the limits of skepticism and the persistence of community, see A. J. Cascardi, *The Bounds of Reason* (New York: Columbia University Press, 1986).

potentially infinite in scope. In response to the claim that the demand
for infinite recognition is nothing more than a reflection of Hegel's
infinite self-consciousness, conceived as an abstract, self-transforming
substance, it may be said that the demand for recognition shows how
the idea of transformation can be made concrete. Taken independently, the idea of recognition is indeed unstable and abstract; but
the potential openness to transformation shows how recognition may
be understood in social terms. More specifically, the normative
standard that the idea of recognition helps establish is one in which
desire could serve an essentially social demand, through an
enlargement of the subject's capacity for recognition.

And yet Kojève's analysis does not quite explain the constitution
of the social as a symbolic order, in and against which the demand for
recognition takes place. Nor does it allow us to answer questions
about power and domination, viz., questions about who establishes,
who controls, and who orders the models of desire for society as a
whole. For thinkers of a tradition that includes Rousseau, Hegel,
Marx, and Durkheim, the answers to these questions are dependent
on the belief that the social subject is modeled after the individual
subject, that the social subject is, so to speak, a macrosubject – the
individual subject multiplied or writ large. For Hegel, the macrosubject
is ruled by the laws of Spirit, Consciousness, or Reason itself; the
social character of its existence is proved, despite the particularism of
subjective desire, by the historical progression of social relations,
which are themselves a manifestation of the "cunning of reason." For
Marx, this Subject is controlled by the laws of economic exchange.
But when thinkers like Weber and Freud address the problems of
social organization and collective will-formation they begin from the
assumption that interests, desires, and ideals establish society as a
symbolic order that is larger and more powerful than any of its
members. In Freud's analysis of organizations like the army or the
Church in *Group Psychology*, for instance, he describes the moral
physiognomy of groups in such a way that the force of desire among
their members results in a cohesion and symbolic power for society
as a whole.[47] In order for a society to exist at all, its members – who
we may assume, with Hobbes, would bring one another to a violent

---

47 For Freud, this cohesion is a function of the force of desire, libido, or Eros, itself,
   "who holds together everything in the world." Freud, *Group Psychology and the
   Analysis of the Ego*, trans. James Strachey (New York: Boni and Liveright, 1921),
   p. 40.

death out of the passions of envy or greed – must succeed in channeling their desires away from self-destructive ends. But in sublimating their violence toward one another the members of society endow a single object with symbolic powers over them. For Freud, the problems of collective will-formation and of social order will remain insoluble unless we can find someone whose power over us can absorb the envy that we as equals naturally have of one another:[48] "Many equals, who can identify themselves with one another, and a single person superior to them all – that is the situation we find realized in groups which are capable of subsisting" (*Group Psychology*, p. 89).

So understood, the constitution of the social as a symbolic structure depends upon the power exerted by superior or exemplary individuals. "Society," writes Ortega y Gasset, "is born from the superior attraction which one or several individuals exercise on other individuals." As he goes on to say,

Superiority, the excellence of a certain individual, automatically arouses in others an impulse of adherence, a tendency to follow. The manners of this eminent person are adopted enthusiastically as super-individual norms by those who are attracted ... This dynamic relation between the superior man and the desire to follow him, to conform to him, which he arouses in others, appears in all societies from the roughest and most primitive to the highest and most materialized societies.[49]

What happens to the symbolic order of society where the hierarchical differences and symbolic powers of authority have been overturned, or where the "naturalistic" principles of honor, charisma, or tradition are no longer in force? With reference to the question of modernity, we can say that the symbolic power of the social is preserved, albeit in a partial and imperfect way, in the association of "autonomous" selves; indeed, it would seem that the social *must* be preserved as something that transcends the mere sum of individual desires, if only because individual desires can be satisfied in such circumstances only

48 This includes of course the love for those early powerful figures who demand obedience of the infant. For further development, see Jessica Benjamin, *The Bonds of Love*.

49 Ortega y Gasset, "No ser un hombre ejemplar," in *Obras completas*, 2nd edn (Madrid: Revista de Occidente, 1965), II, p. 355. See Luciano Pellicani, "Ortega's Theory of Social Action," *Telos*, 70 (1986–87), 123: "The wheels of history are, so to speak, lubricated by the 'disinterested' creativity of exemplary individuals, and put into motion by the enthusiasm of their followers."

by cooperating in a division of the whole (e.g., the division of labor). The problem of desire in its peculiarly modern form is thus "resolved" by a symbolic structure in which desires are expressed and in which authority is imposed according to the principle of *differentiation from within*. In quasi-Hegelian terms, we can say that the principle of heroic exemplarity is recast as a "rationalized" or logocentric version of democratic selfishness, but with the necessary caveat that the symbolic power of society is replaced by the impartial and "efficient" mechanisms of the market and the State. As Stanley Rosen said in a study of Hegel that bears some marks of Kojève's influence, "This mutuality of satisfaction is in effect the return of recognition: I cannot satisfy myself without recognizing the validity of my neighbor's desires"(*G. W. F. Hegel*, p. 192).

To see the symbolic order of society as expressed in the differentiation of society from within, rather than in a rigid hierarchy of ranks, is to accept a functional conception of desire as pleasure and utility. The subject's conception of desire as the ability to order its preferences according to a calculus of pleasure or pain (in the classical formulation of Bentham's "On the Principle of Utility") reflects a freedom from the symbolic structurations of power characteristic of the traditional world. But on further inspection the conception of desire as utility is symptomatic of a more fundamental disorientation and limitation of desire, the effects of which are to be seen in societal rationalization and in the covert authority of the bureaucratic State. This may be explained in the following terms.

Insofar as it is a social force, the individualizing basis of subjective desire leads to a social contract of the more or less Hobbesian form, one that clearly establishes the utilitarian basis of desire, or perhaps more accurately, one that establishes the subject as a utilitarian instrument in the mutual satisfaction of desires: "I will satisfy your desire if you will satisfy mine."[50] But the social contract generated by individuals is enforceable only within a symbolic structure. As we have seen in connection with our analysis of Don Juan, this structure is society itself.[51] In Weberian terms, the symbolic order of society is

---

50 See Stanley Rosen, *G. W. F. Hegel*, p. 209: "In this manner, for the sake of self-satisfaction or pure egoism, my desire becomes useful to you, and your desire becomes useful to me. Man as desire is redefined as utility."

51 As Anthony Giddens points out, Durkheim criticized Tönnies "because the latter's conception of *Gesellschaft* treats society in the manner of utilitarian theory, as an aggregate of independent 'atoms,' which only constitutes a unity insofar

thus "preserved" in the form of a series of rationalized bureaucratic structures and procedures whose power is larger than its subject-authors. In Marxist terms, the social division of labor, enforced by the State, makes the nature of human labor as one-sided and as specialized as human desires and needs are manifold; this is precisely why the product of human labor in the modern world can acquire universal social validity only as exchange-value. Thus while the division of labour is an organization of production that has grown up "naturally," it is a web which has been "woven behind the backs of the producers of commodities" (*Capital*, 1, p. 201). In this way, the transformation of desire into utility or pleasure masks the fact that a desire freed from the hierarchical structurations of power allows for something less than the full expression of the subject's manifold needs and infinite demand for recognition. In analytical terms, the rationalizing interpretation of desire as pleasure is a symptom of the fact that reason (*qua* subjective self-consciousness in need of recognition) and desire have been split apart. Freedom and rationality are no less closely related for Marx than for Hegel.[52] But whereas Marx demanded the reorganization of society along communal lines, Hegel specified only that this reconciliation would proceed from the reflection of the individual, and its desires, in the social-rational whole.

The transformation of subjective desire into social utility represents one of the presiding interpretations of desire in the modern age. In Hegel's critique of modernity, utility is defined in terms of its opposition to a second interpretation of desire, romantic passion. For Hegel, utility is anathema to those forms of Spirit that manifest themselves as sentimentality, faith, and speculation, all of which more fully express the subject's capacity for self-enlargement and change. (In Kierkegaard's analysis, utility is opposed to purity of heart, whose virtue is to be found in the remarkable singlemindedness of its purpose: "Purity of heart is to will one thing.") At the same time, Hegel dismissed the notion, central to utilitarianism, that the subject is "free" to the degree that he can do whatever his inclinations lead him to desire: "The man in the streets thinks he is free if it is open to him to act as he pleases but his very arbitrariness implies that he

as it is cohered by the 'external' influence of the State." *Capitalism and Modern Social Theory* (Cambridge: Cambridge University Press, 1971), p. 226.
52 For further discussion, see Anthony Giddens, *ibid.*, p. 227.

is not free."[53] As such, utility expresses a characteristic truth of enlightenment culture, a truth that follows from the absence of an established hierarchy of desires or a closed relation between desires and ends, viz., the ceaseless, restless oscillation of desire from one object to another.[54]

As long as subjectivity is expressed as utility, desire will act to limit the possibilities for recognition, in effect by *reducing* the differences among objects; accordingly, utility results in a diminution of the capacities for recognition of the self-conscious subject. Insofar as the vision of society seen from the perspective of utility is that of a space in which only empirical differences in pleasures can be recognized, it can offer only scant opportunities to transform the self. Eventually, the conception of desire as utility proves insufficient to the demand for recognition that difference creates; as a result, the utilitarian conception of pleasure characteristically comes to grief on the problem of boredom (cf. Stendhal: "The curse of inconstancy is boredom," p. 211). This would explain the Hegelian critique of the endless vacillation of desire in the modern age in the *Phenomenology of Spirit* (sec. 579), and it would explain as well Stendhal's need to overcome boredom by reformulating subjective selfhood on the basis of some broader principle – in this case, in terms of the crystallizing power of the imagination:

In an access of melancholy Don Juan said to me at Thorn: "There are less than twenty varieties of womankind, and once one has sampled two or three of each variety, one begins to grow sated." I replied: "Only imagination can escape once and for all from satiety. Each woman provides a different interest, and what is more the same woman will be loved in a different way if chance should offer her to you two or three years earlier or later in life, provided that chance decrees you should love her at all. But a sensitive woman, even if she loved you, would merely chafe your pride with her claims to equality." (p. 208)[55]

53 Hegel, *Philosophy of Right*, trans. T. M. Knox (New York: Oxford University Press, 1967), p. 230. I am indebted for this reference to Anthony Giddens, *Capitalism and Modern Social Theory*, p. 227.
54 See *PhS*, especially sec. 579.
55 Stendhal posits that the alternative to a pointless and unsatisfying utility is romantic desire, one which is typified in Werther rather than Don Juan. Thinking of Werther, he writes: "'More brains are blown out every day for love than from boredom.' I can well believe it, for boredom strips away everything, even the courage to kill oneself. There are people constitutionally unable to find pleasure in anything but variety. But a man who sings the praises of champagne at the

It remains of course to be seen whether the concepts of imagination and genius can be used in order to enlarge the subject's capacity for recognition, or whether they are able only to recast the problem of subjective desire in romantic terms, thereby preserving the opposition between romance and utilitarian reason that Hegel saw as internal to the modern age.[56] Does Stendhal's recourse to the imagination succeed in enlarging the subject's response to the demand for recognition, or is it a last-ditch attempt to control the excess of desire over its potential satisfactions, in the hopes of overcoming the symbolic power of an order that seems to create desires whose possible satisfactions it simultaneously denies? A full response to this question would require a theory of romanticism, but for present purposes it may be sufficient to say that the Stendhalian conception of the imagination overturns the conventional conception of romanticism as characterized by "limit experiences of an aesthetic and mystical kind... for the purpose of a rapturous transcendence of the subject," and so as opposed to the Enlightenment.[57] Rather, the distinctive achievement of Stendhal's "happy few," who expire only after they have found satisfaction, is predicated on an imaginative transposition of desire in which the tacit but everpresent demand for recognition can be "read back" into the subject, who is retrospectively (but no less concretely) energized by it. Stendhal's literary realization of the imagination's power provides a discursive "space" in which the differences created by desire can be both preserved and overcome. As I want in conclusion to explain, such a notion is vastly different from the concept of "intersubjectivity" in terms of which the demand for mutual recognition has conventionally been expressed.

In the initial sections of this chapter we saw that regardless of whether we think of subjectivity as "originating" in the renunciation of the psychology of belief, in the political science of Hobbes, or in the Cartesian formulation of self-consciousness in relation to an

---

expense of the wine of Bordeaux is only saying with a certain amount of eloquence: 'I prefer champagne.'" (*On Love*, p. 211).

56 To take but one additional case, for a thinker like Fichte the power of the imagination derives precisely from its ability to achieve a dialectical synthesis: "The task was this, to unite the opposed entities, I and not-I. Through the imagination, which unites contradictory elements, they can be completely united." *Ausgewählte Werke in Sechs Banden*, ed. Fritz Medicus (Darmstadt: Wissenschaftliche Buchgesellschaft, 1962), I, p. 411.

57 Habermas, *PDM*, p. 309.

"objective" world, desire must be considered as internal to its development rather than as posing an external threat to it. Subsequently, we began to locate the beginnings of subjective desire in the seventeenth century with reference to Don Juan and to the court; and finally, we have come to see that while subjective desire demands recognition, it remains unable to meet this demand in the modern world. To be sure, the "social" survives by virtue of the fact that desire always implies another consciousness, hence a plurality of desires. But neither the conception of desire as a natural passion standing in need of social restraint, nor the notion of desire as utilitarian pleasure in need of rational control, allows the endless demand for recognition to be incorporated as part of the model of subjectivity, and neither allows the transformative nature of desire to find expression in terms of a social norm. What are the prospects then for an alternative conception of desire, one in which the demand for recognition might be incorporated as an essential task of the subject of the "disenchanted" world? And how might the endless task of recognition be reinterpreted as a social norm, so that its "infinity" will not be wholly abstract?

In the concluding pages of this chapter, I want to look briefly at the vision of desire implicit in the Habermassian critique of modernity, where desire is incorporated into the scheme of communicative rationality and in which the demand for recognition takes concrete shape in the formation of an "intersubjective" realm. In contrast to Habermas, who succeeds at best in perpetuating the utilitarian conception of desire characteristic of modernity,[58] I would propose an interpretation in which the power of desire as an expression of the differences among individuals is itself projected as the groundwork of

58 This remains so despite Habermas's contrast between a utilitarian ethics and a communicative ethics in, among other places, *Legitimation Crisis*, trans. Thomas McCarthy (Boston: Beacon Press, 1975), pp. 88–90. I believe that Habermas's distinction fails, on the one hand because the defect he identifies in utilitarianism (viz., that it "falls below the stage of internalization attained in the conventional ethics of duty") finds no remedy in the theory of communicative action, which must likewise reject the ethics of duty; and on the other hand because his characterization of communicative ethics as guaranteeing "the generality of admissible norms and the autonomy of acting subjects *solely through the discursive redeemability of the validity claims which norms appear ...*" (p. 89; my emphasis) is virtually empty. As he goes on to confirm, "Generality is guaranteed in that the only norms that may claim generality are those on which everyone affected agrees (or would agree) without constraint if they enter into (or were to enter into) a process of discursive will-formation" (*ibid.*).

social relations, and in which the demand for recognition serves to make the transformation of society concrete. The suspect infinities implicit in the Hegelian interpretation of desire as a motive force in the utopian progression of consciousness toward an Absolute and as a manifestation of the progress of social relations may thus be recast in more pragmatic social terms; in addition, such a model of desire may enable us to reconstitute the symbolic order of society not as Necessity or Law, the Phallus or the *non/nom du père*, but rather as a form of the openness that the task of recognition requires. The speculative dimension of the Hegelian model of self-consciousness is thus retained, but its rational idealism no longer remains fixed in place; this is because while the task of recognition is open-ended, it is also historical and concrete.

Taken within the context of his overall critique of modernity, the Habermassian theory of communicative action is meant to offer an alternative to the philosophy of the subject and to the ethic that dominant visions of subjectivity demand. Subjectivity (which is defined roughly in terms of the objectification of the world) and the philosophy of representation (which posits the knowledge of objects as paradigmatic) are replaced by a model of "mutual understanding between subjects capable of speech and action." As Habermas goes on to explain, the model of participants in linguistically mediated interaction "makes possible a *different* relationship of the subject to itself from the sort of objectifying attitude that an observer assumes to the entities of the external world" (*PDM*, pp. 295–96, 297). The idea of an intersubjective realm, founded on the mutuality of participants in a communicative relationship, represents Habermas's solution to the problem of recognition by creating an "I" whose self-consciousness would embrace the perspective of the Other within itself: "ego stands within an interpersonal relationship that allows him to relate to himself as a participant in an interaction from the perspective of alter. And indeed this reflection undertaken from the perspective of the participant escapes the kind of objectification inevitable from the reflexively applied perspective of the observer" (*PDM*, p. 297).[59]

59 A more radical psychoanalytic criticism of Habermas might take the following form: if all knowledge is laced with desire, then the desire to know could be read as the transformation of a sexual desire, one that deprives the subject of this desire and abandons him or reveals him as *subject to* death. See Julia Kristeva, "Psychoanalysis and the Polis," *Critical Inquiry*, 9 (1982), 83. As I have suggested

And yet it remains clear that in this critique of modernity Habermas assumes the adequacy of a paradigm of intersubjectivity that fails to define the position of the Other as a function of desire; indeed, Habermas omits the question of desire, or at best regards desire as an external threat to the autonomy of the rational subject. As a result, the transformative potential of desire, its orientation to the "beyond" that may be revealed in and through the recognition of concrete others, is lost; it is jettisoned as part of the sweeping critique of "transcendental philosophy." (Habermas writes: "Because such reconstructive attempts are no longer aimed at a realm of the intelligible beyond that of appearances, but at the actually exercised rule-knowledge that is deposited in correctly generated utterances, the ontological separation between the transcendental and the empirical is no longer applicable," *PDM*, p. 298.) In resolving the characteristic antinomies of the subject in relation to a world of objects, Habermas has in essence reduced the Other to a merely empirical or "perspectival" variation of the self, and this reduction is in turn symptomatic of the Habermassian attempt to reconstruct the totality of knowledge based on the accessibility of practical "rules" to rational consciousness. Initially, the advantage of the theory of communicative action over transcendental philosophy is said to lie in the fact that "the intuitive analysis of self-consciousness now gets adapted to the circle of reconstructive sciences that try to make explicit, from the perspective of those participating in discourses and interactions, and by means of analyzing successful or distorted utterances, the pretheoretical grasp of rules on the part of competently speaking, acting, and knowing subjects" (pp. 297–98). Insofar as the effect of this claim is to enlarge the scope of rational consciousness to the point where it encompasses the tacit knowledge expressed in everyday linguistic practice, but ignores the relationship between knowledge and desire, it represents a symptom of what we might call the illusion (some might say the delirium) of enlightenment, i.e., the insistence that light can penetrate everywhere.[60] And yet nowhere does Habermas ask whether the opacities, the resistances, or the transformative energies of desire might be inherent within the Enlightenment subject itself. For Habermas, the unconscious is simply what is hidden, in the sense of "what is kept from public

above, however, this criticism denies the transformative potential of desire that it seeks to assert, in short by reading subjectivity as a form of subjection.

60 See Kristeva, *ibid.*, 84.

communication"; for instance, it stands in contrast to the process of "enlightenment" or "self-reflection" initiated by the analyst.[61] And nowhere does he investigate the role of desire in the formation of the social as a symbolic order which channels and controls the possibilities of communication by positioning subjects with respect to its power in advance. Indeed, the very structure of his questions rules desire out of bounds (what constitutes a "competently desiring subject"?). Second, Habermas's "common lifeworld" is a remarkably static realm. In drawing out a theory of communicative action from the "normative content" of modernity, and vice versa, in deriving a normative vision of modernity from the competencies of communicating subjects, Habermas effectively sweeps the transformative power of desire aside. In so doing, he ignores the possibility that the very opacities of desire – those respects in which there may remain something unrealized within the domain of what has been brought to consciousness, or something unrepresented within the framework of what has been historically achieved – might represent the means or powers by which to transform the world.

The Habermassian theory of communicative action remains wholly within the sphere of modernity even though it carries forward a vision of the relationship between reason and desire that begins roughly where the dominant modern understanding of desire leaves off, viz., with a desire that is split off from reason, and with a conception of "reason" that is deficient insofar as it fails to incorporate the powers and demands of the desiring self. In the theory of communicative action, Habermas in effect confirms the transformation of human desire into a form of social utility. This is to say, Habermas implicitly adopts a "discursive" version of the restrictions on human relations demanded by the Hobbesian analysis of the passions and set in place by the social contract. The moral impulse behind the formation of society as theorized in the Hobbesian ban on mutual aggression – the injunction that subjects should overcome their fear of the destructive consequences of desire in the formation of a symbolic structure (the Leviathan or State) – is reformulated, albeit in a more "civilized" fashion, in a theory of mutual understanding; it is based on a social/communicative subject who is required to trust and understand. So seen, Habermas stands in a far closer relation to the philosophy of Descartes than he has himself

61 See *Knowledge and Human Interests*, trans. Jeremy J. Shapiro (Boston: Beacon Press, 1971), pp. 228–38.

been willing or able to recognize. What, for instance, is the basis of the communicating subject as confirmed by its preoccupation with clarity, understanding, and trust, if not the Cartesian fear of not finding another similar self? In Habermas, the need to certify the existence of the self is projected not in the form of a God, but rather in the form of the wholly secular desire to find an interlocutor. In the association of truth with trust and of trust with clear and intelligible (undistorted) speech – in the association of good speech with communication – one moves quickly from Cartesian self-consciousness to the "communicative rationality" that Habermas has proposed as an alternative to the Cartesian paradigm.[62] In the process, the communicating subject is realigned to the symbolic structure of a differentiated society, as expressed in the controlling authority of the State.

Moreover, it remains symptomatically unclear within Habermassian terms whether the outcome of subjective desire is a state of peace or war, just as it remains unclear whether "intersubjectivity" represents anything more than a compact for the mutual domination of subjects. (One is reminded of Kant's definition of marriage as a contractual arrangement for the mutual use of bodies, a relationship that would easily qualify as "intersubjective" according to Habermas's criteria.) If we begin from a conception of desire as fundamentally aggressive, then the task of intersubjectivity will be the institution of peace, for it is a manifestation of self-consciousness that finds potential satisfaction in the recognition of another desire (read: another consciousness). It is of the nature of desire to want recognition to proceed from the Other, but without becoming wholly absorbed by it. The Other must continue to be present in submission as evidence of the ego's subjectivity, and so as object of the subject's desire. "Intersubjectivity" must be achieved in such a way that subjects both overcome and preserve the differences that desires create, just as Kojève saw that in the struggle of master and slave the Other must be "assimilated" in such a way that he retains his identity within my own. However, since the needs of the Other are the same

---

62 This argument is suggested by a related critique of Descartes in Alan Blum's *Theorizing* (London: Heinemann, 1974). Blum writes: "Man desires to make himself a listener so that he will be listened to. Man's desire is rooted in the fear of not having his voice heard because others are only empirically related to the voice to which he is essentially present" (p. 157). Cf. also Lacan, who writes: "egocentric discourse is a case of *hail to the good listener!*" (*The Four Fundamental Concepts of Psychoanalysis*, p. 208).

as mine, the demand for recognition as expressed in the intersubjective realm is also a recipe for perpetual struggle, and so a ceaseless war.[63] Hence it can be said that the Habermassian theory of communicative action posits an intersubjective consciousness that is no more stable, or fruitful, than the ancient dialectic of master and slave, and that this instability acts to reinforce the societal rationalization that Habermas elsewhere seeks to overcome.

In light of the limitations of the Habermassian critique, it would be tempting to recuperate the transformative potential of desire by recourse to the work of thinkers like Jean-François Lyotard and Gilles Deleuze, who attempt to reimagine desire as a transgressive force akin to that we have seen in the seventeenth-century interpretation of the myth of Don Juan. In my opinion, the vision of desire as a purely utopian, emancipatory force presents problems that cannot be resolved without a fundamental revision of the postulate of transgressive desire itself. As a historical thesis, for instance, the attempt to locate a purely affirmative, emancipatory, anti-Oedipal form of desire must ignore the alternation between periods of stability and moments of transition that are characteristic of history itself. And as a normative postulate, the transgressive vision of desire must negate the dialectic within society between iconoclasm or context-breaking and the need for stability or context-shaping and recognition. As such, it provides an inadequate basis on which to situate the demand for recognition as a social force. But rather than reject the principle of transformation that desire makes possible we might consider how to accept the freedom that is made available in the loss of an intrinsic relation between reason and desire, or in the eclipse of the psychology of belief. How can the demand for recognition be balanced with the need for self-differentiation in the absence of established social hierarchies and ranks demands? Given the detachment of desire from any intrinsic natural or rational ends, how can we come to value desire no longer as simply a transgressive force, as that which threatens to disrupt the unity of consciousness from without, but rather as that which shapes the identities that in turn motivate social change? These are among the questions that we shall pursue in the pages that follow.

63 See Rosen, *G. W. F. Hegel*, p. 157.

6

❖❖

Possibilities of postmodernism

❖❖

History, theory, postmodernity

The foregoing discussion of the problem of desire brings to a close our analysis of the contradictions of subjectivity in relation to the culture of modernity. On the one hand, we have seen that a reconception of subjectivity in terms of desire is essential if the possibility of transformation essential to modernity is to remain alive; yet on the other hand we have seen that the modern conception of desire is subject to the consequences of a chronic indeterminacy in the relationship between desire and its ends, so that transformation can never satisfactorily be achieved. One way of explaining this problem is to say that the modern conception of desire provides no adequate basis for recognition, hence no way in which individual desires can be linked to society as a whole. As a result, desire is conceived as an iconoclastic force, and the desire for transformation is never stabilized. To be sure, one must agree with the Hegelian proposition that desire is integral to subjective self-consciousness and as such seeks satisfaction in another desire, but modern culture confronts the additional, and seemingly insoluble problem of positing desire-driven transformations having first rejected the possibility of transcendence; as a result, modern culture tends toward forms of self-transcendence that turn desire back ceaselessly upon itself. These and similar instabilities help account for the contradictory nature of subjectivity and for the destabilizing pressures at work within modernity itself.

The contradictions of modernity may be further underscored if we recall the conservative critique that has been mounted in the name of the "wisdom" of the Ancients or the virtues of "heroic society." In a pivotal chapter of *After Virtue*, for instance, Alasdair MacIntyre summed up the contrast between the Ancients and the Moderns through the presentation of a stark either/or: either we must accept

275

an Aristotelian morality, which seeks to ground the self in the principles of virtue as made visible in the concept of the social role, or we must fall into moral emotivism, that uniquely modern form of relativism that culminates in the Nietzschean will-to-power. In MacIntyre's terms, *either* one must accept an Aristotelian critique of modern culture, *or* one must accept the Enlightenment's self-cancellation in the form of Nietzsche's critique of moral philosophy as a mere "fiction." As MacIntyre sees the options, there is no third alternative available to us.

Because of the limitations of these and similar critiques, it is tempting to consider the alternative approach to the problem of modernity that stems from Hegel's attempt to criticize the modern paradigm while nonetheless carrying forward the commitments to freedom and rationality that modernity has made.[1] At several points in the chapters above we have had occasion to make reference to Hegel's critique of subjectivity and to Hegel's pivotal place within the culture of modernity. We have seen that the Hegelian critique of modernity represents the first thoroughgoing attempt to reintegrate the various capacities of the subject that, over the course of modernity, had been split off into separate cultural spheres. At the same time, Hegel is among the first to recognize the inadequacies of a critical paradigm that reduces consciousness to its knowledge of an external world; hence Hegel proposes that the consciousness of the subject cannot be separated from transformations in the social and historical contexts in which the subject is set. While Hegel may succeed in reconciling the contingencies of history with the inner logic of speculative thought, the Hegelian critique of subjectivity is dependent on the invocation of a totality that is complete and closed unto itself. Thus Habermas acutely argues against the (implicitly Hegelian) construction of a consciousness embracing the total society, observing that if individual subjects are drawn together and subordinated to the higher-level subject of the "social totality," there is likely to arise a "zero-sum game in which modern phenomena such as the expanding scope for movement and the increasing degrees of

---

1 Richard Bernstein's review of MacIntyre's *After Virtue* (Notre Dame: University of Notre Dame Press, 1981) acutely stresses the Hegelian alternative; see Bernstein, "Nietzsche or Aristotle? Reflections on Alasdair MacIntyre's *After Virtue*," in *Philosophical Profiles* (Philadelphia: University of Pennsylvania Press, 1986), pp. 115–40.

freedom cannot be adequately accommodated."[2] Phrased in other terms, it can be said that the same concept of totality that enables history and speculation to be reconciled works in practice toward the exclusion of one of its terms. Nonetheless we have also seen that Hegel represents the temptation within the history of modernity to infinitize subjective self-consciousness and thereby to resolve the contradictions of subjectivity through the interpretation of Spirit as an all-embracing Absolute. In light of these challenges to the concept of totality – challenges that have been intensified in the name of "postmodern" discourse – we must ask whether it is indeed possible to detach Hegelian wisdom from the presupposition of a Spiritual Absolute.

Hegel's account of Absolute Spirit may from one angle be understood as the cornerstone of a system of thought – the last – in which the principles underlying the Whole are assumed to be accessible to reason. In this respect, Hegel remains committed to reconciling the goals of enlightened modernity with the principles of Ancient philosophy, while offering fundamental corrections of modern, dualistic thinking. Whereas traditional thinking about the whole is characterized by a refusal to recognize its divisions, or by the ability to see the interconnections among its parts, and whereas Platonic philosophy depends upon the possibility of a privileged intuition of the relationship between reason and the good (which is later transformed into the concept of prudence), the philosophy of the subject represents a rejection of these principles in favor of an interpretation of the whole along dualistic lines. Modern philosophers define the whole in terms of the division of body and mind (Descartes), of faith and science (Pascal), or of the empirical and transcendent worlds, or formal and sensuous intuition (Kant). Insofar as the unity of these terms is to be reconstituted at some "higher" level, they demand the creation of categories like Descartes's "subject," Pascal's "hidden God," or Kant's "transcendental ego." In response to these resolutions of the problem of dualism, Hegel seeks to reconcile the contradictions of subjectivity by redefining subject as Spirit. Hegel thus attempts to reconcile subject and object, and thereby to "re-enchant" the world, by viewing these terms not in light of their possible or projected syntheses but rather in terms of the

---

2 Habermas, *Philosophical Discourse of Modernity* (henceforth, *PDM*), trans. Frederick Lawrence (Cambridge, MA: MIT Press, 1987), p. 376.

unity of the first principle of their formation. The onward and transformative motions of Spirit, which are manifested equally through the "subject" and through "history," are thus involved in a process of recovering or remembering an origin, the integrity of which is best visible retrospectively, but which is nonetheless guaranteed in advance.

Hegel's critique of subjectivity thus attempts to reconcile the simultaneous demands of history and speculation that stand at the root of modernity as an historical paradigm. Despite Hegel's attempt to criticize modernity while preserving metaphysics by drawing together those aspects of subjectivity that had been split apart over the course of the modern age, we must face the fact that the Hegelian solution to the problem of modernity issues in the completion of wisdom, the end of history, and the effective closure of the self-inventive possibilities of discourse. Hegel's concept of the totality stands for this reason in a pivotal position with respect to the transition from "modern" to "postmodern" discourse. Lyotard's theory of the *différend*, for instance, represents a paradigmatic expression of the postmodern renewal of the principle of trans-formation, but Lyotard, like Derrida, plays out the "end of philosophy" analogous to the "end of history" indicated by the Hegelian completion of wisdom. If the problem of modernity was to provide for the social and political unity of fundamentally disgregated subject-selves, then the task of postmodernism is to allow for the possibility of transformation where we as subjects find ourselves implicated by and inserted into totalities *in advance*. In Hegel, the unity of many different and independent self-consciousnesses becomes a manifestation of Spirit – in Hegel's terms, of "'I' that is 'We,' and 'We' that is 'I.'"[3] But, to phrase the matter in terms of our discussion of the problem of desire, the postmodern rejection of the Hegelian whole may lead to transformations of the "I" without a program for collective recognition; to the extent that this is true, it fails to resolve the problems of "modern" discourse, which is based on the reality of disgregated subject-selves – but with the difference that the "I" is now both removed from a "natural" context and decentered with respect to the "we." The postmodern attempt to locate terms of criticism, such as the *différend*, outside of the grand

---

3 Hegel, *Phenomenology of Spirit*, trans. A. V. Miller (New York: Oxford University Press, 1981), sec. 177, p. 110.

narratives of Reason and Spirit, may be interpreted as an effort to overcome the suspect totalities that are necessary to the Hegelian critique of the modern age, but this attempt has in turn jeopardized the possibility of finding the normative possibilities of the specific modes of self-assertion in which we find ourselves engaged. It risks a sharp imbalance in the relationship between transformation and recognition described above.

In the attempt to "overcome" Hegel, postmodernism may be characterized by its denial of the potential unity of history and theory, by its rejection of the possibility of ascribing normative force to historical paradigms, and by refusing to frame its critique in terms of a speculative discourse about such things as the ends of history, social relations, or the nature of the self. Accordingly, postmodernism asserts itself oppositionally with respect to the historical and theoretical terms in which modernity has been construed. How does this program take shape and what consequences does it have?[4] Seen from the point of view of theory, postmodernism may be characterized by the attempt to resist any purely speculative reordering of the boundaries between the value-spheres of modern culture, in favor of a post-theoretical and sometimes heterogeneous conception of discourse that is fully informed by the fact that the knowing "subject" of any discourse may just as well turn out to be the deceived subject of that discourse.[5] Lyotard's Wittgensteinian insistence on the place of language-games in philosophy, like Rorty's neo-pragmatist insistence on the role of philosophy "in the conversation of mankind" assert the contingency of all modes of speech and, as such, constitute refusals of the attempt to mediate and thereby recuperate the differences among the divergent expressions of the subject, but this may be because those differences have mostly collapsed.

Similarly, postmodernism has evolved, through the contradictory logic of modernity, into what can only be called a "post-historical" space. If, as the culture of modernity developed, history came to challenge theory for possession of the ground on which the

---

4 I explore some of the consequences of the paragraphs that follow, and draw on the material contained in my "Afterword" to Reed Way Dasenbrock, ed., *Redrawing the Lines: Analytic Philosophy, Deconstruction, and Literary Theory* (Minneapolis: University of Minnesota Press, 1989).

5 See Paul Smith, *Discerning the Subject* (Minneapolis: University of Minnesota Press, 1988), especially p. 78.

disparities of meaning or the pluralities of value-judgments could be recuperated and made whole, it must at the same time be said that this was, in Hegel's assessment, a function of whatever claims to reason could be validated by the actual course of events. History, in Hegel's terms, was itself an expression of the "cunning of reason" and could, in light of the power of speculation, be thought of as having been brought to an end. In the Hegelian sense, the "end of history" is a product of the completion of wisdom that leaves us with no meaningful conflicts, no ground of desire, hence with nothing to say. Following a thinker like Kojève, writing in the Hegelian aftermath, the "end of history" portends the discursive homogeneity, hence the eventual collapse of differences, in the late- or post-modern age.[6] Thus postmodernism may be taken as "post-historical," but in a way that reveals the unique instability of the Hegelian response to modernity. The historical implications of the terms postmodern theory invokes serve neither to provide paradigms for the self-expression of Spirit through our divergent purposes and aims nor to generate categories of judgment for the evaluation of our conceptual differences. "History" may thus assert itself neither as the court of the world's judgment and an expression of reason or truth, nor as an expression of the diversity of human purposes and aims, but rather as the skeletal *fabula*, as the story-line in terms of which its own extinction can be retold.

In the attempt to pass beyond history and theory and into the realm where the figurative and other "aesthetic" powers of discourse allow us the freedom to redescribe ourselves, however, postmodernism deepens a series of modernist commitments to the contextuality of truth and the revisability of all contexts.[7] This commitment has been carried out in, among other ways, the attempt to formulate a transformative social practice in terms of Rorty's "self-creation" and "re-description," or through Lyotard's insistence on the *différend* and the "postmodern sublime." But all these efforts should be taken not as signs that the tensions between history and theory have finally been overcome, but rather, as Anthony Giddens has argued in

6 In addition to Kojève, see Barry Cooper, *The End of History* (Toronto: University of Toronto Press, 1984), and Stanley Rosen's essay on Kojève and Leo Strauss, "Hermeneutics as Politics," in Rosen, *Hermeneutics as Politics* (New York: Oxford University Press, 1987).

7 The contextuality thesis has been admirably defended by Roberto Mangabeira Unger in *Passion: An Essay on Personality* (New York: The Free Press, 1984).

Consequences of Modernity, as an indication that the postmodern subject continues to inhabit a world in which the effects of "disenchantment" remain in place.[8] For example, the concerns of the Frankfurt School heirs of Marx about the reification of social relationships and the rationalization of the world have been reshaped by the emergence of a hyperaesthetic postmodern culture, as late capitalism has moved from the realm of commodity relations to the simulated economy of excess, and as the ethic of liberal individualism has been played out to near exhaustion in a decentered media culture. To judge by the political implications of Jean Baudrillard's work – itself a symptom of the culture it seeks to describe – the postmodern scene represents the form in which the logic of modernity has depleted itself; the "post-historical individuals" of Nietzsche's tribe are the true heirs of the modern ethic; as one recent social critic has said, "we are presented with a culturally refined model of behavior that has left behind the crudity of Bentham's quip that 'pushpin is as good as poetry.' The 'last men' of Nietzsche's herd are content in actively seeking the role of a passive spectator in the democratic process."[9] Baudrillard's judgments (e.g. that "all that remains is the fascination for desert-like and indifferent forms, for the very operation of the system which annuls us"[10]) are at once descriptions of postmodernism and symptoms of the new, self-validating desperation of the postmodern cultural critique; their motto: "Despero ergo sum."[11]

These things having been said, it must be added that in postmodernism, the tasks assigned to modernity's spectator-subject and to liberalism's judge are subsumed by the interdisciplinary critic of discourse. As the preceding chapters will have testified, the postmodern critic is committed to inhabit the space between discourses, but as I hope to be suggesting here, postmodern culture has yet to develop (indeed, *refuses* to develop) a language of judgment corresponding to its critical stance. (This is the language I will attempt

8 Anthony Giddens, *Consequences of Modernity* (Stanford: Stanford University Press, 1990).

9 Arthur Kroker, "The Last Days of Liberalism," in *The Postmodern Scene* (New York: St. Martin's Press, 1986), p. 159.

10 Baudrillard, "Sur le nihilisme," *Simulacres et simulation* (Paris: Editions Galilée, 1981), p. 231.

11 Paul Foss, "Despero ergo sum," in *Seduced and Abandoned: The Baudrillard Scene*, ed. André Frankovits (Glebe, Australia, and New York: Stonemoss and Semiotexte, 1984), pp. 9–16.

to articulate in the concluding section of this chapter through a reinterpretation of Kant's aesthetic judgment.) Having rejected the program to reintegrate the faculties of Kant's divided subject, however, and having lost faith in the possibility of rearticulating the "proper" or "normal" relationships among the various cultural spheres, it is no surprise to find that postmodernism has enthusiastically embraced Lyotard's self-transcending sublime; it should come as no surprise that postmodern social "theory" is to be found in the nauseous allegories and brilliant vertigo of Baudrillard. Indeed, when set against such a backdrop, claims for the reintegrative or redemptive mission of the aesthetic or any other form of discourse are bound to place the new discursive heterogeneity under the subtle erasure of an aesthetic screen, subordinating what Kant saw as the ethical function of the aesthetic sphere to a voyeuristic stance that mimics the seductive cycle of postmodern power as embedded in the disenchanted world of dead labor, "cool theory," the electronic eye, and the steady flow of freely floating, value-neutral signs.

It is within this post-theoretical, post-historical, and post-liberal framework that we may further explore the work of postmodern thinkers like Baudrillard and Lyotard. Since I have suggested that postmodernism is a post-historical phenomenon I would argue that both Lyotard and Baudrillard radicalize the consequences of what Foucault described, in definitively post-Hegelian terms, as the "end of subjectivity" (the "end of man"),[12] that Baudrillard's analysis of the simulacrum, and Lyotard's of the *différend*, represent distinct versions of social theory rewritten from the post-Hegelian perspective of the "end of philosophy," of the totality in brackets, and of the eclipse of the subject as agent of social change.

Consider Baudrillard's vaguely Weberian description of modernity as that period in which the structure and values of the "traditional" world were subjected to a series of destabilizing pressures. In an essay entitled "Symbolic Exchange and Death," for instance, Baudrillard proposed a distinction between caste societies (whether archaic or feudal) on the one hand and class societies on the other. Baudrillard describes societies of caste or rank as structures in which "social

12 See Foucault, *The Order of Things* (New York: Vintage Books, 1973): "one can certainly wager that man would be erased, like a face drawn in sand at the edge of the sea" (p. 387).

assignation is total, social mobility nil." In these societies, signs are secured by a series of "naturalistic" principles and are shielded by archaic prohibitions that assure their absolute clarity: "each sign refers unequivocally to a particular situation and a specific level of status."[13] In contrast stands the world of "unbounded" signs; these create a space for the exercise of subjective freedom, which is in principle supported by a network of free economic exchange, but these are vulnerable to the effects of uncontrolled proliferation: "this multiplication of signs no longer bears any connection with the bound sign of restricted circulation. It is the counterfeit of it, not by virtue of having denatured some 'original'... No longer discriminating (but only competitive), relieved of all barriers, universally available, the modern sign nevertheless simulates necessity by offering itself as a determinate link to the world" ("Symbolic Exchange," p. 136).

The passage from the "traditional" world of caste relations and heroic signs to the world of the free production of signs by no means eliminates the nostalgia for the assurance offered by the "real" (i.e. bounded) sign. On the contrary, this desire is simply displaced: as the force of history, which represents the real as absolute Necessity, in its constitution as the "always anterior" or "archaic" sign; and as morality, which becomes the locus of the absolutely binding sign. Given the social transformations associated with the invention of subjectivity and the formation of what Heidegger calls the modern "world picture," it is not surprising to find a will to return to the world of virtue, duty, and prudence. We can see the expressions of such a will in the work of thinkers as different as Alasdair MacIntyre and Leo Strauss. But as Baudrillard warns, this was a world of restricted signs, and therefore *cruel*: "If we start yearning nostalgically, especially these days, for a revitalized 'symbolic order,' we should have no illusions. Such an order once existed, but it was composed of ferocious hierarchies; the transparency of signs goes hand in hand with their cruelty" ("Symbolic Exchange," p. 136). In thinkers like Descartes, Cervantes, Hobbes, and Pascal, reason is empowered to relocate the "natural" meaning of signs and so to establish and make legitimate its own self-chosen ends; but this power proves insufficient to satisfy the demand for a binding sign. Thus Baudrillard notes that

13 Baudrillard, "Symbolic Exchange and Death," in *Selected Writings*, ed. Mark Poster (Stanford: Stanford University Press, 1988), p. 136.

the modern sign dreams of the sign anterior to it and fervently desires, in its reference to the real, to rediscover some binding obligation. But it finds only a *reason*: a referential reason, the real – the "natural" on which it will feed. This lifeline of designation, however, is no more than a simulacrum of symbolic obligation. It produces only neutral values, those that exchange among each other in an objective world.   ("Symbolic Exchange," p. 136)

So seen, the problem of modernity is to establish the authority of the signs that bind. It is reflected in, among other ways, a crisis in the nature of "exemplary" discourse, which mirrors the symbolic organization of society as a whole. As we have seen in connection with Cervantes' *Don Quixote* above, the binding power of the archaic heroic sign – its ability to exact respect, to command obedience and belief – depends on an unswerving faith in the goodness and power of an exemplar, and on the promise of establishing an unmediated relationship with him. Taken together, these factors contribute to produce the characteristic aura and "charisma" of the hero, whose actions in turn carry moral force for society as a whole. And yet exemplary discourse is inherently unstable, for the hero by definition makes demands that the ordinary members of society cannot fulfill. Moreover, it will inevitably appear from an enlightened point of view that the non-heroes of society deceive themselves when they take a historical artefact, the projection of their own desires and ideals, for a source of ultimate empowerment. Similarly, it seems that the hero is himself bound to discover an ironic relation to his project once he comes to recognize the implausible expectations that exemplarity places on him.[14] Don Quixote's models are the source of all goodness and virtue; but they also make unyielding demands, and so are also the source of his abjection. For a thinker like Descartes, the impossible demand for a binding relation to the exemplar (to Plato, Aristotle, and the philosophers of the Schools) is figured as a crisis of personal identity that is "resolved" by a dramatic reshuffling of the order of signs, the result of which is a "stable" reapportionment between empirical and transcendental signs; the philosophical understanding of subjectivity is its effect. In Cervantes' works, this problem is addressed in terms of a division within "literary" discourse between novelistic narration, with its ethos of subjective irony and the characteristic anxieties that this generates, and the "romantic" desire for inclusion in a universal community of mankind through willing

14 See Unger, *Passion*, p. 56.

submission to binding laws. As an anti-romance, *Don Quixote* shows that those (like Don Quixote) who choose the path of identification with heroic exemplars, as well as those (like the Priest, the Barber, and Sansón Carrasco) who express a confidence in their ability to disrupt or resist such identifications altogether, discover in equal measure the mediated nature of the signs that bind; they experience equally powerful, if opposing, deflections of their exemplary attempts to secure a place within an unambiguous symbolic realm. But in either case, the Cervantean or the Cartesian, the crisis in "exemplary" discourse is precipitated by the "precession" of the model (Baudrillard's term) as a short-circuiting of the project of heroic identification in the modern age.[15]

In contrast to Baudrillard, Lyotard describes modernity as that period during which the legitimation of practices was made via explicit appeal to "grand narratives," and specifically through the terms of history and theory. On Lyotard's account, the transition from modernity to postmodernism was brought about by forms of technical and scientific progress that produced an unregulated competition among explanatory frameworks, which resulted in the eventual displacement of the truth-claims of all of them. This is a story of the latest phase of post-Enlightenment culture as standing at the limit of what MacIntyre describes as "emotivism," as one of fragmentation, or dispersion, roughly akin to what Flaubert foresaw in *Bouvard and Pécuchet*, in which the organizing threads of knowledge (the various "narratives" that comprise the whole) are successively splintered off from the web of discourse. Yet whereas Flaubert's characters are left with the sublime and ironic emptiness of the Idea, the postmodern self is left with the pure heterogeneity of language-games. This, rather than Flaubertian irony or decadence, provides Lyotard with the basis for not simply a secular but a "pagan" conception of value that is meant to challenge the subject's habitual modes of self-assertion:

This is what paganism would be. The point is not that one keeps the games, but that, in each of the existing games, one effects new moves, one opens up the possibility of new efficacies in the games with their present rules. And, in addition, one changes the rules: one can play a given game with other rules, and when one changes the rules, one has changed the game,

15 See Baudrillard, "Simulacra and Simulations," in *Selected Writings*, p. 175.

because a game is primarily defined by its rules. And here again it is a problem of inventiveness in language games.[16]

Lyotard himself recognizes the persistence of the problem of authority inherited from modernity in the formulations just offered – that the moves within language-games are not wholly arbitrary (we cannot make just *any* moves), and that there is a residual desire for some faculty or authority capable of determining the rules that constitute each game. Thus he must at the same time posit a principle that would allow us to regulate the "purity" of the games. For Kant, the regulative idea is the totality of reasonable beings; in Kantian aesthetics and politics, it is defined by the "supersensible unity of humanity." For Hegel, the Kantian totalities are no longer adequate because they still contain traces of a subjectivity divided against itself. But because Hegel does not want simply to refute but rather to incorporate and "overcome" Kant, he looks for a totality that would be able to incorporate difference within sameness, a relationship that he secures through the unity of the first principle governing the transformations and self-divisions of Spirit in the world. For Lyotard, by contrast, the approach to any principle of discursive regulation is premised on a prior rejection of the concept of the whole. When Lyotard asks, "Where, after the metanarratives, can legitimacy reside?... Is legitimacy to be found in consensus obtained through discussion, as Jürgen Habermas thinks?"[17] his point is that the language of consensus, a later version of totality, does violence to the heterogeneity of language-games, i.e., to the very fact that may allow us to introduce the principle of incommensurability into an existing discourse. In place of the whole, Lyotard asserts the power of the *différend* to restore a voice to whatever remains outside Kantian representations and is excluded from the Hegelian concept of the whole as a self-moving, progressive field. Lyotard focuses instead on the "postmodern sublime" as an effort to put forward the unpresentable in discourse itself, or to "work without rules in order to formulate the rules of what *will have been done*."[18] In conjunction

16 *Just Gaming*, trans. Wlad Godzich (Minneapolis: University of Minnesota Press, 1985), p. 62.
17 Lyotard, *The Postmodern Condition: A Report on Knowledge*, trans. Geoff Bennington and Brian Massumi (Minneapolis: University of Minnesota Press, 1984), pp. xxiv-xxv.
18 See Lyotard, "What is Postmodernism?" trans. Régis Durand, in *The Postmodern Condition*, p. 81.

with the postmodern sublime, the principal power of the *différend* is to restore mobility to a system in which each discourse falsely imagines itself as having the power to command the field of culture as a whole. The *différend* will, if critical, result in the introduction into each discursive field of a perspective that is, in part at least, that of another field. In principle, each field remains open to continuous transformation by the others.[19] And yet, as a mode of political discourse, the *différend* is in practice faced with the notoriously difficult task of commanding transformation without the prospect of transcendence, and of thus empowering us to establish the rules for what "will have been done."

In recent debates over the question of modernity and postmodernism, Rorty has tried to strike a bargain with Lyotard by attempting to "split the difference" between the politics of the *différend* and Habermas's adherence to the narrative of emancipation grounded in communicative action and consensus, in favor of the more limited, metaphysically innocuous claims of postmodern bourgeois liberalism. But in resolving (more accurately, in circumventing) the antinomies of modern thought, Rorty has in effect leveled the differences between the terms involved. What remains after the distinctions between history and theory, fact and interpretation, reason and desire, value and rule, and a host of other quasi-metaphysical categories have been dissolved is a post-historical and post-theoretical form of discourse that lacks the power of resistance of the *différend* and thus falls easily in step with the institutionalized values of the rationalized, bureaucratic, technological society at hand. Truth may simply be described as "what works," and the good may be viewed as a function of innovation or novelty realized, as Rorty sanguinely says, in the search for "new and more interesting descriptions" of ourselves: "The sense in which human beings alter themselves by redescribing themselves is no more metaphysically exciting or mysterious than the sense in which they alter themselves by changing their diet, their sexual partners, or their habitation. It is just the same sense: viz., new and more interesting sentences become true of them."[20]

If one were to take Rorty seriously here, it would be necessary to augment a discussion of these (post-theoretical) language-games with

19 See David Carroll, *Paraesthetics* (London: Methuen, 1987), p. 175.
20 Rorty, *Philosophy and the Mirror of Nature* (Princeton: Princeton University Press, 1979), p. 351.

an examination of the aesthetic categories on which they rely; Charles Altieri's reinterpretation of modernism may be taken as representing a systematic effort along these lines.[21] I would refer the reader also to my reinterpretation of Kant in the concluding section of the present chapter. For now, let us simply say that Lyotard is more ambitious than Rorty insofar as he wants to transform the aesthetics of the "new" and the "more interesting" into the terms of a critique of (political) judgment that goes against the grain of the Hegelian whole. In Lyotard's hands, the result is a politics of "difference" carried out in the interstices of existing discourse; but in the process, the modern ideal of transformation has itself been transformed into the pure obligation to be different:

There is no politics if there is not ... a questioning of existing institutions, a project to improve them, to make them more just. This means that all politics implies the prescription of doing something else than what is. But this prescription of doing something else than what is, is prescription itself: it is the essence of a prescription to be a statement such that it induces in its recipient an activity that will transform reality.   (*Just Gaming*, p. 23)

For Lyotard, the postmodern sublime provides a means to shape the aesthetics of innovation into a social and personal vision and so to concretize the modern notion of freedom expressed in Kant's "other (transcendental) world" or in Schiller's ideal of an "Aesthetic State." It is both a continuation and a correction of the "aesthetic ideology" that Habermas has so strongly opposed. Lyotard's interest in a "postmodern sublime" (the terms are contradictory in some respects) begins as part of his attempt to reclaim the transformative power of desires from all efforts to totalize them in the form of a metanarrative (historical) or representational (theoretical) framework and so to realize their virtues by overcoming the "fictional" and "other-worldly" (which is to say, transcendental and speculative) bases on which they had previously been seen to rest. According to Lyotard, modern aesthetics and, presumably, the politics of liberalism as well, are constrained by an adherence to the "good forms" that reflect their nostalgia for the reconciliation of differences within a whole: "It allows the unrepresentable to be put forward only as the missing contents; but the form, because of its recognizable consistency,

21 See, for example, the discussions contained in *Painterly Abstraction in Modernist American Poetry* (Cambridge: Cambridge University Press, 1989), and especially the section on Kant and the Romantic tradition, pp. 99–107.

continues to offer the reader or viewer matter for solace and pleasure" (*The Postmodern Condition*, p. 81). In his advancement of a postmodern project, Lyotard may be seen as carrying forward the modernist vision of a world and of selves which we might be free ever to reimagine and recreate, but he wants to detach these possibilities from any reference to the purely "fictional" schema of Kant's "other world." Thus, Lyotard sees postmodernism as one way to liberate whatever was of value in the modernist vision of the self as open to continuous reinvention from the adherence to a politics of closure and containment, but not simply by reminding us of the possibility of self-revision that exists within the framework of the Hegelian Absolute or by initiating a search, through the sublime, for forms of expression in which the real is ceaselessly transcended and subsumed by the Ideal. These are all the pathways of modernity and are on his account all equally limited by their "nostalgia" for the (social, historical, theoretical, etc.) whole. Rather, Lyotard envisions postmodernism as the site, or multiple sites, which allows the "unpresentable" to be put forth not simply as the "missing contents" of some projected totality; instead, by denying itself the solace of the "good forms" of social, political, aesthetic, and philosophical expression (of consensus, harmony, or taste), he challenges us to encounter a "stronger sense of the unpresentable":

The postmodern would be that which, in the modern, puts forward the unpresentable in presentation itself; that which denies itself the solace of good forms, the consensus of a taste which would make it possible to share collectively the nostalgia for the unattainable; that which searches for new presentations, not in order to enjoy them but in order to impart a stronger sense of the unpresentable.   (*ibid.*)

The self-creative potential of language-games, as realized in the postmodern sublime, is seen as the post-theoretical means by which we may make the future present and so render transformative ideals concrete. According to Lyotard, the postmodernist works in the absence of any rules in order to project the rules for what will, from the perspective of the future, seem necessary: "*post modern* would have to be understood according to the paradox of the future (*post*) anterior (*modo*")" (*ibid.*). According to Kant, we experience the sublime when the imagination cannot find forms of representation adequate to its conceptions, or when we find ourselves confronting an idea for which we can find no adequate example. These circumstances produce the ambiguity of a pleasure that derives from the painful experience of reason when faced with its own limits; they generate a shudder of pain that is a source of elevation and, according to Kant, an indication of human greatness. But as a post-theoretical thinker who wants to transform the painful pleasures of the sublime into a form of the "gay science," Lyotard must efface the difference between our ability to imagine new possibilities on the one hand and our ability to concretize them on the other. To this extent at least Lyotard could be said to follow Hegel; he seeks a form of self-creation uncontaminated by the "bad," Kantian idealism that relies on the fiction of a "transcendental" realm. But because Lyotard also accepts the proposition that there is no Spirit, the postmodern sublime easily becomes a manifestation of the will attempting to realize the absolute novelty that is not ordinarily available to the subject-speakers in language-games.

At the conclusion of this chapter I will present a proposal for the rereading of the category of judgment in political and aesthetic terms that may allow us to negotiate the problems just outlined. For present purposes it may be sufficient to see that in its paradigmatically modern form the aesthetic judgment is bound up with a series of antinomies that are reflected in the liberal attempt to construct a social whole according to universalizable bases of judgment (e.g. Kant's "supersensible substrate of humanity"). It has customarily been thought that the theoretical commitments of modernity could be realized in the form of a society in which the differences among individuals could be mediated and their social purposes harmoniously aligned. For the major portion of its modern history, political theory has seen its task as one of synthesizing the differences among persons or of regulating purposes through a series of abstract principles or rules. The notion of a society in which competing conceptions of the good could simultaneously be pursued thus stands at the heart of liberal modernity not only in Kant's theory but also as a version of Schiller's "Aesthetic State." Liberalism universalizes the ground of individual judgments and of "psychological" differences (e.g., those of taste) but thereby radicalizes modernity's lack of any substantive conception of the good; as we have seen in chapter 5, it easily shades off into the choice-ordering calculus of utilitarianism. At the same time, modern political theory tends to formalize the process of judgment as a mere procedure of choice in an effort to institutionalize a framework that will allow a diversity of goods to be ordered and ranked. In this dimension, the liberal vision reinforces the contradictions of reason and desire discussed above: it remains faithful to the variability of individual desires, but its means of recognition, and its mode of reconciling desires, only fortify the "iron cage" of bureaucracy that Weber described as having a hold on the modern world.

As Charles Altieri has pointed out, the model of judgment represented in the political philosophy of John Rawls may be situated within and against this tradition, both as a manifestation of the contradictions of modernity and as an attempt to resolve those same contradictions from within.[22] Whereas the majority of political thinkers begin with a theoretical principle that would generate and insure a hierarchy of competing value-claims, Rawls attempts to build an idea of justice by accentuating the cardinal premise of modernity, viz., that there is no truly higher, and certainly no *natural* principle for synthesizing our diverse desires and interests. Instead, he positions subjects behind a common "veil of ignorance" and asks them to assert their choices and then play out their differences in a realm of self-expressive action and discourse. In so doing Rawls remains faithful to the goals of the voluntarist line of modern political theory, beginning with Hobbes: to supply a framework in which human subjects, exempt from prejudicial constraints or from pre-existing conceptions about the "nature of man," can be allowed to confirm their autonomy as social beings through the choices that they make.

Whether Rawlsian-style liberalism, which leads in a fairly direct way to the politics of social democracy and the economics of the modern welfare state, is appropriate to the socio-economic conditions of postmodernism, or whether those conditions have now outstripped the powers of liberal theory, remain important questions, and they are as yet unresolved. It is in any case clear that the Rawlsian political agenda encourages us to posit our differences in order to fashion a social whole rather than to find ways to articulate and preserve our differences *given* our interpellation within a series of all too pervasive (social, political, economic, discursive) wholes. But the initial attractiveness of Rawls's position may become clear if we contrast his

22 Altieri, "Judgment and Justice under Postmodern Conditions; or, How Lyotard Helps us Read Rawls as a Postmodern Thinker," in Dasenbrock, ed., *Redrawing the Lines*, pp. 61–91.

account of the hypothetical "original position" of society with the assumptions at work in modern utilitarianism, for it is against the utilitarian analysis of the good that Rawls has made his most powerful claims. According to Rawls,

> it is by the conception of the impartial spectator and the use of sympathetic identification in guiding our imagination that the principle for one man is applied to society. It is this spectator who is conceived as carrying out the required organization of the desires of all persons into one coherent system of desire; it is by this construction that many persons are fused into one. Endowed with ideal powers of sympathy and imagination, the impartial spectator is the perfectly rational individual who identifies with and experiences the desires of others as if these were his own ... This view of social cooperation is the consequence of extending to society the principle of choice for one man, and then, to make this extension work, conflating all persons into one through the imaginative acts of the impartial sympathetic spectator.[23]

According to one line of objections familiar from our discussions above, the trade-offs of utilitarianism are those of the disenchanted world; all that is gained in freeing us from a fixed and rigid conception of the good is lost by utilitarianism's continued reliance on the position of an impartial spectator-subject who is unable to form attachments to any substantive conception of the good. Insofar as the vaunted neutrality of this position may be found to act as a cover for hidden claims to power, the values it generates could best be criticized on ideological grounds.[24] On a view that has closer affinities with the one taken up by Rawls, however, the failures of utilitarianism are registered more directly in the vision of selfhood with which it is aligned. On Rawls's account, the presuppositions of utilitarianism are such that it results in the conflation of all desires into a single system of desire; rather than allow the subject to reproduce the variability of desires, and thereby render the merely abstract diversity of subjective desire concrete, utilitarianism tends to efface the difference between subjects just as it tends to reduce the differences among goods. Yet insofar as the subject *qua* "ideal spectator" is to resemble a "person" at all, the position it describes cannot be wholly abstract: if the subject-spectator's stance is to

---

23 Rawls, *A Theory of Justice* (Cambridge, MA: Harvard University Press, 1971), p. 27.
24 For a sustained discussion of neutrality, see Bruce Ackerman, *Social Justice in the Liberal State* (New Haven: Yale University Press, 1980).

remain sufficiently detached, personal desires must be ignored; yet full self-interest must be assumed if the spectator-subject is to reflect the positions of others in the group and command their respect.[25]

In order to fashion a politics independent of the historical and theoretical assumptions of a spectator-subject and still preserve a place for the desiring self, Rawls must invoke the fiction of an "original position" of society, free of any *specific* commitments concerning the nature of justice or the particular desires of the members of the social group. The "original position" captures, in the form of a hypothesis concerning the access to knowledge of the parties to a contract, the fundamentally modern ideas that we should be free to transform ourselves through the choices that we make and that our political institutions should impose no prior limitations concerning which version of the good life we may pursue. It is thus meant to secure our roles as social but autonomous value-seeking agents, or as Rawls says in another place, as "self-originating sources of valid claims."[26] The original position is more or less equal in power and scope to that occupied by the "ideal spectator" of utilitarianism; but it is not simply a principle of difference, since Rawls must specify equally what the contracting subjects in this position *do* and *do not* know. What they *do not* know is what would distinguish any one of them from the others as the particular human beings they are;[27] it is in this sense a position of epistemological darkness that is meant to contain, rather than embrace, the difference that a knowledge of these differences would make. As Rawls says, "no one knows his place in society, his class position or social status, nor does any one know his fortune in the distribution of natural assets and abilities, his intelligence, strength and the like. I shall even assume that *the parties do not know their conceptions of the good*" (*Theory of Justice*, p. 12, my

25 Rawls also says that "A rational and impartial sympathetic spectator is a person who takes up a general perspective: he assumes a position where his own interests are not at stake and he possesses all the requisite information and powers of reasoning. So situated he is equally responsive and sympathetic to the desires and satisfactions of everyone affected by the social system ... Thus he imagines himself in the place of each person in turn, and when he has done this for everyone, the strength of his approval is determined by the balance of satisfactions to which he has sympathetically responded." *A Theory of Justice*, p. 186.

26 Rawls, "Kantian Constructivism in Moral Theory," *Journal of Philosophy*, 77 (1980), 543.

27 See Michael Sandel, *Liberalism and the Limits of Justice* (Cambridge: Cambridge University Press, 1982), p. 24.

emphasis).[28] Yet at the same time the parties to this position *do* know that they, like everyone else, are rational beings and therefore value certain "primary" goods: "Regardless of a person's values, plans, or ultimate aims, it is assumed there are certain things of which he would prefer more rather than less, on the grounds that they are likely to be useful in advancing all ends, whatever ends they happen to be."[29]

Whether Rawls can coherently maintain these divergent positions – whether he can conceive of a desiring subject apart from any *particular* objects of desire, and whether his concept of distributive justice does not require a "thicker" conception of the self than the "original position" will allow – has already been the subject of much dispute. Bruce Ackerman, for instance, has argued that Rawls effectively establishes the set of the subject's possible choices as infinite while setting the chooser at zero; his inference is that when this Subject Zero confronts the Infinite Choice Set it will be unable to choose *any* principle of justice until *some* set of preferences is put in place (see *Social Justice*, p. 339). Accordingly, Rawls must continuously specify what information will and will not be available to the parties to the social contract. But it is clear from Altieri's discussion of justice and judgment in Rawls that by containing the problem of recognition within the realm of the "hypothetical," Rawls hopes to appeal to a position that resists the political consequences of modernity by embracing its theoretical conclusions in advance, regardless of whether he can resolve the problems of self-contradiction and indeterminate self-characterization mentioned above. It may in this light become clear why Altieri sees Rawls's principal antagonist as Lyotard, for the heterogeneity of language-games outlined in *Just Gaming* may be read as a radicalization of the emotivist stance described by MacIntyre, or of the voluntaristic "behaviorism" criticized by Iris Murdoch in *The Sovereignty of Good*. According to Altieri, "there is no more pressing challenge to political philosophy than to establish normative models compatible with the diverse local positions that we must take as givens within the polity because there

---

28 Cf. Lyotard on the nature of justice in modernity: "since Rousseau, the answer to the question of justice in relation to theoretical discourse is displaced, because it has been thought that the just will be that which can be prescribed by the set of the utterers of the statements. The position is quite different from the Platonic one, because what the utterers state does not necessarily offer any guidance." *Just Gaming*, p. 29. Cf. also A. J. Cascardi, "Genealogies of Modernism," *Philosophy and Literature*, 11 (1987), 207–25.

29 The formulation is that of Michael Sandel, *Liberalism*, p. 25.

is no higher principle for combining interests or imposing shared criteria."[30] This represents a forceful attempt to reassert and radicalize the ambitions of modern political discourse; beginning from the "primacy of difference," rather than from the principle of identity, the task is to construct a "reflective theatre" (Altieri's term) "in which the differences can be negotiated and a complex model of hypothetical identifications elaborated" ("Judgment and Justice under Postmodern Conditions," p. 64).

A conception of the subject as open to the transformative effects of difference but as nonetheless abstract would be the price to pay for the attempt to base a personal psychology, if not also a politics, on Rawls, whose indeterminate concept of identity is further constrained prior to the stage of self-reflection; as another recent critic of Rawlsian liberalism, Michael Sandel, has remarked,

> for a subject such as Rawls' the paradigmatic moral question is not "Who am I?", for the answer to this question is regarded as self-evident [and, we might add, as given in advance by a prior process of individuation], but rather "What ends shall I choose?", and this is a question addressed to the will. Rawls' subject would thus appear epistemologically impoverished where the self is concerned, conceptually ill-equipped to engage in the sort of self-reflection capable of going beyond an attention to its preferences and desires to contemplate, and so to re-describe, the subject that contains them.
>
> (*Liberalism*, p. 153)

And while Rawls does indeed assert that the good most appropriate to an individual is the outcome of "careful reflection," it remains clear that the objects of this reflection can only be either the various alternative plans and their consequences for the realization of the subject's desires, or the first-order wants and desires themselves.[31] The concept of "difference" thus has a primarily empirical and voluntaristic force for Rawls, as the plurality, or diversity, of choices that might go to make a rational life-plan, and in none of these ways

---

30 Altieri, "Judgment and Justice under Postmodern Conditions," p. 69.

31 Because the Rawlsian self is too thin to be capable of desert in the classical sense, it must count on legitimate expectations or entitlements. In this light, it may be possible to see why the subject of the "disenchanted" world invariably inhabits a welfare state. Cf. Sandel: "claims of desert presuppose thickly-constituted selves, beings capable of possession in the constitutive sense, but the deontological self is wholly without possessions of this kind. Acknowledging this lack, Rawls would found entitlements on legitimate expectations instead. If we are incapable of desert, at least we are entitled that institutions honor the expectations to which they give rise" (*Liberalism*, p. 178).

does reflection focus on the self *qua* subject of desires (see *Liberalism*, p. 159).

Because of these and other limitations of *A Theory of Justice*, it is necessary to supplement Rawls with a series of claims about the nature and plausibility of the criteria which the subject must meet in order so much as to fashion an identity or political role from the context of differences available to it. What becomes essential to the operations of justice and judgment in the modern age is not just the "neutral" framework of the original bargaining game or the force of competing wills within a competitive or "agonistic"arrangement, but the assumption that only subjects who can provisionally recognize themselves within some interpretive context can also be the subjects of judgments that are just or fair (cf. Rousseau: "The passage from the state of nature to the civil state produces a truly remarkable change in the individual. It substitutes justice for instinct in his behavior, and gives to his actions a moral basis which formerly was lacking"[32]). We must, on this view, recognize ourselves *as* agents of a particular kind, and these hypothetical identifications, "thick descriptions" of a provisional sort that are available to us by virtue of the social context of our actions and discourse, must be able to meet the tests of what Altieri describes as "plausibility," not objectivity, if they are to have any hope of securing the recognition of others. And yet just as Rawls cannot coherently conceive of a "general" subject of desire, there is nothing to *guarantee* that the identifications thus adopted will remain provisional and not be torn apart into various versions of the historically limited particular and the abstract universal. Accordingly, there seems no way to insure that these "hypothetical" identifications will be either substantive or transformable in any significant way: insofar as they remain unrealized they quickly vaporize into wish-fulfillment dreams, yet insofar as they are concretized they tend to become sedimented as permanent identifications or rigid social structures.

Aesthetic liberalism

In pointing toward identifications that are, strictly speaking, neither historical nor theoretical but hypothetical or "fictional," we leave off roughly where the critique of modern politics begins and with a recognition of the irreducible instabilities and risks inherent in any

32 Rousseau, *The Social Contract*, ed. and trans. Ernest Barker (New York: Oxford University Press, 1962), I, viii, p. 185.

liberal conception of the subject-self; in the process, we shift to grounds that are, properly speaking, neither historical nor theoretical, but rather "aesthetic." These are perhaps best expressed in Rousseau's willingness to confront the problem of justice from a "provisional" point of view by "setting all the facts aside"; Rousseau: "the researches which can be undertaken concerning [the origins and foundations of inequality among men] must not be taken for historical truths, but only for *hypothetical and conditional reasonings, better used to clarify the nature of things than to show their true origin.*"[33] In considering the question of justice, Rousseau takes it as a matter of fact that there are a series of differences (more precisely, of "inequalities") among individuals that cannot be made legitimate or justified. What he seeks specifically to explain are moral and political inequalities and, on this basis, "by what sequence of marvels the strong could resolve to serve the weak, and the people to buy imaginary repose at the price of real felicity" (p. 102), for these are the inequalities that are reflected in the forms of association that have been instituted and agreed to by men ("The various forms of governments derive their origin from the greater or lesser differences to be found among individuals at the moment of institution," *Second Discourse*, p. 171). How can such inequalities be justified or made legitimate? In the *Second Discourse*, Rousseau addresses these questions in a two-stage process that forces us to consider the problem of difference as transcending the merely empirical plane: the one sets its sights toward the "speculative" or "theoretical" problems of man, nature, and method, while the other looks to the genealogy of modern society and avails itself largely of the language of historical critique. And yet it remains unclear from the *Second Discourse* just how the subject can be situated between theory and history or how these languages can be linked.

We have seen that for Lyotard, history and theory remain heterogeneous "language games," neither of which has privileged access to the nature of truth; Lyotard can thus regard the ethical "ought" as bearing on the subject only as a counter-fiction of sorts, i.e., as the point of analogy or transition between descriptive and prescriptive language-games. We can also see that there is nothing save perhaps the will to regulate the purity of these different games, and that the only lasting imperative this vision can evoke is that

33 Rousseau, *Discourse on the Origins and Foundations of Inequality among Men* (*Second Discourse*), trans. Roger and Judith Masters (New York: St. Martin's Press, 1964), p. 103; emphasis mine.

statements be new and different. By contrast, the need to locate a model of identity and a form of discourse within the gap or *décalage* between history and theory is in the deconstructive reading of Rousseau assigned to literature, which on account of the "metaleptic" relationship between these terms is also "condemned" to being the "truly political mode of discourse."[34] In this analysis, the function of the critical reader is not unlike that of the psychoanalyst who has come to identify the "transference" involved in any attempt to posit a transcendent principle of the good; he can see that "the legislator has to invent a transcendent principle of signification called God in order to perform the metalepsis that reverses the temporal pattern of all promissory and legal statements. Since God is said to be, within this perspective, a subterfuge, it follows that the *Social Contract* has lost the right to promise anything. Yet it promises a great deal" (*Allegories*, p. 276). Seen from one perspective, metalepsis reveals the predicament of modern society and addresses the *aporia* of history and theory by uncovering the ruse involved in formulating rules to legitimize what "will have been done" (in Rousseau's somewhat less tendentious terms, "for the effect to precede the cause. For such a thing to happen, the social spirit which can be the product only of a country's institutions would have, in fact, to be present at their birth, and, even, before the laws are operative, the citizen would have to be such as those same laws would make him"[35]). According to this view, political discourse derives neither from the need to reconcile the empirical differences among individuals, goods, or theories about their relative merits, nor from the discrepancy between the pressures of history and the seductions (and possible deceptions) of a purely theoretical, speculative, or utopian ideal, but rather from the fundamentally figural process by which some end-state is projected or transposed under the name of something else.

It is equally clear that in the *Social Contract* Rousseau has undertaken to explain the nature of political association within a framework of remarkable theoretical constraint. As Althusser argued, the entirety of the *Social Contract* may be defined by the limitations of the theoretical field in which the problem of justice is posed:

There is thus no transcendental solution, no recourse to a third party, be it God or Chance. The solution cannot be found outside the existing givens, a ruthless enumeration of which has just been established. The only solution

34 Paul de Man, *Allegories of Reading* (New Haven: Yale University Press, 1979), p. 157.   35 Rousseau, *Social Contract*, "Of the Legislator," v, vii, p. 207.

possible inside the theoretical field constituted by men and the alienated relations whose authors and victims they are is for them to change their "*manner of existence.*"[36]

Yet, as Althusser has also shown, in seeking to bring this social change about, Rousseau is forced to avoid the materialist conception of history that on his account would resolve these antinomies; Rousseau must make a succession of "flights forward" into the speculative ideal of a utopian state, which desperately needs transcendence but cannot, by his own theoretical lights, invoke it, and "flights backward" into history, which take the form of a regressive social and economic program that remains powerless to address the conditions of society as it stands. Since neither of these projects can be framed within the scope of the languages at hand, Rousseau must move toward a new type of writing, a "fiction," whose "success" remains nonetheless clouded by its symptomatic placement outside the bounds of historical and theoretical discourse. "Fiction" is in this vision indicative of the desire to occupy a place that no "history," no theory, has been able to claim:

> If there is no possibility of further Discrepancies – since they would no longer be of any use in the theoretical order which has done nothing but live on these Discrepancies, chasing before it its problems and their solutions to the point where it reaches the real, insoluble problem, there is still one recourse, but one of a different kind: a *transfer*, this time, the transfer of the impossible theoretical solution into the alternative to theory [*l'autre de la théorie*], literature. The admirable "fictional triumph" of an unprecedented writing. ("Rousseau," p. 159)

In other words, Rousseau invents a mode of discourse (that deconstruction will call "literature") in order to resolve the discrepancy between history and theory that in political terms signals the possibility of radical transformation. If it is true, as I have suggested in chapter 1, that the consciousness of modernity is structured by the tension between the desire for absolute genesis or origin and the need for legitimation and recognition – a tension that is "stabilized" through the formation of the liberal State – then the most radical task of transformation would be to discover and preserve this originary tension from all attempts to contain or reduce it.[37] By

36 Althusser, "Rousseau: The Social Contract," in *Montesquieu, Rousseau, Marx*, trans. Ben Brewster (London: Verso, 1982), p. 123.
37 Dick Howard discusses these terms in *The Politics of Critique* (Minneapolis: University of Minnesota Press, 1988); see especially pp. 198–99.

contrast, in the deconstructive reading the metalepsis central to what Paul de Man calls the "figural" or "allegorical" production of transformative, revolutionary, or truly transcendent ends is overcome, yet not without the significant risk that the gap between history and theory that fiction "resolves" may be taken as an incitement to the dangers attached to revolution itself – alternately, to the naive idealism of wish-fulfillment dreams or to the cynicism that breeds despair. While the contradictions of history and theory may thus be magically resolved, we are led to a new and more complex antinomy, in which the tensions of history and theory are reproduced in the form of a text that splinters into fragments of projective (utopian) desire and historical (ascetic) denial.

In light of Rousseau's position as an early critic of the modern age, it begins to become clear that the desire to pass beyond or deconstruct the antinomy of history and theory characteristic of the discourse of modernity by recourse to a "third term" (whether "literature," "discourse," or "language-games") results in a reincorporation of that antinomy as a division within the social, political, or psychological fields. In other words, it returns us to the divided subject; or perhaps more accurately, it sees the creation of a space within and between discourses as creating opportunities for resistance to what it regards as the "unified" subject of the modern age. In the postmodern reading of Rousseau, the will to overcome these antinomies, hence to deny the desire for a unified subject, is characteristically projected onto that form of discourse known as "literature." But whereas deconstruction sees literature as, in de Man's words, "condemned" to a series of projects that it cannot possibly accomplish, it might be more accurate to regard all discourse as shaped by the desire of subjects to find recognition and to see that project as energized by the impossibility of identifying the self as the subject of any one discourse.

Accordingly, I would suggest that: once we begin to think of discourse as providing possible models of recognition, then "fictional" discourse (the "literary"specificity of which would on my account subsequently drop out, as would the need for a "theory" by which to render it legitimate) may be seen neither as the site from which fixed and stable identities might be invoked, existing ideologies reproduced, or a fundamental diversity of goods and values ranked, nor as the means simply to destabilize these pursuits, but rather as the locus of competing judgment-claims made by subjects seeking recognition, as the product of a need that continues to exist as long as we refuse to accept any prior, substantive limitations on the nature of the identities we may pursue. Left to their own devices, the langagues of history and theory will not allow this much: the language of history, which speaks in terms of necessity, will lead us to deny the possibility of transformation and to interpret our inherited modern identity as fate (Marx writes that while men make their own history, "they do not make it as they please; they do not make it under circumstances chosen by themselves, but under circumstances directly encountered, given and transmitted from the past"[38]); the lure of theory will by contrast tempt us to imagine recognition as taking place within the framework of a purely speculative and ideal whole. (What is required, as the final pages of this chapter will show, is a new conception of the aesthetic as a means of linking these two.)

To be sure, it must be said that any reformulation of the antinomies of subjectivity in such terms would have to recognize not only the division of culture into a series of discrete languages or "codes," but also the fundamental ruse that lies at the heart of any attempt to identify an overarching "subject" for all of these. Whereas the preceding chapters of this study have been able to suggest some of the internal contradictions characteristic of the various modern discourses, the heterogeneity of modernity as a whole is something that can best be seen in retrospect, for it shows up in the form of a contradiction whereby the subject of any given discourse tends to forget that he or she may also be the deceived subject of that discourse.[39] At the center of this deception lies the belief that the subject of modernity is single, rather than divided and heterogeneous, and it is on the basis of this illusory certitude that modernity has been reduced to a singular discourse. But the task of recognition is only made more difficult, not relieved, if we concentrate solely on the decentering critique of the unstable relationship among modern discourses. Once we begin to think of discourse as providing possible models of recognition, however, then what we recognize as "fictional," or more generally, "aesthetic" discourse (the "literary" specificity of which would subsequently drop out, as would the need

38 Marx, *Eighteenth Brumaire of Louis Bonaparte* (New York: International Publishers, 1963), p. 15.
39 See Paul Smith, *Discerning the Subject* (Minneapolis: University of Minnesota Press, 1988), pp. 70–82 ("Unconscious").

for a "theory" by which to render it distinct and legitimate) may be
seen neither as the site from which fixed and stable identities might
be invoked, existing ideologies reproduced, or a fundamental
diversity of goods and values ranked, nor as the means simply to
destabilize these various pursuits, but rather as a reflection of the
competing claims made by subjects seeking recognition, as the
product of a need that continues to exist as long as we refuse to
accept any prior, substantive limitations on the nature of the identities
we may pursue. As I hope in the following section of this chapter to
explain, a more systematic understanding of the concept of judgment
that underlies our relationship to the aesthetic field may be pursued
through a reinterpretation of the concept of "aesthetic judgment"
that originates in Kant. Whereas the modern reading of Kant takes the
aesthetic as the name of an autonomous discourse, and sees its objects
as belonging to a distinct cultural sphere, the concept of "aesthetic
liberalism" I would propose represents an attempt to transform the
ceaseless tensions between the various modes of modern discourse
into the conditions of possibility for the exercise of judgments
necessary to the ongoing project of self-imagination in the
postmodern age.

In pursuit of a postmodern critique of modernity, one that would
avoid the pitfalls mentioned above, I want in these remaining pages
to outline a category of judgment that would proceed by a reordering
of the fundamental terms of the *Critique of Judgment* of Kant along the
lines suggested by those thinkers who most seriously take the
aesthetic as providing models of value. More specifically, I would
suggest that the political and ethical consequences of judgments so
modeled can be retrieved by casting the category of aesthetic
liberalism in contrast to the dominant modern project of "liberal
aestheticism," as represented in the prevailing interpretations of Kant,
such as are available in works like Paul Guyer's *Kant and the Claims
of Taste*.[40] The category of liberal aestheticism seems to depend on
the unacknowledged extension of the principles of subjectivity to a
politics which is then brought to bear on the aesthetic "object" – e.g.
its ability to hold together contradiction and coherence, or to admit
a multiplicity of interpretations while preserving its identity as an

---

40 Guyer, *Kant and the Claims of Taste* (Cambridge, MA: Harvard University Press,
1979).

irrefutable ground of value or truth. Rather than begin by accepting a series of (modern) arguments for the existence of a "common substrate of humanity," for an ahistorical human nature, or for a trans-historical community or "tradition," the project of aesthetic liberalism seeks the reverse. Its goal is to reformulate the terms of liberalism on the basis of the very antinomies mirrored in aesthetic experience and judgment, thus attempting to recover the energies that a thinker like Gilles Deleuze acutely perceived as lying hidden within the Kantian system of the "faculties."[41] By almost all conventional accounts, including ones like Guyer's, the aesthetics of Kant established the theoretical grounding for modern art and for the existence within modernity of what we might describe as an "aesthetic moment," one that is derived from certain inherently untranscendent, bodily feelings of pleasure and pain, and that calls forth certain modes of evaluative response or "judgment." But whereas the *Critique of Judgment* is at the same time seen as providing a means by which the divisions characteristic of liberal modernity could be reconciled or made whole, and whereas the postmodern reading of Kant sees the third Critique as itself the source of universalizing tendencies that must be resisted in the interests of cultural heterogeneity or "difference," I would argue for a reading of the third Critique that would allow us to rearticulate, in order to transform, a politics of subjectivity that is implicit in the earlier Kantian Critiques. If some formulation of the relationship between the individual and the community, as between the terms of empirical singularity and conceptual generality, or the categories of freedom and necessity, sense and understanding, reason and desire, value and rule, is indeed central to liberal modernity, then we may think of the Kantian aesthetic as not so much offering a moment of synthesis as an attempt to resist the immanent threat of a radical telescoping or collapse of these terms, such as might occur either by recourse to a falsely redemptive and utopian vision of the mission of art or, conversely, by an implosion of the liberal field and the "supersession" of art in the form of a hyperaesthetic cultural space.

The aesthetic moment in Kant may be seen as replicating rather than resolving the tensions between the individual and community that Kant elsewhere formulates as central to the position of the subject in the modern world. What is required for a recasting of the

41 See Deleuze, *Kant's Critical Philosophy: The Doctrine of the Faculties*, trans. Hugh Tomlinson and Barbara Habberjam (London: Athlone Press, 1984).

category of aesthetic judgment is the introduction of a principle of movement that would allow us to mediate between these terms. Whereas the Enlightenment reading of Kant – as carried forward most recently by Habermas – sees the third Critique as reflecting a development of the "inner logic" of a self-contained aesthetic sphere, and tends to privilege the (public) discourse of taste over the experience of art, and whereas the Romantic response to Kant tends to see the *Critique of Judgment* as a reintegrative and redemptive attempt to restore unity, through the formation of what Schiller called an "Aesthetic State," to a social totality that had been shattered by the disintegrative forces of capital, I would suggest that both the Romantic and Enlightenment readings of Kant represent attempts to flatten or reduce the tensions from which the sustaining ethical force of modernity derives (this is the flattening that thinkers as different as Altieri and Deleuze have learned to resist, and the result is a far more resilient conception of the aesthetic in Kant). These tensions include not only a separation of the public and private spheres, but a dialectic of experience and judgment that reflects the historical ambitions and constraints of modern culture itself. On the one hand, aesthetic experience as described in the third Critique reflects the goals of the modern subject in freeing itself from predetermined rules; these ambitions are preserved in the form of aesthetic judgments, which are characterized by Kant as taking place in a realm that recognizes no pre-established precepts or rules. Moreover, the principles appropriate to the objects of such judgments cannot be derived from a priori concepts; rather, they must themselves furnish a concept, which must be one "from which we get no cognition of a thing."[42] For example, if we wish to determine whether something is beautiful or not, "we do not refer the representation of it to the Object by means of understanding with a view to cognition, but by means of the imagination ... we refer the representation to the Subject and its feeling of pleasure or displeasure" (*CJ*, p. 41). Yet on the other hand Kant recognizes the need to recuperate aesthetic experience through the invocation of universalizable principles; aesthetic experience is thus sublimated or "rationalized" in the form of principled judgments or claims of taste, whose general nature is to conceive the particular as contained in the universal, and by extension to insure the *lien social* (see *CJ*, p. 18). As a result, Kant leads us to

42 Kant, *Critique of Judgment* (henceforth, *CJ*), trans. James Creed Meredith (New York: Oxford University Press, 1928), p. 5.

suspect that the foundations of the liberal ethic reside not in the cognitive powers of reason or the understanding, but in the (transcendental) imagination, which regrounds the liberal state as the unity of wills under the concept of an end which has subjective claim to universality.[43]

To be sure, it must be said that Kant himself tempts us to read the aesthetic moment as possessing a reintegrative force with respect to the cognitive and ethical capacities of the subject. Since the first two Critiques reflect not only a division of the faculties, but also a somewhat more distressing separation of worlds, but since Kant also insists that the various faculties have jurisdiction over one and the same territory, it might seem that some additional power would be needed to provide the possibility of moving from one sphere to the next. If in the first Critique Kant secured our knowledge of the sensible world from a transcendental point of view, and if the purpose of the second Critique was to demonstrate the principles of freedom as grounded in a supersensible realm, then the task of the third Critique is to provide the means of passing from one world to the next. How may the links between the sensible and the supersensible worlds be established? Whereas conventional interpretations of the third Critique tend to regard aesthetic judgment as an autonomous power or force, it would be more fruitful to say that what we call the aesthetic is the reflection of the surplus demand created by every other existing mode of discourse, and that its primary purpose is to provide a means for shifting from one domain of experience to the next.[44] To this extent it functions like Lyotard's *différend*. Rather than invent a new faculty for making these links, Kant argues that the aesthetic judgment serves a relational function; it enables us to introduce a principle of mobility into a system of antinomies and dualisms that is otherwise static; through it, the sensible world (where

---

43 See Kroker, *The Postmodern Scene*, p. 160. As he goes on there to say, "The imagination founds the individual and the state on the basis of the aesthetic informing the judgement of the 'kingdom of ends.' Thus the *Critique* stands as the founding text of aesthetic liberalism." Heidegger points out in his study of Kant's metaphysics that the *Critique of Judgment* establishes the central role of the transcendental imagination. See *Kant and the Problem of Metaphysics*, trans. James S. Churchill (Bloomington: Indiana University Press, 1962).

44 This is the basis of the "Kantianism" of a work like Lyotard's *Just Gaming*. Some of the contrasts between Lyotard's position and mine emerge from the fact that Lyotard flattens the dialectic of experience and judgment into the pure heterogeneity of language-games, whereas I propose to reformulate that dialectic, to recover the mobility of the terms involved.

necessity rules) may be placed in communication with the principles of freedom (which are located in the supersensible domain). Thus he goes on to say that:

There must...be a ground of the *unity* of the supersensible that lies at the basis of nature, with what the concept of freedom contains in a practical way, and although the concept of this ground neither theoretically nor practically attains to a knowledge of it, and so *has no peculiar realm of its own, still it renders possible the transition from the mode of thought according to principles of the one to that according to the principles of the other.* (*ibid.*)

The aesthetic moment in its modern (i.e., paradigmatically Kantian) mode is centrally bound up with a series of antinomies that are reflected in the project to construct a social whole on the universalizable principles of judgment, where the bases for judgment return us to the necessarily subjective and individual experiences of pleasure and pain. This presents the problem of aesthetics in its "liberal" guise, i.e., as reflecting the heterogeneity of desires and the tensions between the public and the private realms. Kant develops this dimension of his theory by returning to the proposition of pleasure and pain which he had earlier banned as a transcendental principle of reason. To be sure, Kant continues to remain bound by his earlier rejection, yet he comes to recognize that the sensible is integral to the demands of universality in a way that resembles the status of supersensible Ideas, which are not known in themselves but are necessary and are known to exist just the same. What must be subsumed in order for this universality to be achieved is the limited and strictly *subjective* nature of pleasure and pain, or perhaps more accurately their subjective *interest*, which leads Kant to formulate his paradoxical notion of the "disinterested interest" proper to art. And yet it remains equally clear that the subjective and sensuous qualities of aesthetic experience must remain retrievable if the aesthetic moment is to be sustained; indeed, it would be fair to say that the universalizing tendency of judgment cannot ever legitimately erase that which is sensuous and "subjective" in the experience of art.

Consider in this regard the "antinomy of taste" as described in the "Dialectic of Aesthetic Judgment" of the third Critique. On the one hand, it would seem that the diversity of judgments about taste, which reflect its "merely subjective" basis, has no power to command the assent of others: "The object is *for me* an object of delight, for others it may be otherwise – every one to his taste" (*CJ*, p. 207). To be sure, this isolated moment of the dialectic of taste may itself be appropriated as part of a Nietzschean "transvaluation" of the dualisms of Kantian aesthetics, a project Roland Barthes articulated in the terms of the "pleasure" of the text. On this anti-liberal view, pleasure forms the ground of self-assertions that are no longer meant to be ethical at all; pleasure stands "beyond" good and evil insofar as it stands beyond the normative standards that the principle of community would impose. And yet the Kantian analysis remains substantially ahead of Nietzsche and Barthes, at least on this point, insofar as it recognizes that judgments of taste must at least admit of controversy, or would not count as judgments at all. For Kant, this means additionally that such claims must be conceptual, and so universalizable and respectful of the demands of community. But if both propositions about the demands of community *and* the subjective basis of judgments are not simultaneously met, Kant argues, the aesthetic moment would collapse; either our claims would not amount to judgments, and we would not be able so much as to quarrel about them, or they would not be of the kind we call aesthetic, i.e., capable of allowing us to retrieve the individual in the experiences of pleasure and pain.

What I have called "aesthetic liberalism" is made possible insofar as the terms of these antinomies can be reconciled while their autonomy is simultaneously preserved. The solution of an antinomy in Kant's understanding turns on the possibility of two apparently conflicting propositions not being in fact contradictory, but rather being capable of coexisting, despite the fact that such a possibility appears impossible within the realm of cognition (see *CJ*, p. 208). Consider in this regard the "solution" of the antimony of taste. On the one hand, Kant recognizes that judgments of taste apply to objects of sense, "but not so as to determine a concept of them for the understanding ... it is a singular representation of intuition referable to the feeling of pleasure, and, as such, only a private judgment" (*CJ*, p. 207). Yet on the other hand it is clear that judgments of taste lay the foundation for the formation of a community, through "an extension of judgements of this kind to necessity for every one" (*ibid.*). Thus Kant argues that the concepts to which we refer the objects of aesthetic judgments are not to be taken in the same sense in both instances. Thus there is, Kant says, a wider "scope of reference" for the representation of both the object and the subject of the aesthetic judgment, in which the terms of these contradictions may be both preserved as distinct and realigned.

All contradiction disappears, however, if I say: The judgement of taste is based upon a concept (of a general ground of the subjective finality of nature for the power of judgement), but one from which nothing can be cognized in respect of the Object, because it is in itself undeterminable and useless for knowledge. Yet by means of this very concept it acquires at the same time validity for every one...because its determining ground lies, perhaps, in the concept of what may be regarded as the supersensible substrate of humanity. (*CJ*, pp. 207–08)

Whereas the conventional reading of Kant takes the claims for the existence of a "supersensible substrate of humanity" adduced in the passage above as an all-too easy target for the counter-assertion of the primacy of heterogeneity and difference, the interpretation I have proposed would preserve the tensions within the Kantian antinomies, recognizing that the concept of a "supersensible substrate" is, in Kant's own terms, like a fiction "which does not afford any proof of the judgement of taste" (*CJ*, p. 207). And whereas the problem of liberal theory, as conventionally conceived within the context of modernity, turns on the question of how one may arrive at universally valid judgments (e.g., about power) based on the experience of fundamentally disgregated subject-selves, and conversely of how collective judgments may bind the individual will, the project of aesthetic liberalism is sympathetic to postmodern conditions insofar as it seeks to reclaim the authority of sensuous experience, of individual desires, and of muted or subaltern voices, as well as the possibilities for recognition and transformation that these may furnish, from the totalities into which they are all too easily, or prematurely, absorbed.

Some of the advantages of reinterpreting Kant in such a way that the critique of aesthetic judgment is tied to an ethic (and, indeed, a politics) appropriate to postmodern social conditions may be made clear in contrast to Richard Rorty's recent arguments for the ethic of solidarity that emerges once one adopts the stance of the "postmodern bourgeois liberal" over all other metaphysical and aesthetic options. The contrast is important to consider, because Rorty's most recent arguments rest on the apparently liberal premise of the necessary separation of the public and the private realms of life. Unlike Kant, however, Rorty rejects the idea that the aesthetic provides the means by which these realms may ever be made transparent to one another. For Rorty, the theory of "postmodern liberalism" (if indeed it can legitimately be counted as a "theory") is designed to correct the universalizing errors of the metaphysical tradition that permeate the old logic of liberalism, viz., the tendency to think that one's preferred vocabulary may be made globally valid, to believe that one's private language may be authoritative for the public as a whole, and to make specious claims for the authority of one's judgments by invoking the concept of a "supersensible substrate of mankind." Thus Rorty guards against these errors by resolutely partitioning off the public use of language from its private use, which in his opinion should not be shared if the goals of individual autonomy and self-creation are to be met.

Unlike the project I have proposed above, Rorty's sharp public–private split involves divorcing the language of community and consensus, and what I would call "recognition," from the language of self-transformation, rather than seeing the ways in which the purposes of these two languages might be aligned. While the mobility I perceive as essential to the aesthetic is preserved in the work of thinkers as diverse as Altieri, Deleuze, and Lyotard, in Rorty's version of postmodernism the political realm of "social organization" not only remains, but is *ideally* one of procedural justice and is, moreover, emphatically distinct from the "aesthetic" realm of private individuals seeking unique, differentiating self-creation and personal fulfillment. Indeed, Rorty argues that there is no way to hold the ideals of self-creation and justice, or of private perfection and collective human solidarity, simultaneously in place.

What I have described above in terms of the concept of aesthetic liberalism represents another means to achieve the goals that Rorty and I would share, at least as far as a critique of the dominant tradition of modernity is concerned. As I have interpreted it, aesthetic liberalism does not ask that we attempt to hold the ideals of self-creation and justice simultaneously in place, but rather derives its force from our inability to do just that. More important, it reflects an effort to grant subjects a transformative power over their identity as individuals seeking at once to ground that identity in the terms of recognition promised by community and to distinguish it therefrom. As I have argued above, this project can be seen as drawing out the political consequences of the judgments we call "aesthetic." In a vision such as Rorty's, however, the dialectic of the aesthetic moment is severely and, I believe, unnecessarily, curtailed; the aesthetic is preserved, if at all, in a reduced form, in a commitment to the particular and the contingent, the private, the local, and what Lyotard would call the small narrative (*petit récit*).[45] The aesthetic project becomes simply one of facilitating individual creations; its premise is one that Rorty shares with the Lyotard of *The Postmodern Condition*, as well as with many of the "high modernist" writers to whom he refers, viz., to "make things new," to make "something that never had been dreamt of before."[46] Its "theoretical" basis lies equally in Nietzsche and Descartes: to redescribe experience in one's own, incommensurable, terms, and so to recreate and master oneself and one's world "by inventing a new language." Understood as "aesthetic," however, this project no longer represents the ideal of a discourse that would shuttle back and forth between the necessarily distinct poles of individual and community, of reason and desire, of empirical singularity and conceptual abstraction; indeed, the theoretical culture now indicates that the differences between these terms have mostly collapsed. In the wake of this implosion, or ruination, however, the aesthetic is easily drawn into alignment with the bureaucratic and technological procedures of a world of decentered signs. In such a world, the politics of "difference" most often takes the form of resistance, rather than self-transformation; its principal goal is to overcome existing modes of identification rather than to invent the terms in which some future recognition might be achieved.[47] It goes without saying that there can be no transformation without a corresponding resistance, but when transformative goals collapse, or when the dialectic of recognition and transformation ceases to have force, we move from the project of aesthetic liberalism to the potentially complicitous practices of the postmodern cultural hyperspace.

45 See Richard Shusterman's discussion of Rorty in "Postmodernism and the Aesthetic Turn," *Poetics Today*, 10 (1989), 605–22.
46 Rorty, *Contingency, Irony, and Solidarity* (Cambridge: Cambridge University Press, 1989), p. 13.
47 The argument against the limitations of resistance have been forcefully made by Altieri in *Painterly Abstraction in Modernist American Poetry*; see for example pp. 489–95.

Index

Index

Index

Index

Index

Quintilian, 30

Rabelais, François, 81, 83
rationalization, 8–10, 16–71 *passim*, 79, 274, 287
Rawls, John, 291–95
recognition, 45, 49, 134–35, 208, 215, 218, 231, 235–42, 244–45, 247–49, 250–53, 257, 259, 261–63, 265–68, 270–71, 273–75, 278–79, 291, 294, 296, 299–302, 308–10
reification, 79–80, 179, 281
Reik, Miriam, 208
Reiss, Timothy, 64–65, 190
Renaissance, 5
Ricoeur, Paul, 40, 61, 129, 131, 176–77, 199, 251
Robert, Marthe, 86, 96
Romanticism, 268, 304
Rorty, Richard, 14, 36, 92, 149–52, 279–80, 287–88, 308–10
Rose, Gillian, 21, 92, 161, 184
Rosen, Stanley, 8, 12, 36, 37, 67, 76, 89, 130–31, 141, 151–52, 188, 197, 208, 235, 237, 265, 280
Rousseau, Jean, 44, 105, 191, 263, 296–97, 299, 300
Royce, Josiah, 90
Russell, Bertrand, 36

Sandel, Michael, 293, 295
Sartre, Jean-Paul, 2, 40
Schiller, Friedrich, 16, 116–18, 288, 290, 304
Schlegel, Friedrich, 103, 110–11
Schluchter, Wolfgang, 10, 16, 17–18, 21, 176, 178, 191, 199, 202
Schmidgall, Gary, 208
Schmidt, Alfred, 70
Schulte-Sasse, Jochen, 55
secular illumination, 142–43, 148, 151
secularization, 43, 46–47, 49, 95–96, 98, 102, 120, 123, 125–78 *passim*, 251, 259
self-assertion, 16–40 *passim*, 108, 125, 203, 279
Serres, Michel, 247
Seznec, Jean, 148

Shaftesbury, Anthony Ashley Cooper, Earl of, 259–60
Shakespeare, William, 5, 54, 245, 254
  Hamlet, 254
  Othello, 245
Shapiro, Gary, 31
Shils, Edward, 154
Shusterman, Richard, 151, 310
Sica, Alan, 95
Siegel, Jerrold, 53
Simmel, Georg, 95
simulation, 282, 284
Sloane, Thomas, 53, 137–38
Smith, Barbara Herrenstein, 122
Smith, Paul, 279, 301
Spinoza, Baruch, *Ethics*, 24, 119
spontaneity, 89, 92
sprezzatura, 254
Starobinski, Jean, 63–64
state of nature, 180, 182, 195, 205, 212, 221
Stendhal (Henri Beyle), 75, 230–31, 248, 253, 260, 267–68
  De L'amour (On Love), 75, 230–31, 248, 253, 260
Sterne, Laurence, 113
Stierle, Karlheinz, 31
Strauss, Leo, 8, 31, 141, 152, 180, 195, 205, 208, 215, 217–19, 283
Struever, Nancy, 53
sublime, 54, 280, 286–90
substantive rationality, 4, 40–56 *passim*

Taylor, Charles, 50, 59–60, 66, 155, 163, 200
Tirso de Molina (Fay Gabriel Téllez), 242
  El burlador de Sevilla, 244–53
Tönnies, Ferdinand, 265
transference, 237, 239
Trauerspiel, 143
Trilling, Lionel, 254
Trueblood, Alan, 84

Unamuno, Miguel de, 122
Unger, Roberto Mangabeira, 7, 23, 41–42, 61, 101, 102, 137, 228, 232, 280
utilitarianism, 290, 292–93
utility, 265–69, 272

1. transform contingency into necessity (5)

    ↳ a paradigmatic feature of modernity ??

2. judgment (15,